OLD LIES REVISITED

OLD LIES REVISITED

Young Readers and the Literature of War and Violence

WINIFRED WHITEHEAD

PLUTO PRESS
London • Concord, Mass

First published 1991 by Pluto Press
345 Archway Road, London N6 5AA
and 141 Old Bedford Road,
Concord, MA 01742, USA

British Library Cataloguing in Publication Data
Whitehead, Winifred
  Old lies : the young reader and the literature of war and
  violence.
  1. Literature. Special subjects. War & peace. Critical studies
  809.93358

  ISBN 0-7453-0428-1
  ISBN 0-7453-0429-X pbk

Library of Congress Cataloging-in-Publication Data
Whitehead, Winifred
   Old lies revisited : the young reader and the literature of war and
   violence / Winifred Whitehead
      p. cm.
   Includes bibliographical references.
   ISBN 0-7453-0428-1 – ISBN 0-7453-0429-X (pbk.)
   1. Children's literature–History and criticism. 2. Children–
Books and reading. 3. Violence in literature. 4. War in
literature. I. Title.
PN1009.A1W495 1990
809'.93358–dc20   90–32770
                                                                 CIP

Typeset by Stanford Desktop Publishing, Milton Keynes.
Printed in Great Britain by Billing and Sons Ltd, Worcester.

Contents

My argument is that War makes rattling good history;
but peace is poor reading.

Thomas Hardy, The Dynasts II.v

My friend, you would not tell with such high zest
To children ardent for some desperate glory,
The old Lie ...

Wilfred Owen, 'Dulce et Decorum Est'

Boys and Girls
And Women, that would groan to see a child
Pull off an insect's leg, all read of war,
The best amusement for our morning meal! ...
As if the soldier died without a wound,
As if the fibres of his godlike frame
Were gored without a pang ...

S.T. Coleridge, 'Fear in Solitude'

'Peace upon earth!' was said. We sing it,
And pay a million priests to bring it.
After two thousand years of mass
We've got as far as poison-gas.

Thomas Hardy, 'Christmas: 1924'

If in some smothering dreams you too could pace
Behind the wagon that we flung him in,
And watch the white eyes writhing in his face ...
If you could hear, at every jolt, the blood
Come gargling from the froth-corrupted lungs,
Obscene as cancer, bitter as the cud
Of vile incurable sores on innocent tongues –
My friend, you would not tell with such high zest
To children ardent for some desperate glory,
The old Lie ...

Wilfred Owen, 'Dulce et Decorum Est'

A strange thing, war, with its bloodshed and cruelty, its pain, grief and tears, it ought to fill every civilized person with the utmost and unwavering revulsion. It ought to and often does. And yet, and yet ...
Yet there is a strange and timeless fascination about warfare and the warrior that has exercised minds and emotions since time began.

Frederick Forsyth, Foreword to
John Keegan and Richard Holmes, *Soldiers*

On the second day
The radios failed; we turned the knobs; no answer.
On the third day a warship passed us, heading north,
Dead bodies piled on the deck. On the sixth day
A plane plunged over us into the sea. Thereafter
Nothing. The radios dumb;
And still they stand in corners of our kitchens,
And stand, perhaps, turned on, in a million rooms
All over the world. But now if they should speak,
If on a sudden they should speak again,
If on the stroke of noon a voice should speak,
We would not listen, we would not let it bring
That old bad world that swallowed its children quick
At one great gulp. We would not have it again.

Edwin Muir, 'The Horses'

Foreword

In 1916 my father, along with many other young men, was sent to prison for refusing to fight and kill for King and Country. In a letter to his mother, sent from Durham prison – my only record of his experiences there – he acknowledges his own shortcomings and failure to live up to his deeply held religious convictions. But at the same time his steadfastness and courage under harsh prison conditions, and his unwavering faith in the rightness and value of bearing witness to his beliefs in this way are also very evident. This book is a tribute to his stand for the pacifist principles which were central to his whole personality and way of life; and also to all those who have suffered in wars past or present, or have striven at whatever cost to themselves to further the cause of peace.

My father died in 1936; and in the years since then I have continued to be acutely conscious that the world has remained a violent place, in which the values for which he suffered – compassion, humanity, care for life, and peaceful cooperation – are as far as ever from being realised. Indeed, in many ways the picture seems even bleaker than when he went to prison in 1916. Wars don't just 'happen'. They are a product of the way we organise our societies, the way we live, the way we think. In her thoughtful book, *Living with the Bomb*, Dorothy Rowe asks: 'Why is there so much appalling cruelty in the world?' Cruelty, she reminds us, 'is not just to those we call our enemies but cruelty to ourselves and the world we live in ...' It is there whenever we accept that the only way to live together is to establish control over others by force, whether that force is exercised in comparatively minor ways within the family, or by public authority – the use of riot police to control crowds; imprisonment, torture or execution of political opponents, or civil or international wars. Today, Dorothy Rowe tells us:

> The warnings are there all the time for us to see. The planes fly overhead, the missiles are installed. Our newspapers, radio and television show us in words and pictures what cruelty we inflict on one another,

either directly by killing and maiming, or indirectly by allowing such cruelty to continue.

We must heed these warnings now, and change the ways in which we think and live, even though this may be difficult and painful. Dorothy Rowe acknowledges:

> Change is a risky business and many people prefer not to take that risk. Change means admitting you might be wrong; change means forgiving and forgetting; change means living with greater insecurity and uncertainty. That is why most people refuse to reflect upon themselves and their lives but instead insist that they are right and others wrong. An inability to see alternatives is regarded as a virtue and admired as a strength.

Yet the uncertainty in which we live at present, not knowing how soon the planet may be destroyed either by the unthinking greed with which we exploit and squander its resources or more suddenly through a nuclear holocaust is surely sufficiently disturbing to provide the impetus to change.

It is fortunately true, as Caroline Moorehead has shown in *Troublesome People*, her impressive survey of the 'enemies of war' from 1916 to 1986, that:

> Of all modern movements pacifism ranks with the battle for women's suffrage as the one most tenaciously, most lastingly and most universally held; and ... it has pushed people to the most remarkable feats of endurance. To profess this faith, people have fasted, marched, survived long winters of extreme discomfort protesting at the gates of military bases, and been arrested more times than it is possible to record. Some have risked the death penalty rather than alter their views; some indeed have died for it. A few, their health and spirit broken by punishment, have gone mad. There is a stubbornness, an obduracy, about pacifism that can be infuriating; it can also be heroic, admirable.

This book has been written in the belief that though it may seem at times immeasurably difficult nevertheless change is still possible. It could begin through an education of the sensibilities of young people, who, though aware that they are facing a threatened future, still retain a capacity for idealism which could be harnessed for constructive change rather than for the destruction of us all.

The ensuing critical study of a selection of literature concerned with the experience of war and violence will be of particular interest to teachers of children at all levels in secondary schools. Many of their junior pupils will already be captivated by stories of past wars, or alarmed by the prospects for their future. Older pupils working for examinations such as GCSE and A-level, and studying texts (poetry, novels, memoirs and histories) from the First and Second World Wars will find the critical examination of a wealth of varied material helpful and relevant to their studies.

It will be of interest also to parents and other concerned individuals for whom the threat of war, of a nuclear-devastated world, is a frightening prospect. Its subject is naturally of interest to all men, who would still be in the front line in any conventional war. Moreover, as was stated in the Constitution of UNESCO in 1946, 'Since wars begin in the minds of men, it is in the minds of men that peace must be constructed.' It is of special concern also to women; for though so far relatively few women have figured as active combatants in time of war, nevertheless during the course of this century an increasingly high proportion of wartime casualties have been women and their young children. As Helena M. Swanwick remarked in 1938 in *The Roots of Peace*:

> Wars have always taken a heavier toll of citizens, especially of the very young, of the old and of women, than they have of soldiers. In the World War it was estimated that, while the deaths of soldiers in all countries might have reached ten millions, those of civilians, by pestilence, famine and homelessness, in addition to direct deaths by bombardment and massacre, reached between two and three times that number ... The losses of women whose children were maimed and killed or slowly starved have a quality of lonely desolation unmatched even by the sufferings of men in battle.
>
> (Quoted in Cambridge Women's Peace Collective,
> *My Country is the Whole World*)

Such losses can only increase in future wars.

Women have throughout history been deeply involved in securing a worthwhile environment for their young children to grow up in. In countless ways so far they have therefore striven to counter war, to lobby and agitate and work for peace, going to prison as determinedly as their male counterparts as conscientious objectors in both World Wars, and they are still ready to sacrifice their comfortable home-life to protest against nuclear armaments at Greenham Common or elsewhere.

The overall intention of this book is to look carefully at the way violence and war are presented or fostered within our society, particularly in fiction and memoirs, and to examine both the macho images which are encouraged in readers (from secondary school age upwards) and also the grimmer realities which lie behind such images and behind the idealisation and social approval of both violence and war. It was General Sherman who, in Ohio in 1880, declared, 'There is many a boy here today who looks on war as all glory, but, boys, it is all hell.' Sherman was right. Yet boys are still encouraged to believe otherwise, through the toys we give them and the play fantasies we indulge in them, and, as they grow older, through film, television and literature. How many books or films exploiting the excitements of the 'Great Escape' stories of the Second World War call attention to the recapture and execution of most of the men involved; or spare a thought for the victims of the heroic 'Dambusters', those thousands of civilians and the 700 Russian POWs who were swept away in the floods when the dam walls were breached?

The opening chapter looks therefore at toughness as a male ideal, exemplified in such cultures as the past civilisations of Sparta, Senegal and the Ojibways, and discusses the relationship between the initiation rites of these people and the 'macho' male image presented today in books by much-favoured writers like Cormier, Golding and Westall. The second chapter pursues this theme to examine the presentation of various societies in historical fiction, and the ways in which seven different writers (mainly for children) approach this question of the role of war and violence in the past, its idealisation or its 'realism'.

The rest of the book engages in various ways with the world since 1914. It looks at some of the fiction, memoirs and poetry arising from the two World Wars in their various aspects – trench warfare, mechanised warfare, air warfare with its accompanying increase in civilian casualties, evacuees, refugees, concentration camps and nuclear bombs. These chapters include first-hand accounts as well as fiction, and suggest some of the differences in quality between the two kinds of writing. Their authors' depiction of the horror, tragedy and courage of war is examined in preparation for a closer look at books which engage with perennially difficult problems of conscience – the problem in particular of whether to agree to join in the battle or to continue to refuse to fight.

The remaining chapters are concerned with the world since 1945, a world of the cold war, of unceasing minor conflicts, of reliance upon the 'nuclear deterrent' and of escalating violence against the individual whether by governments or by other individuals; with various forms of protest against nuclear power and weapons, and with 'fictions of a nuclear disaster' and prophecies of a post-nuclear future after a devastating Third World War. Finally there is a discussion of the role of women both in war and in campaigning for peace during the present century, and a chapter on the poetry of war.

The material presented has been chosen subject to its availa-

bility at the time, and to the limitations of my own knowledge
and abilities. As far as possible I have allowed the books to speak
for themselves, whilst offering my own evaluation of their success
or failure, and of the relative importance of what they have to say
for modern readers. I have also been concerned with the need for
a closer, more responsible look at books which seem to glorify violence, or to imply a virtue in resorting to force and slaughter. In
this context I would quote from the testimony of a former professional soldier, Michael Biggs, recorded by Caroline Moorehead in
Troublesome People. He said:

> 'I cannot be convinced, and the army only made this plainer, that you
> can bring about any kind of happiness, prevent trouble or solve dis-
> putes through force. History has shown that, if anything, it makes
> others more efficient at killing next time. I know, I know that violence
> only legitimizes further violence.'

Or as my father used to say: 'Those who live by the sword will die
by the sword.'

1

A Tough Nut to Crack

In *Firing Line*, a book which presents a fascinating analysis of the military mind, Richard Holmes concludes that we are imprisoned by a cultural belief in violence as an inevitable, acceptable and even laudable way of settling disputes. Though this is by no means the sole reason for our continuing support of the use of force in both domestic and international affairs, it is undoubtedly a strong element in the equation. Certainly toughness as a male virtue has been central to many civilisations of the past. The city state of Sparta was noted for its severe training of its young men, rewarding the endurance of pain with the prized accolade of Artemis victor. In *Theras*, by Caroline Dale Snedeker, a story much read in junior schools in the 1920s and 1930s, Drako explains to the horrified Athenian boy:

> 'While the image [of Artemis] was in Tauris they offered human victims to her. So now she likes human blood. Every year a number of boys are flogged before her altar until the blood flows. The boy who can stand up the longest under the flogging is the victor, and wins the Artemis crown ... Strepon ... is an Artemis victor. We're very proud of him.'

A strikingly similar ritual is described by the Senegalese writer, Birago Diop, in his short story for adults, 'Sarzan'. On the day of the Koteba, the Testing, he tells us, the initiate stood 'legs apart, arms spread in the shape of a cross', in the centre of a circle of 'bare-chested youngsters, each carrying a long branch of balazan wood, stripped clean and supple as a whip ... turning about to the rhythm of the tom-tom.' As the blows fell on the initiate's chest, the 'sharp voice of the flute would go a note higher, the tom-tom would grow softer', thus celebrating this 'test of endurance, the testing for insensibility to pain'. For 'the child who cries when he is hurt will not make a man.'

Sergeant Keita, returning home from the 'civilising' influence of his British army experience, now derides this ritual as 'the ways of savages'. But the narrator protests that Keita himself had benefited

1

from this toughening process, and that it was necessary for survival in the harsh conditions of their lives. He adds:

> The ways of savages? Perhaps. But I was thinking that elsewhere, where I came from, we had left these initiations behind. For our adolescents there was no longer a 'house of men' where the body, the mind and the character were tempered; where the ancient *passines*, the riddles and conundrums, were learned by dint of beatings on the bent back and the held-out fingers, and where the *kassaks*, the age-old memory training songs whose words and wisdom descend to us from the dark nights, were assured their place in our heads by the heat of live coals that burned the palms of our hands. I was thinking that as far as I could see we had still gained nothing, that perhaps we had left these old ways behind without having caught up with the new ones.

A similarly rigorous training is described by Ewan Clarkson in *The Many-Forked Branch*, his novel about American Indians set in Minnesota in the 1830s. He tells how Broken Knife, the Ojibway hero of the story, has learned endurance.

> Up on the ledge, Broken Knife had been enduring both hunger and cold. He was no stranger to either, having been trained from a very early age to undergo hardship. Even as a small boy his parents had encouraged him in this, offering him a choice of breakfast or a handful of ashes. If he chose the food, no comment was made, but if he took the ashes he was complimented and made a great fuss of. Later he learned to go without eating for days at a time, and to sleep out in the open in all weathers, while he waited for the dreams and visions that would foretell his future.

The training of the Dakota, Red Elk, was even more rigorous:

> He had danced at the pole, and felt the bite of the leather thongs tear through the muscles of his shoulders, and not known fear. He had endured hours of torture, but that had been self-inflicted in a frenzy induced by the chanting and the drums, his pain made sweeter by the watchful eyes of the women of his tribe. It had been suffering with a goal, and afterward there had been rest and peace, and the soft caresses of the women to soothe his wounds.

By the end of the story, the value of such training is demonstrated when Broken Knife both endures and survives the harsh weather, hunger and privations of his solitary excursion into the severe Minnesota winter, and also the pain inflicted by his Dakota captors before his courage and steadfastness under torture persuade them to set him free.

In several cultures there is a further dimension to this harsh training; the exclusion from the group of any who fail the test, either by death or by exile. When Drako falls in the Platanistos, a fierce battle between two teams of boys, no one is allowed to help him. Theras is pulled back from his rash attempt to save his friend by a furious Spartan who shouts: 'Killed! Of course he's killed. He'd no business to fall. Do we want a boy that *fell* in Platanistos!'

Theras is devastated by this incident. He feels that 'Sparta, in spite of her laws, her military drill (the best in the world), her splendid, fearless, beautiful men, was really a savage state. But Athens was civilised.' So he runs away, back to Athens, collecting on the way a friend from among the peaceful sheepfarming Achaeans, the original inhabitants of Sparta, now kept in subjection but really, Theras thinks, far more civilised than their conquerors. The subsequent adventures of the two boys call for courage and toughness which match that shown by the Spartan youth, but are called out by necessity, not deliberately inflicted as part of training.

It is interesting to note similarities between this story of Athens and Sparta and *Warrior Scarlet*, Rosemary Sutcliff's story of Bronze Age Britain. There initiation into manhood is achieved partly by a wolf-slaying, which the initiate must manage single-handed. When Drem, handicapped by his withered arm, is in real danger of failure and death, his close friend Vortrix intervenes to save him. Vortrix is punished for his interference by a severe nine-day ritual cleansing; but since 'a boy who failed in his Wolf Slaying and did not die was dead to the Tribe', Drem is cast out to the Half People, a shepherd tribe who stand in the same relation to Drem's folk as the Achaeans did to the Spartans. During the time he spends with the Half People, Drem, like Theras, learns a different kind of courage from the harsh physical testing customary among his own folk: and he learns to value tenderness and patience, and to realise that there are wider issues than physical endurance by which to judge the value of any individual to his community. Like Theras, however, Drem redeems his failure to stay the course laid down – he succeeds against all expectation in slaying his wolf. In spite of the questioning of values in these two stories, therefore, there is in the end an endorsement of the ideals of courage and endurance.

Ever-present death and danger made stern training seem a necessary survival measure for the protagonists of these stories. Even so, when the culture is alien and distanced in time it is easy to dismiss such initiation rites as 'the ways of savages'. It is less easy to detect and evaluate vestiges of similar practices in our own, apparently 'civilised' and cosy modern world. We may no longer accept and defend the ethos of the tough public school world of *Tom Brown's Schooldays* or *Stalky and Co*, with the beatings and bullying, legitimate and covert, which were somehow supposed to 'build character' and produce young men who would be 'the backbone of the Empire'. But neither bullying nor 'initiation rites' are entirely absent from modern Grange Hill-type school stories, nor is the admiration we are expected to accord to those who survive a tough regime – the Duke of Edinburgh award type of hero or heroine, or the toughie admired in stories by writers such as Robert Westall or Robert Cormier. *The Chocolate War*, for instance, opens with an account of a practice (American) football match:

They murdered him.
  As he turned to take the ball, a dam burst against the side of his head and a grenade shattered his stomach. Engulfed by nausea, he pitched towards the grass ... Suddenly, he was caught from behind and whirled violently, a toy boat caught in a whirlpool. Landing on his knees, hugging the ball, he urged himself to ignore the pain that gripped his groin, knowing that it was important to betray no sign of distress, remembering The Goober's advice, 'Coach is testing you, testing, and he's looking for guts.'
  I've got guts, Jerry murmured, getting up by degrees, careful not to displace any of his bones or sinews ... He was aware of the other players around him, helmeted and grotesque, creatures from an unknown world. He had never felt so lonely in his life, abandoned, defenceless.
  On the third play, he was hit simultaneously by three of them: one, his knees; another, his stomach; a third, his head – the helmet no protection at all. His body seemed to telescope into itself but all the parts didn't fit, and he was stunned by the knowledge that pain isn't just one thing – it is cunning and various, sharp here and sickening there, burning here and clawing there. He clutched himself as he hit the ground.

The coach is unsympathetic.

'What the hell you want to play football for? You need more meat on those bones. What the hell you trying to play quarter-back for? You'd make a better end. Maybe.'
  The coach looked like an old gangster: broken nose, a scar on his cheek like a stitched shoe-string. He needed a shave, his stubble like slivers of ice. He growled and swore and was merciless. But a helluva coach, they said.

Sport for savages? The correspondences are all there, in the underlying tone of approval of the boy's efforts to be tough, to endure his pain without flinching or betraying distress, in the free use of war imagery, and in the description of the coach himself, appropriately merciless towards anyone wishing to make the team and battle-scarred from his own past as a football player (American style in this story, but easy to match from British accounts of their own brand of the game in novels like David Storey's *This Sporting Life*). From Jerry's point of view, anything is endurable so long as he makes the team: 'A strange happiness invaded him. He knew he'd been massacred by the oncoming players ... but he'd survived – he'd got to his feet ... Any position, as long as he made the team.' This is the beginning of a story in which Jerry is to be massacred in good truth, in a testing which goes far beyond 'making the team', and which will threaten his life. Unlike *Theras* or *Warrior Scarlet*, however, *The Chocolate War* ends with Jerry's failure.

It is a brutal story: dedicated by Cormier to his son, and defended by him on the strength of his adolescent fan mail – his audience knows what it wants. *The Times Educational Supplement's* review, quoted on the back cover, compares it approvingly with Golding's *Lord of the Flies*, and remarks: 'This is a tour de force, and a tour de force of realism. It is all the more important in that the actual experience of adolescent boys is integral to Cormier's story. The book is uncompromising and unsentimental.' Adrian Chambers writes: 'It is a book about how the bullies always win. It's Tom Brown with Flashman in charge.'

There is a need for books which will help young people to face reality, however distasteful that reality may be. But all books which feature violence, even when ostensibly they are critical of it, inevitably offer an undesirable invitation to share, vicariously, in the violence involved, and tacitly to approve those who inflict it, as well as those who endure. It is always difficult to judge, in any given instance, how much this matters: the dividing line is thin, and it is a shifting line. What will repel one reader will stimulate another to excited sadistic involvement with the bullies, or masochistic involvement with the victims. That this is so cannot justify turning one's back on the problem, or censoring all books which include violent incidents; but it is important to be clear about the precise nature of what is being offered.

If, then, we look first at the opening paragraphs of *The Chocolate War* quoted above, it is clear that Jerry is a sympathetic character, and that his experience of the game, including its violence, is accepted as admirable. Though this is only a team of boys playing ball on a field, the players themselves are given an exciting image – 'helmeted, grotesque, creatures from an unknown world'. They belong to the world of sci-fi fantasy. Their actions therefore are glamorous, and can be distanced from the normal behaviour of responsible flesh-and-blood boys. So there is no reaction to the way they set upon Jerry – three of them, attacking simultaneously his knees, his stomach and his head. Jerry's ordeal, moreover, is likened to adult war experience – 'a grenade shattered his stomach' – and to battling against elemental forces – 'a dam burst against the side of his head', he is 'a toy boat caught in a whirl-pool'. He is a hero, at this moment, the dimension of his pain and his endurance being elevated to a plane far higher than participation in a voluntary ball game. Anyone seeking to question his motives for subjecting himself to all this, or the motives of the adult world in setting up the situation and offering praise and commendation to the participants, would instantly be branded as an outsider, soft and womanish to boot. For this is a man's world, one from which, like the battlefield, women – save for a few deter-mined Amazonian feminists – have traditionally been excluded.

The tone of approving acceptance of this state of affairs, however, cannot but affect the quality and nature of the response to the events of the rest of the book. Jerry and his ball-playing activities are sympathetically reported: the teacher, Brother Leon, and the bullies, Archie and his side-kick Obie, are not – at least there are reservations expressed about *their* goings-on. But on a purely dispassionate level, it is difficult to measure precisely the difference in quality between the opening description of the foot-ball game and the closing episode in which Jerry is hoodwinked into a truly slaughterous fight with Emile Janza. In this fight the audience calls both the punchers and the particular punch, and the victim is expected to receive the blows without defending himself – like the Spartan Artemis victor, in fact. For this arrange-ment meant that 'the fighters on the platform would have no will of their own'. They would have to deliver and receive blows pre-cisely as directed by the audience.

Jerry had girded himself for the blow, but it took him by surprise with its savagery and viciousness. The entire planet was jarred for a moment, the stadium swaying, the lights dancing. The pain in his neck was excruciating – his head had snapped back from the impact of Janza's fist. Sent reeling backwards, he fought to stay on his feet and he somehow managed not to fall. His jaw was on fire, he tasted acid. Blood, maybe. But he pressed his lips together. He shook his head, quick vision-clearing shakings, and established himself in the world once more.

Before he could gather himself together again, Carter's voice cried out, '*Janza, right to the stomach*,' and Janza struck without warning a short sharp blow that missed Jerry's stomach but caught him in the chest. His breath went away, like it did in football, and then came back again.

The comparison with the football experience is made explicitly here, and is there also in the target of the blows – the head and the stomach – the difference being that this time there is no protection. But there is another dimension in Jerry's own response. Whereas in the game his thoughts had been wholly taken up with getting into the team, in this fight he begins to take on the savagery of his enemies.

> He cocked his right arm. He tasted bile in his mouth. He let his arm go. The glove struck Janza full face and Janza staggered back. The result surprised Jerry. He had never struck anyone like that before, in fury, premeditated, and he'd enjoyed catapulting all his power towards the target, the release of all his frustrations, hitting back at last, lashing out, getting revenge not only against Janza but all that he represented.

The reader is here invited to enter into Jerry's justified rage and frustration, and as both participants lose control and go in for the kill, while the crowds are 'in a turmoil now, jeering, urging Janza on', there is no doubt of the quality and direction of the reader's involvement. 'And that crowd out there he had wanted to impress? To prove himself before? Hell, they wanted him to lose, they wanted him killed, for Christ's sake.' And as Goober frantically calls for the rain of punches on Jerry's body to be stopped, 'his voice was lost in the thunder of screaming voices, voices calling for the kill ... *kill him, kill him.*'

From excited participation in this mob frenzy the reader is called back, to be sure, to a pity for Jerry's pain and broken body: but his fractured jaw and possible internal injuries are, after all, 'the risks of the boxing ring', and he has gone down, he is 'chicken', he has failed the test. So Brother Jacques, the 'good' teacher, can only give a 'gentle, guarded rebuke' to Brother Leon, who is ultimately responsible for what has happened, whereas the unspeakable Brother Leon can assert that he is still in control, with his commendation of 'all that energy and zeal and enthusiasm' and his hypocritical acceptance that Archie, though he 'really didn't use [his] best judgment', nevertheless 'did it for the school. For Trinity.'

In between these two incidents, which epitomise the ethos of the book, is the story of Jerry's stubborn but doomed resistance to the subtle, relentless, sadistic bullying of both Brother Leon and the powerful secret school society, The Vigils. Carter, the president of this society, is the physical bully, but Archie, the psychological bully, is the real force behind the scenes.

Archie is 'a bastard', but there is a persistent undercurrent of admiration for him, evident in the love–hate relationship with Obie, his acolyte, whose admiration for Archie's quick wits, quick tongue, and fertile invention of torments for his victims is balanced by his awareness that he, too, is one of the victims. Obie, like everyone else, is 'always waiting for [Archie] to fail, to fall flat on his face', but is also waiting admiringly to see what he would come up with next, and to join from the side-lines in Archie's own feverish satisfaction as, each time he scores, he is 'carried on marvellous waves of power and glory'. The reader shares Obie's perception of Archie: indeed it is a fascinating performance. Jerry, for all his stubbornness and fighting spirit, cannot match it. But then Jerry is cast in the role of loser, the one we are to be sorry for.

Both Brother Leon and Archie are past masters in the art of destructiveness, creating havoc and misery, tormenting their victims by skilful psychological ploys which for sheer evil enjoyment of another's humiliation and distress outstrip the cruder physical bombardment of Jerry's final debacle. Carter, who stage-manages this fight, has no time for the subtler stuff.

> Now, he watched the kid Renault, looking as if he was ready to faint with fright, his face pale and eyes wide with dread, and Archie having fun with him. Jesus. Carter hated this psychological crap. He loved boxing where everything was visible – the jabs, the hooks, the round-house swings, the glove in the stomach.

You can take your pick of torments in this story, but there is no doubt that the sheer inventiveness of mean, spiteful, malicious tricks from both Leon and Archie compels attention even while it disgusts.

So, incidentally, does that thread of adolescent lust running through the book. 'Watching girls and devouring them with your eyes – rape by eyeball – was something you did automatically.' There is plenty of 'rape by eyeball' in this story of male power-fantasy.

The trouble is that by the end of the book Cormier almost persuades his readers that this state of affairs is normal, what goes on everywhere, in and out of school; that it is, in fact, a 'tour de force of realism'. Like *Lord of the Flies* in this respect, the book leaves a sour taste in the mouth, a conviction that in our most secret and persistent dreams we are all drowning in a cynical cesspool of corruption. Within the book, Carter attributes this state of affairs to Archie. 'Archie repelled him in many ways but most of all by the way he made everybody feel dirty, contaminated, polluted.' Jerry, too, is aware that Archie has this effect on him.

> A new sickness invaded Jerry, the sickness of knowing what he had become, another animal, another beast, another violent person in a violent world, inflicting damage, not disturbing the universe but damaging it. He had allowed Archie to do this to him.

As a result, Jerry is not merely defeated in body, but in spirit.

> He had to tell Goober ... to do whatever they wanted you to do ... They tell you to do your thing, but they don't mean it. They don't want you to do your thing, not unless it happens to be their thing, too. It's a laugh, Goober, a fake. Don't disturb the universe, Goober, no matter what the posters say.

This extremely pessimistic view of human nature – which is, of course, ultimately the responsibility of the author, not of individual characters – is unfortunately one which can readily evoke a response from the volatile adolescent reader in his more despondent moods, crowding out the idealism which, at this stage of human experience, is also there to be utilised. It is salutary to remember that the books Primo Levi and Bruno Bettelheim have written out of their experiences in Auschwitz, Dachau and Buchenwald, though unflinching in their description of the inhumanity and degradation of the concentration camps, nevertheless convey a resilience and a toughness of hope and compassion which contrast strongly with the despairing acceptance of human evil in Cormier's novel.

The Machine-Gunners, by Robert Westall, set in the Second World War, a time of violence which affected a generation of British youngsters, is a robust, 'down-to-earth' realistic book with the added excitement of a real war to test the courage of its protagonists. But this book, too, betrays its author's ambivalence towards the violence he portrays. The hero, Chas McGill, is an entirely sympathetic character, popular with his mates and leader of a mixed gang of lads – and one girl. He has the second-best collection of war souvenirs in Garmouth, and busies himself looking for anything else he can pick up after the nightly air raids.

It is his rivalry with the bully Boddser which sends Chas into the wood where he finds a machine gun complete with cartridge belt – and a dead German gunner.

> The gunner was sitting there, watching him. One hand, in a soft fur mitt, was stretched up as if to retrieve the gun; the other lay in his overalled lap. He wore the black leather flying-helmet of the Luftwaffe, and goggles. His right eye, pale grey, watched through the goggle-glass tolerantly and a little sadly. He looked a nice man, young.
>
> The glass of the other goggle was gone. Its rim was thick with sticky red, and inside was a seething mass of flies, which rose and buzzed angrily at Chas's arrival, then sank back into the goggle again ...
>
> He wanted to let go of the fuselage, drop off and run home. But something in his mind wouldn't let him; something found the dead man fascinating. Something made him reach out and touch the gloved

hand. Inside the sheepskin the fingers were hard as iron. The arm and whole body was stiff. The gunner moved, but only as a statue or a toy soldier would move, all in one piece. The flies rose and buzzed. Inside the goggle was a deep red hole full of what looked like ... Chas dropped and was violently sick against a little door marked *Nicht Anfassen*.

Chas's squeamish reactions to this horrible sight do not prevent him from scoring off Audrey when, later, she too finds it more than she can stomach. His remarks, 'Girls aren't allowed to look. They can't stand it' and 'I knew a girl wouldn't be any *good*' both help him to wipe out the memory of his own weakness and indicate the direction of his thinking. Boys are expected to be tough, to take death and its horrors in their stride.

In the course of the story Chas has many opportunities to train himself in such toughness, helped at times by the pretence that he is a French Resistance fighter confronting a Gestapo swine, or by some similar projection into the adult war. When the police sergeant says, 'This war's doing bad things to kids. They're running wild. You don't know where you are with them any more', he gets short shrift from Chas's father, who has no liking for the police. Nevertheless, the story makes clear that he is right. As the narrative proceeds there is a steady progress towards an increased hardening of attitudes in the various members of Chas's gang – in spite of their continuing concern for each other and for the German airman they capture – which persists to the very end of the book, and to some extent redeems it. All the same, the brutality as it occurs and escalates is not pretty.

At one point, for instance, when Clogger has rescued Chas from Boddser:

> He turned to Chas. 'It's up to you, Chas. We can't afford this lad any more. Shall I do him proper?' Chas didn't even think. He was black with hate.
>
> 'Do him proper,' he said.
>
> It had been a fair fight. There had been a time when Clogger's nose had streamed red, and Chas thought, horror upon horrors, that he might lose. But Clogger cared no more for his bleeding nose than a fly. He just kept on and on, white, silent, steady as a man chopping wood. He never touched Boddser's face; always hit his body where it wouldn't show. And Boddser was much too keen not to get hurt.
>
> So, in the end, Boddser was lying on the ground being very sick. Chas watched fascinated as the green strings of slime trailed from his mouth.

Even then, Clogger has not finished with Boddser. To make absolutely sure he will not tell who has beaten him:

Clogger raised his boot and kicked Boddser in the ribs three times. It made a terrible noise, like a butcher chopping a leg of lamb. Then he kicked him three times more, and three times more. Boddser was much more sick now. When he looked up, his eyes had changed. He looked as if he understood something he had never understood before ...

So has Chas. He understands now just how far Clogger is prepared to go, and he doesn't like it. But Clogger refuses to allow him to run away from the implications of what has happened.

'It was you who said to do him proper.'
   'I didn't know what doing him proper *meant*.'
   'Ye didnae think it meant gieing him a clout and sending him bawling to his ma? Ye didnae want the poliss round here in an hour, did ye?' Chas shook his head mutely.
   'Then what other way would *ye* have shut his trap?' Chas shook his head again.
   'Och, you're nobbut a bairn.'

Though once again he is sick with shock, Chas denies this, indignantly, and draws from Clogger the admiring admission, 'Ah guess you're a hard man in your own way, Chassy McGill.'
   This judgement is endorsed by the fathers of both Chas and his friend, Cem, after the action is played out and the children, in an access of panic, have shot their German friend, Rudi, with the captured machine-gun.

'I'll not say *much* for my lad,' said Mr McGill slowly, 'except he thought he was *fighting* the Germans.'
   'Oh, hush,' said Mrs McGill. 'Chassy could have killed somebody.'
   'I'm not talking about his sense, missus. I'm talking about his guts.'
   'Aye,' said Cem Senior, looking hard at Mr Parton. 'That's one thing the kids didn't lack. Guts.' And he spat on the ground.

It is noticeable how quickly Mrs McGill's protest is silenced by this invocation of the male virtue of 'guts'. It is of course desirable that young people *should* have 'guts'. The question is, what kind of guts, and how can this quality be encouraged in a way that is compatible with compassion and concern for others? Neither teachers nor parents nor society at large can safely abdicate responsibility for the attitudes they foster in the young, whether by precept or example or through the literature they offer them to read. By the way the story is told, *The Machine-Gunners* does leave open-ended, and so invites serious discussion of, some of these issues. How far should Clogger's assault on Boddser be condoned or condemned? Should Rudi have allowed himself to be persuaded into mending the machine-gun for the gang? What was the relationship between those attitudes fostered in a society at war and the way the children's own attitudes hardened and their actions developed? What responsibility do the adults bear anyway for their own confusion of motives and beliefs, including the myth which persists even in time of peace that it is admirable for boys to be 'tough' in the ways described? Although these questions are clearly implicit in the narrative, the story is still finally weighted in favour of toughness, so they must be raised deliberately with young readers. And there are many adults, too, in our present society who would fail to see the challenge to their assumptions lying behind Westall's sympathetic presentation of Chas McGill, Clogger and the rest of the gang. There are also questions to be asked from a more detached position outside the story. What is the function of the more extreme scenes of violence, or incidents which excite disgust? Are they really necessary to the story, or is Westall betraying his readers into the kind of fascinated if horrified enjoyment of morbid or cruel detail felt by Chas at the sight of the dead airman or at the beating up of Boddser? Is there not here, too, an assumption that we should *all* be tough enough to take this kind of thing?

These are questions to be asked also of Golding's *Lord of the Flies*, a novel which could be said to be a forerunner of books like *The Machine-Gunners*. There is, of course, a significant difference in intention in one important respect. This novel for adults contains a strong vein of realism and adventure which makes it a compelling story for younger readers as well. But the main emphasis in the story, and the aspect that invites esteem from those who accept its thesis, is its quality as fable, through which Golding reveals Man's unregenerate nature by means of the moral deterioration of a group of schoolboys stranded on a desert island without adult guidance or control.

There is a shadowiness, an air of unreality, in the circumstances surrounding both the boys' arrival on the island and their eventual departure from it which effectively cuts off their experiences there from the rest of the world. Despite allusions to an atom bomb, a passenger tube ejected from a plane that had been shot down, the 'men with megaphones' to whom the boys had given 'simple obedience' and a 'civilization in ruins', it is evident that Golding has chosen his protagonists and their situation to suit his own convenience rather than to give any reality or background to their plight. They are a motley crew of boys, aged between six and twelve years, including, incredibly, a posse of cathedral choirboys, who emerge mysteriously as a group marching in formation, carrying shorts, shirts and other garments in their hands, but still wearing the choristers' regalia – square black cap, and 'the black cloaks which bore a large silver cross on the left breast and each neck ... finished off with a hambone frill'. The effect of this is largely to preclude any of the questions invited by Westall's novel on the influence upon the boys of their normal background and upbringing, a state of affairs reinforced indeed by the naval officer's reproach at the end: 'I should have thought that a pack of British boys – you're all British aren't you? – would have put up a better show than that.' Any deliberate irony in this is discounted by the way in which the boys' steady progress on the downward path is illustrated by a reversion from their early 'civilised' inhibitions to a state of painted savagery. At first Roger is prevented by inbuilt fears of 'the protection of parents and school and policemen and the law' from stoning the small boy, Henry; while Jack, when he first encounters a pig, is unable to kill it, 'because of the enormity of the knife descending and cutting into living flesh; because of the unbearable blood'. It is not until he paints his face that he becomes 'liberated from shame and self-consciousness' and able then to execute a kind of war dance, his laughter changing to a 'bloodthirsty snarling', which will give him and his mates the courage to hunt and kill.

Few critics pause to reflect on the assumptions behind the contrasts here being made between the 'British way of life' and 'painted savagery', though these are stereotypes which reflect a narrow conception of different communities and their values. It does not seem to have occurred to Golding that boys of the same age brought up in 'primitive' tribal societies would be better equipped in survival techniques of the kind which would not require painted faces for their execution, but would certainly include an understanding of the need to cooperate for the common good – a quality signally lacking in these British boys. There is little sense of sustained concern or responsibility towards others in the group, even after the untimely disappearance of one of the 'littluns'.

This is one result, no doubt, of Golding's decision to illustrate his thesis through one half only of humanity – the male half. There are several consequences of this choice, one being the suspicion that under the surface we are seeing another 'testing time' in 'the men's house', and that this is one of the reasons for the novel's obsession with the power struggle between Ralph and Jack and the accompanying escalation into brutality and violence.

There are a number of scenes in *Lord of the Flies* which fall into the same category as those already quoted from *The Machine-Gunners*, and perhaps served unconsciously as a model for them. One such is the episode of the dead airman, and his effect upon Simon.

Simon saw a humped thing suddenly sit up on the top and look down at him. He hid his face and toiled on.

The flies had found the figure too. The life-like movement would scare them off for a moment so that they made a dark cloud round the head. Then as the blue material of the parachute collapsed the corpulent figure would bow forward, sighing, and the flies settle once more.

Simon felt his knees smack the rock. He crawled forward and soon he understood. The tangle of lines showed him the mechanics of this parody; he examined the white nasal bones, the teeth, the colours of corruption. He saw how pitilessly the layers of rubber and canvas held together the poor body that should be rotting away. Then the wind blew again and the figure lifted, bowed, and breathed foully at him. Simon knelt on all fours and was sick till his stomach was empty.

The imagery here is a repetition of the earlier symbolic mounting of the pig's head on a stick, and its transformation thereby into Beelzebub, Lord of the Flies. It is an image which is central to the theme of the book, and points back to the first appearance of the black-cloaked choristers, who, ironically, are to become the 'flies', the spearhead of the evil forces on the island.

The pile of guts was a black blob of flies that buzzed like a saw ... They were black and iridescent green and without number; and in front of Simon, the Lord of the Flies hung on his stick and grinned. At last Simon gave up and looked back; saw the white teeth and dim eyes, the blood – and his gaze was held by that ancient, inescapable recognition. In Simon's right temple, a pulse began to beat on the brain.

There are many such scenes, told with a vividness of detail which betrays the reader into an even greater fascination with evil, brutality, violence and bloodlust than was felt in *The Machine-Gunners*. There are the frequent hunts, with the ritual chanting of 'kill him, kill him'; the death of Simon, when the frenzied crowd 'surged after [him], poured down the rock, leapt on the beast, screamed, struck, bit, tore'; and the death of Piggy.

Piggy fell forty feet and landed on his back across that square, red rock in the sea. His head opened and stuff came out and turned red. Piggy's arms and legs twitched a bit, like a pig's after it had been killed. Then the sea breathed again in a long, slow sigh, the water boiled white and pink over the rock; and when it went, sucking back again, the body of Piggy was gone.

There is also the final savage hunting of Ralph, the climax of the book and of all the violence. It is an orgiastic affair, 'the end of innocence', an exploration of 'the darkness of man's heart' for the reader as well as for Ralph, with none of the compassion or sense of hope which marked the books by Levi or Bettelheim. What, precisely, do advocates of this book expect young readers to gain from it?

It is interesting to compare some aspects of *Lord of the Flies* with Ivan Southall's story of six youngsters – four boys and two girls – stranded on an island 50 to 60 miles off the coast of Australia. In *To the Wild Sky* Southall too explores the problems of survival and cooperation facing his protagonists, but it is a slighter story for readers of 13 or 14, and one without Golding's theological 'message'.

The children concerned inhabit a saner, more matter-of-fact world; one not at war. They are plunged into adventure by the sudden death of the pilot who is taking them to Gerald's home for his birthday party. The ensuing trauma is serious enough – Gerald must somehow pilot the plane to safety, in spite of his limited knowledge and experience, and there will be the pilot's body to cope with, and the perils of a deserted island with slim hopes of rescue. But Southall's story achieves dramatic impact without unnecessary indulgence in violence or disgust. He concentrates rather upon the realistic detail of Gerald's handling of the plane, his subsequent lapse into a state of shock, the fighting and dissension and difficulties initially caused by the highly individual characters of the protagonists, and their fumbling but hopeful attempts to pull together to survive. At the end of the story we do not know whether they will succeed, or what hope they have of rescue, but we do know that they will not give in easily. It is noticeable, also, that the presence of the two girls – not tomboys, this time, like Audrey in *The Machine-Gunners*, and certainly not romantic angels, either – adds a caring dimension to the story which surfaces so rarely, and all too briefly, in *Lord of the Flies*.

Another relatively slight story for young readers which nevertheless invites comparison on its own level is Jan Needle's *A Game of Soldiers*. It is set at the time of the Falklands War, and through their confrontation with Maria, a young Argentinian soldier, explores the implications of the effect of the war ethos upon two boys and a girl. Michael is determined to kill this enemy soldier, but when the time comes finds himself unable to pull the trigger. He is too keenly aware of the soldier's youth and humanity. But the local farmers and the British soldiers have no such inhibitions. They come rushing to the scene with all the panoply of war and shoot the 16-year-old wounded boy out of hand.

Michael lay on his back for endless hours, holding his knife on his stomach as a comforter. He felt sick and stunned with the shock of it all, but with little twinges of excitement, despite himself. The men and the helicopter had been terrifying, true – but marvellous, as well. The noise, the urgency, the ... then he would remember Maria and the shots. Then he would squirm, and twist, and worry.

What had his father said? It served the bugger right. He was a soldier, fighting in a war, and he got what was coming to him. Michael had tried to explain that it had not been like that, but his father had laughed.

'He was there, so he bought it,' he said. 'What did you expect them to do – give him a kiss or something? You know what they say, Mike. All's fair in love and war.'

But he was injured, thought Michael. He was ill. He was a prisoner of war. Well – he should have been. What had gone wrong? Surely that was not what *should* have happened? Surely there were rules.

Since throughout the story Michael has involved himself imaginatively with the fighting, wearing a combat jacket, carrying a commando knife and talking 'tough', his about-face is the more telling. It leaves the reader questioning the morality of this 'game of soldiers', whether it is played by boys or by grown men, in fantasy or for real. The story – the author's novelisation of his television series – is more lightweight than the other books, but it makes a serious contribution to the discussion of conventional attitudes to war and violence, and must lead us to examine carefully the effect upon young readers of novels and stories like these. Do they encourage young people towards a toughness necessary to enable them to face the perils of the adult world, as was the intention of primitive training and initiation rites? Or are they, in reality, a sick indulgence in violent fantasy which undermines the strength of moral compassion, and is alien, therefore, to the needs of the modern world? In a nuclear age desperately in need of finding ways of living in peaceful cooperation, is it not a serious disservice to the future of all mankind to encourage instead a habit of mind which, as Mary Midgley remarked in an article in the *Guardian* (28 January 1987) 'responds to any international problem, not by serious efforts to improve relations, but by ordering more and better missiles'?

2

A Dream of Heroes

Golding and Westall are correct in recognising the fascination that evil has for us, together with its accompaniments of blood, violence and horror. We cannot wish this away by disapproval or censorship, or refuse to acknowledge the need young people have to explore the darker side of their natures, or, for that matter, to elevate natural and innate feelings of hatred and aggression into the heroism of physically beating and battering down the enemy. Aggressive impulses are, after all, important both for survival and for progress: but to these ends they need to be channelled and utilised, not either indulged or suppressed.

Through story, fiction, poetry, drama and autobiography we can explore such feelings in safety, and confront in fantasy the problems which trouble us in our own lives. Literature sometimes presents an ideal of heroism, lent romantic glamour by distance from the sordid present, but we can also find there a salutary realism which clearly presents both sides of the picture. We may remember the stirring speech which Shakespeare gives to Henry V at Agincourt:

> We few, we happy few, we band of brothers:
> For he to-day that sheds his blood with me,
> Shall be my brother: be he ne'er so vile,
> This day shall gentle his condition.
> And gentlemen in England, now a-bed,
> Shall think themselves accurs'd they were not here;
> And hold their manhoods cheap, whiles any speaks,
> That fought with us upon Saint Crispin's day.

But even in this atmosphere of heroic battles and 'manhood', another facet of war is presented by Williams, an ordinary soldier who can see all too clearly the price to be paid.

> But if the cause be not good, the King himself hath a heavy reckoning to make, when all those legs, and arms, and heads, chopped off in a battle, shall join together at the latter day, and cry all 'We died at such

17

a place,' some swearing, some crying for a surgeon; some upon their wives, left poor behind them; some upon the debts they owe, some upon their children rawly left: I am afeared, there are few die well, that die in a battle: for how can they charitably dispose of any thing, when blood is their argument?

This complexity of motivation and awareness has fascinated many writers of historical fiction. They have been acutely conscious of their readers' desire to share vicariously in the world's heroism, to prove worthy and courageous, winning glory and recognition even if only by proxy through the medium of fiction. Many have also been aware of the complementary evil, destruction and devastation attendant in real life upon the lust for glory and power; that however stirring the speeches of the leaders may be, there is always a reverse side, in death and injury and 'children rawly left'.

Peter Carter graphically explores this complexity in *Madatan*, a novel for readers from 11 to 14, through the experiences of Madaah in eighth-century Britain. Madaah's relatively peaceful herdsman's life in the Western Isles comes to an abrupt end when, while still a boy, he is carried off to Orkney and Ragnar's Hall by the fierce, raiding Norsemen. There he learns to survive in the face of adversity. Being young, tough and quickwitted, he soon adapts to his captors' rough, violent way of life. He learns about their gods, 'the great Odin and the mighty Thor, gentle Baldir and cunning Loki', and about 'the dead heroes who feasted in Odin's hall, Valhalla, as the Norsemen feasted in Orkney, and who would, at the ending of all things, fight a last fight against the monsters, the enemies of all men – and of all gods.'

These gods reflect, naturally, the Norsemen's own view of the meaning of life, their values and aspirations, which as portrayed here are essentially warlike. Carter has, to be sure, found little place for the gentler attributes of the Norsemen, described by Henry Treece in his introduction to the first book in his trilogy *The Viking Saga*. There he reminds us that:

When they had settled in this country they became some of its most law-abiding inhabitants. Moreover, their wonderful sagas show that their literature was a highly cultivated one; the splendid construction of their longships demonstrates their intelligence and ingenuity.

Though some of these characteristics are apparent during Madaah's brief encounter with his captors, in *Madatan* it is the harsh toughness of their lives and outlook which is most strikingly portrayed, and which impresses Madaah as he contrasts the brutal self-interest of these bold, dangerous adventurers with his own peaceful culture.

Madaah thought much of these things. At times he would wander away along the coast and hear, in the crying of the gulls, the voices of his ancestors, as if they were calling to him not to forget them and their gentle ways. But he felt in the power of the waves, as they smashed against the rocks, the power of these new gods – the gods of the iron sword and iron hammer.

This is the power which fills him with excitement as he accompanies the Norsemen on their journey southwards, plundering, killing, and battling with the seas as they go; and he looks forward with pleasure to the fight to come.

But even as he takes part in sacrificing three captives to the Norse gods a new influence comes into his life, that of the meditative, gentle men of the new Christian religion. Attracted by the 'curious abstracted look' in the eyes of one of the victims, 'as if his mind had been elsewhere', he impulsively takes from him a heavy, dark, iron cross, still wet with blood, and clips it round his own neck. This action proves symbolic in various ways. For the time being the cross he has taken proves his salvation, and leads him to a complete change of fortune and outlook in the shelter of this new God. He is destined, nevertheless, to find in the Church a more deadly betrayal than any he has yet faced, and one in which his own blood, actual and spiritual, will eventually also stain the cross he has adopted as his symbol.

It is here that we see the central theme of this novel, in the complexity of the contrasting motives and beliefs which Madaah encounters as he searches for spiritual integrity and the true meaning and purpose of life. The violence of his eventual response to the Church's betrayal arises directly from his experience both of the heroic violence of the Norsemen and of the contrasting, but, in the end, fragile tranquillity, peace and beauty he has found in the Church with Brother Ealdred, the Christian scholar and librarian. For soon he finds that even within the Church there are temptations to seek power rather than learning, and that the influence of the gentle Ealdred is counterbalanced by that of the ambitious and ruthless Sigulf.

He thought about it often; was he to be a scholar, like Ealdred? Or a man of power, like Sigulf? He thought, too, of the world in which he found himself. There was the realm of the King, the ruthless despotic world where a wrong word could mean death in a ditch, and there was the world of Ealdred, those pure glittering peaks of scholarship where a wrong word could gain a reproof, often as sharp as any spear, and there was the world of Sigulf, where men laboured and toiled to ward off the wolves of the kingdom and keep in peace and safety the learning of a thousand years.

Through Madaah's musings, Peter Carter expresses with admirable lucidity the conflicting lines of thought which may be rehearsed in the minds of those who wish to make some important contribution to the welfare of mankind, but who are also tempted by visions of personal glory, or who succumb to the belief that the ends justify the means.

Madaah is too honest and clear-sighted to be deceived for long by an outward show of disinterestedness. When he discovers that the Church, though ostensibly aloof from worldly power and considerations, is yet deeply concerned in political plotting, and has not scrupled to use his services in ways which are quite contrary to the trust and faith he has invested in it, he is shocked and outraged. Even more is he outraged by the apparent casuistry of the arguments then presented to him by the man he had trusted, his mentor Ealdred, in defence of Sigulf's actions. As a result, the 'gentle growth of trust, and kindliness, and affection, which had begun to turn towards the light, withered, and in its place a fouler growth of malice and hatred began to sprout and ooze.'

So begins a long, dark time for Madaah, culminating in grim scenes of torture and cruelty, utter despair and evil.

It seemed to him that trust was an illusion, love a weakness, and the only way to live unhurt was to cut oneself off from humanity. But as he had turned away from mankind, become a ghost, a phantom, haunting the forest, living in darkness, so, like a foul and perverted appetite, his need for attention grew. Wounded and warped, he struck at what he considered to be the wounder and warper, although with every blow he struck, he destroyed yet more of himself. If there were books to be burned, he burned them; if there were churches to be destroyed, he destroyed them, seeking, in his own black way, to be revenged on the Church which had first breathed into his ear a promise of a better life.

And yet he was still a spiritual being, although his spirit moved in darkness and fed on revenge.

But though this bitter search for revenge is told with stark realism, the reader never feels that violence is being depicted for its own sake. When they occur, scenes of violence are entirely functional, an essential element in the exploration of good and evil impulses in mankind, recounted with no invitation to vicarious enjoyment of sadistic acts. Indeed, Madaah's own worst excesses, as well as the horrifying tortures he has to endure, are told quietly, in retrospect, when eventually he finds help and reconciliation through his encounter with the hermit, Colum.

He told him of the years of savagery when he had been worse than a beast, when he had turned, not just against the Church which had betrayed him, but against mankind; when humanity had been his enemy, and he had hunted it down with such fury that even the men he led, wolves themselves, had become afraid of him.

Through mutual confession of their respective traumatic failures, Colum is finally able to bring Madaah to an understanding of the truth which lies at the heart of this story, that there is 'divinity and bestiality in every man – perhaps even – and still – in him'.

The story ends in an act of faith and reconciliation, but one which still leaves open the question whether Colum, in the comfort he offers, or Ealdred, in his life, teaching and finally his death in defence of Madaah really can counterbalance the double dealing of the Church and Ealdred's troubling acquiescence in it.

Madatan is a searching story, one which examines closely, with a compelling clarity but also with a sense of hope, the vital issues of good and evil, of ends and means, of the specious justification of violence, cruelty and deceit, and of the temptations towards the ruthless search for power which afflict mankind. It requires a relatively sophisticated response from the young reader, and a willingness to discuss seriously the contrary ideas presented. This makes it less comfortable and also more mature reading than a book like *Knight Crusader*, a story for readers of eleven or twelve by Ronald Welch, which presents the conflict between Christian and Infidel with an emphasis upon military prowess, endurance, valour and glory; but with little attempt to analyse what is entailed in the display of such qualities – and with few concessions to the idea that good is not a Christian monopoly.

As a result of his experiences, Madaah had developed an interested, yet also detached view of religious beliefs.

Madaah had known other beliefs and other ways of life. He was the only novice with a standard of comparison; he could place God against Odin, Christ against Thor, the Apostles against Baldir, and the world of angels and devils against those old beliefs with which he had grown up; that world where there had been no distinction between the natural and the supernatural, between 'them' and 'us', between 'then' and 'now'.

The Crusaders, however, were conducting a holy war against the Infidel, and Welch shows no interest in presenting their quarrel with similar detachment. The hero, Philip d'Aubigny, has lived all his life in Outremer, a tiny kingdom held in the Holy Land by the Christians, and currently under threat from Saladin and his Saracen army. But though it is evident that the Turks' 'exquisite and polished manners' have impressed Philip, they still remain the enemy, given a measure of respect, but clearly felt to be inferior to the pure-bred Norman Christians.

This narrowness of vision is further exemplified by the quarrel between Philip and his fellow-Christian de Nogent, its emphasis upon de Nogent's 'oafishness' in contrast to the 'purity' and 'nobility' of Philip's blood, and the tone in which the ensuing battle between the two is described.

> He brought his sword down on de Nogent's left shoulder, just where the neck joins the collar bone. Not even the finest hauberk could have saved a man from that terrific blow. De Nogent's collar bone snapped like a twig. He reeled to one side, dazed, staggering and barely conscious of what was happening to him. Only his training and strong legs kept him upright.
>
> Philip swung back with a speed and precision that brought appreciative cheers from his critical audience. He slashed sideways at de Nogent's neck, and caught him a sweeping blow under the ear, a deadly stroke at a vital spot. De Nogent was bowled off his feet, the last faint shreds of consciousness hammered out of him. His sword dropped from his fingers, and he crashed to the ground, rolled over on his back and lay there, his helm staring up blankly at the blue sky and the setting sun.
>
> Hands pounded Philip on the back.

It might be a battle of fisticuffs in the school playground for all the significance lent to the deadly cut and thrust which has deprived the 'oafish' de Nogent of his life – or a game of football, perhaps, like that described by Cormier in *The Chocolate War* (see Chapter 1).

There is a similar ruthless lack of pity in accounts of battles with the Saracens.

> The Turk was hurled from his saddle, the spear transfixing him from breast to spine. His horse, caught in the flank by the full weight of Philip's charger, was bowled over like a toy ... The ground was littered with Arab ponies and Infidels. Christian knights were falling back, waving their spears exultantly and shouting incoherent cries of triumph ... 'Philip, Philip! ... I enjoyed that!' he [Joscelin] yelled.

Only when Joscelin meets his own death at the hands of the enemy are we brought to a sense of the horror and pity of war. Even here Sir Hugo, as a seasoned campaigner, will allow his son no time to mourn. 'Never mind, Philip. You will get used to seeing your friends killed before you're much older. I'm hardened to it. At least, I thought I was,' he tells him.

After a variety of adventures, escapes and intrigues in the battle against the Infidel, the book ends with yet another fight to the death – once again between fellow Christians. The pleasure taken in the fight is the same.

> Philip thrust de Braose down, arching his back over the table, and stabbed down savagely, grunting with each furious blow, hacking and ripping at the hauberk around the throat. And then he saw a gap, and the white of the bare skin. He paused, and struck for the last time ...
>
> Richard grinned back impudently, the torchlight shining like dark gold on his hair. 'I wouldn't have missed that fight for three whippings, my lord,' he said.
>
> Philip laughed, and felt the better for it. He saw Sir Geoffrey pick up a hunk of cold meat from the table, and gnaw at it greedily. He had eaten nothing for hours.

Along with Philip's page, Richard, many young readers will no doubt enjoy the grim 'hacking and ripping', and the final triumphant deaththrust in this stirring story. Because the narrative makes no concession to weakness, shows no squeamishness about death and killing, they can remain undisturbed by any doubts about whether war and violence are indeed acceptable ways of settling disputes. Nor does the story at any time raise the possibility that the Crusaders might have been misguided in their forays against the Turks; or betray any awareness that the term 'Infidel', so freely used of the Saracens, could be offensive to modern Muslims, who naturally think of themselves as 'the Faithful', and some of whom now live in Britain alongside the Crusaders' descendants in what needs to become a climate of mutual tolerance.

It could reasonably be argued that Welch is merely reflecting the attitudes and prejudices of the time, that this is a necessary element in fiction which seeks to recreate the past, and that the book was written in 1954, before it occurred to many of us to wonder what might be the reactions of ethnic minorities. Nevertheless, Peter Carter, in *Madatan*, has found many ways in which to insert considerations relevant both to the epoch he is presenting and to the concerns of today. One such episode occurs when Madaah meets the Norsemen again, this time as prisoners of the Christians to whom he is now loyal.

> As the Norse words came from his tongue, he felt an odd stirring of sympathy for the men. That was strange, he thought. For a year he had hated the Norsemen, but, at his first meeting with them again, he saw them merely as men; cruelly pinioned, ill-treated, lost too in the darkness of paganism.

Such compassion for the enemy is unusual at any time; but it is the privilege of writers of fiction to create characters who stand out from the prevailing mental set and to use them as a way of asking questions and provoking serious thought about the burning issues of all times. One of the questions we can legitimately be asking of a book of this kind, therefore, is how far it will prove both attractive to young readers and yet at the same time offer more than an unthinking acceptance of the war ethos and a vicarious participation in barbarous acts of violence.

One writer of historical fiction able to enter thoroughly into the warlike culture she is describing, and yet leave room for questions of contemporary relevance to arise, is Rosemary Sutcliff. Her series of novels about Britain through the ages reflect with remarkable sympathy the tribal culture of the Bronze Age in *Warrior Scarlet*, the matriarchal culture of the third century in *Mark of the Horse Lord* and *Song for a Dark Queen*, the martial ethos of Roman Britain in *Eagle of the Ninth*, and, in succeeding stories, the perpetual unease generated by Viking, Saxon and Norman invasions. In all these books there is, naturally, a warlike spirit, both in invaders and defenders, which is nevertheless portrayed with a greater awareness and sympathy for both sides, and also for the more peaceful and caring communities which persisted in the intervals of war despite the ever-present threats from without.

One of the most complex and rewarding of her books is *Sword at Sunset*, a novel set in the fifth century, in King Arthur's Britain. But the narrator and main protagonist, Artos the Bear, is not the idealised hero of Arthurian legend, nor are his Companions chivalrous knights riding out gaily in search of adventures and damsels in distress. Artos is a man of his times, a tough, seasoned campaigner, who has spent his life with a group of men dedicated like himself to the task of defending Britain against the incursions of the Saxons. He tells his story in retrospect, as he lies at the point of death, looking back with a mixture of pride and clear-sighted regret at his achievements and his failures both in the campaign and in his personal life. Of the campaign he can now say: 'We have scattered the Sea Wolves so that it will be long and long before they can gather the pack again. Together we have saved Britain for this time, and together we will hold Britain, that the things worth saving shall not go down into the dark!' But though Artos does not question the necessity for his life-long dedication to battle, he does see that his success has been limited; and has been achieved at a severe cost in life and in happiness.

The story of his campaigns against the Sea Wolves is told with a spare stern realism, which accepts the slaughter as a necessary evil; but it is never seen as an exciting boys' game, though we are given a clear sense of the attraction Artos finds in the fighting life.

I carried a heavy heart with me down the war-trail that spring, and yet there was relief in the familiar feel of my battle harness. I have always been a fighting man, and for me there was the release, the small sweet death of forgetting, in the clash of weapons and the dust cloud of battle, that other men find in women or heather beer.

But when Gault dies under the surgeon's knife we are not spared the cruelty of war; the grim details of Gwalchmai's vain attempt to extract the arrow in a 'hundred to one chance' of saving Gault's life, or the anguish of Levin at his friend's death. It is interesting to compare the 'stiff upper lip' exhortations of Sir Hugo in *Knight Crusader* with the practical way in which Artos tries to help Levin by setting him immediate tasks to fulfil, and by the harsh yet essentially sympathetic response to his grief.

> 'I cannot do it,' he said pitifully. 'Artos, have some mercy on me – I can't. It is all true as you say, but I *can't go on!*'
> But already, though he was not aware of it himself, I could feel him strengthening under my hands, bracing himself to take up the intolerable burden.

'Oh yes you can.' Artos tells him sternly. 'One can always go on. And as to mercy, I keep that for when and where it is needed.' And unsparingly Artos contrasts Levin's present weakness through his grief for Gault with the courage of Gault's own final moments, in which he got 'the rags of you out of ambush and back to camp with a mortal wound in him'. As Levin responds to Artos's therapeutic scolding, and painfully pulls himself together to take up the struggle again we see that there are no heroics in this scene, only a clear knowledge of what must be done.

The sense conveyed of stern necessity in the business is reinforced by the knowledge that Artos and his Companions are fighting not for personal power or glory, but to preserve some quality of life for their descendants. This is an important theme in the story, and an example of a further dimension to war which is more readily available to writers of historical fiction than to those dealing with the confusing, unfinished business of the wars taking place in their own time. Sutcliff distances the war experience in her books not merely because it lies in the past, but also because she is able to 'place' it in a specific context which permits certain definitive judgements to be made about the ultimate consequences of war and about its role in history. In this story its relevance for us today lies partly in the vision of the links between past and future which Artos can still perceive as he watches the lighting of the Beltane fires in the age-old Midsummer Eve ritual, fires which symbolise 'the Need Fire, the Fire of Life'.

They made the fire at last, after the usual long drawn struggle, the curl of smoke and the sparks that fell on the waiting tinder, the sudden miracle of living flame. A great cry of joyful relief burst from the watching crowd – odd how one always has the fear: 'This year the fire will not come and life will be over.' To me it was this year – this year the dark will close over our heads, this is the black wilderness and the end of all things, and the white flower will not bloom again ... The small licking flame so easily to be quenched, was a promise, not of victory maybe, but of something not lost, shining on in the darkness.

The fear, lying deep inside Artos, that 'this year the fire will not come and life will be over', is one that will be recognised by many readers in this atomic age. But whereas the present fear is of a threatening darkness without hope of survival, Artos expects that the hardships and defeats in the end will prove to have been worthwhile. For the modern reader there is in many of the books written about this period of British history a comforting and relevant theme; the awareness that though the indigenous people fought bitterly against Romans, Vikings, Saxons and Normans they eventually became reconciled to their invaders, and were able to live with them as one nation. Artos says:

'I remember once, long ago, Ambrosius said to me that if we fought well enough we might hold back the dark for maybe another hundred years. I asked him, seeing that the end was sure, why we did not merely lie down and let it come, for the end would be easier that way. He said, "For a dream"...'

For Artos this dream has become a vision of hope. It has come from the sight of two boys, one British, one Saxon, beginning their day in mutual suspicion and hostility but ending it 'sharing the same broth bowl and ... picking bramble thorns out of each other's feet'.

And suddenly I knew, watching them – Ambrosius never knew it – that the longer we can hold off the Saxons ... even at the cost of our heart's blood, the more time there will be for other boys to pick thorns out of each other's feet and learn the words for hearth and hound and honey-cake in each other's tongue ... Every year that we can hold the Saxons back may well mean that the darkness will engulf us the less completely in the end, that more of what we fight for will survive until the light comes again.

One may doubt the logic of the argument, but this sense of the continuity between past and present is what distinguishes the genuine historical novel from the exciting adventure story that is set in the past mainly for the opportunity of nostalgic empathy with the glories of 'battles long ago'. In *Knight's Fee*, a story of Norman Britain, Rosemary Sutcliff brings clearly into focus her strong sense of the continuing relevance of the past, when the old shepherd, Lewin, shows Randal an axe-head he has found buried on the downs. As Randal holds it he 'sees' the man to whom it once belonged – whom readers of this author's other books will recognise as Drem, the Bronze Age hero of *Warrior Scarlet*.

He had an extraordinary sense of kinship with the unknown man who had first closed his fingers over that strange weapon, who had perhaps seen the wolves leaping about the lambing folds as he, Randal, had almost seen them for an instant tonight; an extraordinary feeling of oneness with Dean, of some living bond running back through the blue, living flint, making him part of other men and sheep and wolves, and they a part of him.

Randal's awareness of 'oneness' with the past was first awakened by Ancret, an old woman whose ancestors pre-dated both Normans and Saxons. She had told him:

'We, who are an older people still, who were an old people when they raised the grave mound on Bramble Hill in the days when the world was young, we see the conquerors come and go again, and marry and mingle, but we know that all things pass, like a little wind through the bramble bushes.'

This crystallises in Randal's mind into an understanding that the real life of ordinary people can persist in spite of the surface fluctuations of successive invaders.

'And all the time, the wind blows over,' he thought. 'Ancret's people, and the Saxons, and Harold dead at Hastings over yonder, and now the Normans: and all the while the wind blowing over the downs, just the same.' Half asleep as he was, he was suddenly aware of the new life in the lambing pens, the constant watchful coming and going of the shepherd and dogs and lantern, as of something not just happening now, but reaching back, and forward and forward, into the very roots of things that were beyond time.

In *The Namesake*, a story by Walter Hodges of King Alfred's battles against the Danes, it is King Alfred himself whose vision extends beyond the battlefield where he has, of necessity, spent so much of his time. In an interval of peace he takes his followers to Stonehenge, a place feared by the local inhabitants for its ancient pagan associations. But Alfred sees it differently:

I like to come here, because I know that I am standing where other men like me have stood and thought the same thoughts as I, a thousand years before I was born, and where others like me will stand likewise after I am dead ... Every man is a part of the bridge between the past and the future, and must feel how it stretches out both ways before and behind him.

Although Alfred, like Artos, has devoted his life to the defence of his realm, he is represented essentially as a man of peace, ceaselessly – though vainly – working to secure that cooperation between Saxon and Dane which Artos, too, had hoped for. After his victory over Guthorm he deliberately escorts him and his army out of the kingdom, to prevent the possibility of a massacre of the Danes by his Saxon friends, saying:

'No good can come solely by hastening the deaths of other men. Though the brave man will face his enemy and follow his lord in battle to the death, there is no value in fighting without necessity, and no virtue in either killing or dying for its own sake.'

Guthorm thinks differently. He represents the men 'of the north', whose creed is that:

'to die in battle is the noblest end of a man. The blood-red battlefield is the pathway to Valhalla, where the warrior who has died fighting lives again, crowned for ever in the glory of his battle-deeds. That is why our young men seek the battle so eagerly, why they rejoice to kill and be killed. This is what has made us strong. This in the end will make us masters of the world.'

But Alfred asks him:

'And what will you do in the world when you have mastered it? Will you not then try to live, and keep it in peace while you can? Or is Valhalla all you fight for?'

Through this exchange Hodges too has been able to present values which transcend the expediency of the moment and put into perspective for the reader the values of the fighting man normally associated with the period of which he is writing.

The conflict between the conventionally acceptable dream of the glory and heroism of knighthood and a gentler, less favoured, but more lasting fame through the creative arts is a theme also of *One is One*, by Barbara Leonie Picard. Stephen, the young hero, longs for a heroic future, in keeping with the expectations of most boys of his age. But a traumatic fear of dogs and the relentless teasing of his brothers and cousins have led him to share their belief that he is too cowardly ever to become a knight. So reluctantly he accepts his father's decision that he shall enter a monastery as soon as he is old enough. Meantime, he finds solitary consolation in an increasing perception of the beauty around him.

> Stephen had a more than ordinary awareness of the shapes and colours of things around him, and, left so much alone, he had time to study them. He noticed how the shapes of similar things differed subtly from each other: the wings of a hawk against the sky from the wings of a pigeon; the shape of a leafless oak from the shape of a leafless ash; the leaves of ivy, according to where on the branch one picked them; the head of an ox from the head of a cow. And colours he noticed: how the colour of clothes changed according to whether one saw them by sunlight or torchlight; and the way the flames of the fire made flowers blossom on the plain stuff of a gown ... And then there were other things he noticed, too: the fluid rippling of – what was it? bones? flesh? – beneath the shining hide of a well-groomed horse when it moved; the way one could actually see the invisible wind when it blew over a field of corn ...

This artistic vision helps to compensate him not merely during the hard and lonely years in his father's castle, but also when, in the monastery, he is set to help the dour Brother Ernulf with his richly illuminated manuscripts. But Stephen cannot forget his longing to prove himself 'a man'. He runs away from the monastery, and through a series of adventures demonstrates his courage and skill in the martial arts. But finally he decides to return to the monastery, to Ernulf and his manuscripts. He does not regret his adventures; 'he had found – even if only fleetingly – happiness; and two friends to love', and what he had 'gained and learnt from the world' compensated for the sorrow, anguish and loss sustained in the process. But he recognises that his achievements had finally 'proved of little worth to him ... He thought of his fulfilled ambition and dismissed it as valueless and to be regretted, when weighed against the truer satisfaction of art.'

The balance in historical fiction, however, is by no means always on the side of peace and the arts, even when artistic sensibility is an attractive side to the hero's character. Wulf, in Bryher's *The Fourteenth of October*, loves to watch Brother Thomas draw and paint; he has a vivid sense of colour and pattern in the countryside and in Laurel's imaginative and intricate weaving; and in his bitter hatred of the Normans lies a sharp awareness of their contrasting disregard for the quality of life.

'It's not the Normans themselves,' I said ... 'It is what they do. Life is always hard, but they destroy everything that makes it bearable. What they call discipline is merely a form of slavery. The men are taken from the land and turned into soldiers to blight an ever-wider radius of earth. Then their leader rides through villages of terrified, less-than-human serfs, and calls it victory.'

And who, Wulf asks, even among their priests, knew the meaning of compassion?

Wulf is greatly attracted, on the other hand, by the Syrian trader's eloquent description of Byzantium, its beauty and its civilisation. 'It is not a hall in a saga,' Latif tells him, 'all meat and oxhides, but a palace where even the sunlight is cloth of gold. We quarrel with our neighbours over a philosophical point too tenuous to write down, but we wear no daggers, call out no armies.' Wulf has been brought up in a land where such peace and concern for the arts seem impossible.

There had been no peace as long as I could remember. We never knew where the shield-hung dragon ships would strike. Every spring, as the corn was sowed, we wondered whether we should reap it ... The whole eastern coast was sinking back into wilderness.

He has been embittered, moreover, by the knowledge that so many of their neighbours had given up the fight against the raiders, leaving the burden of defence upon his father. When his father is killed, and he is taken hostage, he is desperately aware that he values freedom above everything else, for, in Latif's own words, 'without it everything is sterile, search is useless, our days merely mortality'. He escapes from captivity only to find the same unwillingness in the men of Cornwall to leave their farms to fight in support of King Harald, so that the Battle of Hastings ends in Norman victory. In spite therefore of the tempting vision of a life devoted to his beloved garden, 'brush in hand, absorbing the dew and the light, so that these pages would flower long after last year's pippins had become withered moss-covered stems', he knows that he can never reconcile himself to life under the Normans.

Mercy, I thought, yes, it is right to be merciful, but have we not also to ask ourselves: where does mercy end? The English had refused to listen, refused to arm; they had been unwilling to defend a way of life centuries ahead of William's brutal plundering, until it had been too late. The Normans had had friends everywhere, weaving a net from east to west; and we had not only let them snare us, we had helped them! What of the web of evasion and appeasement we had spun about our liberties? Only Harald had fought, and, whatever the Godwin sins might be, I was his thane always. To understand too well, to forgive too often, was this a way to peace?

Wulf's sentiments clearly reflect the author's own anger at the appeasement which, she felt, had led directly to the Second World War, and her belief (expressed in '1940', an extract from *The Days of Mars* reprinted in Ronald Blythe's *Writing in a War*) 'that international promises seldom hold unless backed by force'. So her hero, Wulf, believing like his creator in the need to stand up and fight, unexpectedly chooses to go as a mercenary to join the Emperor's Varangian guards. This will undoubtedly take him to his 'last battle and [his] howe'; but will leave him free to make his own choices, to refuse to bow the knee to the conqueror.

Historical novels which present such differing points of view throw into relief some of the deeper issues presented by war in the light of past and present events. They can be used to promote genuine discussion between those for whom the battles, blood, adventure and glory are the most enjoyable parts of the book, and those who appreciate the more thoughtful, gentler passages in which greater emphasis is given to human relationships and friendships, the delights of scholarship, of art and poetry, or the messages of hope, reconciliation and tolerance. The battles are distant in these stories of past times, moreover, and the fighting is undertaken by individuals making their own choices and confronting the enemy in personal combat for personal glory. So it is easier to detect and isolate contrasting attitudes within the story before attempting to discuss their implications for our own time, and for our less glamorous twentieth-century wars which depend upon mass conscription and mass destruction delivered from afar.

3
Mud, Blood, but not much Glory

The books discussed in Chapter 2 belong mainly to that turbulent period of British history when fear of death at the hands of invaders was an ever-present threat. It was also a time of individual commitment to battle and to the hope of personal glory. The battle scene changed dramatically, however, with the invention of gunpowder, and weapons which deal death not in hand-to-hand fighting, but at a distance: there were now fewer opportunities for spectacular acts of valour or heroism. In *Down the Long Stairs*, by Winifred Cawley, set at the time of the English Civil War, this quickly becomes apparent to the young hero, Ralph Cole.

> I do not know what I expected a soldier's duties to be: most likely something romantic such as patrolling the castle sword in hand (though we had no swords), and scanning the horizon for the first sight of Roundheads and I, of course, would be the one to give the alarm; or even, just learning to load and fire a musket; or, at the very worst, drilling in formation in the courtyard. In fact I became one of a small group sent to the unmilitary task of looking after the cattle and poultry.

Two centuries later, this tedium and sense of anonymity in battle is one of the most striking elements in Stephen Crane's remarkable story of the ordinary fighting soldier in the American Civil War. Henry, the hero of *The Red Badge of Courage*, 'had, of course, dreamed of battles all his life – of vague and bloody conflicts that had thrilled him in their sweep and fire. In visions he had seen himself in many struggles. He had imagined peoples secure in the shadow of his eagle-eyed prowess.' Naturally, he knows that such visions belong to the dream world of fantasy and fiction, not to nineteenth-century America. Nevertheless when civil war breaks out, 'He had burned several times to enlist. Tales of great movements shook the land. They might not be distinctly Homeric, but there seemed to be much glory in them. He had read of marches, sieges, conflicts, and he had longed to see it all. His busy mind had drawn for him large pictures extravagant in color, lurid with breathless deeds.'

The reality proves very different. For some time the brigade is moved restlessly from one place to another, with no discernible purpose. No sooner have they dug themselves in with earthen barricades, than they are ordered off to new ground; until Henry declares, 'I'd rather do anything 'most than go tramping 'round the country all day doing no good to nobody and jest tiring ourselves out.'

It is not only the apparent aimlessness and tedium of the operations which exasperate Henry, but the time this allows for treacherous anxieties about his own courage. His fear of proving a coward in the battle is a central preoccupation of the book.

> The youth had been taught that a man became another thing in a battle. He saw his salvation in such a change ... He was in a fever of impatience ... He wished ... to go into a battle and discover that he had been a fool in his doubts, and was, in truth, a man of traditional courage. The strain of present circumstances he felt to be intolerable.

The essence of this story is the contrast between Henry's secret and at times disabling fears, the loud-mouthed bragging indulged by the soldiers, Henry included, when the enemy is not in sight, and the actual experiences of battle. On the battlefield itself, 'there was a singular absence of heroic poses'. There are indeed isolated incidents of cowardice, in Henry's own headlong flight, and when he sees an officer pummelling a blubbering soldier, driving him 'back into the ranks with many blows', and then staying to help the shaking recruit reload his gun. The engagement with the rebel army, when it comes, is chaotic. It is described in deliberately low-key terms, with, at times, almost comic effect.

> The men dropped here and there like bundles. The captain of the youth's company had been killed in an early part of the action. His body lay stretched out in the position of a tired man resting, but upon his face there was an astonished and sorrowful look, as if he thought some friend had done him an ill turn. The babbling man was grazed by a shot that made the blood stream widely down his face. He clapped both hands to his head. 'Oh!' he said, and ran. Another grunted suddenly as if he had been struck by a club in the stomach. He sat down and gazed ruefully. In his eyes there was mute, indefinite reproach. Farther up the line a man, standing behind a tree, had had his knee joint splintered by a ball. Immediately he had dropped his rifle and gripped the tree with both arms. And there he remained, clinging desperately and crying for assistance that he might withdraw his hold upon the tree.

When the youth's first moment of glory does come, it is the result of a kind of mindless frenzy which has seized him unawares, leaving him barely conscious of his own actions, and able to be, for a brief space of time, a 'war devil' only because he is no longer aware of his own danger.

> These incidents made the youth ponder. It was revealed to him that he had been a barbarian, a beast. He had fought like a pagan who defends his religion. Regarding it, he saw that it was fine, wild, and, in some ways, easy. He had been a tremendous figure, no doubt. By this struggle he had overcome obstacles which he had admitted to be mountains. They had fallen like paper peaks, and he was now what he called a hero. And he had not been aware of the process. He had slept and, awakening, found himself a knight.

All the same, there remains with him to the end the 'specter of reproach'. He knows that at the crisis point, earlier in the battle, he had run.

> As he marched along the little branch-hung roadway among his prattling companions, this vision of cruelty hung over him. It clung near him always and darkened his view of these deeds in purple and gold. Whichever way his thoughts turned they were followed by the somber phantom of the desertion in the fields. He looked stealthily at his companions, feeling sure that they must discern in his face evidences of this pursuit.

Only gradually is he able to 'put the sin at a distance', and with it 'look back upon the brass and bombast of his earlier gospels' and despise them in a newfound assurance, 'a quiet manhood, non-assertive but a sturdy and strong blood'. This enables him later in old age to confess at last to others how scared he had been, and that he had run.

Crane gives us a vivid insight into Henry's fluctuating states of mind as he veers between rashness and cowardice, fear, disgust, desertion and courage. His questioning of the conventional nineteenth-century attitude to war has been taken up to some extent in *The Root Cellar*, Janet Lunn's time-shift story for readers of twelve or so. In it, Rose escapes from present-day pressures into the 1860s. With a friend, Susan, she travels to the battlefields of the American Civil War in search of two young men, Will and his cousin Steve, who had run away to fight 'the rebs'. Steve has been the driving force in this mad adventure, but in his determination to be there at the final victory he refuses to take proper care of a festering wound, and dies, without glory, in hospital. Will is shattered by his cousin's death, angry and despairing and disillusioned. He tells the girls:

And it went on for twelve days. Twelve days! And in the nights, when we was frantically digging us trenches with anything we could get to hand, them mortars was flying over with their fuses like angry little red shooting stars through the blackness, and us never knowing where they was going to land. And the sound of battle never once let up – like some devil's music, the screaming bits of shell, the bullets and bars, the bugles blaring, the drums pounding, the horses and the men screaming.

And the men dying. When they die, you know how they die? They jump. They shout. They cry. And they fall. You go in a rage and you want to get them devils who's shooting at you. That's all you think about. Then the battle's over for the day. The smoke and the dust starts to settle. The vultures – them big ugly turkey vultures – starts to wheel and circle around in the sky, looking for their dinners, and the smell of the dead is something awful. You look around and the rage is gone out of you and you don't hardly know yourself or your comrades neither.

Will has found no glory anywhere in this war, only pain, blood and loss. His cousin is dead, and his hero, Abraham Lincoln, for whose ideals he had fought, has been assassinated.

Henry and Will and their contemporaries endured only a brief spell of campaigning. The First World War (still sometimes called the 'Great War') lasted four bitter and weary years, and has given rise to many books of personal reminiscences, novels for adults and young people, and a considerable body of poetry.

Crane's picture of the American Civil War was written without any personal experience of fighting, yet some of its scenes give a vivid prevision of the battlefields of the Somme. One such scene is the account of Henry's awakening, in the early dawn, to a dream-like world of 'gray mists ... slowly shifting before the first efforts of the sun's rays'.

About him were the rows and groups of men that he had dimly seen the previous night. They were getting a last draught of sleep before the awakening. The gaunt careworn features and dusty figures were made plain by this quaint light at the dawning, but it dressed the skin of the men in corpselike hues and made the tangled limbs appear pulseless and dead. The youth started up with a little cry when his eyes first swept over this motionless mass of men, thickspread upon the ground, pallid, and in strange postures. His disordered mind interpreted the hall of the forest as a charnel place. He believed for an instant that he was in the house of the dead, and he did not dare to move lest these corpses start up, squalling and squawking.

In Sassoon's brief poem, 'The Dug-Out', there is a similar vision of the men, huddled in death-like sleep.

> Why do you lie with your legs ungainly huddled,
> And one arm bent across your sullen, cold,
> Exhausted face? It hurts my heart to watch you,
> Deep-shadow'd from the candle's guttering gold
> And you wonder why I shake you by the shoulder;
> Drowsy, you mumble and sigh and turn your head ...
> *You are too young to fall asleep for ever;*
> *And when you sleep you remind me of the dead.*

In Owen's 'Strange Meeting', too, the poet escapes in dream into the 'sullen hall of Hell'.

> It seemed that out of battle I escaped
> Down some profound dull tunnel, long since scooped
> Through granite which titanic wars had groined.
> Yet also there encumbered sleepers groaned,
> Too fast in thought or death to be bestirred ...

For both these poets, the sleepers epitomise the pity of war, the helplessness of its victims as they seek momentary respite in exhausted sleep, the ugly prevision of death in their attitudes, and in their unwillingness to be wakened to the hideous reality of the war which still surrounds them.

Both Owen and Sassoon saw war as a terrible but far from heroic experience, and both briefly became conscientious objectors. They finally returned to the Front, not out of any desire for glory, but from a deep sense of loyalty and comradeship with the men who had fought under their command. Susan Hill's novel, *Strange Meeting*, takes its title and some of its preoccupations from their experiences.

It is the story of two young officers, John Halliard and David Barton. At the beginning of the story John, having been wounded in action, is on leave in England with his family, and hating every minute of it. After his experiences at the Front he can no longer communicate with them – there is now too great a divide between those who have remained safely at home, and the 'veteran' soldier, who knows what it is really like 'out there'. He returns to his regiment to discover that it has been decimated in a senseless carnage which, 'within the space of five weeks, and those after two years of consistent service in the Old Front Line', has reduced his CO to 'an old man in the yellow-grey lamplight.'

Hilliard now shares his quarters with Barton, a new recruit, who, unlike the reticent Hilliard, seems able to communicate his thoughts and feelings without constraint. Hilliard feels that, beneath his surface gaiety, Barton has 'some kind of central poise and calmness'. But Barton has not yet seen active service, and his eventual reactions to his 'baptism of fire' are an important element in the story.

Barton's first traumatic encounter with the reality of war is an apparently minor incident: an 18-year-old lad has bolted into a disused cellar and is refusing to come out. His comrades know that if he cannot be persuaded out, he will face court-martial and death. They are all compassionately concerned for him in a cama- raderie of understanding which Henry, in *The Red Badge of Courage*, would have envied. Where the others have failed, Barton succeeds, and the boy emerges from the cellar only to be killed instantly by a stray shell. It is his sense both of direct responsi- bility for the boy's death and of its meaninglessness which temporarily crumples Barton.

When later he is sent to map the terrain, it is the recurrent sense of futility that hits him hardest. He and the runner, Grosse, making their way through the trenches, dodging shells as they go, suddenly come upon a scene of carnage.

> But as they rounded the next corner ... they came upon a total blockage in the trench-way, a mess of burst sandbags and earth, shrapnel and mutilated bodies. Blood had splattered up and over the parapet and was trickling down again, was running to form a pool, mingling with the contents of a dixie which had contained stew. The men had been getting their mid-day meal in this traverse when the bomb had landed in the middle of them ... Barton ... found himself staring in fascination at the shattered heap of limbs and helmets, at a bone sticking out somehow through the front of a tunic, at the blood. He felt numb ... They turned another corner. A young soldier was up on one of the firesteps, facing them and about to step down into the trench. Barton caught his eye. As he did so, a shot came and the man toppled rather slowly forwards, to land almost on top of Barton and between him and Grosse.

These two incidents are too much for Barton.

> The body was warm, the skin faintly flushed. He had been alive, looking into Barton's face. Then dead. Nothing. Nothing ...
> He did not want to go on, he wanted to go back, not because he had lost his nerve, but because he was sickened, for where was he going, why was he to spend an afternoon making a map, playing a game, spying and reporting about a few square yards of country, why had the men standing in the traverse with their meal, and this Private with the pale eyelashes, why had they been alive when he came down here less than an hour ago who were dead now?

What disturbs Barton even more is the way he, and all the others, are persistently striving to accept this futility as necessary, to 'make a pattern out of it', to find some way to give themselves the courage to go on. Like Sassoon and Owen in real life, he is tempted to surrender 'as a conchy', to get 'out of it all because I feel guilty that I'm here and doing nothing to stop it'. So he is sympathetic when Garrett, his CO, at the cost of his army career, decides that the 'reconnaissance raids are pointless in terms of strategy and a criminal waste of men', and refuses to accept any further 'responsibility for the fruitless loss of life which they entail'. Nevertheless, neither Barton nor Hilliard take the same course: they find ways of coming to terms with their deep resentment at the waste. And though by the end of the story Barton is 'missing, presumed dead' and Hilliard has lost a leg, when we leave Hilliard he seems about to find the reconciliation and acceptance which earlier Barton had found so unthinkable, so wrong, even obscene.

It is worth comparing this story with similar incidents recorded in the prose and poetry of Edmund Blunden, Siegfried Sassoon and Wilfred Owen (see Chapters 4 and 16), particularly with Owen's 'The Sentry', 'Futility' and 'Insensibility', which explore the torment of those who have not 'made themselves immune to pity'.

Trooper Jackson's Story, by Brian Thompson, seems, at first sight, a very different kind of book. Ever since, as a child of four, he had been dazzled by the arrival of a troop of horse 'in the cobbled town square, each man bearing a lance and sitting in the saddle as straight as wood', Sam Jackson has determined to be a soldier. He joins up at 18, in January 1914, and in a few months finds himself in France. His first reconnoitring expedition leaves him trapped behind the German lines, so he joins a band of French resistance fighters. One of these, the dentist, Berthelot, proves to be a kind of Scarlet Pimpernel figure, less flamboyant, perhaps, but a valiant hero. Sam joins him in a series of lighthearted adventures and near escapes, in which there is also, however, a keen awareness of sudden, sordid death, of cruelty and ruthlessness, and of the misery of the Belgian people under German occupation. But it is not until Jackson, Berthelot and the girl, Elise, are flying out of Belgium in a balloon (the most hare-brained adventure of them all) that the full horror of the war really hits them. As they fly over the ancient city of Rheims, they are appalled by the devastation they see.

> The cathedral and the area round it were the worst shelled places in the whole town. Many of the buildings had their exterior walls still standing, but were gutted like herrings by the blast. In other streets, the Germans had made the citizens pile the rubble into neat house-shaped

piles where they stood, travesties of bookshops, cafes, houses, surgeries, like a cruel child's playthings ... The whole district had been overturned.

Berthelot's grief soon gives way to a determination to fight back, and he is heartened by the resilience and defiance of the inhabitants, who, 'staring upwards incredulously' at the balloon, 'waved their hats or ran along the slushy streets, cheering and shouting in amazement and disbelief'.

But soon the balloon is flying above the Allied lines, and into an artillery barrage, and this is a very different scene, one which changes their sense of elation to one of shocked despair.

We crouched in the bottom of the basket and held on to each other for fear of our lives, and I will not pretend that we were brave or even rational about it. We screamed. The three of us screamed and screamed and screamed, until the froth flecked our lips and our throats ached.

But it is what they see of the Allied lines below that most afflicts them.

I think when we first saw it – and for us it was coming in late to a horror story without the chance to get acclimatized – I think even then we knew that the whole thing was futile. We had spent months watching the shells and guns going up to the front ... we had guessed that a battle was taking place, a big one – but we had dreamed in our innocence it was a battle, just one battle, not a way of life.

What we saw from the balloon was like nothing human. It had no scale that we could measure it by. The ground danced like surf in the centre of a sea of mud and broken trees and smashed villages a mile or more wide. It was like a huge, grey, suppurating slash across the face of the earth, a foul obscenity scrawled on nature. We screamed because we were in terror of our lives, and because we had been robbed of something – our joy in life, our right to live – while those poor demented bastards down below clung to their inch of mud, or were pitched up by the fury of so much bloody froth.

They land, safely enough, and are taken in and feted at the French Headquarters, but Elise puts into words what is in all their minds.

'I would rather have died in that valley this morning than to be alive now,' she said. 'This. This map. How long is it going to stay like this? A two-hundred-yard salient as a Christmas present for the troops! The same again next Christmas?'

More graphically perhaps than any other character Elise has brought into focus one of the most devastating and frustrating aspects of this war, fought for so long, yet over comparatively so restricted an area of land, back and forth, at such unthinkable and fruitless cost in young lives.

Brian Thompson, like Susan Hill, ends his story on a more optimistic note, but the message is there all the same in the French Colonel's sympathetic reaction to their distress: 'What you experience today has shocked you. I do not wonder. It is disgusting, evil ... It is beyond belief. Nobody, in years to come, will ever be able to get it right.'

We might expect to find this same sense of shock in *Tank Commander*, by Ronald Welch. But any indignation which does occur is muted by the fact that his hero, John Carey, comes from a long line of fighting men, stretching back to *Knight Crusader*, who are part of the military tradition, of the officer class, trained therefore to accept – even though with private grumbling and criticism – the decisions of superior officers. So although the book has been meticulously researched, in Welch's usual fashion, and no doubt also sifted through his own later experiences as an officer in the Territorials and during the Second World War, it presents no such devastating overview of the war. It does give a wealth of information about Regular Army life, from the traditions and manners of the officers' mess in peacetime to details of loading and firing rifles and of the first deployment of tanks in 1917. We are told of Carey's experiences in action from 1914 onwards, his wounds, his medals, his courage, his steady progression up the hierarchy to the rank of Colonel of the Tank Corps, his care for his men, and at times his compassion, which is apparent even in the incident with the cowardly Tyler, who is court-martialled and shot. It is interesting to compare this incident with the similar occasion in *Strange Meeting*. In Susan Hill's story the two young officers and the men had all worked hard to assist the terrified young lad, and save him from the consequences of his paralysing fear. Tyler, however, has from the beginning been characterised as 'useless', and a potential threat to the good name of the regiment.

> John knew his background, a Swansea dockside slum area, a father with a prison record, his mother a drunken slut and a horde of ragged, dirty brothers and sisters. Tyler had three regular meals a day now, clean clothes, regular pay, small as it was, and the orderly routine of army life. He would never make an NCO though: he was almost illiterate, slow of thought, ready enough to obey orders but probably incapable of ever accepting responsibility and leading others.

So it is small surprise to John – or to the reader – when he breaks, once this so desirable 'orderly routine of army life' has given way to the mud, blood and terror of death at the Front. His desertion, of course, cannot be concealed, so John can do little at that stage to help him: there is little hope of mercy for anyone who runs. Jones, his Sergeant-Major, defends him, once. 'If you ever 'ave to stand for an hour up to your knees in mud, listening to a lot of bloody great shells falling around you, then you might learn what this bloody war is all about', he barks at the MP who has called Tyler a 'little coward'. But Jones is here less concerned to show understanding towards the wretched Tyler than to defend his regiment against the imputation of cowardice in its ranks.

No one much cares for the business of executing Tyler: he is filled to the brim with brandy so that he will be too drunk to notice what is happening to him, or to make a nuisance of himself to his guards; and the officers, NCOs and firing squad are all given a ration of rum to see them through it, too. And that is that. Discipline and duty prevail, and Tyler is dead, 'pour encourager les autres'.

In *Tank Commander* it is always clear that the business of the professional soldier, John included, is to obey orders and get on with the war, whatever the circumstances. John has early learned to take 'searing rebuke from a Senior Officer', deserved or not, 'in silence and stiffly at attention'. Experience counts for nothing against rank, as we discover when John is trapped behind the German lines with Sergeant Jones and Private Thomas.

> Both of them had seen more than three years of active service in South Africa, and many more of peacetime soldiering and manoeuvres, while John had taken part in three days fighting only so far. But he was the officer. It was for him to decide what to do next, unless he asked them for their opinion.
>   It never occurred to John to do so. He had been trained to lead.

This is fine when the officer, in spite of his relative inexperience, gives the right orders, but as Peter Parker points out in his book, *The Old Lie*, many young officers had been given commissions with little adequate training on the assumption that their public school background had sufficiently fitted them for command. Time and again John and his men see the consequences of ineptitude, stupidity and lack of imagination on the part of their superiors. But, as Parker suggests, though 'the "moral" preparation within the schools was as outmoded and redundant as the military one ... a large number of combatants were sustained by their belief in the ideals for which they were fighting'. So, as he wryly remarks, 'In spite of circumstances which provoked scepticism amongst the less devout, the majority of young officers seemed to

have maintained their faith throughout the War,' and continued
to accept the defects of the command structure in spite of its
evident and sometimes disastrous flaws.

'Faith in the War' and in 'the old lie' is a major theme in
Welch's story. There is little chance of finding in it an officer who
will, like Colonel Garrett in *Strange Meeting*, put his career on the
line in protest. This is particularly apparent when John takes
command of a newly created Tank Corps. Even from a limited
experience with the new tanks, John knows immediately that they
will not perform well on 'the Salient'. He is appalled that 'intelligent' men have spent so much time making an 'immense model'
of the battlefield, 'a hundred yards square, covered with dug-outs,
trenches, ruined houses and villages, craters, pill boxes, and even
a lake filled with real water'. He knows how soon all this will dis-
appear once fighting begins, and make nonsense of the plans from
HQ. But he says nothing at the end of the Staff Officer's lecture,
only grumbles quietly afterwards to his fellow officer, Bill, who
will have to help him put the plan into operation. His cause for
complaint, nevertheless, radically questions the whole basis of the
attack. 'I can't see anything very professional about this offensive.
It's like a driver trying to smash his car through the garage doors.
He doesn't seem to realise he needs a key to unlock them.' But
although he knows that the generals who had planned this battle
from their 'safe and comfortable HQs' were probably sending his
tank crews on a fatal mission, John only reflects, glumly, that
'Generals must not flinch from the thought that their orders
would send thousands of men to death. He was a professional
soldier too, and perhaps he might become a General in course of
time. He tried to console himself with the fact that though his
orders might cause the death of those tank crews nearby he would
be sharing the risks with them.'

It is troubling that Welch leaves the reader with no more than
these stifled regrets at the unnecessary loss of so many men. I.F.
Clarke, in his fascinating book, *Voices Prophesying War*, has made a
much more trenchant comment on this kind of situation. In his
analysis of pre-1914 fiction attempting to prophesy the shape of
wars to come, he writes:

The period from the 1880s to the long-expected outbreak of the next
war in 1914 saw the emergence of the greatest number of these tales of
coming conflicts ever to appear in European fiction. Save for rare
exceptions, they are distinguished by a complete failure to foresee the
form a modern war would take. The slaughter of the trenches, the use
of poison gas, the immense damage caused by submarines, the very
scale of a world-wide industrialized war were mercifully hidden from

the admirals, generals, politicians, and popular novelists who joined in the great enterprise of predicting what was going to happen.

This war was inevitable. It was the result of the now familiar time-lag between the rapid development of technology and the belated abandonment of ideas, mental habits, and social attitudes that the new machines and the new industries had rendered out of date. When men thought of war they did not foresee the struggles of great armies and anonymous masses of conscripts that finally came to pass. Instead, drawing on an imagination still burdened by a long tradition, which presented war as an affair of brief battles and heroic deeds by individuals, they underestimated the scale of actual warfare.

Welch's book amply illustrates the truth of this indictment of the military command; but invites little effective protest against it. It offers an equally simplistic view of the causes of the war; that the assassination of the Archduke of Austria by the Serbs was used by the Austrians as an excuse to quell the troublesome Slavs within and outside their borders, so putting 'a match to a trail of gunpowder that linked the great capitals of Europe'. To be fair, Welch has been the only writer discussed so far to attempt to give even this much explanation for a war which, as he says, was to 'cause the deaths of millions of people and change for the worse the entire future of the world'.

If you accept that the story is told within the parameters of a Regular Army officer's vision, it is an excellent yarn, likely to appeal to readers of twelve and over more readily than the sensitive, perceptive questioning of the novels by Hill or Thompson. For sophisticated readers, however, it offers a striking contrast to *Across the Black Waters*, a novel (for adult readers this time) by the Indian writer, Mulk Raj Anand.

As a boy Anand lived with his parents in north Punjab in the barracks where his father was a havildar (or sergeant). There he would listen to the tales of sepoys who had seen service in France in the First World War. Their stories and his own shrewd assessment of the lowly status accorded to the sepoys within the British army were to provide him with material and inspiration for his account of the experiences at the Front of the peasant lad, Lalu Singh, the main protagonist in a trilogy of novels, *The Village*, *Across the Black Waters* and *The Sword and the Sickle*.

Anand's attitude to the humble, often illiterate sepoys is quite different from the contempt implicit in Welch's account of the unfortunate, underprivileged Tyler. Of the men in his story Anand says:

A passionate people, prone to sudden exaltations and depressions, more faithful than any other if they believed, they were neutral in this war, because this was not a war for any of the religions of their inheritance, nor for any ideal which could fire their blood and make their hair stand on end. Ordered about by the Sarkar, they were as ready to thrust their bayonets into the bellies of the Germans as they had been to disembowel the frontier tribesmen, or their own countrymen, for the pound a month which the sahibs paid them. But they were like conscripts, brutalized and willing to fight like trained bulls, but without a will of their own, soulless automatons in the execution of the army code, though in the strange dark deeps of their natures, unschooled by the Sarkar, there lay the sensitiveness of their own humanity, their hopes, their fears and their doubts.

Anand records the sepoys' resentment at the stand-offishness of the reticent Tommies which contrasted strikingly with the behaviour of the kind, polite, gesticulating 'Francisis'; but also their resilience of spirit, sensitivity of mood, and lively awareness of life and of each other. He describes his various characters with affection, never mocks their ignorance, and presents their differing beliefs with respect. So we are genuinely involved with Lalu's grief and unease when he finds Daddy Dhanoo floating in the water, looking up 'with the widened stare of a horrible and lonely death', his body denied the rites his religion demanded. We participate fully, also, in the bitterness with which Uncle Kirpu responds to Babu Kushi Ram's unwelcome questions about the fate of dead comrades, and grieve with Lalu at his old friend Kirpu's suicide, driven thereto by his malicious arrest on a false charge.

Like the Tommies, the Indian sepoys saw their regiments decimated in fruitless attacks and counter-attacks. But though they were caught up in a wholesale slaughter they were not prepared for, in a cause none of their own, they are shown wresting from it comradeship, affection, and a refreshing delight in the moments snatched behind the lines in the farmhouse, in the cafes, even in the brothels of Marseilles where they were fleeced and then unceremoniously turned out. Lalu in particular is able to stretch his hands out to the men, women and children from other religions and nations, even to those Tommies who could respond with like friendliness in recognition of their common plight. In spite of the horror, the bombs, the burning flesh, the ceaseless roaring of the guns, the summary execution of the gentle Hanumant Singh for cowardice, the 'hundreds of old and new mounds of graves, where the spirits of the dead seemed to crowd together waiting to possess the living who came that way', this remains a heartwarming book, making a unique contribution to the literature of the First World War.

The First World War saw the introduction in Britain of universal conscription to replenish the ranks following the massive casualties suffered at the Front. Consequently it also marked the appearance of the first conscientious objectors: young men who refused for reasons of conscience to kill their fellow men. Two books for younger readers – of 13 and over – which explore the position of these men in the First World War are *A Long Way to Go*, by Marjorie Darke, and *An Inch of Candle*, by Alison Leonard. Though pacifism is clearly a less exciting and compelling theme than active service in a novel for young people, both writers have made a praiseworthy attempt to involve their readers in the fortunes and difficulties experienced by their protagonists.

A Long Way to Go is the story of 18-year-old Bella and her twin brother Luke, descendants of the escaped slave and the pert young Bristol orphan who were the main characters in *The First of Midnight*. The story opens with Bella seeing off her older brother, Jack, onto the troop train for France, and wishing she could go too. She is full of patriotic fervour, and the desire to do something 'active', away from the household chores which seem to be her lot. But Luke has different ideas: he has decided to resist the draft and refuse to fight. This is not from cowardice, as he proves by his courageous rescue of a small girl from the dangerous ruins of her house. But he cannot believe in the war, or consent to destroy life without good reason. He tries, with some difficulty, to articulate his feelings, both to the strongly disapproving Bella and later to the hostile Tribunal.

Naturally he fails to impress the Tribunal with his fumbling, hesitant concern with the 'beauty' of the world in contrast to the ugly wastefulness of war, and his declaration that no one has any 'right ... to go round killing and killing. There ain't no worse sin and I can't ... *won't* take part.' But the Board is not impressed, either, by the more conventional religious or political convictions of the others at the hearing. All of them, including Luke's friends Stan and Norman, are summarily ordered into the army and shipped off to France where refusal to obey orders can be met with death as deserters. There they are forcibly taken to the Front Line trenches, where they still refuse to fight. Stan and Norman are killed by shell-fire and Luke, wounded, is returned to England to solitary confinement until the end of the war. Bella, meantime, has become a munitions worker; but gradually she, too, begins to question the morality of the war, and to share Luke's pacifism.

This is a lively story, in which the arguments on both sides make their impact through the events and characters in a way which invites sympathy, and so opens up debate.

An Inch of Candle also features a heroine who is scornfully unsympathetic towards her pacifist brother. Dora, at 15, has romantic ideas about war and heroism, fed by her reading and by her naturally lively, rebellious nature. Richard's father is even more unsympathetic, a strict Methodist, authoritarian, rigid and narrow in his views, and no easy man to oppose. Nevertheless Richard, like Luke, is no coward, and eventually wins respect for his stand.

Dora learns from Richard's experience just how hard the role of conscientious objector can be. She also learns the true nature of life at the Front when the Reverend Bosanquet begins to show her letters from his son, Humphrey, who is an officer in France. At first they are conventional and neutral, disappointingly unheroic, making 'no mention of wounds, dead comrades, or even of the enemy'. When during Humphrey's brief leave Dora surprises a look of fear and misery in his eyes, she concludes:

> 'He was so windy that he could not even write to his devoted father and his ailing mother. He was leaning against the side of the trench, hour after hour, day after day, mud-soaked and lice-ridden in the gas-filled air, sweating with terror while the brave tough Tommies went on watch and made tea and knocked off Huns all around him.'

But Humphrey's true feelings are revealed to her when the shaken rector receives a sheaf of papers recording what his son has been silently enduring. The young man suffers not so much from fear, as from a total horror of what is happening. He has written:

> The only comfort in all this, strange to say, is the sky overhead. Stand-to being at dawn and dusk, we see, on days when it is not raining, the first light rising behind the German lines, that light which is pale and yet intense ... Even when the clouds are thick and the unremitting rain torments us, I look up into that sky, and think of hymns sung in childhood about a Friend for little children, and ponder on those men in all the miles and miles of trenches up and down the Line who also look up into that relentless sky. Of those who look up into the sky from the strange territory on the other side of no-man's-land, I cannot bring myself to think, any more than I can think of those who sit by their fires at home in ignorance of how we suffer here.

Humphrey's father is deeply distressed by this revelation of his son's anguished doubts about the righteousness of the war. He had served on the Tribunal which sent Dora's brother to prison, and had argued down with derision Richard's religious scruples. Dora is acutely aware of this, and of the additional tragedy when the rector's wife commits suicide, unable any longer to bear the anxiety of having a son at the Front.

One of the strengths of these two books is their endorsement of quiet unheroic decency which refuses to kill, or to be carried along

in unthinking acceptance of conventional catchwords of patriotism and heroism. The very ordinariness of the young men and
women as they begin to think things through, even their fears,
inconsistencies, self-dramatisation or follies, emphasise the
humanity and courage of their position, and make their point. As
Edmund Blunden wrote later:

> By the end of the day both sides had seen, in a sad scrawl of broken
> earth and murdered men, the answer to the question. No road. No
> thoroughfare. Neither race had won, nor could win, the War. The War
> had won, and would go on winning.
>   (Quoted from *The Mind's Eye* in Paul Fussell,
>   *The Great War and Modern Memory*)

Summer of the Zeppelin, by Elsie McCutcheon, is a story of the
Home Front for readers of twelve or so. Several of the characters,
unfortunately, are little more than stereotypes – the bullying
headmaster, Mr Christmas, and his pert, obnoxious grand-
daughter, Sophie, for instance – and the slight plot element is
implausible. But this is one of the few novels to give a genuinely
sympathetic portrait of a German soldier, though Bill, like the
German in Bette Greene's novel of the Second World War, *The
Summer of my German Soldier*, is a highly idealised character.

The story is set in a small village in Suffolk. The young heroine,
Elvira Preston, her father at the Front, is left to make the best of
life with an apparently unsympathetic and moody stepmother,
who is away all day working in a munition factory, and, Elvira
feels, values her mainly as unpaid domestic help and childminder
in the evenings after school.

When Elvira first becomes aware of the presence of German
prisoners of war in the neighbourhood, she is in full agreement
with local beliefs about them.

> She remembered the tales she had heard of how they had murdered
> Belgian babies and children. And Mr Christmas had brought in a post-
> card one day showing a group of monstrous-looking German soldiers,
> with red bloated faces and glassy green eyes, waving swords and
> wearing spiked helmets.

She remembers also her father's very different comments on his
last leave, that 'this was all nonsense, that German soldiers were
much the same as British ones and hated the fighting and the
trenches every bit as much'. But she remains unconvinced until
she meets Bill, a POW, but a quiet, gentle man, a medical student,
a fine organ player, with a 14-year-old sister in Germany about
whom he is understandably anxious; and though from time to

time Elvira's doubts and suspicions are revived, her friendship with Bill finally convinces her that Germans are human, too.

In spite of its shortcomings, this is a welcome novel because of its unusually humane and tolerant attitude to conscripts of either side. It gives also a lively account of wartime Suffolk, the rationing, the local munitions factory, the anxieties of the families of serving soldiers, the rumours and gossip, and the kindliness which nevertheless emerges when anyone is in trouble – during the influenza epidemic, for instance, and when Elvira's father is posted missing. Like *An Inch of Candle* and *A Long Way to Go* it will appeal to young readers with a taste for domestic fiction, and can serve as a relief from the grimmer aspects of war.

Although these three novels offer less excitement than books dealing more directly with action at the Front they provide young readers with insight into an important aspect of this war – the stirrings of conscience against the continuing slaughter and an accompanying compassionate awareness of the sufferings of the 'enemy'. This is shown to be in marked contrast to the deeply disturbing patriotic fervour, the unreasoning hostility towards all dissenters or supposed 'aliens' and the acceptance of cruelty which, as will be seen in records of firsthand experience discussed in the next chapter, was fostered by war even in normally gentle and peaceful people.

4

From the Horse's Mouth

The books reviewed in the last two chapters have been historical novels in the sense that they were written out of research and imaginative recreation of events the author had not lived through. But there is also a body of literature from the First World War, sometimes disguised as fiction, sometimes written directly as personal memoirs by men who themselves experienced the events they describe. In the decade after the War, Peter Parker tells us in *The Old Lie: The Great War and the Public School Ethos*:

> A wave of anger and bitterness broke ... with a spate of novels and memoirs in which the authors' days as schoolboys and subalterns were recalled in a jaundiced frame of mind. As the first War memoirs began to appear, in which honour and idealism were depicted floundering in the filth of the Western Front, voices were once again raised against the schools in which such illusions were bred.

Some of these books were written to help their writers to come to terms with experiences which had been deeply troubling and traumatic; and which continued to have a profound influence upon their lives long after the war was over. They are, therefore, a unique and invaluable record of the effect of war upon its participants. They reveal not only the courage and heroism it elicits, but also the terror and suffering, and the shame and guilt of being perpetrators as well as victims of acts of cruelty and horror. The issues they raised were to be reflected in later fictional writing by novelists who had no first-hand experience of war. So they afford a measure against which to evaluate the quality of the war fiction we offer young readers; and a challenge to those novels which foster a false belief in the glory and heroism of war.

Rudolf Frank was born in Mainz, Germany, in 1886, and in 1914 was sent with the German artillery to the Eastern Front, as military correspondent. His novel *No Hero for the Kaiser* (1931), which he describes as 'an anti-war novel to warn young people', is based on his own experiences. His hero, Jan, however, is a Polish boy of 14, who, with Flox, the shepherd's poodle, is left alive after the small Polish hamlet of Kopchovka has been destroyed in a battle between German and Russian forces. Jan is adopted as a mascot by the German unit, and stays with them for two years, sharing their fortunes and guiding them through the Polish woods and countryside.

Jan quickly becomes a favourite with the men, and in return gives them unstinting loyalty. Then he sees the dead body of Vladimir, Flox's original owner, and realises that his efforts on behalf of his new friends have caused the deaths of men from his own village, who, like his father, were fighting on the other side. Though he remains with the German unit, this thought continues to haunt him. He recalls an earlier experience when he had been foraging for food for the unit in company with the Jewish Corporal Jacob. Jacob then was sternly taken to task by the elderly Jewish shopkeeper for wearing a soldier's uniform in defiance of the commandment: Thou shalt not kill. 'I must,' Jacob answers. 'In Germany every man must become a soldier.' But the old man replies, 'You must? What means you must? ... No man must.' This reply too stays in Jan's mind, along with the old man's uncompromising admonition:

> 'What is a coward? You need more courage than a whole regiment of soldiers to say: I shall not touch a gun, I shall not shoot. You need more courage for that than to run about with the others at the children of fathers and mothers who brought them up in care and sorrow.'

Moreover, he prophesies, whether Germany wins or loses the war, this will not profit Jacob: his reward from those in authority will be a new war 'against the Jews in our country', whom they will destroy, 'and that will be their thanks to you for wearing that bloody uniform'.

In 1933 Hitler banned this book, had it publicly burned and the author imprisoned.

Jan soon realises the true horror of war, and the ways in which language is used to hide the truth. As he meditates on the military uses of words like 'bull's eye', 'salvo', and 'in the field' he perceives the deceit which glorifies war and its slaughter. 'A real field does not kill,' he declares, 'a field lies at peace under God's sun, rain, and wind, a field is where things grow.' But the soldier's 'field' is quite a different place.

> The mists thickened as they walked towards the ditch from which [they] had driven the Russians the night before. Driven? No, everything was still there: weapons, helmets, caps, and sabers lay in wild confu-

sion on the edge of the ditch: eating implements, clothing, boots, spades, and bloodstained dressings. And in the ditch and in holes made by the grenades, great God, there they all were. The men were there, brown and grey like the earth and rubble, crumpled or stretched out in dust, blood, and dirt. Men's faces gaped, human trunks stuck out of the ground like tree stumps, human arms and legs lay like hacked branches, human hands and fingers grew out of the earth like plants. This was the field they had dug and planted; this was the harvest that had sprung from the seed of their bullets, filling the whole ditch.

Worse still, 'among and beneath the dead lay the men who still had life in them ... with mangled and riddled limbs', begging only for death.

Jan's journey through the battlefields takes him also to the western front, to still greater slaughter, to the anguish of families when news comes of the death of husband, son or father at the front, to a birdseye view of the trenches and shrapnel fire from a reconnaissance plane, to the deaths of many of his comrades in the unit, and finally to the decision to take seriously the words of the old Jew: 'No man must.' After two years Jan has had enough of fighting, and with Flox he leaves the battlefield, and disappears 'into the darkness'.

No Hero for the Kaiser is an avowedly propaganda novel, a little heavy-handed at times, but vividly presenting the point of view of the ordinary conscript. *Old Soldiers Never Die* (1933) is also about the men in the ranks. Its author, Frank Richards, had served eight years in the Regular Army, and had been a reservist for five and a half years when war began. He was called up at once and sent straight to France. In the words of Robert Graves, who was for a short time an officer in the same regiment, Richards 'stuck it out until the Armistice, never missing a battle or raid, never getting wounded, never applying for promotion or a transfer, serving under a dozen successive commanding officers, seeing the Battalion constantly smashed up and constantly reorganised'. In 1930 he began to write in direct, straightforward terms his own unemotional, matter-of-fact account of the war, and with Robert Graves's help and encouragement *Old Soldiers Never Die* was finally published in a duly 'cleaned up' version.

As an old soldier, Richards's comments on the conduct of the war are always succinct and trenchant; told with a dry humour, a keen eye for character or for humbug, and a rare ability to convey in a few words the feelings of his fellow-soldiers. As a veteran of India and Burma, it is true, he has little use for the Indian sepoys he encounters at the Front – Anand would recognise wryly the derogatory tone of his comments on them. He is as forthright, however, about the 'Public Schools Battalion', who were 'very decent chaps but hopeless as soldiers'; or the Territorials, whom he defends at times from the old soldiers' prejudice against them, but also castigates as a 'windy crowd' whom his CO, 'Buffalo Bill', would have 'shot at sight' had he been there. But his chief scorn is reserved for the war correspondents. He accuses them of inventing their stories from well behind the lines, and recommends them for a special medal 'For Distinguished Lying off the Field'.

Though he is keenly aware that one man's cowardice can cost the lives of braver soldiers, he can also show understanding of the pressures of that terrible Front.

> One afternoon a couple of guns in front of us were blown to bits and two young artillery officers were led past us, hysterical and horribly shell-shocked. They were the two worst cases I ever saw, and anyone would have been doing them a kindness if they had put them out of their misery.

His reports of some of the old hands who decided to get out of further fighting one way or the other are even at times tinged with admiration. There was Morris, who was detailed to help a gassed soldier down to the Casualty Clearing Station, and, though not gassed himself, 'dug up a series of coughs that were as loud as high shrapnel exploding', and 'in less than twenty-four hours he was in England as a bad gas case', whereas the genuine gas case was soon back in the line, only to be 'severely wounded at Givenchy'. Then there was the signaller:

> He told me that if he had the luck to get through the bloody barrage, and the luck also to be sent home, J.C. and all his angels would never shift him out to France again. He was true to his word. He got through the barrage and was sent home. His wound soon healed up and he was pronounced fit for the blood-tub. Draft after draft going overseas he was absent from, and he was finally sentenced to six months imprisonment. After a week in prison he was taken in front of the Governor, who informed him that if he volunteered to go back out to the Front he would be released. He informed the Governor that he had done close on two years active service, and that he considered he had done his whack, and that he didn't mind if he was kept in prison until the bloody War finished. The last I heard of him was about a month before the War finished, and he was still in England.

Naturally, Richards has little good to say about the bright ideas of the brass hats behind the lines, and he gives a caustic account of the abortive British gas attacks.

Dann and I were closely watching to see our gas going over, which we were told would kill every German for over a mile in front of us and which none of us believed in ... It looked like small clouds rolling along close to the ground. The white clouds hadn't travelled far before they seemed to stop and melt away. I found out later that the wind that should have taken it across no-man's-land hadn't put in an appearance and the gas had spread back into our trenches ... I met some of the lightly wounded men of the Middlesex and enquired how the show was going. 'A bloody balls-up' was the reply ... In less than an hour from the commencement of the attack the Brigade had lost fifteen hundred men, the majority being killed.

After the attack:

All the good gas cylinders were carried to the left flank and if the man who invented them had all the good wishes of the men who were carrying them he would have been in untold agony both before and after his death.

Richards is unsparing in his commendation of courage and coolness under fire, even when the soldier in question is German, like the officer who had hidden out in a shell-hole behind the British lines to report back the positions of British batteries. But after his account of one Somme offensive he remarks:

It seemed that every German artillery gun ... was firing direct on the Argyles ... I waited awhile before making my way back, and when I did pass by the Argyles' position I could only see heads, arms, legs and mangled bodies. I have often wondered since then, if all the leading statesmen and generals of the warring countries had been threatened to be put under that barrage during the day of 20th July, 1916, and were told that if they survived it they would be forced to be under a similar one in a week's time, whether they would all have met together and signed a peace treaty before the week was up.

In his autobiography, *Goodbye to All That* (1929), Robert Graves gives an officer's eye-view of the war. He joined the Royal Welch Fusiliers in 1914, straight from Charterhouse. In the Second Battalion he experienced at first hand the rigid hierarchy of the Regular Army, and the same supercilious treatment of junior officers as was described by Ronald Welch in *Tank Commander*. A friendly officer from a Surrey Regiment explains:

'They treat us like dirt ... The senior officers are beasts. If you open your mouth or make the slightest noise in the mess, they jump down your throat ... We've got to jolly well keep still and look like furniture.

It's just like peacetime ... The funny thing is that they don't realise how badly they're treating us – it's such an honour to be serving with the regiment.'

But he adds: 'Still, in trenches I'd rather be with this battalion than with any other I have met. The senior officers do know their job, whatever else one may say about them, and the NCOs are absolutely to be trusted, too.'

Graves shared in several of the operations described by Richards, and it is interesting to compare the two men's accounts of the first gas attacks. As an officer Graves was present at the briefing meeting beforehand, and records the hilarity, disbelief and distaste with which the officers heard their orders.

Thomas said: 'It's damnable. It's not soldiering to use stuff like that, even though the Germans did start it. It's dirty, and it'll bring us bad luck. We're sure to bungle it. Take those new gas-companies ... their very look makes me tremble. Chemistry dons from London University, a few lads straight from school, one or two NCOs of the old-soldier type, trained together for three weeks, then given a job as responsible as this. Of course they'll bungle it. How could they do anything else? But let's be merry.'

Thomas's predictions were confirmed once the attack began.

Thomas had not over-estimated the gas-company's efficiency. The spanners for unscrewing the cocks of the cylinders proved, with two or three exceptions, to be misfits. The gas-men rushed about shouting for the loan of an adjustable spanner. They managed to discharge one or two cylinders; the gas went whistling out, formed a thick cloud a few yards off in No Man's Land, and then gradually spread back into our trenches. The Germans, who had been expecting gas, immediately put on their gas-helmets: semi-rigid ones, better than ours. Bundles of oily cotton-waste were strewn along the German parapet and set alight as a barrier to the gas. Then their batteries opened on our lines. The confusion in the front trench must have been horrible; direct hits broke several of the gas-cylinders, the trench filled with gas, the gas-company stampeded.

Like Richards, Graves gives a graphic account of the resulting horrifying carnage which was compounded by the failure of the artillery to destroy the barbed wire entanglements.

Like Richards, too, he speaks scornfully of the war-fever he encountered back home when on leave: 'We could not understand the war-madness that ran wild everywhere, looking for a pseudo-military outlet. The civilians talked a foreign language; and it was newspaper language. I found serious conversation with my parents all but impossible.' At the end of the war he comments sourly on the life which greeted the survivors:

> The *Herald* [a new, anti-militarist newspaper] spoiled our breakfast every morning. We read in it of unemployment all over the country due to the closing of munition factories; of ex-servicemen refused reinstatement in the jobs they had left when war broke out, of market-rigging, lockouts, and abortive strikes. I began to hear news, too, of the penury to which my mother's relatives in Germany had been reduced, particularly the retired officials whose pensions, by the collapse of the mark, now amounted to only a few shillings a week.

In addition, he notes the doubts beginning to arise about whether Britain had been fighting the right war!

> Anti-French feeling among most ex-soldiers amounted almost to an obsession. Edmund [Blunden], shaking with nerves, used to say at this time: 'No wars for me at any price! Except against the French. If there's ever a war with them, I'll go like a shot.' Pro-German feeling had been increasing ...

The suspicion that 'we had been fighting on the wrong side' was to recur after the next major conflict, which some were to claim should have been fought against the Russians. What point can there be in a war which drives men to such an obscene expenditure of young life if even a small section of the combatants can later conclude that they had been killing the wrong people?

Blunden's own account of events, in *Undertones of War* (1928), is notable for its cameos of the shock and horror of sudden death, which seem, incidentally, to have inspired some of the incidents in Susan Hill's *Strange Meeting* (see Chapter 3).

> Not far away from that shafthead, a young and cheerful lance-corporal of ours was making some tea as I passed one warm afternoon. Wishing him a good tea, I went along three fire-bays; one shell dropped without warning behind me; I saw its smoke faint out, and I thought all was as lucky as it should be. Soon a cry from that place recalled me; the shell had burst all wrong. Its butting impression was black and stinking in the parados where three minutes ago the lance-corporal's mess-tin was bubbling over a little flame. For him, how could the gobbets of blackening flesh, the earth-wall sotted with blood, with flesh, the eye under the duckboard, the pulpy bone be the only answer? At this moment, while we looked with dreadful fixity at so isolated a horror, the lance-corporal's brother came round the traverse.
>
> He was sent to company headquarters in a kind of catalepsy.

Blunden too shares the scorn of the man at the Front for the bungling and incompetent plans formulated behind the lines, and the almost universal sense of alienation from the Home Front.

> During my leave I remember principally observing the large decay of lively bright love of country, the crystallization of dull civilian hatred on the basis of 'the last drop of blood'; the fact that the German air raids had almost persuaded my London friends that London was the sole battle front; the illusion that the British Army beyond Ypres was going from success to success; the ration system.

Blunden tells us of the 'peculiar difficulty' he found as an artist in selecting 'the sights, faces, words, incidents which characterize the time'. His solution was 'to collect them in their original form of incoherence'. So his narrative reflects in life-like fashion the confusion experienced at the time, and vividly describes the beauty of the French countryside in contrast to the devastation and ugliness of the battlefront. This gives an immediacy to his writing, but also a shapelessness, a disordered and highly allusive impression of incidents crowding together for attention, the effect of which is nevertheless different, in a way hard to define, from the quiet but poignant freshness of detail of Wilfred Owen's letters home from the Front. Nor can he quite match the force of such passages as Owen's cry from the heart:

> I suppose I can endure cold, and fatigue, and the face-to-face death, as well as another; but extra for me there is the universal pervasion of *Ugliness*. Hideous landscapes, vile noises, foul language and nothing but foul, even from one's own mouth (for all are devil ridden), everything unnatural, broken, blasted; the distortion of the dead, whose unburiable bodies sit outside the dug-outs all day, all night, the most execrable sights on earth. In poetry we call them the most glorious. But to sit with them all day, all night ... and a week later to come back and find them still sitting there, in motionless groups, THAT is what saps 'the soldierly spirit' ...

It is not always easy to make a clear distinction between directly autobiographical memoirs and the writings of those who have given a fictional form to their memories. For as Paul Fussell shows in *The Great War and Modern Memory*, there is always a strongly fictional element in memoirs, too. Fussell points, for instance, to the inextricable mixture of serious impassioned reporting and melodramatic myth-making anecdote in *Goodbye to All That*, and suggests that Graves's book 'is no more a "direct and factual autobiography" than Sassoon's memoirs. It is rather a satire, built out of anecdotes heavily influenced by the techniques of stage comedy.' In support of this he quotes Graves's own remarks in *But it Still Goes On* (1930):

> The memoirs of a man who went through some of the worst experiences of trench warfare are not truthful if they do not contain a high proportion of falsities. High-explosive barrages will make a temporary liar or visionary of anyone; the old trench-mind is at work in all overestimation of casualties, 'unnecessary' dwelling on horrors, mixing of dates and confusion between trench rumours and scenes actually witnessed.

The autobiographical novels, then, may be more open in their inclusion of such 'falsities', but are no less authentic as a response to the war experience of their authors. They have in addition the force and direction of experience organised into 'Art-speech'. Moreover, as Rutherford says in *The Literature of War*:

> The inherent superiority of the novel lies in its not being necessarily confined to the single consciousness of an author-protagonist, and in its not being limited, as autobiographies are by their very nature, to the author's actual experiences.

Rutherford adds:

> Honesty, inclusiveness, psychological and moral insight, and the accurate notation of experience are all desiderata in war literature, but they are not sufficient in themselves: they must be combined with the search for an appropriate form and the struggle to articulate through this the author's complex vision of the truth. Such a combination is achieved most notably by Frederic Manning, in *The Middle Parts of Fortune* (1929).

In this admirable novel, Manning's analysis of the effects of war upon the combatants is one of the most sharply focused of the various books under discussion. In his preface he says:

> War is waged by men; not by beasts, or by gods. It is a peculiarly human activity. To call it a crime against mankind is to miss at least half its significance; it is also the punishment of a crime. That raises a moral question, the kind of problem with which the present age is disinclined to deal.

Manning reflects upon the complexity of war through the creation of a variety of characters, each with a distinct perception of what is happening to him. In addition, both through direct authorial comment, and through the meditations of his central character, Bourne, he is able to offer a more detached commentary on the war than has been achieved through the more personal memoirs of Richards, Graves or Blunden.

Bourne – like Graves and Blunden – is a man of some education and capacity for sophisticated, abstract thought, who has nevertheless – like Richards in this respect – chosen to remain in the ranks. This puts him in direct communication and relationship with the men, in particular with his two friends, the Cockney Martlow and the Jewish Shem. But at the same time he remains detached from them, an observer. He maintains this double stance also towards the NCOs and officers, who perceive, sometimes uneasily, his superior education, and therefore permit him to talk to them on a level of equality not usually allowed to ordinary soldiers. This equivocal relationship with all ranks sets him apart, and gives him a unique vantage point for his reflections. He listens carefully to Sergeant Tozer's rambling, discursive outburst against conscientious objectors and others who inveigh against the wastefulness of this monstrous struggle, and extracts the nugget of sense and feeling from the diatribe. He perceives it to lie in the sergeant's closing remarks:

> 'Some folk talk a lot about war being such a bloody waste ... But when you send 'em over the top with a rifle, an' a bayonet, an' a few bombs, an' they find a big buck 'un in front o' them, they don't care a fuck about wastin' the other bugger's life, do they? Not a bit of it; it's their own bloody skins they think about, then. That's what they call their principle ... But what about us? Who 'as the better principle? Do they think we came out for seven bloody bob a week? I'm not troublin' about my bloody conscience. I've got some self-respect, I 'ave.'

Life, Bourne sees, is 'a hazard enveloped in mystery', and war 'quickens the sense of both in men'; but though they seek to make sense of it from divergent points of view, in the end people differ 'only in the angle and spirit' from which they survey 'the same bleak reality'.

Similarly, his ability to communicate, even haltingly, with the local inhabitants enables him to penetrate the thoughts and feelings of the French women, who, their menfolk at the Front, are left to survive on their own in their shattered villages, their homes invaded by waves of Tommies 'resting' from the battle. He can perceive with the same sympathetic detachment the near-fatalistic resignation of the French peasant, still doggedly tilling his land in defiance of the battle raging over it.

> 'C'est la guerre,' they would say, with resignation that was almost apathy: for all sensible people know that war is one of the blind forces of nature, which can neither be foreseen nor controlled. Their attitude,

in all its simplicity, was sane. There is nothing in war which is not in human nature; but the violence and passions of men become, in the aggregate, an impersonal and incalculable force, a blind and irrational movement of the collective will, which one cannot control, which one cannot understand, which one can only endure as these peasants, in their bitterness and resignation, endured it. *C'est la guerre.*

Most of the story is concerned with specific and detailed accounts of daily life behind the lines, in search of rest, escape and 'a bon time'; in rebellion against the endless parades and fatigues, and in personal relationships. In his account of the officers, NCOs and men, their view of each other, their fluctuating comradeship and exasperation with each other, the unlikely friendships thrown up by proximity in a shared danger and a shared perception of the nearness of death, Manning is unrivalled. He gives us also some of the most powerfully evocative descriptions of the horror of the Front Line, in which terror and tragedy mingle with farce.

Hurry? One cannot hurry, alone, into nowhere, into nothing. Every impulse created immediately its own violent contradiction. The confusion and the tumult in his own mind was inseparable from the senseless fury about him, each reinforcing the other. He saw great chunks of German line blown up, as the artillery blasted a way for them; clouds of dust and smoke screened their advance, but the Hun searched for them scrupulously; the air was alive with the rush and flutter of wings; it was ripped by screaming shells, hissing like tons of molten metal plunging suddenly into water, there was the blast and concussion of their explosion, men smashed, obliterated in sudden eruptions of earth, rent and strewn in bloody fragments, shells that were like hell-cats humped and spitting, little sounds, unpleasantly close, like the plucking of tense strings, and something tangling at his feet, tearing at his trousers and puttees as he stumbled over it, and then a face suddenly, an inconceivably distorted face, which raved and sobbed at him as he fell with it into a shell-hole. He saw with astonishment the bare arse of a Scotsman who had gone into action wearing only a kilt-apron; and then they righted themselves and looked at each other, bewildered and humiliated.

Manning is always painfully aware of the effect of this mind-shattering experience upon men existing now in a kind of no-man's-land in their lives.

Bourne could realise completely the other man's present misery; could see him living, breathing, moving in that state of semi-somnambulism, which to each of them equally was their only refuge from the desolation and hopelessness of that lunatic world ... The girl beside him ... knew nothing of their subterranean, furtive, twilight life, the limbo through which, with their obliterated humanity, they moved as so many unhoused ghosts, or the aching hunger in those hands that reached, groping tentatively out of their emptiness, to seek some hope or stay.

From the distillation of so many different experiences Manning is able to make trenchant comments about warfare in the modern world, and to perceive – in terms similar to those used by Rosenberg in 'Break of Day in the Trenches' – the impartiality of death.

> After all, the dead are quiet. Nothing in the world is more still than a dead man ... Suddenly he remembered the dead in Trones Wood, the unburied dead with whom one lived, he might say, cheek by jowl, Briton and Hun impartially confounded, festering, fly-blown corruption, the pasture of rats, blackening in the heat, swollen with distended bellies, or shrivelling away within their mouldering rags; and even when night covered them, one vented in the wind the stench of death. Out of one bloody misery into another, until we break. One must not break.

Like Clarke in *Voices Prophesying War*, Manning too sees that the professionals in command were still fighting the last war, and did not know how to use the new technology of killing. But Bourne also observes that 'resentment against officers, against authority', even when justified, 'meant very little'. They were a convenient target for the men's grumbles, but the real problem lay deeper, in 'the sense of being at the disposal of some inscrutable power, using them for its own ends, and utterly indifferent to them as individuals'. For war, he feels, is merely a statement of 'the ultimate problem of all human life'. It is a particularly stark and extreme statement, however, because it puts men under an ever-present and inescapable threat of death, 'pressing for an immediate solution' without giving them time to find one.

War is not, though, a manifestation pressing upon the individual from the outside only: it is a facet of his own personality; coming from within. 'A man might rave against war; but war, from among its myriad faces, could always turn towards him one which was his own.' This is a reflection which is troubling, but it is endorsed by the fascination with violence betrayed in the books by Cormier, Westall and Golding, referred to in Chapter 1.

Bourne's own death causes scarcely a ripple. Sergeant Tozer, though viewing his dead body with 'pitiful repulsion ... moved away in quiet acceptance of the fact'. Briefly Tozer reflects on the 'mystery' which had surrounded that 'queer chap', Bourne, and on the surprising extent of his personal sorrow for him. Then, in keeping with Bourne's own awareness of the transitory, fleeting value attached to life and death in time of war, he turns to the next thing to be done, expending no more thought on this individual death in amongst so much slaughter.

This is a book which offers a ready empathy with events and characters, but also, for those who can encompass it, a deeply disturbing analysis of the temptations to battle and the role of war in human society.

Henri Barbusse, in *Under Fire* (1916), tells his story from the viewpoint of the French *poilu*. Although fighting on his own territory, the ordinary French soldier felt the same distrust and alienation towards the civilian population: their rapacity in charging high prices for goods and services; their belief that civilian danger from occasional bombing raids could be equated with the danger and suffering of the troops at the front, and their ability to shrug off the absence of their menfolk in the company of others.

'You take your damned hook from home to go to the war, and everything seems finished with; and they worry for a while that you're gone, but bit by bit you become as if you didn't exist, they can do without you to be as happy as they were before, and to smile.'

This feeling gave rise to the sardonic phrase '*Pourvu que les civils tiennent*' – 'if the civilians hold out'. But the anger and cynicism directed against civilians and shirkers was not extended indiscriminately to all those who succumbed to fear. Like their British counterparts, the *poilus* were too well acquainted with the terror of the front line; and there is a touching account of the execution of a trench-dodger.

'He tried to dodge the trenches. During relief he stayed behind, and then went quietly off to quarters. He did nothing else; they meant, no doubt, to make an example of him ... He wasn't a ruffian, he wasn't one of those toughs we all know ... He was a decent sort, like ourselves, no more, no less – a bit funky, that's all. He was in the front line from the beginning, he was, and I've never seen him boozed, I haven't.'

So the 'fellows of his squad who killed him ... scrawled inscriptions and protests' on the post to which he had been tied. 'A *croix de guerre*, cut clumsily of wood and nailed to it, read: "A. Cajard, mobilised in August, 1914; France's Gratitude." '

Particularly poignant is the episode in which the men digging trenches find themselves subjected not merely to a relentless hail of bullets and shells from the German lines but also to a torrential downpour which turns the land into a swamp, literally drowning them in mud.

We drag ourselves to the spot. They are drowned men. Their arms and heads are submerged. On the surface of the plastery liquid appear their backs and the straps of their accoutrements. Their blue cloth trousers are inflated, with the feet attached askew upon the ballooning legs ... They are the men who were watching there, and could not extricate themselves from the mud. All their efforts to escape over the sticky escarpment of the trench that was slowly and fatally filling with water only dragged them still more into the depth. They died clinging to the yielding support of the earth.

Not only the French soldiers are submerged in this swamp.

There, our first lines are; and there, the first German lines, equally silent and flooded ... Out of the horror of the night, apparitions are issuing from this side and that who are clad in exactly the same uniform of misery and filth.

Next morning, surveying the desolation of water surrounding them, Paradiso concludes:

War is frightful and unnatural weariness, water up to the belly, mud and dung and infamous filth. It is befouled faces and tattered flesh, it is corpses that are no longer like corpses even, floating on the ravenous earth. It is that, that endless monotony of misery, broken by poignant tragedies; it is that, and not the bayonet's silvery glitter, nor the trumpet's cock-crow in the sun!

The misery common to both contending armies is further high-lighted by a pilot flying above the trenches, who becomes aware of two religious services, 'so exactly alike that it looked silly', being conducted within a stone's throw of each other, one in the French lines, one in the German. Barbusse concludes, passion-ately, 'No more war! No more war! Enough of it!'

'Men are made to be husbands, fathers, – *men*, not beasts that hunt each other and cut each other's throats and make themselves stink like all that.'
   'Two armies fighting each other – that's like one great army commit-ting suicide!' ...
   In their troubled truce of the morning, these men whom fatigue had tormented, whom rain had scourged, whom night-long lightning had convulsed, these survivors of volcanoes and flood began not only to see dimly how war, as hideous morally as physically, outrages common sense, debases noble ideas and dictates all kinds of crime, but they remembered how it had enlarged in them and about them every evil instinct save none, mischief developed into lustful cruelty, selfishness into ferocity, the hunger for enjoyment into a mania.

As Barque has remarked earlier, every act of warfare is unclean.

> 'When you've seen men squashed, cut in two, or divided from top to bottom, blown into showers by an ordinary shell, bellies turned inside out and scattered anyhow, skulls forced bodily into the chest as if by a blow with a club, and in place of the head a bit of neck, oozing currant jam of brains all over the chest and back – you've seen that and yet you can say "There are *clean* ways!" '

And Volpatte declares sourly that his country is divided into two nations, 'the Front, over there, where there are too many unhappy, and the Rear, here, where there are too many happy'.

Although Barbusse's rhetoric suffers in translation and sometimes seems inflated in comparison with the robust prose of Richards and Manning, his indignation is as sharply directed against those armchair readers who can still delude themselves that war is an opportunity for valour and glory.

Siegfried Sassoon's trilogy, *Complete Memoirs of George Sherston* (1937), is one of the best known of First World War novels. In it we return to the officers' viewpoint, and, initially, to a boyishly innocent attitude towards war as a potentially heroic game. Through his young hero and narrator, George Sherston, Sassoon recaptures some of the breezy callowness and bravado of youth, giving a surface impression of being able to take in his stride experiences which were clearly profoundly disturbing and traumatic. Even when Sherston returns wounded to England, and voices an urgent pacifism born of his outrage at the senselessness of the suffering and the enormity of the sacrifice he has witnessed at the Front, he maintains a self-deprecating awareness of his youthful capacity for dramatising his situation. This appears in phrases like 'working myself up into a tantrum' and 'If I wasn't careful I should be yelling like some crank on a barrel in Hyde Park'; or, in speaking of his 'statement as an act of wilful defiance', 'how inflated and unconvincing it all looked'; later, having decided to return to the Front, in describing himself as 'that somewhat incredible mutineer who had made up his mind that if a single human being could help to stop the War by making a fuss, he was that man'. These phrases give the air of truth to Sherston's narrative, but make his gesture appear less serious, considered, and sustainable than was really the case. His confused and irrational state of mind persists to the end of the book, when he concludes:

> I saw myself as one who had achieved nothing except an idiotic anti-climax, and my mind worked itself into a tantrum of self-disparagement. Why hadn't I stayed in France where I could at least

escape from the War by being in it? Out there I had never despised my existence as I did now.

The wholly serious tone in which Sherston declares that 'my soul had rebelled against the War, and not even Rivers could cure it of that' is rarely given sustained expression, except in passages which concern others rather than himself.

Shell-shock. How many a brief bombardment had its long-delayed after-effect in the minds of these survivors, many of whom had looked at their companions and laughed while inferno did its best to destroy them. Not then was their evil hour, but now; now, in the sweating suffocation of nightmare, in paralysis of limbs, in the stammering of dislocated speech. Worst of all, in the disintegration of those qualities through which they had been so gallant and selfless and uncomplaining – this, in the finer types of men, was the unspeakable tragedy of shell-shock; it was in this that their humanity had been outraged by those explosives which were sanctioned and glorified by the Churches; it was thus that their self-sacrifice was mocked and maltreated – they, who in the name of righteousness had been sent out to maim and slaughter their fellow-men. In the name of civilization these soldiers had been martyred, and it remained for civilization to prove that their martyrdom wasn't a dirty swindle.

The final volume, *Sherston's Progress*, concludes with a further meeting with Rivers, the doctor at the Slateford War Hospital where Sherston was sent to be cured of his 'defiance'. Rivers is now seen as an exorcist, 'a refutation of wrong-headedness', someone whose good opinion Sherston valued, and who could 'show him the way' to 'a new life'. What is apparent from this reliance upon Rivers is that the contradiction of loyalties remains unresolved – loyalty both to his newfound hatred of war and to his comrades at the Front, some dead, some crippled, whose sacrifice in years, health, both mental and physical, or life itself, it was painful to have to regard as a cruel waste. Like the *poilus* in *Under Fire*, Sherston desperately needs to find some way of going forward to that 'completed peace' which he declares to be the only thing he now wanted. But such peace required reconciliation with what had happened.

It is at this point that we return to Barton in Susan Hill's novel, *Strange Meeting*, to his perception of the insoluble nature of the problem. How is it possible to join in the killing, knowing its futility, recognising the greed, deceit and brutality which gave rise to it and which in turn it fosters in the combatants? How, on the other hand, is it possible to remain aloof whilst the rest of one's generation is being slaughtered? Most of the fighting men – again like the *poilus* in *Under Fire* – settled for winning the war first: only then, they felt, could they begin to unite against war. The more realistic, however, foresaw no end to war; even though the only hope for the future, the only meaning of their sacrifice, lay in an end to wars for ever.

In his more directly personal memoir, *Siegfried's Journey* (1945), Sassoon returns to these problems, subjecting his feelings to a critical scrutiny which reflects his continuing uncertainty and unease about his motives: the 'disturbing and disorderly ideas' which had made him vulnerable to 'Robbie's rather unconstructive and petulant pacifism', and 'all too ready to accuse the governing powers of injustice and improbity'. Nevertheless his serious, deep convictions are further stirred and fed both by his reading and by careful consideration of the issues involved which, now that the war has ended, can be detached from his personal plight. In the course of his analysis he quotes from H.G. Wells' *Mr Britling Sees It Through* (1916), recognising there an expression of his own feelings.

> It is a war now like any other of the mobbing, many-aimed cataclysms that have shattered empires and devastated the world; it is a war without point, a war that has lost its soul; it has become mere incoherent fighting and destruction, a demonstration in vast and tragic forms of the stupidity and ineffectiveness of our species.

Later, after an hour-long talk with Winston Churchill, Sassoon counters the remark that 'war is the normal occupation of man' with a quotation from Hardy's *Dynasts*:

> I have beheld the agonies of war
> Through many a weary season; seen enough
> To make me hold that scarcely any goal
> Is worth the reaching by so red a road.

And subsequently in a lengthy lecture tour to America he read to a variety of audiences, both sympathetic and hostile, a selection of his war poems, interspersed with comments supporting an anti-war stance. He recalls one such session:

> I have preserved the notes for my speech, which ... still strikes me as a very decent, unrhetorical presentation of my evidence against war. It was a ramblingly descriptive, anecdotal account of life in the infantry. I laid stress on those elements in war service which brought out men's finest qualities of cheerfulness and endurance, but expressed a conviction that the indictment of war was to be found in the exploitation and betrayal of those qualities. For the common soldier, the glory of war was an expediently invented falsehood. And I said that no one who

had been in a shell-shock hospital, as I had, could be entirely reasonable about the 'uplifting effects' of war on the individual. It was a genuine attempt to balance the good and bad elements, but I made it provocative by the poems which I read as illustrations. These were interpolated at points calculated to startle complacency.

At the end of the Second World War he remarked:

> If I were asked to make a speech about war now, it would consist of a couple of sentences. 'The only effective answer that a poet can make to barbarism is poetry, for the only answer to death is the life of the spirit. Explosives cannot destroy the immaterial or dumbfound the utterance of inspiration.'

He added: 'At the present time [1945] nobody needs disillusioning about war. The danger seems to be that they accept it in a fatalistic way and that future generations may regard its recurrences as inevitable.'

Has anything changed since then? Nearly half a century later, the view of war as 'inevitable' is still with us.

Erich Remarque's novel, *All Quiet on the Western Front* (1929), was written from the German side of the conflict: his family had emigrated to the Rhineland at the time of the French Revolution. His central character, Paul, joins the army straight from school, with many of his classmates. From the German trenches he too reports the discomforts of mud, lice, rats, food shortages and shelling; the eventual disillusionment with the motives and conduct of the war; the alienation from the civilian population whilst on leave. As a private he sees more clearly than Sassoon that the structure of the army itself corrupts those in command.

> With our young, awakened eyes we saw that the classical conception of the Fatherland held by our teachers resolved itself here into a renunciation of personality such as one would not ask of the meanest servants – salutes, springing to attention, parade-marches, presenting arms, right wheel, left wheel, clicking the heels, insults, and a thousand pettifogging details. We had fancied our task would be different, only to find we were trained for heroism as though we were circus ponies.

Such sadistic exercise of power over men can only occur in the army: 'It goes to the heads of them all,' he declares, 'and the more insignificant a man has been in civil life the worse it takes him.'

In spite of the comradeship of the front line, the ordinary soldier, too, is corrupted and brutalised by his experiences.

> We have become wild beasts. We do not fight, we defend ourselves against annihilation ... crouching like cats we run on, overwhelmed by

this wave that bears us along, that fills us with ferocity, turns us into thugs, into murderers, into God only knows what devils; this wave that multiplies our strength with fear and madness and greed of life, seeking and fighting for nothing but our deliverance. If your own father came over with them you would not hesitate to fling a bomb at him.

He describes not only the horrors of being under attack, but also of killing; of delivering the bayonet jab to the back of your opposite in the Allied camp, cleaving through his face with a spade, smashing it to pulp with a rifle butt, bayoneting the gun crew and then thirstily drinking the water they have for cooling the gun, springing over the wounded as they cry for help and clutch at the legs of the living, the men swept forward, 'powerless, madly savage and raging' as they kill. He describes in graphic terms the torment of the hours Paul spent in a shell-hole in company with the man he had stabbed, as he lay slowly dying. In his anguish of remorse Paul cries out:

Forgive me, comrade ... Why do they never tell us that you are poor devils like us, that your mothers are just as anxious as ours, and that we have the same fear of death, and the same dying and the same agony – Forgive me, comrade; how could you be my enemy? If we threw away these rifles and this uniform, you could be my brother just like Kat and Albert. Take twenty years of my life, comrade, and stand up – take more, for I do not know what I can even attempt to do with it now.

Of necessity Paul crushes down his compassion and remorse in the battles to come, but returns to it with his comrades in the quieter intervals, and most of all in the hospital where he is recovering from his wounds.

A man cannot realise that above such shattered bodies there are still human faces in which life goes its daily round. And this is only one hospital, one single station; there are hundreds of thousands in Germany, hundreds of thousands in France, hundreds of thousands in Russia. How senseless is everything that can ever be written, done, or thought, when such things are possible. It must be all lies and of no account when the culture of a thousand years could not prevent this stream of blood being poured out, these torture-chambers in their hundreds of thousands. A hospital alone shows what war is.

Paul despairs also for his future, in a world after the slaughter, in which, still, 'the keenest brains of the world invent weapons and words to make it yet more refined and enduring'. He laments:

Through the years our business has been killing; – it was our first calling in life. Our knowledge of life is limited to death. What will happen afterwards? And what shall come out of us? ... We will grow older, a few will adapt themselves, some others will merely submit, and most will be bewildered; – the years will pass by and in the end we shall fall into ruin ... Let the months and the years come, they can take nothing from me, they can take nothing more. I am so alone, and so without hope that I can confront them without fear.

Paul did not survive the war; but his creator lived to face the problems of adjustment Paul had foreseen in his prophetic threnody for a lost generation, left 'weary, broken, burnt out, rootless, and without hope'; unable to find their way any more.

Two other books from Germany, *War* (1929) and *After War* (1930), by Ludwig Renn, reinforce the insights offered in Remarque's book. In *War* Renn (whose real name was Arnold Vieth von Golssenau) gives his account of the initial German advance through Belgium, with its ruthlessly punitive attitude towards the civilian population, especially those who offered resistance. Renn feels compunction towards the girl and her dying mother whose house the men invade in search of shelter from snipers; and even towards other, less 'innocent' civilians. Though he also records more routinely episodes in which farms and houses were set on fire and civilians shot, Renn's spare, lucid and searching account reveals a man whose native compassion and concern for ordinary people survived the brutalities of war.

In *After War*, he returns to distressing memories of these incidents. As he is reminiscing one day, a man at the next table remarks:

'I learned to think about things in one day. That was in 1914 as we were crossing the Maas. Our Colonel had a lot of Belgians shot there, men, women and children. Our field-kitchen was halted just in front of the place. And as I was passing the heap of bodies that night I saw a head moving in it. It was a woman, and her face was all bloody. And her eyes – I'll never forget them! They weren't so much dotty or awful, but as you might say without any expression at all. Lots of people in the batch, it turned out, hadn't been killed. And when night came they crept out. And in the morning there they were sitting on the wall opposite the pile of dead bodies, looking around them in the queerest way. I began to think about things then! It was never proved that the Belgians there had really shot at us ... There was no investigation, of course; the people were just set against a wall several deep, and shot into until there was no movement among them, and allowed to lie where they were.'

The speaker contrasts this summary execution of possibly innocent civilians with the fate of war profiteers, some of whom

escaped detection altogether, whilst others were briefly imprisoned. One such had 'smuggled through whole railwaywaggons
full of old goods from French factories and sold them in Germany
and pocketed the proceeds'.

Renn chronicles the increasing disillusion, cynicism and dis-
array of the army in defeat: of men deserting wholesale to the
enemy, leaving their rifles stacked in the trench; of falsification of
reports; of the breakdown of discipline and of increasingly severe
shortages of food and goods. Men began to cut out the soles of
their own boots to send back to their families, and on his return
to Germany, Renn, like Remarque, observes the distressing consequences of a disastrous war upon both civilian population and
returning soldiers. He comments bitterly:

> And yet Germany was supposed to pay? The idea made me dizzy. That
> meant for us poor starving devils that year after year our noses would
> be kept at the grindstone, and that we wouldn't be able to buy a new
> suit even. My good suit had been bought before the war, in 1912.

Conditions in Germany are rapidly deteriorating into a state of
confused revolution, power-seeking, chicanery, self-seeking greed
and hopelessness. Renn disengages himself first from the army,
now being used for ends he cannot support, and then from the
police force, which he has joined instead. Finally, his protests
against corruption and against continuing violence towards the
workers result in his dismissal. He ends his account:

> Now an unsettled life began for me. I found work sometimes here,
> sometimes there, but never for any length of time. And in addition I
> was unsettled within myself; I felt uprooted and hopeless. For seven
> years I lived this life, until I finally found my way to Communism.

Renn tells the story of the years during and after the war with
objective simplicity, allowing fellow privates and NCOs to speak
for themselves, to reveal without polemic, but with mounting bitterness, their sense of the futility of the war, and of grief at the
fate of their Fatherland and people. Always Renn is aware of the
feelings and fate of the ordinary people, their suffering, both at
the hands of the enemy and of those of their own countrymen
who were cynically exploiting the situation for their own gain. He
sees that the punitive attitude of the victors merely reinforced the
corruption and hopelessness, which was to result, in the end, in
the triumph of the Nazis in Germany, and culminate in the
Second World War: for the 'war to end wars' proved no such
thing.

From all these books it is clear that war in its complexity provokes varying and conflicting responses not only between different participants, writers and readers, but also in the same individuals at different times. Thus Rutherford in *The Literature of War*, rightly draws attention in his 'five studies in heroic virtue' to the admiration expressed even by Sassoon and Owen for a 'heroic ideal, stripped of glamour certainly, but redefined convincingly in terms of grim courage and endurance in the face of almost unbearable suffering and horror.' He points to the suppression in Sassoon's poetry of 'the Sassoon who patrolled blood-thirstily in No Man's Land to avenge the death of friends – the Sassoon his comrades nicknamed "Mad Jack" for his reckless bravery in battle – the Sassoon who took German trenches single-handed on the Somme, shouting a "view halloa" as the defenders stole away' – the Sassoon who, as Graves puts it, alternated between the roles of 'happy warrior' and 'bitter pacifist'. He quotes the official citation for Owen's MC, which tells of his 'personally manipulat[ing] a captured enemy machine gun in an isolated position and inflict-[ing] considerable losses on the enemy'. But he dismisses too lightly 'the emphasis on degradation, demoralisation and futility, and the repudiation of any conception of the heroic' in *All Quiet on the Western Front*, suggesting that Remarque's characters 'were debased and brutal before they ever went to war', and citing in proof 'the beating up of a sadistic corporal by the young recruits' – an incident which was itself surely a response to the training intended to 'harden' them for action at the Front.

The fact is that both aspects of war experience are true; the ability to take part almost exultantly in its ferocities and the contrasting sense of the pity of war and revulsion from its cruelties. Men and women, civilians and soldiers are deeply ambivalent about war. But no amount of incidental heroism experienced, reported and admired can justify indulgence in such wholesale slaughter: the more positive, constructive and humane impulse to outlaw war deserves all the support it can get. This is a cogent argument for introducing young readers to books which, though they may offer some of the excitement and drama which attract young people to reading, nevertheless firmly counter 'the old lie', so fiercely denounced by Wilfred Owen and so fervently upheld by the public schools.

5

The War Machine

The 'Great' War shocked the world by the scale of its operations and its casualties. In the Second World War the theatre of operations was even more wide-ranging – in Europe, the deserts of North Africa and the jungle terrain of the Far East; on land, on sea and in the air. It was a war notable for the mechanisation of slaughter, in which the man operating the machine was frequently at so great a remove from his victims that he could blot out from his consciousness their existence and their deaths. The poet R.N. Currey, who served in Anti-Aircraft Artillery, pertinently remarks:

> In *This Other Planet* I tried to express my sense of exile in this world of machines and exact calculation, where you used guns that might be a mile away to fire at a plane represented for you by a disturbance on a cathode ray tube. This seemed to me, and still does, the pattern of the war of the future. A man who is too squeamish to kill a rabbit can launch a rocket.
>
> Ian Hamilton (ed.), *The Poetry of War 1939–1945*

It was also a war which involved civilians to a greater extent than ever before; not only as casualties in the bombed cities, but also as refugees, or as people deported in large numbers from the occupied territories either as slave labour or to the concentration camps and gas chambers where six million people perished. It was a war, too, which culminated in the dropping of nuclear bombs on Hiroshima and Nagasaki, where those exposed to radiation were still dying decades after the end of hostilities.

How, first, did these changing aspects of warfare affect the fighting forces?

In his novel, *Distant Drum*, Manohar Malgonkar explains the principles behind the training described by First World War writers, but still being given to British army officers in the years immediately preceding the outbreak of the next war. This long-established tradition of training, he claimed, was what 'had made the regular officers of the British army the fine leaders of men they were'. It was a crude process, he concedes, but one which achieved 'splendid results'.

> As Bum Warts, you were dirt and less than dirt, never to speak at meal-times unless spoken to. They insulted you at every step, they were never satisfied with your best efforts, for the slightest real or imagined irregularities they gave you extra parades, your smartest salute was soundly berated as sloppy and you spent hours under a sergeant learning to salute, your uniforms made by the most expensive tailor in Delhi were labelled outrageous and had to be altered to suit the regimental way of dressing, and they left you in no doubt that the sight of your face in the mess was unbearable.
>
> On your part, you could do little more than curse them and curse the system with all the invective your Academy-trained vocabulary was capable of. You went about feeling angry and bitter and trying not to show it, consoling yourself with the thought that even the British Bum Warts, their own kith and kin, were given exactly the same treatment. It was only later, as time passed, that you realised that all this was a part of the process – a process which had only just begun and would be continued for several years after you joined your permanent regiment – of putting you through your paces, a process of hardening you up, of increasing your resistance to stress; it was all an essential part of your grounding as an officer and a gentleman, fit to command the King's men.

This 'grounding as an officer and gentleman' finally accepted by Malgonkar's hero, Kiran, with pride as a process of 'hardening you up', was designed to make men 'fit' to kill without any of the scruples normally felt by ordinary, untrained civilians. Malgonkar describes the feelings generated in Kiran by his experience in action.

> It was also Kiran's first successful attack, and its memory brought on a heady feeling of unmixed exultation. He was convinced that nothing else could give an infantry officer the same sense of fulfilment as success in an attack. It was like a submarine commander sinking a ship, an air force officer demolishing a bridge or a dam, or bringing down an enemy bomber. It was the very purpose of existence; the crowning achievement of an infantry officer's life: a successful attack!
>
> And on a day, too, in this his first attack against a Japanese position in a foreign jungle, Kiran had killed a man in hand-to-hand fighting; thrusting his bayonet again and again, savagely crashing his rifle-butt into the fallen, lolling head, not knowing when death had come.
>
> But even that memory did not bring on a sense of guilt. It was somehow all a part of fulfilment, a grisly and ghastly detail in the process of learning to become a soldier.

Kiran was a regular soldier, the army his chosen career. Nevertheless it took several years of intensive training to enable him to develop such professionalism towards the art of killing at close quarters. For the conscript in the Second World War as in the First, training was condensed into a matter of months – at times even less. Hans Peter Richter and David Holbrook describe their initiation into the German and British armies respectively from the point of view of the ordinary civilian.

The Time of the Young Soldiers is the third in a trilogy of autobiographical novels about Germany under Hitler. Recalling his final days at school and his war experiences, Richter says:

> When the war broke out, I was fourteen years old; when it ended I was twenty. I was a soldier for three years. I thought that the things I saw and the things I did were justified because no one spoke out openly against them.

Richter volunteered for the army at 17, and accepted without comment the brutalities of the training – the senior leader 'licking into shape ... the toughest man in our room, for dropping his rifle during drill'; the ruthless instructions to 'kill the swine' if any civilian dared insult their uniform. He describes being made to drink a tumbler full of brandy by his sadistic sergeant: ' "Good!" said the sergeant, satisfied. "I don't stand for any dodgers in my platoon," he told us. "Red-blooded men, that's what I want, see?"'

Like Renn and Remarque, Richter reveals the effect upon the boys of this training, toughening them into men without concern or compassion, ready and willing to take part in similar brutalities. He tells his story in separate anecdotes, related without elaboration, but set alongside each other to make the appropriate impact on the reader. So he tells of the recruit who volunteers to crouch in a slit trench to demonstrate that it has been correctly made and will protect him against tanks passing overhead. But the tank sticks, sinks down into the sand, and crushes the man's arm into 'a bloody mess of bone splinters, torn flesh and rags of uniform'. The narrative moves on without more ado to bayonet practice, in which the corporal's instructions are suitably ferocious and bloodthirsty. Injury, blood and death are, after all, it is implied, the business of war: you accept them and turn to the next thing.

Similarly juxtaposed for effect, are two incidents from a train journey with unfriendly Polish-speaking conscripts. The first is comic: two conscripts suddenly seize the officers' boots and make off with them, but while the officers are still wondering how to explain their loss to their superiors, the boots are brought back and replaced, cleaned and polished. 'They're not a bad lot after all!' the sergeant remarks with some relief. 'Too good for cannon-fodder really!' But in the next incident someone – presumably from the same group of 'not bad' recruits – seizes an anti-aircraft gun from the end wagon, and shoots up the train, old men, women, children and soldiers alike.

Many incidents, comic, or serious, could have come as easily from British or French memoirs:

> The corpses were lying by the tracks in the meadow, about twenty of them, men, women and children.
> We walked down the line.
> 'Danes, all of them. What had they got to do with the war?' muttered the captain. He saluted the dead and turned away. 'Just going for a Sunday outing!'

The enemy plane on this occasion was an allied plane; those horrified by its senseless action of slaughter were German.

When at the end of the war Richter and his men have arrived in Copenhagen, and he is sent to look for quarters: 'There was what looked like an impenetrable wall of human beings on the far side of the barrier, men and women with bitter faces, all staring at me. Their eyes were hostile, their fists clenched.' But as he approaches them, apprehensively:

> An old woman ran towards me, her hands stretched out, her fingers spread.
> I ducked, raising my arm to protect my face ...
> She flung her arms round my neck and hugged me; she was crying. 'Peace!' she shouted, in broken German. 'It's peace!'

The attitudes and behaviour of individuals in peace or war, this novel is suggesting throughout, transcend merely national boundaries, and, for some at least, compassion and longing for peace have survived the harsh, brutal training and the atrocities. Richter's final words are a quotation from Benjamin Franklin: *There never was a good war, or a bad peace.*

Richter's accounts of the German army under training differ little from Holbrook's experience. In his novel, *Flesh Wounds*, Holbrook gives a lively, sharply pointed account of relentlessly punitive drill, calculated to reduce any recalcitrant recruit to such helpless exhaustion that he no longer has the strength to give expression to his murderous hatred of his sadistic sergeant, or to question the ends to which his training is leading.

> Of course, the young men were being made bodily fit and strong, swinging down trees on ropes, scaling cliffs, leaping over plank

runways high above-ground, running through woods and leaping ditches. But the strain of the harsh testing discipline was tremendous – the crushed inward tumult of feelings of impotent vengeance and resentment at being 'bashed' on the square, twice daily, exhausted them. None of them felt he was himself any longer. Personality was subdued to the driven life of the body: even the body could barely keep up – all else that was human in them was relinquished.

This alienation from himself follows the hero, Paul Grimmer, even outside the training ground.

Gradually he submitted his independent self to the Royal Military College, and his scruples sank low within him. A crude animal energy took the place of his more tender feelings, and he came to despise the soft life of those outside the barrack walls, those whose trousers were uncreased, who did not 'belong' to the khaki squads, and who did not carry a pistol at the belt.

It was finally at Battle School that he discovered with a shock that his contempt for the tender life extended even to his relationship with Lucy.

It is important to recognise that, in spite of reiterated condemnations of German atrocities, the German military machine had no monopoly of ruthlessness. Yet, like Richter, Holbrook shows repeatedly that not all human feeling is obliterated – as when Dowsett jibs at driving his tank over dead bodies. For Paul Grimmer belongs to a Tank Corps, which is sent to France in the D-day landings in Normandy. As the tanks lurched and jolted ashore, Paul experiences his baptism of fire, which:

changed [his] sensibility for ever, for ever to be a little deadened. He tasted the full price of death, the abominableness of which human nature was capable, the immense destructivity of man, and the frail predicament by which in the midst of the apparent stability of life we are always in the instability of possible immediate obliteration.

The men in the tanks soon discover that they are not as fully protected as they had hoped, either from knowledge of the deaths they are inflicting or from an overwhelming sense of their own vulnerability.

It seemed hideously wrong that the mastodon-mother herself could be destroyed: and so the first sight of a burning tank dislodged a fundamental security in the trooper's soul ... A burning tank ... looked like a monster, a dying dragon, vomiting up the life within it in black gouts, and blowing aloft ghostly rings which mounted, curling in on themselves, high into the air. Beneath these sad signals, a red and white glower would roll in the eyes of the dead monster, the hatch holes, through which the crew had entered, never to emerge again. For there within, where once was chattering comradeship, offers of chocolate and tea, gossip and chaff, where the men had sat with their head-phones on and worked with maps or preparing meals, was a tempestuous fire, licking the red hot or blackened steel.

Paul finds his own way of surviving the panic of mortar bombardment, and the threat of death by immolation in his tank.

But now Paul Grimmer cut off his feelings for himself: he no longer loved himself. He allowed himself to become expendable. He hated the Army for bringing him into this hell. He lost all trust in the regiment, in comradeship, in action against the enemy. He was utterly divided and alienated, bent only on survival.

Even then the beauty of a beetle, a 'large, green creature, shaped like a shield, jewelled like a brooch, catching gleams from the morning sun', can penetrate his armour of indifference, becoming a symbol pointing to the possibility of surviving even this deluge of projectiles, this 'inferno', raging, it seemed to Paul, 'simply to tear into the vitals of one unhappy man, by whom, afterwards, squatted the tank regiment's Irish padre, offering what solace he could in his genial way, for all the last pain, the final brokenness'. As the sun continues to shine 'brightly on the shattered wood and the fear-crouched men', Paul 'felt split, demoralized and disloyal'. At this moment the squadron leader emerges from the wood, saying cheerfully, 'Looks like we shall soon have a bit of a party'. Such courage as Major Bumpton's, such ability to remain kind, energetic, brave, competent, Paul feels, 'could only go with a darkening of certain areas of human perception: you could only stand war so by splitting yourself into fragments, or by being dead at the centre'.

The theme of Holbrook's story is not merely the inhumanity of the violence done to the infinitely vulnerable, suffering flesh of his men within the inferno of their tanks, and the stark contrast of the beauty of the countryside. It is also the violence to the human spirit, which does not recover, even when the flesh survives. His grief for his men, and for the fatherly old sergeant, Whatmough, and for Whatmough's desolate, bereaved family, stretch him to breaking point, and though he tries to recover himself, saying, 'Be all right in a minute', he 'knew he would never be all right again'. His men, too:

were all dreadfully different from the men they were when they sailed. They were now men who had aged, men who had had more than the most hideous experience of a whole normal lifetime crammed into a few days, so that there was no further capacity for alarm, surprise, joy or pity.

Moreover, there is a pervading feeling that all this pain, horror and destruction had achieved so little. 'And there was something worse than pain: there was the penalty of being brought to realize each his insignificance in the great events, and the meaninglessness of their own acts, terrible or futile as they may have been.' For their contribution to the advance of the battlefronts was insignificant; and half their casualties chance accidents, some, indeed, inflicted by their own side. The battlefield had been 'chaos, confusion, squalor', each man 'lost in the impersonal hell where metal chased flesh, in one great melee', where chance was the greatest enemy, and where no individual 'made effective decisions', but could only assent to 'submerging the individual life in the bloody fracas' because he could see no other way of combating 'the organized and maniac hatred of Nazism'. As he travels home through Europe, seeing 'crowds of grey-faced, thin and dwarfed children' begging by the railway lines, he realises afresh:

War solved nothing, except gross negative matters: the greater human concerns had lain in limbo, until the end of the savagery. Now they came to the surface. The hungry eyes of the lean grey children followed him in his inward vision, over the North Sea, in the oily darkness surrounding the ship, in the drizzle.

Paul returns to a civilian existence in which he has no role, no status. At first he longs to go back to the safety of his position and rank within the army, to its organisation of his life and actions. Instead he has to take his own decisions, to become again an individual, opening up 'dead and unexercised areas of feeling'. He must set aside the 'brutality in personal relationship' fostered by army life, encourage in its place the 'soft and kind' delicacy he had learned to despise, and reassert the need for a 'whole relationship' with some woman he could love, not 'the mere gross and brief satisfaction of the soldier's hunger'.

Vernon Scannell and Keith Douglas were also sent to the Second Front on D-day, and Scannell gives an account of his brief weeks there in *The Tiger and the Rose* and *Argument of Kings*. Both men served also in North Africa, a very different terrain from the green fields of Normandy. Of 18 months of action in the African campaign Scannell remembers, 'in precise detail, not more than a few hours, though the experience has left in the memory a shifting impressionistic canvas of enormous size but seen in a bad light and too far away'. Thus, in *The Tiger and the Rose* he records briefly digging trenches; laying mines; dropping a handful of anti-personnel detonators in panic under mortar-bomb attack and following Scorpion tanks through an enemy minefield. In *Argument of Kings* he tells in more detail of an incident at the foot of the Roumana Hills above Wadi Akarit which led him to walk away from the battlefield to a three years' sentence for desertion (see Chapter 8).

But for a more vivid account of this Front we must turn to *Alamein to Zem Zem*, by Keith Douglas, which complements Holbrook's experience of tank warfare in Europe. In his Introduction Desmond Graham remarks:

> The Desert War was a war like any other: there people killed and were killed; but it was also an extraordinary war. It was fought in a territory 'neutral' to both sides, and being barren, a landscape almost neutral to man. In Douglas's experience of it no civilians were involved; each action he took part in was part of a victory or an advance; as commander of a tank troop in open terrain he had unusual freedom of movement.

Douglas explains that a tank:

> equipped with a wireless, has an advantage over the infantrymen, and over all the soldiers and generals of earlier wars. Before his mind's eye the panorama of the battle is kept, more vividly even than before the general of other times who watched his soldiers from a vantage point, or was kept posted by telephones and runners.

To 'a Crusader troop leader, well out in front of the regiment' this action can be viewed 'in quite an impersonal way' as if it were 'a pageant prepared for his entertainment'. He sees the enemy tank only as 'a suspicious blob on the horizon ... halts his squat turret almost level with a ridge ... scrutinizes the blob through his glasses', and alerts his commanding officers who will issue orders without necessarily seeing the enemy for themselves. This leads the tank crew to a sense of isolation, of being enclosed in a world of their own within the confines of the turret:

> The view from a moving tank is like that in a camera obscura or a silent film – in that since the engine drowns all other noises except explosions the whole world moves silently. Men shout, vehicles move, aeroplanes fly over, and all soundlessly: the noise of the tank being continuous, perhaps for hours on end, the effect is of silence.

This lends a quality of unreality to the situation:

Out of each turret, like the voices of dwarfs, thin and cracked and bodiless, the voices of the operators and of the control set come; they speak to the usual accompaniment of 'mush', morse, odd squeals and the peculiar jangling, like a barrel-organ, of an enemy jamming station.

In the course of a typical action, Douglas tells us:

> Control now instructed us: 'Open fire on the enemy. Range one zero zero zero. Give the buggers every round you've got. Over.' ... I ordered Evans to fire. 'I can't see a muckin' thing,' he protested. 'Never mind, you fire at a thousand as fast as I can load.'

Commanded by a disembodied voice, the tanks fire into the void, often not knowing what they have hit. When they encounter death it is often men – friend or foe – they see too late to avoid, and recognise as already dead only when they have rolled over them. And there are long hours spent in the endless routine of reprovisioning and of maintenance, or within the turret, stationary or in movement, chatting or reading, contrasting sharply with the few excitements of engagement.

> The turret was full of fumes and smoke. I coughed and sweated; fear had given place to exhilaration. Twilight increased to near-darkness, and the air all round us gleamed with the different coloured traces of shells and bullets, brilliantly graceful curves travelling from us to the enemy and from him towards us. The din was tremendously exciting.

Set against this thrill, and this detached perception of the beauty of combat observed from within the turret, are the sour discomforts of the desert, the scarcity of water, the monotony of tinned food, the flies around inflamed sores which refused to heal, the continual dust and sandstorms, and always the awareness of their own vulnerability.

The immediacy of this account, which Douglas wrote so near to the events, lends it a quality of involvement and a freshness which has not been modified by the passage of time. Douglas had only a few months to complete the writing and partial revision of his first drafts before, on 6 June 1944, he was was sent to the Second Front in France, where he was killed three days later.

The harsh army ethos described by Richter, Malgonkar, Holbrook and Douglas is a complete contrast to the comparatively relaxed atmosphere between all ranks in *The Naked and the Dead*, a powerful novel reflecting Norman Mailer's experiences with the US Forces in the Far East. But though there is little of the rigid hierarchy or of the toughening training and discipline exacted in the British and German armies this does not mean an absence of brutality within the regiment as well as towards the enemy. In spite of the relative freedom of speech that he is initially allowed by General Cummings, Lieutenant Hearn in the end suffers the consequences of his temerity. He has finally both to recognise the underlying sadistic impulses to power which have enabled the general to rise to a position of command, and to realise that they are latent also in his own involuntary contempt for the enlisted men. The relations between the men, too, from the moment they disembark on to the beach, keyed up with the tension engendered by anticipation of the coming battles, are frequently soured by hostility and quarrelsomeness towards each other, and by an all-pervasive anti-Semitism which afflicts the two Jewish members of the platoon, Roth and Goldstein. This tough, raw book, full of the ugliness and violence of the battlefield, nevertheless makes a searching attempt to probe the thoughts and feelings of men and officers, and to discover what lies behind their individual ways of responding to situations of stress.

The close, constricting and hostile terrain they face on the Pacific island is quite different from that experienced either by Paul Grimmer in France or by Douglas in the deserts of North Africa, and the nature of the fighting has to change to suit. There is little possibility of mechanised warfare.

In the deep jungle it was always as dark as the sky before a summer thunderstorm, and no air ever stirred. Everything was damp and rife and hot as though the jungle were an immense collection of oily rags growing hotter and hotter under the dark stifling vaults of a huge warehouse. Heat licked at everything, and the foliage, responding, grew to prodigious sizes. In the depths, in the heat and the moisture, it was never silent. The birds cawed, the small animals and occasional snakes rustled and squealed, and beneath it all was a hush, almost palpable, in which could be heard the rapt absorbed sounds of vegetation growing.

No Army could live or move in it. The men skirted the jungle forests, and moved through second-growth brush, past smaller woods of coconut trees. Even here they could never see for more than fifty or a hundred feet ahead, and the early stages of the operation were conducted by groping movements of tiny groups of men.

The story follows the fortunes of one such group, always exposed to the elements and to the exotic and alien plant and animal life which hemmed them in; painfully building a road through the jungle; hauling guns through the mud, drenched by relentless rain; their tents blown from over their heads, leaving them wet, cold and sleepless; encountering the enemy in skirmishes and ambushes and finally sent out on an exhausting and disastrous six-day patrol across the gruelling mountain ranges, headed by Lieutenant Hearn and Sergeant Croft. They suffer repeated casualties; but are finally defeated by 'the flanks of an ancient resisting mountain' and a nest of hornets.

The few survivors return to find the campaign is over, a 'mopping up' operation already under way, the Japanese casualties listed without any sense that these were men, not animals – after so much frustration 'the killing lost all dimension, bothered the men far less than discovering some ants in their bedding'.

> Towards the end the casualty figures were unbelievable. On the fifth day two hundred and seventy-eight Japanese were killed and two Americans; on the eighth day, the most productive of the campaign, eight hundred and twenty-one Japanese were killed and nine captured for the loss of three American lives ... One patrol out at dawn discovered four Japanese soldiers lying ... across the trail, their ponchos covering them ... The lead man waited until the Jap saw him and then, as he was about to scream, the American sent a burst of tommy-gun slugs through him. He followed this by ripping his gun down the middle of the trail, stitching holes neatly through the ponchos. Only one Jap was still left alive, and his leg protruded from the poncho, twitching aimlessly with the last unconscious shudders of a dying animal. Another soldier walked up, nuzzled the body under the poncho with the muzzle of his gun, located the wounded man's head, and pulled the trigger.
> There were other variations.

This long, dense novel is not without flaws. Hearn's protracted private battle with the general could with advantage have been condensed, and the frequent flashbacks to past events in the lives of the main protagonists verge on the sentimental and disturb the flow of the main events. But the accounts of the campaign are vivid and telling, and create an unforgettable impression of jungle warfare and its dire effects upon the participants, who, like Holbrook in the tank force, also find it necessary to distance themselves from all feelings of humanity or compassion.

Holbrook and Douglas were keenly aware of the increasing impersonality of the battlefront brought about by mechanisation, and of the particular damage caused thereby to the humanity of those taking part in this killing at a distance. But the crews of the lumbering and ungainly tanks were still, nevertheless, in closer communication with the enemy than were the pilots, gunners and bomb crews of the aeroplanes of the Second World War. The glamour of these swift, new, graceful and deadly fighting machines, and their even greater distance from the devastation they could cause added a further dimension to the cruel impersonality of modern warfare.

What this meant for the young pilots of the Second World War is made explicit in *Closer to the Stars*, a novel for younger readers of eleven and over by the Australian writer Max Fatchen. The young trainee John Grice may remind readers of Yeats's Irish airman, whom 'A lonely impulse of delight / Drove to this tumult in the skies.' For John the glamour has come back into warfare, the mud and blood of the trenches has receded. He and his companions in the Australian air force camp 'were young and eager. They had not seen the battle or felt the terrible tensions of aerial combat. They knew only the excitement of the sky, the wild thrill of a roll or the crazy landscape-turning manoeuvre of looping the loop.' Though they, too, are required to undergo discipline in their training, the atmosphere is very different from the spirit-breaking indignities of Richter's or Holbrook's experience. Their superiors realise that 'you had to be careful with spirited young men, for it was their spirit harnessed to their skill that could make them good fliers, and they were needed desperately.' So their individuality is cherished.

As the story opens, John is flying solo, 'exhilarated by the rush of the wind past his open cockpit, by the noise of the busy engine, by the feel of the controls in his hands and the fact that he was alone and solely responsible'. In his youthful ebullience he dives down over a haystack, to roar over it at an altitude which will 'make the straw lift ... like hairs on a frightened head'. But twelve-year-old Paul Sims is on top of the stack, forking down the sheaves to Curtiss Longfer on the dray. Paul leaps off the stack on top of Curtiss, and the horse bolts with the dray, smashing it against a strainer post. It is an incident which, though slight enough in itself, and fortunately with no serious consequences, illustrates the way in which the pilot's innocent delight in his flying machine blinds him to its potential for destruction.

John's punishment for this escapade, cunningly devised by Paul, is to muck-out the pigsty; his reward is meeting Paul's sister, Nancy, with whom he has a brief, passionate relationship before being sent to England and the war.

Curtiss, now a solid reliable sharefarmer who also helps out on Paul's mother's farm, has memories of the destruction at close quarters in the First World War. He tries to explain to Paul and Nancy:

'It was the screams of the horses.'
And then he stopped and thought: How can I tell them?
How can I tell them about the noise of the shells, the great gouts of mud, your heart beating as if it was about to leap out of your body, the terror to find cover, pressing yourself down in a shellhole, mud in your

mouth, the barbed wire ripping your clothes, the splintered fangs of the tree trunks round you?

And the horses struggling, struggling up to their bellies, the terrible ripple and stretch of their muscles in the mud, their ears bent back, and your shoulders against the wheels of the gun carriages, the guns cold and metallic. And then flinging yourself down again with your mouth full of filth and mud, mud, mud.

And it all came back to him across the years, across the scarred reaches of his mind where nothing could quite heal it, not even time.

Curtiss had not been separated by machines from the effects of war: he had been a driver, not of tanks, but of horses, 'and he'd loved horses. War was no place for horses any more than it was a place for men.'

Neither John nor Nancy, of course, are able to blot out all awareness of the war for which John is training. Though they see it primarily in terms of its effect on their private lives, nevertheless Nancy could see 'something in John Grice's eyes that wasn't all fun when the war was mentioned'. And the young lieutenant too, who takes Paul up on his first rapturous flight, thinks sadly as he watches Paul:

He's only a kid ... but he's been bitten by the flying bug. Up there it waits for you ... Up there with a cockpit of dreams that you're the best flier in the world.

What a pity we just can't all fly and be happy. Instead of going up there to kill someone ... someone who just might like to be happy in a cockpit too.

All too quickly John Grice is sent to England to this other, less exhilarating aspect of war. 'We don't get much sleep ... We seem to be always in the air,' he writes to Nancy. 'Sometimes we are the hawks looking for prey and sometimes we are the prey.' In the end the 'hawk' takes John Grice; he is killed, leaving Nancy with his baby to give her what strength she can muster to face the future without him.

This story is well tuned to a twelve-year-old readership, mingling in a thoughtful way the adventure and joy and hope of living with 'the futility and separation and sadness' of war; and with glimpses here and there of the tragedies enacted on the other side of the battle.

What about Tomorrow?, another air force story for readers of twelve and over by an Australian writer, Ivan Southall, begins in 1931, when the hero, Sam, runs away from the consequences to himself of an accident while on his paper round. His adventures on the run, trying to pick up the pieces of his life, are interspersed

with his later experiences as captain of a flying boat on his forty-
seventh mission. His navigator copes with the terror, strain and
fear of death by stupefying himself each night with alcohol, but
Sam lies awake, memories of his past and fears for his future (what
about tomorrow?) chasing round his tired mind.

The juxtaposition of Sam's present desperate plight with his
earlier painful but more manageable attempts to resolve his
private, ordinary and everyday troubles brings into sharp relief the
contrast between the two experiences. For Sam is now close to
breaking point, far from the small problems of his growing years
or, indeed, from the ebullient adventurousness of John Grice
during his training weeks in Australia; and Southall spares us none
of the fear and agony and cynicism of Sam's final flights, and of
his clearsighted appreciation of both sides of the slaughter.

> 'Greater love hath no man than this,' the parson used to say, 'that a
> man lay down his life for his friends ... Let us always be aware of the
> freedom we inherit from the love of the glorious heroes who so gladly
> died.'
> *Gladly* died?
> Heroes must have changed.

This story, written out of Southall's own anguished memories of
the war in the air, forces the reader to consider the full implications of words like 'fear', 'courage', 'the achievement of manhood
through ordeal', 'glory' and 'heroism', and the real nature of war.

These questions are also implicit in Richard Hough's story, *Razor
Eyes*, in which a retired English farmer, Mick Boyd, tells of his
wartime experiences between the ages of 18 and 23. Mick and his
friend Bruno were 'fanatical' about planes, and determined to join
the Royal Air Force. But, unlike Bruno and Jo, Mick's high-spirited,
forceful sister, Mick is easily scared – as on the occasion on
Striding Edge in the Lake District when he failed to retrieve a
fallen rucksack:

> Not scared especially of heights, or even of death, but of being hurt. I
> could not bear hurt, injury to anyone, or to animals, above all to
> myself. Always, as a boy, I was afraid of anything that might lead to
> blood and pain. Even someone else's cut finger would make me feel
> sick. And a recurrent nightmare featured lacerated flesh, broken bones,
> innards torn asunder.

So although the 'romantic half' of Mick 'longed above all else in
the world to be in the cockpit of a fighter', he has to contend with
'the frozen agony of fear, like a dagger-sharp icicle plunged into
my body' that assails him whenever he contemplates the possi-

bility of being hit in chest or hip by bullets from a pursuing fighter plane.

His courageous, daredevil sister Jo joins the WAAF at once. But for Mick, first, comes the unendurable experience of seeing a Hurricane crash and go up in flames, incinerating the pilot.

> I lay on my bed and sobbed for that pilot, and his poor, mutilated, burnt body. I felt the fear breaking over me like waves when you're lying on the shore and there is nothing you can do to stop them, except to get up and run. And I couldn't do that either.

It is in this mood that he joins the Air Force.

The succeeding story is one in which he learns to control his fear – through 'flights of ecstasy, especially on rare clear moon-light nights, when I was alone ... and I knew that I had mastered this sweetly responsive little fighter'; but also through determina-tion and endurance. He forces himself to concentrate on the practicalities of the matter in hand, and so to exclude his fear. Hough recreates vividly the atmosphere of the airfields, the endless operations, and the inevitable casualties. Bruno is killed in front of the horrified Mick, who races to the aircraft to see that 'three shells had torn into the starboard side of the fighter, wan-tonly ripping the alloy panels and rib structure apart, exposing Bruno and his terrible wounds ... the awful reality of my worst fears'. Jo – 'tough, inflexible, fast-moving Jo' – has a breakdown from her experiences in the WAAF of the bombing and the war. But Mick manages to survive, even to win the DFC. He sums up his growth to 'manhood through ordeal', however, in dispas-sionate, level terms.

> It was nothing to do with the stunning fear which had once hit me, nothing to do with courage, any of this, I now knew. Nothing deserving special praise or gongs. I was no more than a small cog in the war machine system, more complex even than a Tiffy's engine, my pace conforming with the opening and closing of the throttle. Conformity, that was what it was all about. You conformed to what was expected of you, to the system, to the machine's need, and to the forces of fate. That day, if we had been on Striding Edge, I suppose I would have recovered that rucksack. Not because I was more or less brave (whatever that means) but because I had learned to do what was expected of me. That's all.

Conforming 'to the machine's need' is an image appropriate to his experience of the battle. This sane, soberly realistic assessment of the meaning of war, of war's deaths, agony, 'heroism', deserves careful consideration, coming from a writer who had himself experienced events like those described so movingly in this tense, gripping story.

Two adult novels from America present a slightly different picture of the Air Force. In *Catch-22*, by Joseph Heller, there are no heroes, no 'bright young men' full of energy and straining at the leash to get at the enemy. Indeed, Yossarian, the main protagonist, spends the entire time thinking up ways to avoid going on his next mission. Sometimes he retreats into hospital, with real or imaginary complaints, but his most enduring ambition is to complete his required number of missions and get himself grounded. Always he is defeated at the last minute, as the number required is inevitably raised just as he is near to fulfilling his stint. The Catch-22 in which Yossarian finds himself trapped is symbolic of the Air Force. Doc Danneka explains:

> There was only one catch and that was Catch-22, which specified that a concern for one's own safety in the face of dangers that were real and immediate was the process of a rational mind. Orr was crazy and could be grounded. All he had to do was ask; and as soon as he did, he would no longer be crazy and would have to fly more missions. Orr would be crazy to fly more missions and sane if he didn't, but if he was sane he had to fly them. If he flew them he was crazy and didn't have to; but if he didn't want to he was sane and had to. Yossarian was moved very deeply by the absolute simplicity of this clause of Catch-22 and let out a respectful whistle.

In this long, jokey satire everybody is seen to be crazy: either they are deadly serious about their positions of power and their missions, or they are totally irresponsible, in either case wise-cracking their way through the war in an endless sequence of wacky conversations which sound like an extended, never-to-be-concluded comedians' turn. This demonstrates their determination not to be serious about anything because it would involve being serious about the destruction they are responsible for and the unnerving likelihood of dying on the next mission. But though they are absorbed only in having as good a time as possible in between frantic efforts to get out, to survive the war somehow, the reality of their position obtrudes at times into the narrative with a force which is greater because of the zaniness of its context. There are terrible scenes of rape and murder and drunken riot even during their brief moments of leave, but their main obsession is fear of their own inevitable deaths. One by one, inexorably, all Yossarian's pals are killed. Perhaps the most detailed and sickening account is the death of Snowden, Yossarian's gunner. At first, Yossarian is appalled by the visible wound, 'as large and deep as a football, it seemed. It was impossible to tell where the shreds of his saturated coveralls ended and the ragged flesh began.' But finally, after desperate efforts to staunch this wound, Yossarian discovers a wound inside Snowden's flak suit from which 'his insides slithered down to the floor in a soggy pile and just kept dripping out'. It is in face of realities like this that the overall zany tone is maintained. As James Gould Cozzens explains in *Guard of Honour*:

Flying in those days was a business set apart by its unexampled dangers; and those who flew were joined in the bond of their undefined, informal co-operative effort to shut their minds to the plain fact that if the war continued they were all going to die – perhaps by enemy action, perhaps by accident; perhaps this week, certainly next month. They supported each other in fending off the normal animal despair; now by braving it with cumbersome and elaborate humor – *take the piston rods out of my kidneys and assemble the engine again*; now by a solemn, deprecatory indirection which did not blush to use such euphemisms as 'grounded for good'.

The humour in *Guard of Honour* is different in quality from the wisecracking of *Catch-22*, and its overall tone more serious. But it also takes into its orbit the paradox of the good flier, whose uncontainable high spiritedness was essential to his success as a bomber pilot, but yet a problem to those sober and responsible enough to see its dangers as well as its value. As in *Closer to the Stars* the action takes place in a training base, this time at Ocanara, Florida, in 1943. Its calm reasonable tone, however, is in strong contrast to the deliberate craziness of *Catch-22*.

The Commanding Officer, General 'Bus' Beal, has seen active service, and his experience makes him both respectful and tolerant towards the 'spirited and imperious' Lieutenant Colonel Benny Carriker, whose actions nevertheless cause him considerable embarrassment during the three tense days covered by the narrative. Beal's glowing account of Benny's daring, split-second timing, courage, endurance and intrepidity in combat testifies eloquently to the qualities which made him a valued flying officer. Colonel Ross, however, an older man who had been a judge in civilian life, reflects drily that:

The account of Benny's African service told you that Benny, assured and probably arrogant, always acted as he pleased ... From the incident of the fire in the plane, you learned, along with the fact that Benny's courage and endurance were great, that regulations about wearing flying clothes were not for him.

The reverse side of Benny's character lies indeed in the arrogance with which he takes the law into his own hands. He summarily punches an officer in the face because he had been 'wholly responsible for a stupid and dangerous act' which, 'even if it hadn't killed his chief, might have killed him'. His action – unnecessary because there were obvious disciplinary methods of dealing with the incident – is this time not merely an example of an excusable high-spirited 'loyalty' to his comrades. The officer Benny had punched was leading a team of Black American fliers, brought into the base to become 'an all-Negro medium bomber group'. Benny's action is also, therefore, the first in a series of events which highlight the position of Black Americans in the US army, particularly when they came into contact with white soldiers from the deep South.

The unpleasantly racist attitude to Black American soldiers is comparable with the anti-Semitism revealed in Mailer's book. It has also been carefully documented by Graham Smith in his book *When Jim Crow Met John Bull*, an account of racist incidents occurring in Britain during the Second World War. Its irony as well as its relevance becomes even more striking when one remembers that – in retrospect at least – horror at Nazi treatment of the Jews and other supposedly 'inferior' peoples was used to provide some justification for so destructive a war.

Guard of Honour is a complex book, which explores the experiences of many different commissioned and non-commissioned officers at the base, both conscripts and regular army men, and it is one of the few books to include also some of the women in uniform. It is an admirable exposition of the day-to-day routine of a typical American airbase, with its complex structure of command in which the strengths as well as the serious weaknesses, muddle, incompetence, arrogance, prejudice, self-interest, combine and interlock into a cohesive effort to win the war. In this respect it gives a picture of a community coming together, in spite of differences and conflicts, with a common purpose, an aspect of wartime experience which is still remembered with affection and nostalgia.

But the common purpose at the Ocanara base as at all training bases is to find and perfect the most efficient ways of killing people, civilians as well as military, and to foster attitudes of mind in keeping with this aim – an insensitivity towards other people and a disregard for human life or suffering. In company with the other books mentioned so far, it has relatively little to tell us of the victims of the bombing raids for which these men were being trained, and which in the event were so intrepidly undertaken. In responding to the fortunes of John Grice, Sam Clemens, Mick

Boyd, Yossarian and his comrades or of the varied protagonists of *Guard of Honour* the reader, too, can easily forget that beneath the gallant and glamorous Air Force boys lay the devastated cities: London, Coventry, Warsaw, Rotterdam, Stalingrad, Berlin, Hamburg, Dresden, Essen, Cologne. Under the ruins of churches, historic buildings, factories, hospitals and homes of every description were the dead and injured, men, women and children, soldiers and civilians, hidden, for the most part, from those responsible for their deaths.

6
A Civilian's War

In *My Country is the Whole World*, an anthology of women's writings about war produced for the Cambridge Women's Peace Collective, Helena M. Swanwick is quoted as saying that in the First World War, 'while the deaths of soldiers in all countries might have reached ten millions, those of civilians, by pestilence, famine and homelessness, in addition to direct deaths by bombardment and massacre, reached between two and three times that number'. This estimated total of civilian dead was to be immeasurably exceeded in the Second World War from bombing raids alone.

There are, now, many stories, both true and invented, of the fate of civilians on both sides of this conflict. Some of these are invested with the glow of heroism and drama, of glamour and nostalgia as well as of sadness and horror. This can be a way of helping ourselves to survive, to live with the agony and trauma suffered, and with the deep guilt at what we have done, or allowed others to do for us. But at the same time, we unwittingly lay a trap for future generations, who readily concentrate on the glamour, and forget the lesson learned at such cost – that the ugliness, futility and evil of war far outweigh its few possibilities for glory.

Few of the books discussed in this chapter, whether fiction or semi-autobiographical, invite complacency of this kind. Their special value for young readers lies rather in the way in which they facilitate empathy with war-sufferers because of the youth of the central characters.

One of the most telling impressions of London at war is given in *The Other Way Round*, by Judith Kerr. This is the second in a trilogy of autobiographical novels in which Anna tells how she escaped with her German-Jewish family when Hitler came to power in 1933, and eventually, in 1936, settled in England. It is the story of Anna's growing years as a refugee in a country now at war with her native land: an aspect of the book which will be discussed later. But Anna also records her experiences of the London

Blitz, the nightly terror of increasingly heavy air-raids. After the first all-night raid:

There was glass everywhere, doors hanging on their hinges, bits of rubble all over the road. And in the terrace opposite where there should have been a house there was a gap. The entire top floor had gone, and so had most of the front wall. They had subsided into a pile of bricks and stone which filled the road, and some men in overalls were shovelling them into the back of a lorry.

You could see right inside what remained of the house. It had green wallpaper and the bathroom had been painted yellow. You could tell it was the bathroom because even though most of the floor had gone, the part supporting the bath tub appeared to be suspended in space. Immediately above it was a hook with a flannel still hanging from it and a toothmug in the shape of Mickey Mouse.

'Horrible, isn't it?' said an old man next to Anna. 'Lucky there was no one in it – she'd taken the kids to her sister's. I'd like to give that Hitler a piece of my mind!'

Then he went back to sweeping up the glass outside his shop.

It is the small details which make such an impression upon Anna, and remind us, too, of the everydayness of the family whose house has so suddenly been demolished.

Anna is startled to discover how quickly people can adjust to tragedy – like the old man she, too, gets on with her own life and is surprised, and a little ashamed, to find her pity 'swallowed up by her happiness' at being young and alive in the warm sun, under the blue sky. She can even find beauty in the midst of a raid.

The night outside was brilliant. The sky was red, reflecting the fires on the ground, and in it hung clusters of orange flares which lit up everything for miles around. They looked like gigantic Christmas decorations floating slowly, slowly down through the night air, and though Anna knew that they were there to help the Germans aim their bombs she was filled with admiration at the sight ...

Suddenly a searchlight swept across the sky. It was joined by another and another, crossing and re-crossing each other, and then a great orange flash blotted out everything else. A bomb or a plane exploding in mid-air – Anna did not know which – but the accompanying crash sent her and Papa scuttling away from the window.

When it was over they looked out again at the illuminated night. The orange flares had been joined by some pink ones and they were drifting slowly down together.

'It may be the end of the civilized world,' said Papa, 'but it is certainly very beautiful.'

As the raids persist and progress in intensity, however, Anna begins to find them less easy to take.

> If I think about it now, thought Anna, if I imagine it, then when it happens, when I'm trapped in a little hole with tons of rubble on top of me ...
> Again the terror surged over her.
> She tried to fight it down. I mustn't fight and scrabble to get out, she thought, I must keep quite still. There may not be much room, much air ...
> Suddenly she could almost feel the tight, black cavity shutting her in and it was so frightful that she leapt into a sitting position as though she had been stung, to make sure it hadn't happened ...
> Perhaps it won't be so bad when it happens, she thought. Perhaps it's worse thinking about it. But she knew that it wasn't.

Though Anna is not the only one in the shelter struggling for control, her terror is so overwhelming that it seems as though she is lying 'alone in the dark, trying to shut out the terrible picture of herself screaming mutely in a black hole'.

> At last she became so exhausted that a kind of calm came over her. I've got used to it, she thought, but she knew that she hadn't. And when at last the shuddering crashes stopped and a little light filtered into the cellar with the sound of the All Clear, she thought, well, after all, it wasn't so bad. But she knew that this, too, was untrue.

There are no heroics in this bleakly realistic and sober account of her experiences. Instead the reader shares her vivid perception of the devastating effect of war upon the lives of innocent people: of Mrs Hammond, whose only son was killed during a practice flight; Mrs James, who has lost both her sons, and only comes to life briefly whilst attending to the needs of still-living soldiers; Otto's father, rescued from a concentration camp, but still haunted by his nightmare experiences, and too brain-damaged to realise that he is free, or to recognise his wife and son; and the other refugees in the hotel, all valiantly trying to make sense of their existence in Britain, but knowing that they will never return to the homes and lives they had once enjoyed. Anna is acutely conscious of the tragedy she sees around her, even while she is able to respond with compassion, interest, laughter, and growing maturity to people and events.

In *Fireweed*, Jill Paton Walsh has used a wartime background for the story of two young people, Bill and Julie, evacuees who sneak back to London on their own, and meet by chance during the Blitz. They seek refuge from the raids in the underground until

Julie takes Bill to her aunt's bombed and abandoned house, where they live in the basement. They become part of wartime London, with its atmosphere of friendliness, determination, courage, vitality, quiet heroism and laughter. Bill observes: 'Laughter seemed suddenly to blow up around us, like the swirling wind-borne leaves. It caught other people too ... Yet all around us death and ruin rained out of the sky.'

Like Anna, Bill and Julie, too, can see beauty in burning London, 'the immensity' of which, Bill recalls, 'quenched my own fear in a wave of awe; it seemed like the end of the world. Our danger was only, after all, a small thing seen in that light.'

The Other Way Round undoubtedly impresses the reader as a more faithful, sober record of London during the Blitz; but the 'romanticising' element in *Fireweed* will probably appeal to a wider audience. It vividly recaptures that feeling of a people united in a determination to resist the terror of the Blitz which has become part of the folk-lore of the war years. And for all the jokes, the beauty of the night scene amid the flames, and the romantic nostalgia surrounding the stout-hearted endurance of the people, there is also a keen awareness of suffering and tragedy, which provides a salutary and sobering reminder of the realities of war.

The contrast between the sense of excitement – of glamour, even – which war can generate and the reality of individual tragedy is also brought sharply into focus in a novel for younger readers, *Dawn of Fear*, by Susan Cooper. The main protagonists, Derek, Geoff and Peter, are still at primary school, young enough to be thrilled by the battles in the sky ('that super dogfight yesterday and the spectacular collapse of that poor old balloon'), and by the novelty of a Morrison shelter in the dining room and disruption to lessons during a daylight alert. But in London, 20 miles away, it is apparent that 'he's throwing over everything he's got now', and Derek's father is sombrely anxious that his son should not soon learn to be more afraid than excited by what is happening.

For the time being, nothing is more important than the small local events. The boys are absorbed in building their 'camp', and battling with the obnoxious Wiggses who destroy it. In a way, though, their comparatively innocuous fight with mud-balls is a miniature of the adult war, as is quickly perceived by Derek's friend and neighbour, Tom Hicks, who is approaching military age. His personal enmity with Johnny Wiggs brings a different dimension to the quarrel; for the initial 'anger and the vengeful concentration of wanting to hurt' soon slip over into 'real hatred ... more than a kind of climax to years of enmity; almost as if the whole world had suddenly divided into two and the two halves were here flinging themselves one against the other'. Perceiving this dimension brings a 'dawn of fear' to Derek, too, quickly reinforced by an incident which reveals inescapably the appalling consequences of adult enmity. For Peter's house suffers a direct hit, and he and his family are all killed in the Morrison shelter of which he had been so proud.

This story makes clear that fear, though less glamorous, is a more appropriate reaction to the threat of injury or death in war than the boys' initial – and natural – excitement, and invites careful discussion of hatred, aggression and war at a level within reach of primary school children of ten or over.

London was not the only city to suffer destruction. *The Exeter Blitz*, by David Rees and *The Machine-Gunners*, by Robert Westall, tell of the experiences of Exeter and Tyneside respectively. There are also a number of stories from Germany, to remind readers that the obscenity of bombing civilians was committed by the Allies, too.

Elizabeth Lutzeier, the author of *No Shelter*, was born in Manchester, but now lives in Berlin, the setting for her poignant story of the effects of war upon two innocent young children, Johannes and Kathrin. When war began, Johannes was four. His small sister, Kathrin, was born in October 1940, by which time their father was already at the Front. Like Derek, Johannes, through whose eyes we see the events, at first understands little of what is going on. He only knows that he is terrified of the raids, and terrified, too, when soldiers come to take away Daniela, the Jewish woman whose German husband is in the same regiment as their father, and in whose flat the children and their mother are now living. But Johannes soon learns what war is all about. By 1943 he is a seasoned survivor of air-raids experienced even on Christmas Eve; of evacuation; and of a return to Berlin to yet more raids where he watches fearfully as his mother helps to search for people still alive under the ruins.

She had made him stand on the opposite side of the road with Kathrin, but he was still able to see them bringing the people out. Some of them were dead with their eyes open, some with their arms flung out or their legs bent up, but these were already so stiff that it was impossible for the people who unearthed them to straighten their tortured limbs. They made strange horrid shapes under the blankets which were thrown over them, so that Johannes had nightmares for months afterwards about the people under the blankets, some with blood on their clothes and their faces and some looking as clean and peaceful as though they were asleep.

All too soon, their mother is killed helping to rescue victims of a raid, and the children, Johannes only eight and Kathrin four, are left to fend for themselves. The solitary plight and youth of these children, forced into premature maturity by terrible scenes of death and grief, suffering, starvation and personal desolation is even more bleak and devastating than the corresponding pictures of London in the Blitz. Berlin, facing defeat, is by no means the buoyant place London, in *Fireweed*, had seemed to be.

At first Johannes has no doubts about the rightness of the German cause. While his mother is at work he spends much of his time listening to the radio and absorbing its propaganda. His mother, also, has taken care to tell him only of the good things Hitler has done for the Germans. For although she is undoubtedly aware of the implications when Daniela is arrested, and is deeply grieved for her Jewish friend, she recognises the need to protect her son from hearing dangerously subversive talk. After her death, however, Johannes' innocent blind faith in Hitler leaves him at a disadvantage when he and Kathrin eventually find shelter with a family opposed to the Nazi regime. At first Frau von Kempner condemns this unhappy, lonely little eight-year-old as an 'awful little Fascist!' and declares that she 'wouldn't have him in the house for one moment longer if it weren't for his adorable little sister'. Her hostility to him grows when her son is betrayed by one of Johannes' school friends and is executed. For although Herr Kempner was in government employ, he and his friends listened to the BBC, and were quietly scheming to get rid of Hitler.

This situation allows the author to reveal by implication as well as directly the thoughts, feelings and fears of ordinary German citizens; those who, like Johannes's mother, are 'not political', but, though anxious, uneasy and sometimes grieved by what they see happening to friends and neighbours, keep quiet for fear of the consequences to themselves or their children. It enables her to indicate the continued existence in Germany of others who – from a position of apparent security – were still working discreetly to overthrow the regime: and to show the gradual progress of innocents like Johannes to a greater understanding of the regime they have supported.

The war ends for Johannes with the violent death of Frau Kempner from a stray shell.

In the garden, where the cherry blossoms still waved their branches, undisturbed by anything but the wind, they found Frau Kempner's body.

Johannes lost all control. He screamed and screamed. Like a two-year-old child in a tantrum, he flung himself on the ground and screamed, 'I want my mother. Where's my mother?' Kathrin stood silently beside him as he cried out over and over again, 'Where's my mother?'

She was still standing over him protectively an hour later when two Russian soldiers walked through the gate, with machine guns ready to fire.

The soldiers, who can speak no German, soon discover 'bits' of what they mistakenly suppose to be his mother 'all over the place ...' But the broken body of the woman he has come to love and respect, and who finally had accepted him, has indeed revived nightmare speculations about what had happened to his own mother, when she vanished without trace on her errand of mercy.

The fact that this heartbreaking story is about German children who are innocent victims both of the crimes of their own country's leaders and of British and Allied bombers is a strong point in its favour. It underlines what is too often forgotten: it is the ordinary people of *all* the nations at war who suffer. This was frequently remarked in the memoirs and novels of the First World War, but in the Second World War this truth has sometimes been obscured by a belief that the whole German people were either directly implicated in the horrors of the Nazi regime, or were guilty by association.

The next two stories from Germany are of particular interest because though the protagonists are themselves at odds with the Nazi regime, they too are aware that the Axis powers were not alone responsible for all the horrors committed in the war.

Survive the Storm, by Wolf Klaussner, is a fictional narrative of Wilhelm, a boy whose maternal grandparents were Jewish. He remains in the community, however, at first unaware of the reason for the jibes and bullying directed at him by his school-mates and by some of the teachers. But although he becomes enraged by the persecution he suffers, and deeply involved in the fortunes of a Greek gypsy boy whom he discovers in hiding from the Nazis, Wilhelm is also alert to the atrocities of the American bombers, as they remorselessly flatten the village in preparation for the advance of their land forces.

Compared with what happened next, last night's attack had been no more than a feeble curtain-raiser. Squadron after squadron flew in low, dropping their bombs from almost rooftop level without being inter-cepted. If the survivors in Neustadt had thought that after last night their ordeal was behind them, how mistaken they were. Hundreds of tons of high explosive were aimed at the Neustadt railway junction, dispersing the last fragments of flesh dangling from the leafless trees ... The room swayed. I opened the windows. 'Freedom!' peeled the message of the bombs, no more torture. I sweated with fear, though. This was what saturation bombing meant. They couldn't be more than ten kilometres away.

A little later, when Wilhelm is on his way home from school:

A low-flying fighter had caught up with me and had let fly with all its ammunition. I lay in the ditch, watching the bullets peppering the asphalt in front of me. When the danger was over, I crept home, unhurt, but shattered.

As, on yet another occasion, he watches 'those low-flying pilots with their cannon barking, who fired at everything, even a wild hare for want of a better target', he realises that 'there's no such thing as a just war'. So when the American, Lieutenant Kunz, tells him that the villagers have murdered an injured US pilot, Wilhelm's immediate response is unsympathetic.

'I'm not surprised,' I said. 'Not after all the low-flying pilots were doing to us. They used to fly in and pick us off like so many clay pigeons, with virtually no risk to themselves. Nazi methods.'
'What did you say?'
'Nazi methods,' I repeated defiantly.
'Us?' asked Kunz, offended.
'I don't know about you, but certainly the hedge-hopping pilots used them. Oh, sure. I know we were at war. But your war was a just war. And men like that turned it into an unjust war. A farmer was fired at while he was ploughing. I saw it for myself. They say three people were killed in Kammerwind. By then the farmers couldn't see any difference between the Nazis and the Yanks, so they simply went for him.'

No doubt Wilhelm's language and comments are here a little too mature for his age, but the message is one to be heeded.

In the ensuing events 'barns, dwelling houses and baroque monuments' are destroyed as part of the reprisal for the airman's death and Wilhelm is brought before the military CIC for condemning the actions both of the pilot and his avengers. This leads him to 'the bitter conviction that justice is an illusion. It's only a question of who has the upper hand. People like us, justified a thousand times over, would always land in jail if we insisted on justice.'

In this complex story Klaussner brings home the effect of war and persecution on the lives and personalities both of those who suffered and those who inflicted violence, using his own wartime experiences and diaries and stories told him by others who had suffered and endured during the war years.

In her autobiography, *Mischling, Second Degree*, Ilse Koehn explains that though her paternal grandmother was Jewish her father survived because his work repairing high voltage wires was essential in Berlin at war. Like Wilhelm, therefore, Ilse remained in the community throughout the war, and gives vivid accounts both of the unremitting raids by Allied bombers which devastated Berlin and the traumas of the final days of the war as the Russian soldiers advanced into the capital.

Like many of her British contemporaries, Ilse was sent for a time away from the dangers of the bombing. There is a growing number of popular stories for young people about the experiences of evacuation in the Second World War. In comparison with other tragic consequences of the rise of fascism and the outbreak of war, evacuation presents a relatively cosy experience, and in many of the stories, though the children are clearly under stress, their problems have as much to do with growing up and adjusting to the expectations of the adult world as with the trauma of evacuation. Nevertheless, for many children it seemed an unexpectedly harsh and difficult time of change and upheaval. For never before had a whole generation of children been summarily evacuated from cities under threat of bombardment, and billeted away from their parents on strangers in the countryside.

It is interesting to compare Ilse's account of the ordered but secret transportation of her school to Czechoslovakia with the often haphazard movement of British children to Wales or elsewhere. Ilse and her friends were kept together in camps, under the almost military-style discipline of Hitler Youth counsellors, who had more authority than their own teachers. The children were thus isolated in their camps from the hostile population because, after the ruthless invasion of their country and the atrocities of Lidice, some Czechs were prepared to shoot at the hated German children under cover of darkness.

British children, on the other hand, were thrust into the homes of anyone who had room to receive them, and so were isolated in a different respect, living in billets separated from their companions in 'exile'. So they had to face on their own the twin problems of being away from home, often for the first time, and of fitting in with the unfamiliar customs and values of hosts who – though British themselves – were sometimes reluctant and unwelcoming. In *No Time to Wave Goodbye* Ben Wicks has recorded the true stories of some of the 3,500,000 children who were evacuated, and a number of the novels on the subject are also based on the author's own memories and experiences. Naturally, experiences varied. The evacuees in *Carrie's War*, by Nina Bawden, and in *Fireweed*, by Jill Paton Walsh, for instance, found it hard to settle;

whereas for the young hero of *Goodnight, Mr Tom*, by Michelle Magorian, evacuation was a much happier experience – a relief from the harshness of his unloving mother. Liz, the heroine of Hester Burton's story, *In Spite of All Terror*, welcomed the opportunity to escape her aunt's carping charity, and to stay on at school. Though at first she, too, encountered unexpected problems, in the end she gained from her experience, eventually finding comfort with her hosts. For Rusty, the heroine of *Back Home*, also by Michelle Magorian, it was the return to England in 1945 after years of evacuation in Canada which presented problems of readjustment. In all cases, however, war and evacuation meant radical changes, a disruption of normal expectations which had lifelong effects.

Even so, the experiences of evacuees could hardly be compared with the trauma of those refugees who were leaving their native land for good, sometimes leaving behind families they would never see again, always facing an uncertain future in a country with a different culture and probably a different language. This was Anna's situation in Judith Kerr's novel, *When Hitler Stole Pink Rabbit* and its sequel, *The Other Way Round*, when her family escaped from Hitler's Germany and lived in poverty, first in Switzerland, then in Paris and finally in London.

Though Anna and her brother manage to cope successfully with school in England, and Max wins a scholarship to read law at Cambridge, none of the family can wholly escape their refugee status. Their parents remain in a hotel of refugees from France, Poland, Germany and Czechoslovakia, and more than ten years later, when the war is over, and their arch enemy, Hitler, is defeated, they are still unassimilated, on the edge of British society. Max says to Anna:

> 'You remember … what you used to say in Paris? That as long as you were with Mama and Papa you wouldn't feel like a refugee?'
> She nodded.
> 'Well, now I suppose it's the other way round.'
> 'How, the other way round?'
> Max sighed. 'Nowadays,' he said, 'I think that the only times *they* don't feel like refugees is when they're with us.'

Max and Anna have had their own difficulties – that Max is interned as an enemy alien shortly before his finals is only one example of the strangely insensitive, unwelcoming and bureaucratic attitude of those in authority towards them. Anna is even more grieved and indignant at this treatment of the refugees when she reads in a letter from Max:

One of the internees had committed suicide – a middle-aged Jew who had been in a German concentration camp before escaping to England. 'He just couldn't face being in a camp again – any camp. It was nobody's fault, but we are all very depressed ... '

Although, finally, Max is released from internment, he continues to find great difficulty in being accepted into the Air Force because of his German birth, and Anna is barred repeatedly from the very employment where her knowledge of languages and experience abroad would be most useful. At one point in the story she explodes into anger at the obstructions put in her way.

'My father's name was on the first black list published by the Nazis,' she said quite loudly. 'After we'd escaped from Germany they offered a reward for his capture, dead or alive. I'm hardly likely, therefore, to sabotage the British war effort. But it's extraordinary how difficult it is to convince anyone of this.'

This frustration at the suspicious attitude of the British towards them, at being regarded as 'aliens' and potential enemies is echoed in Charles Hannam's account of his years as refugee in *A Boy in Your Situation*. He had come to Britain on his own, leaving behind his father, grandfather and other relatives who later perished in concentration camps. Karl was placed first in a hostel for refugee children, and later in an approved school building which he and his fellow-refugees shared with 'English boys who are orphans, or who have been in some sort of trouble'. In both places the refugees are put to manual work, and used, they feel resentfully, as slave labour. But their real potential is ignored:

'We could join the army, but they don't want us. It seems ridiculous. Here is a country at war with the Germans, here is a group of us who hate the National Socialists and who are prepared to fight and they won't even look at us.'

The position for male refugees worsened as they grew older:

After the fall of France the police came and took away the two refugee boys who were over sixteen ... Karl ... missed being interned by just a few months, but now he had to register as an alien ... he was not to leave the town for longer than twenty-four hours without reporting to the police station, he was not allowed to ride a bicycle and he was not allowed to move beyond a radius of five miles ... He had to appear before a tribunal that was going to decide if he was dangerous as well as being an enemy alien.

Refugee status, as it happened, made both Karl and Anna more acutely aware than their British friends of the progress of the war in Europe. The evacuation from Dunkirk, for instance, which, for the British, turned 'an ingenious escape from defeat' into 'a great victory', was, for Anna and her fellow-refugees, a disaster, both because of their grave concern for friends left in Paris, Belgium and elsewhere on the continent, and because of their fear of what might happen should their own refuge in Britain be invaded. It led Anna's father to provide an escape-route for himself and his family, a quick, sure poison, for use 'in an emergency'.

In contrast to this grimly realistic attitude, Anna finds an element of comedy in the British response to the fear of invasion.

> Everyone was talking about the invasion of England, for now that Hitler was only the other side of the Channel he would surely want to cross it. To confuse the Germans when they came, names were being removed from street corners and Underground stations, and even buses lost their destination plates, so that the only way to find out where they were going was to ask the conductor.

In spite of her own fears, Anna allows herself a wry smile at this and at tall stories about parachutists disguised as nuns, but betrayed 'by their carelessness in wearing army boots under their habits'.

In the event, though Britain was not invaded, the Channel Islands became one of the many territories occupied by the enemy. Geoffrey Trease has based his novel, *Tomorrow is a Stranger*, on 'the events and conditions of 1940–1945' in Guernsey, which was invaded after the fall of France in 1940. He tells of the evacuation of all who could leave, of the sad procession of people first taking their pets to be put down, of the departure of British troops, the bombing and strafing of the streets by the Germans before they landed, and what happened to those left behind under Nazi occupation. He also skilfully inserts into the narrative information about what was happening in other theatres of war, which gives young readers a valuable perspective on the progress of events in Britain and Europe.

Trease is subtle in his presentation of war, and rarely horrific, so that the inattentive reader can easily miss the underlying trage-dies, revealed not only in the deaths and dangers to the inhabitants and to the few Jews on the island, but also in the help-lessness of the German Oberleutenant Fischer, caught up in a war which destroyed for ever his ability to play his beloved piano, and goes cruelly against the grain of his gentle personality. It is revealed also in changes Tessa perceives in her parents, in, for example, her mother's growing bitterness under the strain of the struggle 'to keep the home going, seeing their children with sunken eyes and matchstick legs', enduring the hunger, cold and dark, 'the wearing out of clothes', and 'the perpetual problem of keeping clean without soap or enough hot water'. In addition, 'schooling was disrupted, teachers too weak and ill to teach, children unable to concentrate ... '

The strain is reflected also in the family quarrels, now increasingly frequent:

> She hated to hear them quarrelling. It happened more and more nowadays. It was the same in many families. Paul's Gran blamed the Occupation for spoiling their childhood. Tessa was beginning to see what it could do to older people's personal relationships.

This is a sensitive, well-written and compasssionate story. But in spite of hardships endured, the people in this novel escaped lightly compared with the Balicki family in Warsaw, who, in *The Silver Sword*, by Ian Serraillier, faced an ever-present threat of capture by the invading German army, deportation as slave labour, or death. Ruth was nearly thirteen, Edek eleven and Bronia three when their father was taken to a concentration camp in 1940. Soon after, their mother was taken off to work in Germany, and they were left in Warsaw alone; hiding out, smuggling food into the Warsaw black market with the connivance of friendly peasants, withstanding starvation, cold, gunfire and bombs. In 1944 Edek, also, is taken off to work for the Germans, and contracts tuberculosis. Eventually at the end of the war the three children are reunited, and, with Jan, a likeable but disturbed orphan they have befriended in Warsaw, undertake the slow, hazardous journey to Switzerland where they are lucky enough to find their parents, and join with them in setting up a Polish House in a village built for the orphans of all the warring nations. This, too, is a moving story of courage and endurance, with some clearsighted awareness both of the ruthlessness of the occupying army and of the effects upon children of too early trauma and responsibility. For all her fortitude and leadership in Warsaw, Ruth reaches breaking point when her responsibilities are over and she is back with her parents. For a brief time 'she behaved like a young child, clinging to her mother and following her about everywhere'. Jan and Edek also suffered in different ways, one in health and the other in personality, and took longer than Ruth to rehabilitate themselves.

Both *Tomorrow is a Stranger* and *The Silver Sword* are fictional reconstructions of actual events not directly experienced by their authors; a factor which inevitably affects the reader's reliance upon the relative 'truthfulness' of the picture they present. But Gertie Evenhuis based her story, *What About Me?*, on her own memories of Holland in 1943. Her hero, Dirk, is eleven, living in Amsterdam under the Nazis, and like the youngsters in *Dawn of Fear* does not yet fully understand the seriousness of what is happening. But he has become aware that his older brother, Sebastian, is leading a secret and presumably thrilling life in his spare time, receiving mysterious parcels, delivering secret messages, and filling his room with maps and forbidden newspapers. Dirk's innocent longing to be in on the action too – a natural reaction in a young boy which can be compared with Derek's youthful enjoyment of the dogfights in the skies in *Dawn of Fear* – leads him headlong into activities which endanger not only his own life but those of his family, friends and teachers. This is a simple, eventful story for readers of ten and over, but one which underlines once again the grim reality behind the occupation and the glamour of adventure.

In Hilda van Stockum's novel, *The Winged Watchman*, ten-year-old Joris and fourteen-year-old Dirk Jan are the two brothers who engage in subversive activities. They help a British airman whom they find hiding in a windmill, and take messages for their uncle, who is a member of an Underground organisation which supplies weapons to other groups and organises escapes and resistance. The Winged Watchman of the title is an old wind-driven poldermill, operated by the boys' father, and used to send secret messages revealed by the set of its sails. This is an exciting but also a thoughtful story, which tells of the compassion, courage and ingenuity of ordinary Dutch people and explores some of the human and moral problems of living under Nazi occupation. For not all Dutch people were willing to work against the German forces. One of the hazards of the war was the spread of Nazi ideology to the occupied countries, and the consequent collaboration of some of their citizens either through fear or conviction.

Though many of the ordinary Dutch people recognised with shame that they had not the courage to protest at the treatment of the Jews and at the repressive measures against them, in *What About Me?* and *The Winged Watchman* only one of the boys actually becomes a Nazi sympathiser. But Arnold, the young Dutch hero of *War Without Friends*, by Evert Hartman, is wholly taken in by Nazi philosophy, and has to learn, painfully, to reject its teaching. Arnold's father is a member of the NSB, the Dutch National Socialist Movement, set up in 1931 by Anton Mussert. The 'NSB-ers' were reviled in Holland as traitors and collaborators but in this book Arnold's sympathies are used to remind readers that cruelty in war is not the monopoly of the 'other side'.

At the beginning of the story, Arnold narrowly escapes being caught by a stream of bullets strafing a ship in harbour. As he contemplates the ship, 'riddled through and through', tilting slowly to its destruction, with its bridge in ruins, he sourly notes: 'So it was true what they said – what his father had said too: the British shot at everything in sight, without considering whether innocent people were the victims', and recalls tales of 'large cities being bombed, killing hundreds of people'. This makes him feel justified in helping the German soldiers to find and capture a British airman whom he has seen bailing out of his stricken plane.

A feature of this book is that although in the end Arnold changes his allegiance and refuses to escape to Germany with his parents as the Allies advance, neither side is presented as wholly evil or wholly good. The arguments of Arnold's father, Mr Westervoort, are obviously specious and self-seeking, and many of his actions show him to be callous, mean-spirited and ruthlessly authoritarian. He is rarely allowed any saving graces, though his point of view, particularly on the need for clear authority, can seem persuasive in wartime. But even in his NSB days, when many of his beliefs and actions are seen to be indefensible, Arnold himself is still a sympathetic character, a victim both of his unpleasant father and of the boys who self-righteously bully him. In separate incidents he is threatened with a knife, brutally attacked by two anti-Nazi classmates, and kicked and beaten with a spanner. Then, in hospital after one attack, Arnold meets Jeroen, a heroic resistance fighter, and eventually helps him to escape. But Jeroen, too, shows that he has been infected with cruelty. When Arnold hears of the death of a former schoolmate who had died in action with the SS at the Russian front, he gets no sympathy from Jeroen.

'They ought to slaughter that lot,' Jeroen continued mercilessly.
Arnold turned his face to the wall without answering.
'It's the same mob that do the killing in the concentration camps. String the beggars up, the lot of them! And I'd be glad to hang on their legs!'
Arnold said angrily, 'That makes you a worse killer than them!'
The silence lasted for minutes. Then Jeroen said, much more quietly than usual, 'Yes, you might just be right for once.'

Arnold's story is of the loneliness of a boy whose beliefs run against the trend, and of his courageous struggle to find the truth for himself. We do not know what will happen to him as he defiantly allows the train to take his parents to Germany without him, or whether Jeroen's testimony on his behalf will save him from the vengeance of his former enemies at school and in the town. But his story should engage the reader with fundamental problems about the nature of and motivation for some of our beliefs and actions, and the extent to which they are influenced by the good or ill fortune of our place and time of birth.

All these stories draw attention to the effect of war upon young people, to the mixture of excitement and glamour which infected them, and which still exerts its dangerous appeal, and to the real tragedies and disruption to their growing-up years. But in the occupied countries those in most immediate and pressing danger were the men, women and sometimes children who continued to oppose the enemy forces either actively as resistance fighters or in quieter ways, who were known opponents of fascism or who were marked out for extermination by their race. Indeed it was the fate of the Jews, gypsies, communists and dissidents of all kinds in Germany and the occupied territories that shocked and outraged the world when the full extent of the heartless cruelty of the concentration camps and the gas chambers finally became known. This time there were no machines to separate the camp guards from their prisoners, or to insulate them from knowledge of the cruelties they perpetrated.

7

The Final Solution

It seems ironic that were it not for the war, 'the final solution' could not have assumed such horrific proportions. The gas chambers were built and fed by citizens from the territories the Germans had conquered and occupied as well as by German nationals.

The systematic persecution of Jews began in the streets of Germany on 1 April 1933, with Hitler's proclamation of a one-day boycott of all Jewish shops. Then laws were enacted one after the other, relentlessly depriving Jews of the normal rights of German citizens. In *A Boy in Your Situation*, Charles Hannam describes his growing isolation and bewilderment as he progresses from the comfortable life and status of a rich Jewish banker's son in Essen to outcast Jew, and finally to refugee in Britain; and explores the traumas left by growing up under constant fear and threat. In his introduction he says:

> I suspect that most children are teased; it may be because they are thin or fat, clever or stupid, fair or red-headed. They hate it but in time the teasing stops, leaving some secret wound. But being teased for being Jewish was physically dangerous in the Germany of the 1930s. If I had not caught the train to England in May 1939, I would have been on one going to the Nazi death camps with millions of other Jews. Several members of my family perished, and I know now that for me it was a near thing. So what appeared at the start as malicious teasing by some boys and a few teachers ended in a deadly serious way. It was a preparation for their indifference to the fate of the Jews, and it laid the foundation for genocide. I have learnt since that unreasoning prejudice against *any* minority group can lead to such death and destruction.

Today his warning still needs to be heeded. His sober, straightforward account of his schooldays in Germany, trying with his family and friends to lead a normal life in spite of the worsening situation, is moving in its simplicity and deeply disturbing in its implications. He has little to tell of actual atrocities – his father, 'a very calm and brave man', protected him as much as possible from such events and from being made fearful by what was happening. And 'many of the non-Jewish people of Germany were good and decent – not all of them approved of the brutality and misery which in the end they were unable to stop'. Nevertheless, he rightly warns: 'Big events have small beginnings; what happened to me is a small detail of the great catastrophe which in the end wiped out most of German and European Jewry.'

The Devil in Vienna, by Doris Orgel, is a comparable story of a young Jewish girl growing up in Austria. Although based on the author's own experiences and memories, it is cast in the form of a journal begun by a fictional character, Inge Dornewald, in 1938, shortly before her thirteenth birthday. Its focus is her close and lasting friendship with Lieselotte, a girl of precisely her own age. But Lieselotte's family have recently moved to Munich, where her father is a Storm Trooper, and where Lieslotte is constrained by him to join the Hitler Youth.

There is an extraordinary vitality in Inge's frank and artless narrative, much of which is taken up with very ordinary events, part of the life of any young girl at school and at home. But it soon becomes evident that many of these events will have serious, even tragic implications for the future, a significance not yet part of Inge's awareness. On 14 March Hitler triumphantly enters Vienna, and the open persecution of the Jews begins in Austria. With Hitler's advent, Lieselotte and her family return to Vienna; but now the friendship between the two girls has become dangerous. Inge is forced to realise that Lieselotte's father would stop at nothing to put an end to it; he would, in fact, see to it that Inge and her family were sent at once to a concentration camp.

As an account for younger readers (of twelve or thirteen) of the progress of Inge and her fellow-Jews towards terror and near-despair, and of the unleashing of the worst instincts in those who acquiesce in the persecution of '*any* minority group', this story is one of the most powerful and compelling.

In *Friedrich* and *I Was There*, the first two books in his trilogy of autobiographical novels (for readers of twelve or over), Hans Peter Richter tells from the 'Aryan' angle the story of a friendship between the narrator and a Jewish boy, Friedrich Schneider, who lives in the flat above him. In these two stories the gradual deterioration of conditions for Jews is chronicled in a quiet, detached manner which makes it all the more poignant and horrifying. In *Friedrich* the focus is on what happens to the Jewish boy. *I Was There* covers the same period of time but concentrates on the narrator's own experiences, so that the emphasis has shifted to record the acceptance and even participation of ordinary citizens like himself in the brutalities committed against the Jews. In his preface Richter says: 'I am reporting how I lived through that time and what I saw – no more. I was there. I was not merely an eyewitness. I believed – and I will never believe again.'

It is the first-hand witness and admission of implication which makes this narrative so impressive. Richter was only eight when Hitler came to power, and fourteen when war began. Like Arnold in *War Without Friends*, therefore (see Chapter 6), he was at an extremely vulnerable time of life during the Nazi years. And though he and his family made little active protest against Nazi ideology, they were not blind to its excesses.

Regine, the German heroine of *A Night in Distant Motion*, a novel for teenagers by Irina Korschunow, is also a sensitive, sympathetic character. But at first she too accepts without question Nazi beliefs about German racial superiority. It is not until she gets to know Jan, the supposedly 'subhuman' Polish POW, that she begins to doubt: Jan's own philosophy was so different. ' "I don't want to hate," he said once. "There's so much hatred in the world. I don't want to add to it. I want there to be less of it." ' For years Regine had believed 'what my parents believed, what we read in our books, what we sang, heard on the radio, saw in the newspapers, what they preached to us at the German Girls' League', that:

> The Jews are our misfortune.
> Germans are better than everyone else.
> The *Führer* knows everything.
> The *Führer* will lead us to victory.
> You mean nothing, your people mean everything.
> One people, one empire, one leader.

She believed also at first that Jews and communists were sent to concentration camps 'to learn to work'. But under the influence of her love for Jan, and with the help of the French POW, Maurice, and the sensible, down-to-earth German farm girl, Gertrud, she finally realises just how blindly and unthinkingly she has allowed herself to support Nazi ideology.

Gertrud looks at life with a fund of common sense, which is invaluable to Regine during the terrible days after her illegal association with Jan has been discovered. She tells Regine:

> 'When Hitler came to power in thirty-three, [my father] said there would be a war. But no-one in the village listened to him; they were dazzled with their National Peasants' Cooperative and their National Food Estate and all that trash. They thought, now every cow will grow five udders.'

Many Germans, including Regine's own parents, had been seduced into supporting the Nazis out of self-interest – the promise of jobs and security for themselves and their families – even at the cost of those selected as 'enemies of the state'.

After Regine has seen Jan taken away to almost certain death, and has herself escaped from prison, she joins Gertrud and Maurice in listening to forbidden foreign broadcasts, from which she learns also the truth about the progress of the war, about the increasing numbers of refugees, and 'the collapse on all fronts'.

A Night in Distant Motion is a poignant love story in which important issues of fascism and the war are skilfully introduced as an integral part of Regine's own experiences. But though she was gradually forced to acknowledge the falsity of all she had believed, her mother still found the truth impossible to accept. 'If that's true,' she said. 'If we've been so wrong ... No, it's not true. We can't be that wrong. How could we go on living?'

In a novel for slightly younger readers, *Survive the Storm* (see Chapter 6), Wolf Klaussner also discusses the war and the position of those persecuted under fascism. Wilhelm has first to come to terms with his inheritance of part Jewish blood, and then with his recognition that his experiences have infected him, too, with vindictive desires to exterminate his tormentors and, after the war, to exact revenge on anyone he sees as 'left-over from the Nazi dung-heap'. The discussion of this complex mixture of feelings in Wilhelm is an important aspect of the story. Even as he helps the Americans and watches them 'run amok in their zeal to exercise justice', Wilhelm is sickened, 'racked and broken'; but it is not until much later that he is able to grope towards an understanding of the way in which people living under oppression can be hardened by their miseries into becoming as cruel to others in their power. He says:

> Today I can see it in a different light. For centuries they had been beaten and downtrodden, had knuckled under to harsh authority, had learnt that you had to keep out of harm's way. They had come to terms with those who held the whip hand. And now they didn't know where they stood. They had done away with a wounded pilot who had strafed them, and now the village was alight. Once again they had been delivered into the hands of the mighty. Could they be expected to distinguish between justice and injustice? ...
>
> All these people had been called on to do when the airman crashed was to have mercy on a dying man. But they'd forgotten what mercy meant.

Survive the Storm is also the story of Psomi, a Greek gypsy, whose family have been victims of the 'final solution'. Wilhelm discovers

Psomi hiding in a disused quarry, and the growing friendship between the two boys and the profound influence they have on each other are central to the theme of the book. It is often forgotten that the gypsies were included in the Nazis' extermination plans, and there are few books of memoirs or fiction in which they play a significant part or are allowed to show the courage and intelligence attributed in this story to Psomi.

Certainly the impression is usually given that the Nazis reserved their most fanatical hatred for the Jews, whom they systematically deported from all the countries they occupied, searching them out even, Margaret Balderson suggests in *When Jays Fly to Barbmo*, from the far north of Norway.

At first, the problems consequent upon occupation enter less starkly into this novel, the main theme of which is the growing to maturity of the heroine, Ingeborg, and her discovery of her mixed Lapp-Norwegian birth – readers will note wrily the relevance of her reactions to this equivocal racial inheritance. But for most of the book, war seems remote from the island of Draugoy and the farm where she lives. It bursts in on the inhabitants finally when four German soldiers suddenly arrive at the farm, seize a helpless, defenceless old Jew who had been working there, set fire to the boat shed and slaughter the animals to teach the Norwegians not to defy their orders. As Ingeborg listens to the dreadful sounds of destruction, and sees 'these four great heroes of the new modern world, prodding in front of them one frail, defenceless old man', with 'the evidence on their faces that they had enjoyed their work' she feels both anger and contempt.

> They had left us nothing – and yet they had left us everything. For now in our hearts was hatred – not the emotional hatred that dies when the storm is over – but hatred cold as steel which would stay with us for ever and which, when multiplied throughout our entire country, would one day spell their doom.

We are not told what happened to the old man, but his likely fate can be conjectured from the many stories and memoirs of those who survived the holocaust or left behind a record of their experiences before they died. *The Diary of Anne Frank*, the story of a Jewish family in hiding in Amsterdam, was one of the first to be published after the war, though by then Anne, her mother and sister had perished either in Auschwitz or Belsen.

From her hiding place, as early as 1942, Anne could see 'rows of good, innocent people accompanied by crying children, walking on and on ... bullied and knocked about until they almost drop. No-one is spared – old people, babies, expectant mothers, the sick

– each and all join in the march of death.' For the next two years Anne and her family endured the close confinement of their hiding place, meeting only their few courageous helpers, living through the heavy bombing and terrible destruction of Amsterdam in 1943, under perpetual constraint to remain quiet and undetected, and fearing hourly discovery or betrayal.

The Frank family stayed together until they were captured. In *The Upstairs Room*, on the other hand, Johanna Reiss tells us that her family decided to split up, Johanna going into hiding with her older sister, Sini. But, as they discover later, their whereabouts was known to others in the neighbourhood: it was chance or luck that they too were not betrayed. Johanna, like Anne, records the problems of claustrophobia from their close confinement, of living in perpetual fear of discovery, of anxiety for their hosts as well as for themselves, exacerbated always by news of the fate of friends and relatives who had not found secure refuge.

One alternative was to send a child 'to live with [a non-Jewish] family as their own child'. This was the solution sought in Yuri Suhl's novel, *On the Other Side of the Gate*, by a young Jewish couple, Hershel and Lena Bregman. When their son, David, is born in a Polish ghetto, they decide not to have him circumcised, and keep his existence a closely guarded secret. Then, when David is 18 months old, and the Germans are instituting days of 'action' to round up and take off from the ghetto the 'nonproductive element', they begin the sad, slow planning necessary to find a home for the baby with a non-Jewish friend they had known before the Nazi invasion.

This is a clearly told, straightforward story of Hershel's successful mission to secure a safe home for his son. But, as the author points out in his Afterword, even when, in the real life episodes which inspired this story, the parents lived to claim back their child, 'not all reunions between children and surviving parents went smoothly'. In some cases, too, failure to keep up the agreed payments meant that the children 'were turned into the streets to fend for themselves', and, consequently, were 'picked up by Polish or German police and returned to the ghetto where they were then first in line for the next deportation'.

Few of the children in Dr Korczak's orphanage in the Warsaw ghetto were to survive the deportations. In order to write *Shadow of the Wall*, a novel for readers of twelve upwards, Christa Laird researched memoirs and diaries, and tells us that although her central characters, 13-year-old Misha and his family, are fictional, many of the other characters in the book, including the director, Dr Korczak, and the helpers and children of the orphanage, are based on real people.

Misha and his two sisters are taken into the orphanage because
their mother, though still living nearby, is already too weak and ill
to look after them. Misha tries to help her during her final weeks
of life by smuggling food into the ghetto, at considerable risk to
himself, and manages also to smuggle his baby sister, Elena, to
foster parents outside the ghetto. He then escapes in the nick of
time to work as contact-man for an underground organisation.
But he watches in helpless anguish as those left in the orphanage
are rounded up and marched off to Treblinka to their deaths.

> At the head of the column, Misha saw the old Doctor, the man who
> had been both his guardian and his friend ... Beside them, upright and
> proud as ever, Musik carried the orphanage flag, the blue Star of David
> ... bright against its white background ... There was Abrasha, struggling
> along exhausted between Sami and Viktor, his violin clutched under
> one arm ... The children's wooden shoes beat out a dirge as they
> trudged slowly along in the midday heat. With a wild surge of hope,
> Misha prayed ... that Rachel would somehow not be there.
>   But of course she was there. Right at the end of the line, carrying one
> of the new tiny tots from the hospital.

This is a story, simply told, of small everyday happenings which
contrast sharply with the children's desperate and dangerous
attempts to survive; and of courage in the face of tragedy.

Most of the books discussed so far have been novels, which certainly contain painful reading, but yet are within the compass of
readers between the ages of twelve and fifteen. They can be seen
as opening up issues which it is important for young people to
know about, but which are too horrifying for most of them to face
without such preparation or until they are more mature. The
books which follow, written mainly as direct records of experience
by survivors of Nazi persecution and the death camps, plumb the
depths of human depravity and of human misery. The fact that
the events described were actually experienced by their authors
immeasurably increases the pain with which they are read.

In *Winter in the Morning* Janina Bauman records her personal
recollections of 'life in the Warsaw Ghetto and beyond'. Janina
was the daughter of a Jewish doctor in Warsaw, with a comfortable home and rich relatives, though even before the Germans
arrived there were distinct disadvantages for Jews in Poland.

> At that time, it was hard for anyone to get into medical studies at
> Warsaw University – for a Jewish boy or girl it was almost impossible.
> Though total exclusion had never been introduced in Polish universi-
> ties, there was none the less a clear unofficial restriction on the number
> of Jews admitted for studies, particularly those leading to professional
> degrees, such as medicine. Practically the only way a Jew could get in

was to gain a good certificate from a state high school. But there the same obstacle lurked again: there were severe restrictions on the number of Jewish children admitted to state secondary schools. One had to be truly brilliant and pass the qualifying exams with top marks to be accepted.

Nor was life wholly comfortable once she was admitted to the school, since she was the only Jewish pupil there. Nevertheless, when the time of trial begins under German occupation Janina finds friendly classmates who walk home with her and advise her to slip off the tell-tale armband, so that she can attend school unnoticed.

Throughout this deeply disturbing and absorbing account we are shown the complexity of individuals, Polish and Jewish; their kindness and compassion, even at great risk to themselves, but also their hysteria and brutality, their meanness and greed. This mixture of motives is apparent in the varied behaviour the family encounters when they have been hounded into the already over-crowded ghetto. There are horrifying accounts of the months during which the Nazis were selecting victims for deportation to the gas chambers. Janina is appalled to discover that a former classmate is now in the Jewish police force, and to see him gratui-tously cruel to a helpless old man. She is deeply uneasy when she realises that her Uncle Julian, also in the police force, accepts bribes from those he helps to escape. She records the hysterical denunciation of herself and her sister by another Jewish woman, whose accusation, 'They have no right! Innocent people may die instead of them!' rings in her ears long afterwards. 'Was the woman right?' she asks herself in anguish. 'Might someone die instead of me?' When, later, they succeed in escaping to the 'Aryan' side, they find some people who are willing to hide them out of genuine feelings of pity and conscience, but some who are motivated solely from greed. Repeatedly the family escapes by a hair's breadth as, one after another, their places of refuge are dis-covered by heartless blackmailers, who gradually strip them of all they have left in return for silence. These are some of the many incidents which led her to declare in her Introduction:

> During the war I learned the truth we usually choose to leave unsaid: that the cruellest thing about cruelty is that it dehumanises its victims before it destroys them. And that the hardest of struggles is to remain human in inhuman conditions.

Janina remained human: but many of the stories of survival from concentration and death camps confirm the truth of what she had learned at such cost.

Kitty Hart, a Polish girl like Janina Bauman, was twelve years old at the beginning of the war. At the threat of invasion, she and her family fled to Lublin, and tried unsuccessfully to escape across the border into Russia. Finally, after months on the run, Kitty and her mother were caught by the Gestapo and taken to a concentration camp. The story of her experiences are told in her autobiography, *Return to Auschwitz*.

During her months on the run, Kitty learns the basic lessons of survival:

> It was now that I began to understand how much like an animal a human being is: You *have* to be, in time of stress. Basic animal requirements are food, sleep, and the ability to excrete. Everything else is a bonus. Nobody who has not been on the run across hostile countryside, then driven to exhaustion as a slave labourer, then bullied and driven closer to death in an extermination camp, hungry for months on end – so hungry that most of the time it is impossible to think of anything else – can know how trivial everything else is. Permitted those three you can survive: food ... sleep ... shit.

Kitty learned that in order to survive in Auschwitz she must constantly fight for these basic needs: but both she and her mother were determined to do this 'without hurting anyone else'. Many of their fellow inmates, however, had no such scruples. 'It was hideous to see how readily one of your own people would turn against you in return for a few privileges and the chance of a few more months of life', Kitty remembers. But this degradation of the inmates was the deliberate policy of camp officials.

> I had already grasped the value of being invisible. Not being around when the hunters came. Having an unidentifiable face. There were thousands and thousands of women in the various sections of the camp, and even the *Kapos* were unable to tell one from another. With shaven heads, ravaged faces and ill-fitting garments, everybody looked so much alike. That was part of the Nazi plan, after all: to reduce all of us to impersonal, downtrodden nothingness.

In *The Informed Heart*, his book about his experiences in Dachau and Buchenwald, Bruno Bettelheim analyses in careful detail this aspect of the 'Nazi plan'. He recalls the 'standard initiation of prisoners', which took the form of forcing them 'to hit one another and to defile what the SS considered the prisoners' most cherished values. They were forced to curse their God, to accuse themselves and one another of vile actions, and their wives of adultery and prostitution.' He adds:

Besides traumatisation, the Gestapo relied mainly on three other methods of destroying all personal autonomy. The first of these ... [was] that of forcing prisoners to adopt childlike behaviour. The second was that of forcing them to give up individuality and merge themselves into an amorphous mass. The third consisted of destroying all capacity for self-determination, all ability to predict the future and thus to prepare for it.

Primo Levi also records the many ways in which the guards carried out this destruction of individuality. Levi, who spent two years in Auschwitz, writes in *If This is a Man*:

Then for the first time we became aware that our language lacks words to express this offence, the demolition of a man. In a moment, with almost prophetic intuition, the reality was revealed to us: we had reached the bottom. It is not possible to sink lower than this; no human condition is more miserable than this, nor could it conceivably be so. Nothing belongs to us any more: they have taken away our clothes, our shoes, even our hair; if we speak, they will not listen to us, and if they listen, they will not understand. They will even take away our name: and if we want to keep it, we will have to find ourselves the strength to do so, to manage somehow so that behind the name something of us, of us as we were, still remains.

Some of the prisoners were destroyed in a different way: they were placed in positions of power within the camps. Of these, Levi writes:

The Jewish prominents ... are the typical product of the structure of the German Lager: if one offers a position of privilege to a few individuals in a state of slavery, exacting in exchange the betrayal of a natural solidarity with their comrades, there will certainly be some who will accept. He will be withdrawn from the common law and will become untouchable; the more power he is given, the more he will be consequently hateful and hated. When he is given command of a group of unfortunates, with the right of life and death over them, he will be cruel and tyrannical, because he will understand that if he is not sufficiently so, someone else, judged more suitable, will take over his post. Moreover, his capacity for hatred, unfulfilled in the direction of the oppressors, will double back, beyond all reason, on the oppressed; and he will only be satisfied when he has unloaded on to his underlings the injury received from above.

Kitty Hart was never in such a position of power, but the experience which most devastated her, and for a while deprived her of the will to go on living, was being forced to load her two dearest friends in the camp on to the death lorry. She writes:

It was the same with the sick as with the corpses: it took two of you, one at the shoulders and one at the legs, picking up the limp or struggling body, swinging it once, twice, to and fro, and then throwing it up on to the heap in the lorry.

We screamed and wept as we did it. And when I saw that Hanka was one of those I had to toss up in that way, I knew I would have to go with her. Instead of picking up another victim, I made a dash for the lorry and tried to scramble up behind my friends.

Kitty is prevented from going deliberately to her death by her mother and two of her friends, who hold her down until the lorry has gone. 'Still I wanted to die. With my own hands I had helped to send two dear friends to their death. I could never forget the pleading, terrified look in their eyes.'

Her mother sees her through the dreadful days which followed this incident, in which she was in acute danger of giving up altogether and becoming a 'Muselmann' or Muslim. This name was given to those who had abandoned all hope and become walking automatons. They were so called, Bettelheim explains, because of 'what was erroneously viewed as a fatalistic surrender to the environment, as Mohammedans are supposed to blandly accept their fate'. But, he adds, these people had made no conscious decision to submit to the will of God: they had simply given up, becoming no longer capable of responding in any way to the intolerable environment of the camp, and, with no hope to sustain them, had deteriorated into 'walking corpses' who soon died. Levi writes:

They crowd my memory with their faceless presences, and if I could enclose all the evil of our time in one image, I would choose this image which is familiar to me: an emaciated man, with head dropped and shoulders curved, on whose face and in whose eyes not a trace of thought is to be seen.

Having been forced to become implicated in her friends' liquidation, Kitty too narrowly escapes being reduced to that fearful deprivation of 'affect, self esteem, and every form of stimulation', that total mental and physical exhaustion which would inevitably have led to death but for her mother's strenuous efforts to rouse her.

She is persuaded to leave the scene of her friends' departure for that of the *Kanada Kommando* – but she is then housed close to the gas chambers and crematoria, and set to sorting the possessions of the victims, a mountain of 'suitcases, bundles of clothing, shoes, prams and even toys'. From the windows of her new living quarters she can see those who had owned these goods march to their deaths.

A column of people had been shuffling from the direction of the railway line into a long, low hall ... What I was witnessing was murder, not of one person, but of hundreds of innocent people at a time ... On the outside of the low building a ladder had been placed. A figure in SS uniform climbed briskly up. At the top he pulled on a gas mask and gloves, tipped what looked from here like a white powder into an opening in the roof, and then hurried back down the ladder and ran off. Screams began to come from the building. We could hear them echoing across to our hut, the desperate cries of suffocating people. I held my breath and pressed my hands over my ears, but the screams were so loud you'd have thought the whole world must be able to hear them.

'It's over.' Someone was shaking me. 'It's all right, it's gone quiet. They're all dead now.'

It could not have taken more than ten minutes.

Jews and gypsies were not the only people to suffer and perish in the camps. Weislaw Kielar, Fania Fenelon and Wanda Poltawska were all arrested, charged with aiding the Resistance Movements in their native France or Poland, and sent to concentration camps at Auschwitz or Ravensbruck.

Weislaw Kielar was arrested in May 1940 as a member of the Polish Resistance, and his book, *Anus Mundi: Five Years in Auschwitz*, records his daily struggle to survive in the steadily deteriorating conditions in the camp. During his stint of work first as hospital orderly and then as corpse bearer, Kielar was well placed to remark the escalation and increasing efficiency of the extermination programme in Auschwitz. At first the camp held mainly male political prisoners and criminals; but it was gradually expanded to take in French, Polish, British and Russian prisoners of war, women, gypsies and Jews. At first prisoners died mainly from disease, exhaustion following beatings or punishment sessions, or weakness from lack of food; some were deliberately shot, allegedly whilst escaping, some were injected, one at a time, with phenol. But soon the gas chambers were built, to accommodate an increasing death toll as the extermination programme got under way. Kielar narrowly escaped extermination on several occasions, and recounts objectively the ingenuity and also at times the ruthlessness with which he saw and used the smallest opportunity to improve his lot within the brutal camp conditions. Every such effort added fractionally to the mixture of luck, courage and toughness necessary to his survival. His account, written from the point of view of a young man (he was 20 at the time of his arrest), one of the first to enter Auschwitz, and not primarily destined for the gas chambers, complements the experiences of Bettelheim, Levi and Kitty Hart.

Kielar also records the unexpected acts of compassion; the genuine love and affection between individuals; the grief as they watched the deterioration of young, beautiful girls into emaciated, withered skeletons before they too were sent 'up the chimney'; the remaining shreds of humanity and solidarity surprising in such inhuman conditions. The final pages tell of the remorseless way in which the surviving camp inmates were herded in front of the advancing American armies – at one time they were only ten miles away, yet the starving, emaciated men were repeatedly and ruthlessly marched out of reach of liberation, the bodies of those too weak to continue piled high at each brief stop made on the journey.

Fania Fenelon was arrested as a member of the French Resistance, and spent nine months in Drancy prison in Paris before being taken to the women's camp at Auschwitz. By chance she was recognised as a musician and taken into the women's orchestra. Though its members fared ill in various respects – they were starved and punished as ruthlessly as their companions in the camp, and remained under constant threat of liquidation – they had slightly better accommodation and clothing, and more of them survived. Their role was to play occasionally to their masters, the SS, and to play fellow-victims to the martyrdom of forced labour or the gas chambers.

> Here, in the icy air of this winter morning, in this geometrical land-scape of squat, stumpy sheds with barbed wire above them, the watchtowers, without a single tree on the horizon, I became aware of the extermination camp of Birkenau, and of the farcical nature of this orchestra conducted by this elegant woman, these comfortably dressed girls sitting on chairs playing to these virtual skeletons, shadows showing up faces which were faces no longer ...
>
> And, painfully, I realised that we were there to hasten their mar-tyrdom. One, two ... one, two ... Alma's baton set the pace for the endless march past. With the tip of his boot an SS beat time while the last woman, followed by the last soldier and last dog, went through the camp gate.

In *The Musicians of Auschwitz*, Fania describes the torment of playing the music she loved for such hellish purposes. Anguish attended also the occasions when she had to sing to men like Joseph Kramer, the commandant of the camp of Birkenau, under whose orders so many were exterminated.

> I was going to sing; it was a simple, normal action. It was also simple and normal that I should cast an eye over my audience. I saw Kramer and my heart began to beat violently; my hands, normally perfectly

dry, were damp now. It wasn't stage fright, the stakes were no higher than usual: it was quite as dangerous to comport oneself in such a way as to displease a warden as to embark on the great aria from *Butterfly* before the camp commandant. It wasn't that. For me, singing was a free act, and I was not free; it was above all a way of giving pleasure, giving love, and I felt a frantic desire to see those three SS men stuck like pigs, right here, at my feet.

Standing in front of those men with their buttocks spread out over their chairs, with that parody of an orchestra behind me, I felt as though I were living through one of those nightmares in which you want to cry out and can't. That cry would save your life, enable you to escape from the attendant horrors, and yet you lie there open-mouthed with no life-saving sound emerging.

Behind these details of daily degradation; of friendship and loyalty in the midst of fear and squalor; of 'chimneys smoking day and night'; of betrayal and steady deterioration physically, mentally, emotionally; of playing not only for those going to their deaths but for those who sent them there, lies the heartbreaking sense of a perceptive, honest, direct, sensitive and loving young woman, deeply involved with the music which in this dreadful place was both her saviour and her torment.

Her friend Florette's arrival at the camp epitomises the horror and the callous disregard for all humanity. She tells Fania:

> 'I arrived here with my mother, my father, my boyfriend, my whole family: twenty-one people in all. We'd been rounded up. I didn't know where they were going. When I saw them get into the trucks I didn't understand. So when I arrived at the quarantine block, I actually dared to ask about my parents. Then the blockowa grabbed my arm, pulled me towards the door, and said in her foul German jargon, pointing towards the chimney with her filthy finger: "You see that smoke? – that's your father coming out of the right chimney and your mother out of the left." I screamed like a mad thing, I was hysterical ... '
>
> She calmed down, her startling green eyes filled with tears. She lowered her head, suddenly humble. 'Because of that, I think I'll rail against everything all my life. You don't get over a thing like that ... '

Thirty years later, Fania too was to say: 'I've never left the camp; I'm still there, I've spent every night of my life there, for thirty years.'

Wanda Poltawska, arrested in 1941 for aiding the Polish Resistance Movement, also found herself haunted by memories – in this case of Ravensbruck: 'The dreams were so frighteningly realistic that I was nightly reliving the appalling reality of the camp.' It was to exorcise these nightmares that she wrote *And I am Afraid of my Dreams*, an account of her experiences as a 'guinea pig' subjected to some of the cruel experiments made upon the inmates.

The experiments were mainly injecting bacteria into bone marrow, or removing sections of bone or muscle from the legs of healthy young women. The results were excruciatingly painful, crippling, and sometimes fatal.

In a few short days, we had lost five women who had so recently been in good health. The shadow of their deaths struck chill into mind and body, and all of us, whether or not we had yet been operated on, found it harder to go on living. Terror had entered our barbed-wire compound and held us in its unrelenting grip. We could no longer find the courage to smile or sing. We couldn't even cry.

Herded together and driven to work like cattle, adrift among hostile strangers, we were young women without a future. Things were so bad now, it was hard to see how they could possibly get worse. And yet every day brought news of fresh calamities.

One girl, 'hardly more than a child, who adored dancing and was life and movement personified', had a large section of bone removed from her legs. 'Then, for good measure, they injected them with bacteria. She lay there, butchered, her legs in plaster – still trying to smile.'

Although convinced that they would never survive the camps, these women courageously kept alive some measure of hope. In a collective will, they requested that 'a school should be founded, a first-class establishment for women, ... to educate girls in such a way that they would be incapable of fighting wars or of lending themselves to criminal experiments on human beings'.

Those who did survive found that their trials were not over; even when they had escaped the camp there were other perils awaiting them at the hands of those from whom they might have expected protection. As they travelled the roads on the way back home at last, Wanda tells us, they found 'hands ... men's hands, reaching out for [them] ... lustful glances ... oily smiles ... There were so many variations on the theme, so many seemingly inno-cent approaches to defenceless women ...' She adds:

I looked at my group of weary, exhausted girls and saw terror in their eyes. Where were we going to sleep? By this time we were frightened of all men, no matter who they were; soldiers, civilians, Frenchmen, Serbians, Poles or Russians. Not one of those fellows who were looking us over right now, seeing us as just another group of eighteen-to-twenty-year-old girls, could have any idea of what we had been through. There was nowhere to go, no barrack huts, nothing but open fields. And those camp-fires, those tents, those eager, groping hands ...

At long last, I don't remember exactly when, we got to Arnswalde, the first railway station in operation since the war. Our feet were torn and bleeding. We sat on the station platform all day waiting for a train. But when one finally steamed in, we were horrified to find it full of men.

The panic-stricken girls were in despair; but to their relief, through the good offices of the station master, Wanda found a refuge for them in a goods wagon with six soldiers and an officer.

The aftermath of the Nazi holocaust – the legacy it has left in Europe and elsewhere – has also been well documented in a spate of novels and memoirs by people who, in Germany or the occupied countries, had been associated on one side or the other with the 'final solution'. The theme of Peter Carter's complex and serious novel for teenagers, *Bury the Dead*, is the way the Nazi past, the extermination camps, the anti-Semitism and the unspeakable cruelties of the war continued to affect the lives of the Nordern family in East Germany. Frau Helga Nordern was a young girl at the end of the war, one of 'the desperate army of refugees' trudging to an elusive safety through endless forests in bitter sleet and mud in company with her mother and 'the scarcely less desperate rearguard of the Wehrmacht'; with always on their heels 'the terror from the East'. Though Helga's mother, the aristocratic Frau von Ritter, had kept her daughter safe during their flight, she herself had been raped by the 'liberating' forces, and her husband, a *Junker* and a major, had been shot by a drunken soldier as he was surrendering.

Subsequently, safe at last, Helga married Hans Nordern, a working man and a socialist, and with him turned her back on the Nazi era to lead a serious, earnest, conscientious – almost too exemplary – existence, firmly supporting and working for the new German Democratic Republic. But this does not save the Norderns or their children, Erika and Paul, from the consequences of their country's past. Into their lives comes Frau von Ritter's brother, the Nazi Karl von Bromburg, for whom nothing has changed. He remains convinced that the 'final solution' was a justified 'purification of the race, wiping out a plague'. His continuing activities in support of still-living Nazis eventually also involve his sister, a seemingly gentle old woman who has nevertheless forgotten nothing of her own aristocratic past and forgiven none of the atrocities she had suffered. Worse still, driven into a corner, implicated against their will and blackmailed by Karl, the whole Nordern family, including Erika and her innocent younger brother, Paul, face the prospect of retribution along with the hateful Karl.

At the crisis point of the story Herr Nordern says: 'It's endless. Endless. Forty years since the war ended, forty years! And still ...

still ... You think that the past is dead and buried, but the ghosts come back, and back, and back.'

It is not merely the ghosts of Nazi atrocities which have come back in this way, but of those committed by the other side. Frau Ritter's recall of those terrible days of flight and of her own sufferings at the hands of the soldiers have shocked her son-in-law out of all complacency.

> 'It's all right, Father.' Erika's voice was that of a ghost. 'It wasn't your fault.'
> 'No? That's what we keep telling ourselves,' Herr Nordern said. 'But it happened, when the Russians came in ... the women ... it did happen. It was part of our past and we denied it. We haven't told the truth really. But what else could we do? ... They'd been through it, the Russians. When you think what happened to their country, and the troops – the Red Army – they'd seen it, and they didn't get leave, you know. Some of them had spent three years in the front line. Not that it excuses – oh God. Oh God Almighty.'

The 'message' of this book is conveyed in the way the separate elements of its protagonists' experience are gradually revealed and found to be interlinked in an inextricable chain of cause and effect, which culminates finally in an awareness of mutual complicity. We are *all* responsible for what has happened in the past, and for what lies in wait for us in the future.

This should be true of our past heroisms, probity and virtue as well as of our selfishness, cruelty and lack of concern: but in this novel the evils of fascism are seen to have been more powerful than the feeble virtues opposed to it, now or then. Frau Nordern in her distress is almost incoherent but yet can make the relevant connection between violence past, present and future:

> 'It's the past ... They had a rally in Bromberg ... They were there with their banners and swastikas and singing the Horst Wessel song. They sent an SS squad, all blond hair and blue eyes, and, dear Christ, what they were doing. And we let them, let them do it, because they were doing it to other people. Getting rid of trouble-makers, we said, agitators; bringing order. Yes, we said that and let them murder and torture and now we are paying for it, over and over. And they say that in the West some kids admire them. Dear God.'

This inability to escape from the past is the theme also of Christa Wolf's autobiographical novel, *A Model Childhood*, in which she says: 'What is past is not dead; it is not even past. We cut ourselves off from it; we pretend to be strangers.' Symbolically, Christa Wolf (who now lives in East Berlin, the scene of Carter's

novel) distances herself from the child she once was in the narrator, Nelly, through whom is she nevertheless telling her own
story. So it is Nelly but also Christa who knew 'or sensed – for in
times like these there are many gradations between knowing and
not knowing' – that when her aunt fell victim to the 'euthanasia
programme ... there was more to Aunt Dottie's death than met
the eye'; and it is Nelly but also Christa who is aware, then and
later, that her elders at the time knew more than they said, but
did nothing.

Throughout this novel Nelly veers between memories of the
past and her present life, grappling endlessly with feelings of guilt
and oppression as she recalls her own fervent participation in the
Nazi youth organisations, and recalls, also, people and incidents
which should have indicated clearly what was happening and
aroused her horror and opposition. She remembers the words of a
former teacher, Maria Kranhold:

> But of course believing was no excuse, Kranhold then said. You had to
> look at what you believed. Nobody had ever been lied to about the
> most important issues. Hadn't Hitler demanded more Lebensraum for
> the German people from the very beginning? To any thinking person
> that meant war. Hadn't he repeated over and over that he wanted to
> exterminate the Jews? That's what he had done, as much as he could.
> He had declared that Russians were subhuman, and that's how they
> had been treated, by people who wished to believe that they were. And
> people of her old teacher Julia Strauch's caliber had fallen into the trap
> themselves, with their belief in everything. Who can absolve them for
> having sent their minds on a vacation?

In this fascinating, complex book Christa Wolf tries to come to
terms with the child who had also 'sent her mind on a vacation',
though with the greater excuse of the comparative innocence of
childhood.

These books are essential reading for all who would know what
evil things can be done or connived at by ordinary people. For
perhaps the most disturbing aspect of these accounts is that they
reject the notion that this was an aberration of the time, something peculiar to Hitler and the Germans in the 1930s, which the
civilised world can now shudder at and complacently forget. In
Return to Auschwitz Kitty Hart says:

> It could have happened anywhere. It can still happen anywhere if con-
> ditions are right. There are awful signs, in fact, of it beginning to
> happen in various parts of the world yet again, and getting worse ...
> France, for example, and England. When you hear someone speak
> slightingly of 'That Jewish lot down the road' or rant 'It's high time

those bloody blacks were rounded up and sent back where they belong', you are listening to the very people whose prejudices can so readily be inflamed by propaganda at the right moment.

Levi too warns; 'In every part of the world, wherever you begin by denying the fundamental liberties of mankind, and equality among people, you move toward the concentration camp system, and it is a road on which it is difficult to halt.'

At the time when the truth about the camps first became known, many refused to listen. They turned away with 'the most appalling indifference to the Holocaust' which persisted, Kitty Hart claims, for 35 years. Then her television appearance awakened at last a genuine interest, especially from young viewers 'anxious to know more and wondering why they had so far been given so little information'. For those seeking information, her story is one of the most accessible of the autobiographical accounts currently available. Even so, it requires a maturity (to be found, perhaps, in some 17- or 18-year olds) which can face the extremes of evil of which we are capable, and absorb the lessons which must be learned if we are to survive.

There are also two novels from America for teenage readers which reinforce the message that no part of the world is immune from travelling along the same road. *Alan and Naomi*, by Myron Levoy, and *The Wave*, by Martin Rhue, illustrate the effects of Nazism and anti-Semitism in an American context, thus demonstrating the universal nature of problems and attitudes which too many still find it easy to dismiss as having no relevance for themselves.

Choosing stories such as these can help to dispel any such complacency. They require us to face squarely the unpalatable truth that cruelty is a human weakness which can affect us all, and which it is all too easy to justify in the name of patriotism or self-preservation.

8

Hiroshima and After

At the height of its operation, Kitty Hart calculated, Birkenau's extermination buildings at Auschwitz alone were receiving up to 20,000 people daily. The gas chambers could accommodate 2,000 people at one time, the ovens of the crematoria could dispose of about 18,000 bodies every twenty-four hours, and the open pits coped with a further 8,000 in the same period (*Return to Auschwitz*, pp. 117–18). Millions of people went through the various extermination camps, abused, degraded, humiliated, reduced to the lowest state of existence possible by deliberate and systematic cruelty, and finally murdered. These brutalities were committed at close quarters by men and women upon other men, women and children.

Millions had already been killed from a distance in bombing raids over the major cities of Europe, or died in the battles which raged throughout Europe and North Africa. To these must be added those who died also in the Far East in the war with Japan, both in battles on the ground and in raids on Japanese cities.

In March 1945, we are told in Peter Townsend's book, *The Postman of Nagasaki*, General Curtis Le May, commander of the US bomber force in the Marianas, 'ordered his B29s to be stripped of all guns except the rear turret, as well as of all superfluous equipment, and to be loaded to capacity with bombs filled with napalm, jellied fuel which ignited on impact – the most deadly of all incendiary devices'. More than 300 B29s were then sent 'to set fire to the heart of Tokyo', where:

> in houses made of wood and paper, there lived, until that awful night, a quarter of a million low-paid workers. By dawn, 130,000 of them with their families lay strewn about the city in heaps of charred, unrecognisable corpses. During the nights that followed, B29s burnt to death thousands more civilians in Nagoya, Kobe and Osaka.

In face of so many deaths suffered in so many ways in this war, how does one make comparison with the slaughter perpetrated

upon the citizens of Hiroshima and Nagasaki by two atom bombs?
I.F. Clarke writes in his book, *Voices Prophesying War 1763–1984*:

> In the abominations of modern warfare, in the inhumanity of Dachau,
> Buchenwald and Oswiecim, in the mass extermination of millions of
> Jews, and in all the brutalities of a new iron age, man was forced to rec-
> ognise a capacity for evil that had, so it was thought, vanished forever
> from the earth ... And then, after all the changes and disasters of the
> first really world-wide war in human history had had their effect upon
> the mind, the imagination had somehow to find a place and an expla-
> nation for the last news of all. Shortly after 09.00 hours on the
> morning of 6th August 1945 the United States aeroplane *Enola Gay*
> began its bombing run over a Japanese city. At 09.15 hours the first
> nuclear bomb exploded over Hiroshima at a height of 31,000 feet and
> ended life for 80,000 men, women and children.

The second nuclear bomb fell on Nagasaki three days later.

Was it the millions of deaths which had preceded this final act
which had numbed the minds of politicians and military to the
horror of what they were about to do? The decision to drop these
bombs was taken by a few individuals behind closed doors, and
carried out by a handful of crewmen in two bombing runs. At the
lowest estimate, 140,000 people from Hiroshima alone were to die
by the end of 1945, and a further 50,000 by the end of 1950. More
still died over the years following, including some who had not
yet been born. Churchill's famous phrase could have been
adapted to this situation, but naturally, no one thought to do so –
never, in so short a time, was so much suffered by so many at the
hands of so few.

At the time we were told there was no other way to end the war
quickly and save the lives of our troops. We were not told that
Japan was already seeking peace talks; or that atomic scientists
had suggested that the threat of a nuclear device or a demonstration of its powers without loss of life might be as effective a way of
securing peace. This idea was later to be used to defend our reliance on a yet larger arsenal of such weapons.

One of the earliest, and still the most moving detailed account
of the bombing of Hiroshima was written for *The New Yorker* by
John Hersey, and published on 31 August 1946, a year after the
dropping of the bomb. *Hiroshima* was reprinted by Penguin Books
the following November.

In his Introduction to *One Family's War*, 40 years later,
Christopher Mayhew wrote:

> We can miss the true meaning of war when we read about an army
> fighting rather than a particular soldier, of a city being blitzed rather

than a single house, of the 'Battle of Britain' rather than of Paul in his Hurricane, fighting down his fears ... It seems particularly important today to avoid thinking about war in general terms. The first nuclear exchange will obliterate all questions of victory or defeat, attack or defence, right or wrong; only the suffering of this or that particular person or family (multiplied an unimaginable number of times) will have meaning.

Perhaps in making this comment Mayhew was looking back at Hersey's account, for this is the form it takes; a 'vivid yet matter-of-fact story' which selects six people and 'tells what the bomb did to each of them through the hours and days which followed its impact on their lives'.

Hersey begins his account with the precise location and every-day actions of each of the six 'at the moment when the atomic bomb flashed above Hiroshima'. These quite ordinary details must have been etched on the memories of the survivors: a clerk in the personnel department at the East Asia Tin Works; a doctor at his private hospital; a member of the surgical staff of the Red Cross Hospital; a German Jesuit priest; a tailor's widow; and the pastor of the Hiroshima Methodist Church. Their experiences epitomise the suffering, injury and death caused by the bomb both then and later.

Towards evening, the Rev. Mr Tanimoto, who had worked tire-lessly all day to give what help he could, found about 20 men and women on a sandspit, unable to move, and in danger of drowning as the tide flooded in.

He reached down and took a woman by the hands, but her skin slipped off in huge, glove-like pieces. He was so sickened by this that he had to sit down for a moment. Then he got out into the water and, though a small man, lifted several of the men and women, who were naked, into his boat. Their backs and breasts were clammy, and he remembered uneasily what the great burns he had seen during the day had been like: yellow at first, then red and swollen, with the skin sloughed off, and finally, in the evening, suppurated and smelly ... He had to keep consciously repeating to himself, 'These are human beings.'

But most of the injured found no one to help: there were few available to attend to them even at the Red Cross Hospital:

The lot of Drs Fujii, Kanda, and Machii right after the explosion – and, as these three were typical, that of the majority of the physicians and surgeons of Hiroshima – with their offices and hospitals destroyed, their equipment scattered, their own bodies incapacitated in varying degrees, explained why so many citizens who were hurt went untended and why so many who might have lived died. Of a hundred and fifty doctors in the city, sixty-five were already dead and most of the rest were wounded. Of 1,780 nurses, 1,654 were dead or too badly hurt to work. In the biggest hospital, that of the Red Cross, only six doctors out of thirty were able to function, and only ten nurses out of more than two hundred. The sole uninjured doctor on the Red Cross Hospital staff was Dr Sasaki.

Even Sasaki was shocked and dazed, and so overwhelmed by the size of the catastrophe that he 'worked without method' amongst patients lying

> on the floors of the wards and the laboratories and all the other rooms, and in the corridors, and on the stairs, and in the front hall, and under the port-cochere, and on the stone front steps, and in the driveway and courtyard, and for blocks each way in the street outside ...
> Tugged here and there in his stockinged feet, bewildered by the numbers, staggered by so much raw flesh, Dr Sasaki lost all sense of profession and stopped working as a skilful surgeon and a sympathetic man; he became an automaton, mechanically wiping, daubing, winding, wiping, daubing, winding.

A month after the explosion 'something like order had been re-established in the hospital', but medicines were still in short supply and patients still lay in the corridors.

Hersey follows each of the six survivors in turn, repeatedly halting his narrative at a moment of crisis – the moment of the flash, or nightfall, or when the end of the war was declared – so that the reader is sent back again in time to live over the same events in slightly different circumstances. Thus there is a steadily accumulating build-up of the endless multiplication of distress, shock, anguish, terror, bewilderment, and helpless seeking for medical aid, information, lost loved ones, safety, consolation amid a general inability to take in the scale of the disaster, or to assist each other.

> Mr Tanimoto saw, as he approached the centre, that all the houses had been crushed and many were afire. Here the trees were bare and their trunks were charred. He tried at several points to penetrate the ruins, but the flames always stopped him. Under many houses, people screamed for help, but no one helped; in general, survivors that day assisted only their relatives or immediate neighbours, for they could not comprehend or tolerate a wider circle of misery.

He records also the silent, numbed courage of the wounded.

> To Father Kleinsorge, an Occidental, the silence in the grove by the river, where hundreds of gruesomely wounded suffered together, was

one of the most dreadful and awesome phenomena of his whole experience. The hurt ones were quiet; no one wept, much less screamed in pain; no one complained; none of the many who died did so noisily; not even the children cried; very few people even spoke. And when Father Kleinsorge gave water to some whose faces had been almost blotted out by flash burns, they took their share and then raised themselves a little and bowed to him, in thanks.

Added to all the personal pain and suffering was the anguish of knowing nothing about friends and relatives, some of whom had simply disappeared. This aspect of the tragedy is the central theme of *The Miracle Tree*, an illustrated story by Christobel Mattingley, with fine charcoal drawings in Japanese style by Marianne Yamaguchi. This is one of several books written on a simpler level for younger readers.

It might be asked how an episode of such unimaginable horror could be made the subject of books for young readers. But, as in the case of the Nazi holocaust, it is an aspect of human experience and of human history which must be made known to young people, so that they can be helped to grasp its significance and its implications for the future; and so that they may also be helped to face, in some degree, the emotional trauma of realising of what we are capable. It has been the mission of several story-writers to attempt this almost impossible task.

The Miracle Tree vividly evokes the almost pastoral atmosphere of Nagasaki in the years after the bomb. But the story is less successful in its emphasis on the role of the 'miracle tree' as *deus ex machina* in the final dénouement. Hanako is still in Nagasaki living as a recluse, scarred physically and emotionally by the bomb, and barely recognisable, when her mother and husband come separately to look for her. But although for 20 years the paths of all three cross and recross it is not until it is almost too late that they are brought together by the 'miracle' tree which Tano has planted and tended in token of his enduring love for his wife.

Toshi Maruki, the author and artist of another picture book, *The Hiroshima Story*, went to Hiroshima with her husband soon after the bomb fell to help the survivors. Subsequently, they held an exhibition of the paintings which had arisen from their experiences in the devastated city, and these, together with the true story of a woman they met at the exhibition, formed the basis of the book. The direct simplicity of this excellent story and the colour, delicacy, compassion and charm of the illustrations would have a powerful effect upon readers of any age.

Eleanor Coerr's moving story of *Sadako and the Thousand Paper Cranes* is also beautifully illustrated, this time in black and white by Marianne Yamaguchi. Eleanor Coerr tells us that Sadako was two years old when the bomb fell. Nine years later, when she was eagerly training for a relay race, she began to have dizzy spells, and before long was taken into hospital with leukaemia, the 'atom bomb disease'. Eleanor Coerr has researched into her family background and into the letters she wrote and which were later published by her classmates in order to recreate for readers of ten and over the story of her final months of life.

It begins with the lively, alert eleven-year-old excitedly looking forward to the celebrations of Peace Day, seeing it, with all the high spirits of youth, as a day of carnival, rather than as a day of memorial for those who had died when the atom bomb fell on the city. Indeed, for her, 'the worst part was seeing people with ugly whitish scars. The atom bomb had burned them so badly that they no longer looked human. If any of the bomb victims came near Sadako, she turned away quickly.' At this stage Sadako seems unscathed and carefree: it is not until the following year that she has to face the prospect of her own death from leukaemia.

Eleanor Coerr describes simply the progress of the disease. As Sadako came closer to death, we are told:

> She never complained about the shots and almost constant pain. A bigger pain was growing deep inside her. It was the fear of dying. She had to fight it as well as the disease. The golden crane helped. It reminded Sadako that there was always hope.

The golden crane had been given her by a friend, to remind her of an old Japanese belief that 'if a sick person folds one thousand paper cranes, the gods will grant her wish and make her healthy again'. The effort to complete this number helped to sustain her in her tragic fight against death, but, we are told, she had made only six hundred and forty-four when she died. Her classmates folded the remaining three hundred and fifty-six cranes so that the full number could be buried with her. They also initiated a collection for a memorial statue to her courage and to 'all children who were killed by the atom bomb', which was unveiled in the Hiroshima Peace Park in 1958.

Karl Bruckner has set himself a difficult task in his more detailed, complex and strongly anti-war children's novel. Sadako is the central character in this story too – it was originally published in Vienna as *Sadako will leben* and translated (into rather stiff prose, unfortunately) by Frances Lobb under the title *The Day of the Bomb*.

There are a number of minor differences in his account of Sadako's family and life, though these are not significant to the overall impact of his story – according to Bruckner Sadako was four at the time of the bomb, had one brother about six years older, was a cyclist not a runner and had completed 990 cranes before she died.

Bruckner ambitiously attempts a wider survey of people and events in Hiroshima before and after the bomb was dropped. He gives his own version of what happened at the high level discussions behind the scenes both in USA and Japan, and tries to recreate the thoughts, feelings and movements of the crews of the bomber and of the reconnaissance planes making a preliminary survey of the target. He imagines a variety of responses to the situation from the various crew members, some, like the observer and photographer, seeing their activities purely as a job – 'what he photographed was a matter of indifference to him'; some, like Hawkins or O'Hagerty, having considerable reservations about the 'war machine'. Colonel Tibbets, the pilot of the bomber, is credited with ignorance of the significance of the bomb he was carrying, and only begins to consider the implications of what he has accomplished when the bomb has exploded, and his bombardier, Major Ferebee, is 'half out of his mind' at the 'dreadful mushroom of smoke and flame' which indicates that 'anything that is still left of Hiroshima is on fire'. Then he decides: 'I am innocent. I carried out an order', a defence which reminds one of the Nuremburg trials. But, overall, Bruckner is compassionate in his assessment of the moral dilemma facing the bombing crew.

Though one can fault Bruckner's book in several ways – its heavy prose style and the stilted, at times exaggerated, tone of the dialogue are a distinct disadvantage in a book for young readers – its anti-war stance is firm and decided, and it raises many issues which are worth serious consideration.

Peter Townsend is similarly ambitious in the scope of his book for adults, *The Postman of Nagasaki*. He combines an account of the history of Japan's entry into the war and the American research into nuclear fission with the story of a 16-year-old postman, Sumiteru. His narrative embraces the author's horror at the ruthless militarism of Japan as well as at the Allied decision to drop the bombs upon urban targets. It reveals also his respect and admiration for the ordinary Japanese people he met in Nagasaki, their warm hospitality, their courage and the sincerity and sensitivity with which they told him what had happened.

Townsend gives his own version of the two bombing-runs over Hiroshima and Nagasaki which in each case 'obliterated the entire city and nearly half of its inhabitants'. A professional airman who 'proved himself a brilliant fighter pilot in the Battle of Britain', Townsend is less kindly disposed than Bruckner towards those who carried out the raids. Of the first run he writes:

At Tinian Island ... the base chaplain blessed the eleven-man crew, captained by Colonel Tibbets, of the B29 bomber. 'May the men who fly this night be kept safe,' he prayed, but breathed not a word of compassion for their tens of thousands of intended victims ...

When they had accomplished their mission, Townsend tells us:

As *Enola Gay* turned for home, the crew cheered; Tibbets lit up his pipe once more and its blue smoke drifted across the flight deck. Behind him a column of purplish black smoke, mushroom-shaped at the top, rose up several kilometres above Hiroshima. All that remained of the city was a smouldering waste-land upon which rain soon began to fall, no ordinary rain, but heavy drops, black and greasy – 'black rain' precipitated from the atomic cloud and full of radioactive particles.

Three days later, without giving the Japanese government adequate time to negotiate a peace settlement, the second bomb, 'Fat Man', was dropped on Nagasaki. Sumiteru Taniguchi was severely injured when the bomb fell, but survived to tell 'the smallest details' of his story to Townsend 'during those hot, busy days and nights of August 1982' which the author spent in the city 'finding the ones who could tell me about all aspects of the A-bomb'.

Sumiteru was delivering letters at the time of the explosion.

As he turned into the street, he saw children in white shirts playing; they saw him too – he was their friend who passed by every day. They waved to him: 'Hullo Sumiteru, see you tomorrow.'

At that instant, the children and everything else around him disappeared in a blinding flash, bluish-white, like a gigantic arc-lamp, and accompanied by deafening unearthly thunder – survivors would remember it as *Pika-don*, the flash-boom. Then all was dust and darkness as a wind more violent than any typhoon blasted Sumiteru off his bicycle and hurled him to the ground some metres away. Through the murk, he glimpsed small white shapes, reminding him of leaves scattered by an autumn wind, being swept along the ground until they came to rest and lay still.

Sumiteru was severely wounded by a flying boulder, the skin of his left arm 'had been scorched off and hung down in shreds from his finger-tips', and 'the skin had been flayed clean off his back, from his neck to his waist-line, where it hung, parchment-coloured, like a ragged length of cloth.' It took two days for Sumiteru to reach help; and it was March 1949 before he finally left hospital to return to work.

Sumiteru's ordeal is told quietly; the days when he was in so much pain that he could only beg his nurses to kill him; when though he was still so young 'it looked as if pain and sorrow were to be his lot for the rest of his life'; when in spite of operations and skin grafts he knew that his left arm would remain half useless. It was 'a long and agonizing battle against death, a wearisome, almost impossible climb up out of hell to a sane and normal existence'.

Once out of hospital, Sumiteru faced the next stage, a future in which he had to 'remake his life, shattered as it had been at the beginning of his manhood'.

Remaking shattered lives was to prove a problem for all those who had been exposed to the bomb. Townsend explains:

> A-bomb survivors were extremely vulnerable in a society which tended to regard them as a people apart; tainted by the atom bomb and its effects – disfiguring burns, psychological problems and radiation sickness; tainted by death itself. More and more they met together to talk, not so much about their past experiences, as about the consequences of the bomb on their daily lives. In the minds of many of them there still remained an inkling of that complex called 'death guilt', a sense of shame at having survived mass extermination. Why had they not died with the rest? The thought obsessed many of them.

One pressing problem was that of marriage: the ugliness of bodies that had been exposed to the flash burns or fear that future children might be malformed deterred many from marrying survivors of the bombs. Sumiteru faces both these handicaps in his attempts to find a wife. Eiko, whom he eventually marries, courageously comes to terms with the revelation of his ugly, scarred back, and her devotion and wisdom 'enabled him to make a success out of his ruined youth'. But Townsend tells of her anguish over his constant ill health, and their terrible fears for their unborn children.

> Sumiteru kept a diary in which he daily recorded his fears concerning the inherited effects of radiation on the child both he and Eiko longed for. One day he forgot to lock up his diary. Eiko came across it and began glancing through its pages. It was not long before she put it down, cold with fear for her expected baby. Her anguish increased as the days passed until, hardly able to bear it any longer, her thoughts turned to abortion – it was not an uncommon practice with mothers faced with the same problem, the *hibakusha* complex. It would free her from her anxiety, now amounting almost to terror; free the baby, too, if it were to be born handicapped, from an incomplete and probably miserable life.

Eiko and Sumiteru are fortunate: both their children are born perfect.

It struck Sumiteru as he looked down on his son and fondled the swaddled infant, as almost miraculous that he himself, who years ago had been given up for dead, had now succeeded in breathing life into another man, a child, innocent and immaculate, of his own poor mutilated flesh.

He took Eiko's hand and caressed it. Chosen as his wife by hazard when so much else in his life had been destroyed, she had bravely and faithfully partnered him in his act of creation, borne him these two lovely children. Into Sumiteru's life, to which he clung so precariously, she had brought an undreamed-of sense of fulfilment.

Eiko, though not directly a bomb victim, nevertheless in electing to stay with Sumiteru chose. also to share his sufferings: in her own words it was 'like holding a time-bomb in her hand, never knowing when it would go off'.

This sense of the bomb relentlessly haunting the lives of those who survived runs also through the selection of short stories about Hiroshima and Nagasaki which was edited by Kenzaburo Oe and published in English with the title *Fire from the Ashes*. At the beginning of 'The House of Hands', the author, Mitsuharu Inoue, quotes the comment of a woman from a rural village in Nagasaki Prefecture:

> Nobody's going to marry those Nagasaki girls. Even after they reach marrying age, nobody's going to marry them. Ever since the Bomb fell, everybody's calling them 'the never-stop-people.' And the thing that never stops is their bleeding. Those people are outcasts – damned Untouchables. Nobody's going to marry one of them ever again.

'The House of Hands' is the story of four girls, caught in this trap, one dying of her latest miscarriage and consequent haemorrhage, another whose marriage is being negotiated, but who is desperately fearful lest this might be her fate too. The remaining two are torn between sympathy for their friends and anxiety for their own prospects.

In Yoko Ota's story, 'Fireflies', the narrator returns to Hiroshima to visit her younger sister, Teiko. She too is haunted by memories. 'Come to think of it,' she remarks, 'wherever I happened to be in Hiroshima, although seven years had passed since the bombing, my eyes seemed to see only masses of fire and blood everywhere.' Yet this is a tender, quiet story, full of gentle self-deprecating humour and keen compassionate observation as well as deep anger and despair. This mixture of feelings surrounds her observation that seven years later her sister, Teiko, still lives in 'a shack, a barrack, some kind of little living unit appropriate to this devastated city', with only one source of water from a pipe at the army horse stables, and infested with slugs which 'slithered round in droves' and were dropped into a 'small can of thick salt water behind the curtain'. Later in the story these slugs assume a symbolic dimension.

During her visit the narrator meets Miss Mitsuko Takada, a young woman terribly scarred by the bomb. Her reaction is the more poignant because it comes from someone who had shared the experience of the flash.

> It was not a girl but a monstrosity. Her deformed face stood out even more grotesquely because she had put on her best clothes, a pure white blouse and a skirt with a flower pattern in crisp white ... I broke down weeping, slumped on the wooden board, shuddering but unable to stop my tears. I wished I could stand up, reach out to the monstrous body of the young woman and embrace it ... 'It's all right. I've learned to accept it,' Mitsuko said, and lifted me up in her arms. I was going to say, 'Don't accept it!' but the words wouldn't come out.

As the narrator contemplates the slugs in her sister's house that night, she says to them: 'You must have been soldiers. You come here every night because you have something you want to say. Can't you ever rest in peace?' But there is no peace for the survivors of the bomb.

The final story in the book, 'The Rite', by Hiroko Takeishi, gives perhaps the clearest insight into this restlessness, this failure to find peace. Aki is pursued by nightmares. Though to all appearances she takes part normally in life, repeatedly she, too, is haunted by the consequences of the bomb. She visits Tomiko, and noticing that she is pregnant finally nerves herself to ask, 'When is it?' Tomiko tries to assert confidence in this, her third pregnancy, in spite of the two small jars on the Buddha altar, containing 'fetuses that had miscarried'. But at the question 'the light had gone out of Tomiko's face', and Aki feels 'as if she had suddenly been thrown into the middle of a thicket of prickly cactus', with no way of escape. The image of 'all those miscarried babies', and her subsequent visits to another friend, Setsuko, who is dying of cancer, hem her in like the cactus thicket, with visions of endlessly varied funeral rites.

> There are caskets in hearses that glide gently forward, followed by the long chain of the funeral procession, and there are coffins dragged along on screeching pushcarts, tied down roughly with a common rope. There are people who gouge out the viscera of their dead and then wait upon the mountains for the birds, and there are people who scale precipices, their dead stuffed into leather bags upon their backs. There are secluded tombs away at the far end of well-kept avenues of

approach flanked with statues of lions and camels and of elephants, while by the shores of northern seas, are graves marked only by the native rocks forever lashed by stormy waves.

There are all kinds of rites to go with death.

But what haunts Aki, and has prevented her from being able to come to terms with life after the bomb, has been the instantaneous disintegration of so many of her friends, leaving no possibility of proper funeral rites for them.

Aki has never seen Kazue's dead body.

Nor Emiko's dead body.

No, nor Ikuko's.

Nor has she ever come across anyone else who witnessed their end or verified the deaths of Junko or Kiyoko or Kazue or Yayoi.

This has made it impossible for her to accept the reality of their deaths. She continues to feel, against all her knowledge of what has really happened, that 'one of these days, surely, she'd meet Junko. Maybe she'll run into someone who has news of Kazue!' So she lives almost in a state of suspended animation, waiting.

If the dead, as they say, are never truly dead and will not rest in peace until the appropriate rites of mourning are performed for them, then the deaths of Junko and of Kiyoko and Kazue are not, so to speak, fully accomplished.

Yet even while at one level she is refusing to accept these deaths, the ever-present memory of 'the great flash, the big bang, the squall of wind', and the scene of devastation that followed fills her 'with the dread premonition' that the tall buildings she now sees around her will suddenly disintegrate, too, in a nightmare repetition of the original disaster. Life has, for her, become permanently threatened. She feels that if only she could identify the real enemy, 'and fling the fullness of my anger and hate at it', she would find relief from her torment. But she cannot, and her nightmare of disintegration affects also her vision of the man she loves. She sees him, too, 'hideously changed beyond all recognition', and cannot live with this 'dread awareness' of the death that must overtake both of them, the 'terror of being sucked into that void that blocks out the light and of falling down, down into that black abyss.' Amid the ordinary everyday scenes she witnesses or in which she joins, calmly enough on the surface, Aki's capacity for living free from the nightmare of the bomb has gone forever.

The stories in this book are varied, with humour, warmth, compassion, as well as fear, tragedy and pain. But they all tell the same story, of the incredible inhumanity of the atom bombs, of perma-nent, persisting emotional and physical scars left upon their victims, and of the urgency of their message now 'as the threat of nuclear war increases with each new task force dispatched to a tropical sea, with each Cruise or Pershing missile implanted in Europe', as Wilfred Burchett remarks in his book, *Shadows of Hiroshima*.

What emerges also from many of these stories and accounts is the continuing inhumanity towards the victims of the bomb, the *hibakusha*. There were indeed many individual Americans and Japanese, doctors, surgeons, nurses, journalists, writers and con-cerned members of the public who worked tirelessly to give them what help they could. According to Wilfred Burchett, however, the first foreign journalist to enter Hiroshima after the explosion, the American authorities tried from the beginning to prevent the world from learning of the severity of the damage done to people as well as to buildings. In *Shadows of Hiroshima* Burchett tells of the difficulties put in his way when he attempted to send accurate reports of what he had seen to the *Daily Express* in London. In the end, he tells us, General MacArthur effectively 'banned reporting on what had happened in Hiroshima and Nagasaki'. Burchett ends his book by saying:

> We should never cease to meditate on the fact that there has already occurred a first nuclear war, and, because of this precedent, there is little reason to doubt the possibility of a second ... On the other hand, Hiroshima also represents the indestructibility of human resistance. Despite their ordeals, the cover-ups, even the ostracism from 'normal' society, the *hibakusha* survivors have fought back, becoming the most stalwart and militant of peaceniks. Through them and their on-going struggle, the *urgency* of Hiroshima is transmitted to all of us.

It is also important to remember that the *hibakusha* will not be with us forever; their number diminishes daily. It is therefore incumbent upon the rest of us to keep alive the memory of what happened to them, and to take up with the same determination the struggle to ensure that such terrible suffering and destruction can never happen again.

In *Over Our Dead Bodies*, Dorothy Thompson's collection of 'informed argument, personal accounts, poetry and polemic' written by women against the bomb, Bel Mooney reminds us:

> The philosophy we are forced to live by – that there could well be justi-fication for wiping out millions of our fellow-humans – has no place in civilisation ... That is the power of the nuclear bomb – to pollute our atmosphere, our language, our minds and our souls.

It is clear that in a century which has already seen the gas chambers, the massive bombings of civilians by 'conventional' forces, the destruction of two non-military Japanese cities by atomic bombs, and an escalation of terror and violence threatened and committed by governments as well as by individuals, the 'pollution' of which Bel Mooney speaks has reached nightmarish proportions. The need therefore to summon all our resources against the acceptance of a nuclear arsenal and with it the possibility of a future nuclear war remains as pressing as on the day when the first outcry and protests were heard against the dropping of 'Little Boy' on Hiroshima and 'Fat Man' on Nagasaki.

9
Fighting Back and the Challenge of Conscience

In 1739 Anna Laetitia Barbauld wrote: 'When we pay our army and our navy estimates, let us set down – so much for killing, so much for maiming, so much for making widows and orphans ... We shall by this means know what we have paid our money for.' (Quoted in *My Country is the Whole World*, an anthology assembled by the Cambridge Women's Peace Collective.) The twentieth century has been notable for the struggle of conscience between those men and women who, though normally pacific, have nevertheless decided to take an active part in war or in advocating a build-up of conventional or nuclear arms, and those who refuse under any circumstances to countenance war or preparation for war. This problem and its challenge to the individual conscience of conscripts has been the theme of several of the novels and memoirs of the First and Second World War already discussed in earlier chapters.

But the Spanish Civil War, which broke out in the 1930s, attracted to its ranks many young men and women from outside Spain who were not subject to conscription, but decided to join in the conflict as volunteers. In *The Freedom Tree* (for readers from 13 to 15), James Watson tells of one such group who travelled illegally to Spain to fight on the Republican side against Franco, and engages with the problems of conscience which impelled them to the fight but continued to beset them at the battlefront. Watson explains: 'In Europe the shadows of military tyranny had lengthened. Hitler had achieved total power in Germany. He had destroyed parliamentary government, liquidated his opponents and started to build the infamous concentration camps.'

The young men of Watson's story saw in the Spanish conflict a chance to fight this fascist tyranny. His hero, Will Viljoen, dreamed of joining the battle because his mother had been Spanish, and his father had died in Spain fighting for the Republican cause. Will, together with a chance acquaintance, Griff, joins 'Candy' Sam who is taking a group of volunteers to Spain in an armoured truck full of guns and ammunition. Griff is,

139

in many ways, a contrast and a foil to Will. He joins the expedition mainly to escape the police, and because he is a lively, rebellious Cockney lad avid for adventure. Will on the other hand is idealistic, readily moved by cruelty and injustice, and reacts strongly to the picture of their fascist enemies which Sam paints as he sets them to bayonet practice.

> Sam gave the sandbags another vicious swing. 'Our enemies, lads. In Seville they slaughtered nine thousand men, women and children. They stacked their bodies in the streets and cemeteries. And for extra fun, they went round the poor quarters lobbing grenades through house windows.'
> Will closed his eyes. As Sam described them, he saw scenes of merciless cruelty, of Fascist machine-guns cutting down innocent and helpless civilians, continuing into the night illuminated by searchlights; of hundreds made to dig their own graves before being murdered; of many buried alive.

So Will takes part enthusiastically in the training. But when he is confronted with the reality of killing, he knows that in spite of his firm belief in the justice of his cause, he will never make a soldier. 'The enemy soldier lay belly down ... He was as terrified as Will – and as young: wan-faced, pop-eyed, immovable as though his limbs had been driven into the ground with wooden stakes.' Will cannot fire at him; it is Griff, who had had no ideological reason for entering the war, who kills the boy. Will is horror-stricken and nauseated by this death, 'sixteen years of caring and loving and feeding ... turned, in a single moment, to cold flesh ...'

> His mind had never prepared itself for this. It had imagined other, nobler pictures – all shattered ...
> He took out his pistol. He handed it to Sam once they had climbed to safety in the Republican lines. 'Give it to somebody else, please. I want none of it.'

So Will's future contribution to the cause is as a stretcher bearer only.

He becomes hardened to the constant danger, 'the menace of bullets no longer worried him', and he develops 'not so much courage as cold nerve' which is to stand him in good stead in recovering casualties under fire. Gradually he discovers also the deep comradeship which had been so striking in the trenches during the First World War – and with it a new fear, for his friends' lives.

But though Will fervently endorses the reasons for fighting presented in his dead father's letters and by his various friends in the

Seven Bells Brigade, his further experiences on the battlefield – bringing in the wounded, or having to abandon them; seeing his friends die one by one until only he and Sam's sister, Molly, are left; experiencing the nightmare of capture and the execution of Sam and Frederico – only confirm his resolve. 'He wanted none of this war. He had had enough. There must be other ways to win justice, protect liberty.'

Then comes the raid on Guernica, which is worse than anything he has experienced before; worse even than seeing his friends die, 'stagger and fall in blood'.

> They watched the bombs fall in a single, streaming cascade. They saw whole streets shudder with the impact of high explosives. Houses split in two, lifted from their foundations. Great walls keeled over into the streets. Solid bricks and stone disintegrated. Plumes of black smoke shot upwards through the jagged ruins ...
>
> The trenches held no terror like this terror. In the trenches you could duck, hide, be confident in the protection offered by mother earth. This was a new kind of war, no longer soldiers against soldiers, but the deliberate extermination of civilians. And Will wondered, when solid stone could resist attack no better than a sandcastle survives the lapping sea, what future was there for man?

After the bombers came the Heinkels, completing the extermination of young and old with machine-gun fire. But what finally breaks Will is his own failure to save a toddler, who is killed not ten paces from him. He fires frantically at the Heinkel until his pistol is empty, for the first time intending to kill, his initial scruples evaporating in the anguish of the moment. This is a crisis point in the novel, epitomising the struggle of conscience of those who hate war.

The author underlines this conflict of convictions in an historical note which says:

> Edmund Burke, the English philosopher, wrote: 'All that is necessary for evil to thrive is that good men do nothing about it.' For such a belief, men left their jobs, their families, their homes, to fight and die in Spain. If Fate had granted them victory, all that followed might have been averted.

The Freedom Tree firmly links the injustices and horror of the Spanish Civil War to the disregard for human suffering which led finally to the Hunger Marches in Britain; the poverty, unemployment and suffering throughout Europe which followed the First World War; the rise of fascism and the failure of the rest of the world to fight back before fascism had grown strong enough to unleash the horrors of the Second World War and the concentration camps upon Europe. But it also examines, thoughtfully, the way in which Will's own initial impulse to 'fight back' conflicts with his natural revulsion to killing.

A similar revulsion was experienced in real life but in a different context by Kitty Hart, when, as she tells us in *Return to Auschwitz*, she found herself unable to take revenge on those who had acquiesced in her persecution. She and her fellow survivors went on the rampage through Slazwedel, their anger at the appalling things they had been made to do and suffer leaving them few scruples about destroying German property – but, she was to discover, it was a different matter when it came to destroying German life.

> In the semi-darkness I could make out a huddle of people in one corner: an elderly man and woman, a younger woman, and two little girls.
> 'Kill them,' my friends were screaming. 'Go on, kill them.'
> I gripped the knife and moved towards them.
> The little girl was howling with terror. As I got used to the gloom of the basement I found that looking into her eyes was no different from looking into the eyes of doomed children in Auschwitz. But this one was German.

Recognition of the child's common humanity with the doomed Auschwitz victims holds Kitty's hand, but she also realises that, as Arnold understood in *War Without Friends*, if she killed this child she would be imitating the evil actions of the SS.

Facing up to this central question of a specific capacity to kill, either as a moral problem to be confronted before consenting to engage in war, or in its practical dimension when the enemy is actually there in front of you, is one of the most difficult problems to resolve. In *Women in War*, a book of firsthand accounts of women's experiences in wars from the Second World War to El Salvador, Shelley Saywell writes:

> I travelled throughout the [USSR] and interviewed women who had served in many different capacities, from partisan to bomber pilot. Most of them wanted to talk not about themselves but about the war and its effect on the country, on civilians – to give me some sense of the scale of destruction and loss of life. When I asked about their personal experiences they showed a modesty that is frustrating to an interviewer, yet endearing. Simply, they fought out of necessity ... The women I expected to meet, the tough, hardened individuals who had fought in trenches alongside men, simply did not appear. Instead I met women whose passions and sensitivities reflected a real horror of war, who cried through much of our time together and who remembered death, not glory.

Some of these women 'spoke of the brutalization, the numbing effect of the war on their personalities', but one woman remarked: 'War requires the ability to kill, among other skills. But I don't think you should equate killing with cruelty. I think the risks we took and the sacrifices we made for each other made us kinder rather than cruel.' Another said: 'I heard men say that the first killing is very difficult emotionally, but after that it becomes automatic. I never felt that way. Each day, with every death, I went through hell. It never became automatic or instinctual for me.'

In *Greenham Women Everywhere* Alice Cook and Gwyn Kirk explain their belief that the willingness to take part in war on the one hand, or to refuse to have any part in it on the other, assumes two totally different attitudes to the purpose, meaning and value of life:

> People assume that violence is a central part of human nature, or that because there has always been violence there always will be ... Nonviolent confrontation assumes that nonviolence is at least as accessible ... a part of human nature as violence is ... Nonviolence, far from being weak, actually feels very strong to participate in.

They feel, moreover:

> Nonviolence is not just the absence of violence or simply a tactic, but a total approach to living, both an ideal to live for and a strategy for change. We cannot achieve peace through violence. It is a fundamental contradiction in terms. Means and ends merge into one another and cannot be separated, so that *anything won by violence has the seeds of that violence contained within it.* [my italics]

For people who think this way, participation in war becomes an impossibility.

In *Challenge of Conscience* Denis Hayes, himself a conscientious objector, has written a careful, sober and dispassionate account of the various religious, political or humanitarian positions taken up by different COs, and defends both their right to act in accordance with their views and their moral and physical courage. Many of them, he tells us, willingly faced danger in air raids or at the front as fire-fighters or in ambulance units or in other non-combatant roles. In *Troublesome People*, Caroline Moorehead has also written about the experiences of COs from 1916 to 1986.

These people, however, are represented in only a few novels or memoirs, and even in these their position and problems are rarely given a satisfactory presentation. It is easier, naturally, to write of the excitements of war than of the problems of conscientious objectors. As Hardy comments: 'War makes rattling good history, but peace is poor reading.'

In *The Lost Voices of World War I* (edited by Tim Cross), Robert Wohl remarks:

> The war experience, then, was terrifying, dehumanizing, demeaning and in sharp and ironic contrast to the heroic images of war that had circulated before 1914 and that continued to be current behind the lines. 'Glory'... was hard to come by on the Western Front ... Yet even in the midst of this industrialized hell, intellectuals and artists discovered values they admired. Among these were manliness and comradeship ... [which] could be exhilarating. So could the submergence of the self into a tightly-disciplined mass.

And these, indeed, are the aspects of war traditionally given more emphasis in fiction and memoirs than the less evidently 'exhilarating' or 'heroic' trials of conscientious objectors.

Pat Mayhew is one of the few COs of the Second World War who recorded his experiences as they occurred. They appear in a collection of family letters, *One Family's War*, which he edited and published in 1987. He registered as a Christian pacifist at the beginning of the war, but decided nevertheless to serve in a position of danger first in the Auxiliary Fire Service, and later in the Royal Army Medical Corps in France. He received the Military Medal for his courage under fire with the ambulance unit during the evacuation of Dunkirk. But in the end he abandoned his pacifism, and on 23 June 1940 applied for a commission as a combatant. He had seen the carnage on the beaches at Dunkirk as the Messerschmitts relentlessly machine-gunned the escaping troops and the small boats and destroyers that were desperately seeking to rescue them, and had become concerned lest he was adopting a 'holier than thou' stance, whilst accepting the 'less holy' war efforts of others to keep him safe and 'protect all his other beliefs'.

Indeed, this thought troubled many COs in real life and in fiction. In *The Dolphin Crossing*, a novel for younger readers by Jill Paton Walsh, it was a dilemma which arose both for John Aston, the 17-year-old hero, and for his elder brother, Andrew. Andrew – a shadowy figure uneasily in the background of the story – has registered as a CO, an action with which John has little sympathy. So he finds it difficult to know what to say when Pat, an evacuee whom John befriends, clearly shows his contempt for 'Conchies'.

> '*This is where I say "Every man has a right to follow his own conscience",*' thought John desperately. He bit his lip and said nothing ... At last [Pat] said, 'You one of them too?'
> 'No, no I'm not. I'm going into the navy as soon as I can.'
> 'It'll be the army for me. That's all right then. I wouldn't take help from one of those.'

No more is said. John has no wish to defend his brother.

The evacuation of Dunkirk is a central episode in *The Dolphin Crossing*, bringing Pat and John into the same sphere of danger and heroism which had proved a crisis point for Pat Mayhew. The two boys set sail crazily in a small boat on their own to save as many soldiers from the Dunkirk beaches as they can. There is a graphic account of the frantic crossing, the desperate, weary and defeated crowds of men waiting quietly to be taken off to the waiting destroyers, the machine-gunning and bombing by enemy planes, the agony of refusing room to yet one more badly wounded survivor, and the final trauma when, after their day's hard work and danger, they realise that most of the men they had saved had been drowned when the destroyer was sunk before it could make for home.

It must have been a U-boat. John thought of the men in the U-boat looking into their instruments, carefully taking aim, hitting, sinking, killing. He hated them. He imagined being able to revenge himself, with savage pleasure he thought of kicking them in the face, breaking arms, letting rip with the machine gun, watching pain and blood. Then his frantic train of thought stumbled and stopped. Andrew said, 'You can only kill a man if you hate him first. And it is always wicked to hate.' Well this was hate. Now he knew what it felt like he realised he had never hated before. The cool, carefully measured tones of Andrew's voice crossed his mind like a subtitle to a picture of himself, hitting a German face with the butt of a pistol. 'However wicked someone is, when you hate him you make yourself as bad as he is, or worse.' *I am wicked to feel like this*, thought John.

But John does not really believe that his hatred is wicked. Instead, his rage against the crew of the U-boat flares up to encompass his elder brother also, whom he now sees 'sitting comfortably at home, talking holy like a saint. He doesn't have to see this. How the hell would he feel, if this happened to him? I'd like to see him trying his ruddy forgiving!'

It does not occur to John, or, presumably, to the author, that when he joins the navy he, too, may be required to take careful aim, 'hitting, sinking, killing'; or that this is precisely why Andrew has refused to take up arms. But Andrew's 'measured' pacifism in no way stirs the imagination like the tense and gripping drama of the two boys' journey across the Channel to the rescue of the British Expeditionary Force. Nor is there any adequate or sympathetic exploration of his beliefs to help the reader to understand or respect his position, or to assess and discuss the attitudes expressed towards him by both John and the impetuous and rashly 'heroic' Pat. This is a pity, since *The Dolphin Crossing* is a stirring story of adventure and courage, and one which could have engaged more trenchantly also with this important issue.

There are no COs in Hester Burton's story, *In Spite of All Terror*, but the reader is confronted nevertheless with the problems of conscience and choice aroused by war. When the 15-year-old orphan Liz is evacuated from London to live with the family of the old, retired Brigadier-General Sir Rollo Bruton she finds herself in the middle of a family row. For in spite of their military background, the Brutons are not anxious to allow their eldest son, Simon, to rush off to join the RAF. For them, and in the event for Liz, too, it seems a senseless waste of Simon's ability, and of his ambition to become a doctor and save lives instead of taking them.

> There was no doubt in her mind of the horror to come; of gas attacks; bombs; destruction; death. For three years now she had sat once a month in the ninepenny seats at the Plaza cinema watching the bombs fall on Barcelona, Guernica, and Madrid, and hearing the madman shouts of the German nation as it roared *Sieg Heil! Sieg Heil!* at the Nazi rallies. She had seen the jackboots marching into Vienna, into the Suedetenland, into Prague. And now, this morning, they were on the march again – over the Polish border on the road to Warsaw. A great evil was abroad in the world. Something that sickened and frightened her. Something that had to be withstood.
>
> And then, wretchedly, she thought of the people she knew who had to go out into Europe and fight this evil. Young Jim Bagshaw from the turning. And Naomi's brother, Abe. And then she thought again ... of the gentle, unwarlike Simon with his long, thin hands and face.

This highlights the dilemma which faced all thinking people: could the evil of the Nazi jackboot only be resolved by the twin evil of bright, sensitive young men taking up guns and bombs in answering destruction?

When Simon returns home on embarkation leave after three months in the army, Liz notes that the anxiety has left his face: he looked 'happy, brown and well'. But it is his 'long, gentle, unwarlike face' that haunts her during the agonising weeks when he is posted missing. Though we are thus made vividly aware of Simon's special character, we are unfortunately not told what effect his subsequent experiences had on him. Was he, in the event, sustained by his belief that he was 'doing something useful to win the war'; and – unlike Wilfred Owen – able therefore to blot out from his consciousness the knowledge of having caused the deaths of young men in the enemy lines whose real vocation, like his own, was saving life not taking it?

Simon went to war to defeat the evil of fascism. There were

Germans, too, who were opposed to fascism, and yet volunteered to join the army as soon as they were of age. In his autobiographical novel, *I Was There*, Hans Peter Richter examines some of their motives. His friend Gunther's father, the narrator tells us, was totally opposed to Hitler's regime. Yet in the end he finds himself supervising Russian prisoners of war, and supporting the war effort. His compassion towards the prisoners, and his condemnation of the way they are treated is as forcefully expressed as ever, but yet it leads him to a determination that Germany *must* win the war. He says:

> 'God have mercy on us if we should lose this war ... If they ask us to account for everything we have done to them [the POWs], then ... I don't dare to think it through ... We mustn't lose this war! Not at any price. If they'd take me, I'd go to the front again! We must win!'

When the narrator remarks, surprised, 'But you were always against war', he answers: 'For me it hasn't been a question of war or Hitler for a long time now! ... If we lose this war, we lose Germany. And that's why we must be victorious!'

For him, love for the Fatherland, in spite of its present unacceptable position, is stronger than all other considerations; and this instinctive feeling for one's own country is always, one must recognise, a powerful persuasion to join in fighting its enemies, no matter how unjust the cause or distasteful the killing may seem.

Yet whatever the motivation, war must have a profound effect upon those who take part in the action. In his autobiographical *Argument of Kings* Vernon Scannell describes the 'dehumanising' effect of war upon a sensitive personality. (Though he uses a third person narrative, John Vernon Bain, the name of his central character, was his own name before he changed it to Scannell whilst on the run from the military police.) He writes:

> Once he was out of hospital blues and back into khaki he seemed to put on, with the uniform, a change or reversion of personality. He was drawn back into the harsh and brutalising ambience of barrack-room and camp. Hospital life soon seemed as remote and idyllic as his civilian existence and he felt the tough rind of deliberate insensitivity growing over the areas of feeling which had begun to reawaken while he was in Winwick. He spent what little money he received on drink and tobacco and he often became violent when he was drunk.

This army personality is far removed from the John Bain of the beginning of his account. Then he was still capable of deep shock at the sight of the dead bodies of the Seaforth Highlanders, whom he had seen only a few hours earlier marching to their deaths on the ridge they had been detailed to defend. It is his state of shock at this and at the sight of his own comrades 'bending over them, sometimes turning them with an indifferent boot, before they removed watches, rings and what valuables they could find' which makes him turn and walk away from the scene.

> All he cared about was moving back, away from where the dead Seaforths were disposed on the sand and rocks in their last abandonment, in their terrible cancellations, their sad mockery of the living. And he saw again the living themselves, his comrades, moving among the corpses, settling on their prey like vultures or jackals.

When, later, he tries to recall this event, and analyse what had made him desert his comrades 'in a forward position', he concedes to himself there might have been some elements of fear for his own mortality, but concludes:

> Cowardice did not seem to have anything to do with what had occurred. He had been afraid often enough to know that what he felt at Wadi Akarit was not fear, or not the kind of fear he could recognise. What he had felt was a kind of hopeless disgust, disgust with his comrades who were looting the corpses, with the lunacy of war, with his own impotence.

Nevertheless, throughout his subsequent imprisonment, he seems haunted by the fear that he may indeed be a coward and by a consequent need to prove to himself that it was not cowardice which had led him to walk away from the fight. In the context of the appallingly sadistic military prison – which reminds one of the concentration camps of Nazi Germany – these fears seem reasonable enough. Still, when Bain is eventually released so that he may be sent to the second front as cannon fodder, his main anxiety is to 'find out if those bastards in the nick were right or wrong'. Is he really a coward?

Once at the front he sees real fear, as Denham, the cocksure young 'macho' man crumples into a 'quivering and sobbing wreck'. As he watches the boy's 'shameless surrender to his terror' he felt 'a faint but positive echo of the cook's unequivocal contempt and vicious dismissiveness, even a stab of sadistic hatred'; but he also admits to 'an intolerable suspicion that he was witnessing something of himself, that he was somehow implicated and had been forced to accept the shame that Denham had moved beyond'.

It is worth considering the true implications of Bain's continuing anguish about 'courage' or 'cowardice', and what is here meant by these terms, what in fact is being asked of these young men. Scannell himself says in his Prefatory Note: 'I hope, too, that it might throw a little light on the nature of human courage and its lack and the terrible uses to which the young are put when the last argument of kings pursues its loud and murderous course.'

Even while questioning the ethos which makes acceptance of the unacceptable possible for the young and sensitive, like Simon in Hester Burton's novel, or Scannell, one must also recognise that anger and hatred at atrocities committed by the enemy arouse desire for retaliation in kind even from normally kindly people. It was in a situation of extreme anger that Kitty Hart could make her abortive attempt to kill; and it is in a similar situation that the young Jewish violinist, Motele, in Yuri Suhl's novel, *Uncle Misha's Partisans*, makes up his mind to take part in the violence of war, and avenge the deaths of his parents and his sister, Basha. He joins the partisans in the forest somewhere in Poland, manages to secrete explosives in his violin case, and finally blows up the Officers' House. He waits carefully to make sure none but the German officers are still in the house before lighting the fuse – even in his overwhelming desire for revenge he is not careless of innocent life.

> Could ten minutes be that long? He thought it would never happen when the first blast came and shook the ground beneath him. A flash of light streaked the sky like lightning. Then another and another. He ran without being aware that he was touching the ground. He was flying through the streets. He shot a backward glance and saw a roaring Gehenna behind him. He heard sirens whining in the distance but was not afraid. Their sound seemed to lend strength to his legs and breath to his lungs. Another street ... another blast ... another alley ... another blast ... 'Basha! Basha! Can you hear it?'... The burning Officers' House lighted up the sky like a giant torch. 'That's some candle you lit there,' Yoshke said, pulling Motele close to him.
>
> 'A *yahrtzeit* candle for our dead,' one of the partisans added.

Motele's hatred has been roused by what he has seen of enemy action and by their massacre of his own family: his desire for revenge is wholly understandable. It is left to the reader to feel a sense of horror at this young boy's satisfaction as he sees the enemy blown to smithereens by his efforts. His corruption to such violence at the tender age of twelve reinforces our sense of the cruelty bred by war, and, at the same time, of the agonising moral dilemma it poses.

Hatred and anger, though part of all war novels or memoirs, nevertheless can in the end give way to a sickening revulsion from killing. *If Not Now, When?*, by Primo Levi, is the story of another group of partisans active in Poland. But though Levi had as good cause as Kitty Hart to seek revenge, we are aware from the beginning of the story that killing is regarded as a cruel necessity, not to be shirked if it has to be done, but to be avoided where possible. This is not only because it brings reprisals on the local peasants, whose goodwill they need. Mendel, the main protagonist of the story, has thought very carefully about the question of killing. He knew that:

> A soldier of the Red Army – such as he was, and was proud of being – if he is missing must go underground and continue to fight. And at the same time he was tired of fighting: tired, empty, bereft of wife, village, friends.

When he first joins Ulybin's band of partisans he tells them:

> 'I was in the artillery, you know. It's not like having a rifle. You set up the piece, you aim, you fire, and you can't see a thing. When all goes well, you see the incoming rounds five or ten kilometres away. Who knows how many men have died at my hand? Maybe a thousand, maybe not even one ... It's like bomber planes; or when you pour acid into an anthill to kill ants: a hundred thousand ants die, and you don't feel anything.'

But, he explains, he still feels differently about killing at close quarters. After the Germans had forced the Jews in his village to dig a pit, had lined them up at its edge, and killed them all, men women and children, including Mendel's own wife, Mendel had decided that 'killing the Germans is something we cannot avoid'. But he still felt that in itself killing is 'bad', is 'horrible'.

Because he knows of his reservations, the partisan leader takes Mendel on an expedition and requires him to kill the Ukrainian spy they have captured in the forest.

> Ulybin handed the gun to Mendel, without saying a word.
> 'You want me to – ?' Mendel stammered.
> 'Go ahead, *yeshiva bucher*,' Ulybin said. 'He can't walk, and if they find him, he'll tell what he's seen. A spy never changes; he stays a spy.'
> Mendel felt a bitter saliva fill his mouth. He stepped back two paces, aimed carefully, and fired. 'Let's go,' Ulybin said. 'The foxes will take care of him.' Then he turned again to Mendel, illuminating him with the flashlight. 'Is it the first time? Don't think about it. It gets easy afterwards.'

Mendel accepts the necessity of this killing; but though he obeys Ulybin's order, understanding why he has been selected as executioner, he never becomes reconciled to it.

Gedaleh, leader of the Jewish partisans whom later Mendel joins, explains his point of view to the village mayor:

'As partisans, our war is different from the one the soldiers fight: ... we don't fight it at the front, but behind the enemy's back. And as Jews, we have a long road ahead of us. What would you do, Mayor, if you were alone, a thousand kilometers from your village, and you knew that your village, and the fields, and your family no longer existed?'

This is why, he says:

'We will fight until the end of the war, because we believe that making war is a bad thing, but that killing Nazis is the most just thing that can be done today on the face of the earth; and then we'll go to Palestine, and we'll try to build the house we've lost, and to start living again the way all other people live.'

Few of these Jewish partisans survived the war. Gedaleh, Mendel and a small group of the others gradually made their way through Germany towards Italy and their passage to Palestine. But first, for these few too, came their moment of revenge. In Neuhaus, near Dresden, they find German civilians defeated, confused, but still hostile to the Jews. Someone in the crowd shoots Black Rokhele, one of the women in the band. That evening she dies:

A woman, twenty years old, not even a combatant, a woman who had survived the ghetto and Treblinka, now killed in peacetime, treacherously, for no reason, by a German hand. A woman unarmed, hardworking, lighthearted, and carefree, the one who accepted everything and never complained, the only one who didn't know the paralysis of despair.

The band goes in furious determination to the Rathaus, where they kill all they find, ten hostages, they say, not only for Rokhele, but for 'the millions in Auschwitz'. But though he has taken part in the revenge killing, Mendel still says:

'Blood isn't paid for with blood. Blood is paid for with justice. Whoever shot Black R was an animal, and I don't want to become an animal. If the Germans killed with gas, must we kill all the Germans with gas? If the Germans killed ten for one, and we do the same as they, we'll become like them, and there will never be peace again.'
   Gedaleh intervened: 'Maybe you're right, Mendel. But then how do you explain the fact that now I feel better?'

Though Mendel admits that he, too, feels better, he does not concede his point. He continues to feel that the Germans also have suffered in the terrible raids on Dresden and elsewhere. Answering violence with violence may make one feel better, for a time, but it solves nothing. It leads only to further wars, never ending, as Edek, a lieutenant in the Polish Internal Army, had told them earlier, in 1944.

Mendel's own personal decision to accept the necessity for violence is reflected in 'The Song of the Partisan' from which Levi has taken the title of his novel. The question asked is pertinent to any of these deliberations on the rights and wrongs of reprisals or of answering aggression with aggression. It runs:

> If I'm not for myself, who will be for me?
> If not this way, how? If not now, when?

Levi ends his story on a mixed note of hope and despair. A baby is born to the young partisans Isidor and White Rokhele: but as his woman is struggling to give birth, Isidor is camped in the corridor of the hospital with four friends, all armed and threatening reprisals against the terrified nurse and the doctor if the baby dies. It is as though, after so many years spent in the wilderness, armed, fighting for his own right to live, Isidor has come to believe that weapons are the only answer.

The nurse eventually emerges with the newborn child. 'Male,' she says, 'like him!' But Mendel sees that the hospital staff have now turned their attention to a newspaper. It 'bore a very big headline, whose meaning he couldn't understand. The newspaper bore the date of Tuesday 7 August 1945 and carried the news of the first atomic bomb, dropped on Hiroshima'.

The child, their common hope for the future, has been born into the nuclear age.

This opens up a new dimension to the argument. We are no longer in a situation in which universal conscription is likely to pose problems for the individual conscience. Conventional wars will probably be small enough to be conducted largely by the regular armed forces, while the decision to drop nuclear bombs or fire long-range missiles is likely to be taken out of our hands in the future as it was in 1945. There will be few fingers required to press the buttons, and these will belong to the professionals.

This does not make conscience superfluous. In *One Family's War* Stephen Howarth wrote about the bombing of Berlin, 'It seems a hopeless mental exercise to try and draw a clear shining line through the fog and say "This side, the act of a Christian; that side, of a barbarian."' The truth of this has been clearly shown in all these books, and presents a dilemma which has been answered in different ways by different writers and their various protagonists. But however we seek to answer it, whether by killing or by refraining from killing, in the atomic age even more urgently than in the age of mechanised armies there is still no escaping the need for each one of us to make an informed decision about where we now stand. In *Challenge of Conscience* Hayes writes:

> The pioneers of the First World War laid the trail through the steadfastness of their suffering, the COs of the Second followed as best they could – will the torch be carried clear and steady through the perplexities of the aftermath to ages yet to come? A tremendous responsibility rests upon each one of us to renounce any natural diffidence and to witness fearlessly to the supreme relevance of conscience's challenge.

10

Anti-Nuclear

In spite of the recent revival of interest in the two World Wars, the agonies of conscience suffered both by participants and by COs may now seem remote to the concerns of today's teenagers. But for many young people the problems of nuclear power and the fear of nuclear war have an immediate and pressing interest. In a number of teenage novels anti-nuclear protest is a central theme, coupled usually with a strong story-line of family or peer-group relationships deployed in different ways and with varying degrees of success. These books can nevertheless provide a first step towards a more serious and informed discussion of the realities of the nuclear age.

Nuclear power and the nuclear deterrent are inextricably linked in the public mind: and with reason. It is becoming increasingly clear that nuclear energy is not the safe, cheap, alternative source of power we were led to believe it was in the 1950s; and that the pace and extent of its development owe more to the need to fuel nuclear warheads than to provide electric current for domestic and industrial use. The costs incurred in building, maintaining and, soon, in decommissioning nuclear power stations have so far outstripped expectation that now, at last, it has been admitted that they are not an attractive business proposition. More importantly, nuclear accidents (at Three Mile Island and at Chernobyl in particular), in calling attention to the seriousness of the damage sustained by people and by the environment both close to the affected plant and also at a distance from it, have alerted the public to a renewed sense of the danger to the entire world should nuclear conflict break out. The fact of Chernobyl, indeed, has been less easy to dismiss from public consciousness than the vaguer possibility of a nuclear war at some time in the future; for the accident at Chernobyl actually happened, and its consequences remain with us. The psychological and economic impact of this disaster both within and beyond the borders of the USSR has already led to a heightening of public concern for successful negotiations to reduce the world's nuclear arsenal.

The link between these two aspects of nuclear energy are apparent in various novels for children and adults, and are therefore discussed together in this chapter.

In *There Will Be a Next Time*, by Tony Drake, five youngsters celebrate the end of O-Level exams by organising a week-long sit-in in a 'nuclear shelter' constructed in the main square according to specifications set out in the newly issued civil defence booklet. The idea is to show how little real protection it could give in case of atomic attack, and to alert the general public to the futility of the nuclear deterrent, and the need for world-wide disarmament.

They are all reasonably sincere in their hostility to the bomb: but while Barney 'came from a home that was steeped in political activism', Karen 'went because Barney expected her to', Doug 'had been branded a rebel as far back as his infant school days and he saw no reason to change his attitude now', Jennie is a serious-minded, ardent CND supporter who 'believes in unilateral disarmament' and Skip is a Christian pacifist who, incidentally, is keen on Jennie. This variety enables Drake to suggest, skilfully, the mixture of (sometimes dubious) personal motives and sincere conviction which activates people in their behaviour.

Barney draws up a leaflet to hand out to passers-by, outlining some of the arguments against the bomb and asking for support in getting rid of all nuclear weapons, since 'only then can we begin to make the world safe from the holocaust that threatens us all if present policies are pursued'.

Many passers-by ignore the leaflet and the young protesters, some stop and talk, a few become aggressive, some cannot be taken seriously, but none offers any real challenge to the position the group has taken up. Only Lou, a footloose young man who 'travels the road' and has a good opinion of his own worldly-wise knowledgeability, begins to disturb Jennie's faith and judgement. But this is more through his personal attractions than the points he makes – there is little really informed or deep-rooted argument offered in the book, save perhaps for Skip's moral line that 'killing was wrong, and killing people by incinerating them in a nuclear war was the worst possible evil'. To this Lou responds simply by declaring that he doesn't agree: 'some things are worth dying for, and if they're worth dying for, they've got to be worth killing for too'.

Lou's own attitude to life does not, it must be said, incline the reader to suppose he would find many things 'worth dying for'. He has opted out of a conventional existence and lives by busking, working occasionally when nothing better turns up, but is not above turning a dishonest penny if the opportunity offers. He cheerfully scoffs at Jennie's life-style, and at her rather priggish attitude in hoping to save the world by living for a week in the shelter. His breezy dismissal of all this earnestness, coupled with his evident interest in her attractions quickly seduce Jenny into agreeing – for a short time – to desert the demonstration and go off with him to Devon.

Though this story succeeds in bringing the nuclear issue vividly to the attention of young readers, it nevertheless leaves the impression that, after all, those who persist in their protest are uselessly idealistic, and less interesting and exciting than those who turn their backs on it all, shrug off any responsibility, and get on with the 'real' business of living and loving while there is yet time. It is clearly a difficult subject to write about in a lively, compelling way, and Drake is not the only novelist who has found it hard to strike the right balance between maintaining interest in his characters and story and conveying a sufficiently serious approach to his theme.

Linda Hoy dedicated her book, *The Damned*, to 'my many friends and comrades, citizens of the People's Republic of South Yorkshire, who are working together for peace'. But she, too, evidently has little confidence in the power of her theme to appeal to the young without some leavening of excitement, and genuine peace-seekers must have reservations about the kind of excitement she introduces. For a subversive nucleus has penetrated into the local CND group, and is determined to take the movement over and steer them into using violence in their campaign for peace; even though, as Linda Hoy herself points out in small print tucked away at the front of the novel, such activities 'would not be condoned by the Campaign for Nuclear Disarmament or any other known peace organization'.

The narrator of this story, Chris Fieldsend, has been stirred into joining his local CND group by a film about 'what the effects would be if a nuclear bomb was dropped … in Britain'. Chris is a lively youngster, with a racy, initially attractive style of narration. But from the beginning we also see in him an unpleasant streak, revealed in his chauvinistic attitude to girls and in his casual remark, 'I like watching other people know they're beaten.' So it does not surprise us when he is readily seduced by DAMN, the group in favour of 'Direct Action Against the Missiles Now', and allows them to use him to further their attempts to subvert the peaceful protests of the other CND-ers. He joins them in a violent demonstration which ends in injury and arrests, and a sickening account of the group working over a prone policeman, while Chris watches with growing horror:

I stand motionless and stare as Mike, Trevor and Ralph take turns in kicking at the policeman's body. With every blow he shudders and cries out. He raises his right arm to ward off the blows, but Mike grabs hold of his wrist and holds it steady in the air to make space for the boots to kick and trample, thudding into his body. I stand transfixed.

The policeman is crying out loud for them to stop. He tries to curl up his body to protect himself, but Mike seizes his broken arm from underneath him and yanks it fiercely upwards, forcing the blue uniform into a straightened line for the kicks to hammer home. I catch a glimpse of the policeman's face – swollen, red and bleeding – before Mike smashes into it with his boot.

Ralph and Trevor have their heads down, aiming blows with precision, but Mike's face is clearly visible. His eyes are gloating. He looks elated, glowing with fervour and delight. Suddenly, I hate him.

Though Mike's enjoyment of violence certainly gives Chris pause, he is unable to break free from this gang, who engineer him into an uncomfortable position as accomplice in a cruel plot against Sarah, the girl Chris is becoming attached to.

Sarah, like Jenny in Drake's book, is serious about CND, but she is more attractive and, for the most part, less priggish than Drake's heroine. The daughter of an MP who is also a member of CND, she has more of the arguments at her finger tips, and puts up a good case for non-violence. But when she rejects Chris, with some justice, as a 'chauvinist ... playing soldiers and army with the other overgrown kids in DAMN', he decides to destroy and humiliate her as he had wished to humiliate his chess opponent at the beginning of the story, and becomes a willing participant in Mike's plan to attack her with physical violence and so force her to abandon her principles by fighting back.

If the coming confrontation were to be between Chris and Sarah alone, there is little doubt that the weak, easily influenced Chris would quickly crumple in front of her. But with the unspeakable Mike and Trevor waiting somewhere round the corner for their share in the action – and still with a hold over Chris – the outcome is not likely to be pretty. In the interests of a suspense-laden ending Linda Hoy does not tell us what happened next, or how far and in what ways Sarah's courage, determination and steadfast hold on the principle of non-violence really could enable her to 'win through in the end'. And this is a pity; since though the issues thus left unresolved could certainly provoke animated discussion, the impression left most strongly with the reader is once again that violence is more insidiously powerful – and makes livelier reading – than the movement towards peace.

The emphasis in Caroline Pitcher's brief story, *On the Wire*, is on Rosa's adventures in her desperate attempt to get her mother's film of the latest nuclear weapons safely into the hands of their friends, John and his wife, Madeleine, who is an investigative journalist. The scene is Britain in the 1990s. The government has recently pledged to dismantle Cruise missiles, but is, in fact, secretly installing new weapons at the base near the Peace Camp where Rosa and her mother have been celebrating. When her mother is arrested, the onus falls on Rosa to evade the police and other enemies and find a way to expose the government's duplicity. In spite of some unlikely episodes and characters, *On the Wire* is an eventful and skilful little story, which raises the issues of nuclear weapons for young readers without undue solemnity or polemic.

Though some of his characters are involved with the peace movement, James Watson's main concern in *Where Nobody Sees* is with nuclear waste. But he is more successful in solving the problem of maintaining a level of interest, excitement and tension without either making his characters seem unduly priggish or involving them in violence in ways which betray the principles of the movement they are supporting.

The story opens with a telling scene in which Luke is walking through the woods, quietly minding his own business, when he is suddenly accosted by two men, roughly challenging his right to be there. The strangers are guarding a newly fenced-off area, in which nuclear waste is being dumped illegally in old lead mines, with the connivance of the local MP who owns the land. The extent and secrecy of the operation, and the involvement of establishment figures in it are gradually revealed during the story; so also are the lengths to which they are prepared to go in order to suppress all legitimate protest.

This part of the action is linked, by chance, with the peace women on Greenham Common in the South of England. Among them is Luke's mother, who has deserted her family in a state of exasperation with both husband and son, whom she describes, crisply, as 'a couple of octogenarians in a geriatric ward'. Luke's mother, in many ways, is no more of an advertisement for the peace movement than Chris Fieldsend; yet her ruthlessness towards her husband, the 'bumbling red Reverend', and towards Luke himself does not discredit the Greenham Common protesters because it is seen in a larger context of conflicting, imperfect personalities, who yet have courage, sincerity and credibility.

Also at the Greenham camp are the Siren Sisters, a group of radical entertainers, and their young script-writer and dogsbody, Petra. It is she who makes the book come alive and helps to create its sense of irrepressible vitality. Petra is a Kent miner's daughter, and she 'has ways of making things happen' – nothing is quiet for long when she is around. She takes Luke in hand, and resolutely prevents him from evading the consequences of his chance discovery of illegal nuclear dumping. In spite of becoming deeply scared as the thugs set to work to suppress the two youngsters, Petra refuses to be silenced. She acts out the situation that Linda Hoy evaded in *The Damned*, not with answering violence but with unquenchable determination and with the weapon the author himself is using – the power of words. She produces a sketch for the town's carnival which will blow the secrecy and, with its fierce and pointed satire, rally local opposition to the dumpers.

The characters in this story and their uneasy, sometimes stormy relationships are vividly relevant to the theme. This includes an understanding of the human frailty which continues to permit the unpermissible to go on happening. As an important politician explains cynically to the director of the wealthy and powerful company behind the dumping operations, there is no need for him to panic over any possible disclosure of his activities. He need only 'sit tight' and 'deny everything'.

> 'In a month the issue of nuclear dumping will be cold potatoes. How long did Chernobyl stay in the news? Till Wimbledon, if that. There's nothing so safe as yesterday's news. Before the summer's over, there'll be an inner city riot or the announcement of a royal baby. Profits will flow as usual.'
>
> Rhodes smiled, though not amused. 'Some democracy you've got here.'
>
> 'It works, Charles.'

It works indeed, as Watson's book demonstrates, on human fallibility, stupidity, ignorance, greed and apathy.

Watson's story gets its message across because it is full of action, the characterisation is acute and subtle and the relationships at the heart of the story are convincing, poignant and relevant. At the same time it presents forcefully and more effectively than the other three books the arguments against our heedlessly dangerous nuclear age in all its aspects, including the ruthlessness and lies of those whose power and wealth are tied up with the nuclear industry.

The Watch on Patterick Fell, by Fay Sampson, is also a story about nuclear waste which involves fear and suspense, but does so without the excitement of disturbing scenes of violence. The story is told, this time, from the other side. Roger and Elspeth live in a high-powered scientific family, within sight of a Magnox power station, and near the fell where waste is being stored. Their father is an eminent nuclear physicist who is seeking to solve the problem of the safe disposal of nuclear waste, and Roger himself is hoping eventually to join in this work. Their mother is a bio-chemist at the research station, investigating the genetic effects of radiation upon living organisms.

But though Roger is initially wholly committed to nuclear power, he is conscious of the controversy surrounding it, and of the very different feelings of his younger sister, Elspeth, who is all too vividly aware of the dangers.

> 'I hate it,' said Elspeth fiercely. 'I hate living next-door to it, knowing that it could poison the whole country. Sometimes I'm even afraid to open my bedroom window in case some of it's floating about in the air.'

Although Roger takes every opportunity to scoff at Elspeth's 'unscientific' attitude, and to set her right on matters of 'scientific fact' and logic, she nevertheless has a number of perceptive comments to make throughout the story. She is acutely aware that 'scientists are human beings like the rest of us, not some special breed of supermen' – and it *is* human error which brings about the final catastrophe; she can be as quick as her brother to sense when her parents are concealing something important from their children, and more direct in challenging them; and it is she who perceives at the end the intolerable weight of responsibility her father has assumed. Though, as the trainee teacher, Colin, remarks, Roger and his parents tend to talk 'about Elspeth as though she was stupid, because she thinks in different patterns' from them, we are led in the end to agree with Colin that 'that doesn't make her a fool. Very far from it!'

Given Roger's own emotional involvement with his father's work, though, it is his gradually increasing worries about the safety of Patterick Fell which make the greatest impact. In the very first chapter, we become aware of his unease at the number of lorry-loads of nuclear waste relentlessly making their slow way up to the site.

> In his mind's eye he saw a picture of ports around the country. Of finned tanks of liquid waste swinging above the quayside. Of lorries, code-marked and discreetly escorted by the Nuclear Police, threading through city streets busy with mothers shopping, swinging round corners past home-going children, speeding out along the open roads towards the motorways where casual drivers flashed past unaware of the deadly consequences of a crash.

From his own observation of his accident-prone mother his imagination can also encompass Elspeth's infuriated comment on the fallibility of scientists; and the magnitude of the problem his father has set himself to solve.

Whatever happened to Britain, Patterick Fell must remain intact. The cooling ponds, the vast storage tanks, whatever devices Dad had designed to shield the radioactive waste, these must stand immune from harm even for thousands of years ... As long as there was no accident. No mistake. No attack by sabotage or war ...

In the end it is the danger of sabotage which wrecks Roger's sense of pride and security in his father's work. The story at this point does become exciting in a fairly conventional way, with edgy police, fears of hostage-taking and mysterious men 'shadowing' the children. But Elspeth's hysterical flight from all this, the desperate search for her over the fell, and the final explosion in the laboratory where Dr Lowman works are all both credible and telling. The final solution, the permanent exile of a group of dedicated scientists to a tiny island cleared of local inhabitants and filled instead with nuclear waste, is less credible, but effective in the message it contains of the waste of human lives and potential in a vain attempt to contain the uncontainable and solve the insoluble problem we have allowed ourselves to create for future generations.

The threat of possible sabotage to plant or disposal sites has been used in several novels for teenage readers. The casual introduction of nuclear waste dumping into *A Serpent's Tooth* may make this problem seem incidental to Robert Swindells's story; but it enables him to make several telling points which stir the reader's interest and conscience. Lucy Topham's father is a serious – indeed painfully solemn – hard-working careerist. But his wife, Margaret, is an independent-minded woman, not unlike Luke's mother in *Where Nobody Sees*. She has no intention of being merely an adjunct to her husband's life and career; she is an activist who throws herself into causes and committees. When the Nuclear Effluent Recycling and Disposal Services (appropriately known as NERDS) proposes to use the nearby Pit Field as a burying place for nuclear waste, she is in her element. She sets up a Greenham Common-type group of protesters, who lie in front of the NERDS lorries, and finally decide to live on the site in benders (makeshift tents which can quickly be erected or dismantled between police raids). This infuriates her narrow-minded, career-bent husband; but brings more serious disruption into Lucy's personal life. Lucy is now in 'no man's land' between her warring parents and deeply resentful towards them for what she feels to be a neglect of her real interests.

Her problems, fortunately, are resolved as she grows in maturity and becomes better able to place them in a wider context; to see, in fact, that 'maybe there aren't any goodies or baddies – just people, doing the best they know how and screwing other people up in the process'.

The person who contributes most to Lucy's growth in understanding is 'Daft Alice Hazelborne', an eccentric old woman whose dreams and visions connect the past use of Pit Field as a burial ground for the victims of the Black Death with the present intention to use it to bury nuclear waste. The central similarity between these two events lies in the 'burial', which is 'real' enough, but is also a symbol of the persistently stubborn refusal of people to believe the warnings and prophecies of those who can 'foresee' disaster. Alice explains that an ancestor of hers had tried in vain to warn the villagers of the coming of the Black Death. She was mocked and ignored and accused of being a witch. But when her Cassandra-like prophecies proved true, and 'hundreds died', this brought her no gratitude. She was hanged, for having 'brought the plague on the village with her magic'.

Like the people of that day, we are to understand, the villagers are once again hiding their heads in the sand and refusing to heed prophecies of the disaster which is certain to result if nuclear waste is buried in Pit Field along with the plague victims. It takes not only a nuclear catastrophe caused in France by terrorists, but also a more dubious outbreak of local hysteria over a suspected renewed outbreak of the plague to drive NERDS away from their intended burying ground. As Alice had repeatedly warned, 'Things don't cease to be, just because we hide them in the earth'. The fact that this seems more clearly relevant to the nuclear theme, where the dangers continue to be real enough for centuries to come, than to the possibility of any plague infection still concealed with its victims in the Field has to be accepted in the context of the story – the imagery used to connect the two serves its purpose in pointing the moral.

Monster in Our Midst by Peggy Woodford is an anti-nuclear power/waste story with a more conventional storyline – a mixture of fluctuating teenage relationships and family problems, with troubling examinations nagging in the background. At first the narrative lacks pace. The anti-nuclear propaganda is played out against news extracts about the Three Mile Island and Chernobyl disasters which have been placed at the head of each chapter; and is inserted, also, in the form of excerpts from physics lessons and speeches at anti-nuclear meetings sandwiched a little uncomfortably between the more ordinary everyday affairs of the teenage characters. About half-way through, however, the story takes off with a visit to the power station where the unpredictable Kathy lets off a stink-bomb, and devises various similar ploys to attract attention at demonstrations. As the commitment of the central character, Alan, to anti-nuclear protest becomes more closely interwoven with his personal life, and the reader's involvement in his fortunes develops, the nuclear issue also begins to take on life.

Undoubtedly, though, Joan Lingard in *The Guilty Party* is the more skilful storyteller. Her heroine, Josie, though also sharp-tongued and rebellious, is from the beginning a warmer, more likeable character than Kathy. Her passages-at-arms with her sour, self-righteous aunt and uncle and with her initially pro-nuclear boyfriend Rod have a sparkle which is lacking in *Monster in Our Midst*. This story is lighter in tone, with plenty of laughter and fun. Admittedly it is lighter in information, too; there is little attempt here at technical explanations of nuclear power. But it has its sombre and serious side in Josie's Belfast background and her prison experiences. Both through scenes of police confrontation (common to all these books) and through the prison episode Joan Lingard explores with her usual perception the way we treat dissidents in Britain today.

The explosion in *The Watch on Patterick Fell* was limited in scope and effect, and the sabotage occurring in *A Serpent's Tooth*, though a more serious affair, is given significance only for its effect upon the British protesters. Annabel and Edgar Johnson have tried to imagine in more detail the consequences of a real act of sabotage on a nuclear power station. In *Finders, Keepers*, a story which would appeal to readers of 14 or so, but also at an adult age-level, a suicidal terrorist crashes his plane, with a full load of dynamite on board, into the containment building of a power plant just outside Denver, Colorado. The narrator, 13-year-old Burr McKenna, his older sister, Alex, a motor-bike rider, Si, who joins them and Lorna, an elderly writer full of compassion and wisdom who is already dying of radiation sickness are the main characters in this story of panicstricken flight from the deadly cloud of radioactivity.

The story is tense and exciting, one of the best and most powerful of its kind, a compelling cautionary tale which creates an unforgettable picture of the hysteria, selfish greed and violence of modern society. Few of the people Burr encounters in his flight have any care for the lives and well-being of anyone but themselves. The story is, of course, entirely fictional – in a final note the authors say:

Denver has its dangers: the Rocky Mountain arsenal where, for years, nerve gas bombs were stacked beside the runway of one of the busiest airports in the country; the Rocky Flats nuclear weapons facility, dealing with plutonium, where a few years ago a fire almost caused a major catastrophe. Some miles to the north is the Fort St Vrain nuclear power installation. But the MECO plant in this story is a matter of pure fiction – we earnestly hope it will stay that way.

There have, of course, already been a number of accidents of varying degrees of seriousness within nuclear installations or involving nuclear weapons. One of the most serious and well publicised of these occurred at Chernobyl in the USSR on 26 April 1986, and had a profound effect upon public perception both of nuclear power and of the possible consequences of a nuclear war. In her recent (adult) novel *Accident*, Christa Wolf explores the implications of this event through the meditations of her narrator in the course of the day on which news of the disaster was first broadcast outside the USSR. It is also the day on which the narrator's brother is undergoing six-hour-long surgery for a brain tumour. As she pursues her everyday activities in house and garden, her own mind roams restlessly between the potentially deadly effect of radioactive particles in the plants or food she is handling, the progress of her brother's operation and the current state of the world. As she follows in imagination the progress of the surgeon's knife slicing through her brother's brain towards the tumour, delicately avoiding damage to sensitive tissues, she contemplates also the relationship between the brain's physical composition and the thoughts, emotions and personality it controls. This leads her to consider those individuals on whom the fate of the earth depends, in particular those concerned in nuclear discoveries, in the building and manning of power stations and in the development of nuclear weapons and strategies, and to deplore that hyperactive restlessness of the human brain which threatens to lead the entire world towards its destruction. She questions above all the nature of those at present engaged on the US 'Star Wars' programme. How, she asks, can 'highly gifted young men' allow themselves to be 'shackled' to their 'beloved computers' in an attempt to realise 'that fantasy of an America rendered totally secure through the relocation of future nuclear battles to outer space'?

Julia Voznesenskaya's thoughts on the Chernobyl disaster take, as might be expected, quite a different direction from the meditations of Christa Wolf's heroine. For whereas Christa Wolf is a powerful novelist from the East German Republic, Julia Voznesenskaya was born in Leningrad, imprisoned in the late 1970s and later, in 1980, exiled 'for her social and literary activities'. She now lives in Munich. Her novel, *The Star Chernobyl* (also for adults), centres round three sisters, the eldest a committed party member, the next a dissident and exile like the author, and the youngest married to a physicist at the Chernobyl plant. The story follows the anguish and desperate attempts of the two older sisters to discover what has happened to the youngest, Alenka, her husband, and her two small sons amid the welter of rumours, confusion and official secrecy which surround the incident.

This part of the story is moving and poignant, and reminds one of the confusion, separation of children from parents, official silences and bureaucracy attendant upon many other major disasters, in Hiroshima, the Marshall Islands and elsewhere. And the inclusion of extracts from radio broadcasts, press reports and political speeches made in the Soviet Union at the time lend an air of authenticity to the novel.

But readers of Arkady and Boris Strugatsky's science fiction novel, *Roadside Picnic*, will be struck by a family resemblance between the excursions of 'Stalker' Redrick Schuhart into The Zone with inexperienced companions and the episode in which Anastasia rashly persuades the young looter, Shlik, to take her into the forbidden 30-kilometre zone around Chernobyl; and this is a timely reminder that *The Star Chernobyl* is, after all, fiction, not reportage. This is particularly important since the author's own understandable bitterness against the Soviet Union has led her to relay, through her characters, all the current rumours and accusations, with little in the way of serious counterbalancing argument or proof. There is none of the wide-ranging meditation on the universality of the human condition which characterises Christa Wolf's novel. Voznesenskaya writes as though personal and national greed and aggression, corner-cutting and shoddy workmanship, endeavours to conceal the extent and nature of such disasters, bland reassurances to the anxious public that 'there is no cause for immediate alarm' or that 'it couldn't happen here, or again', or the overriding bureaucracy which always seems so cruelly impervious to individual needs and anxieties are unique to the Soviet Union. In this she does a disservice to the wider public outside the USSR, who also suffer from these ills, and for whom there is still no promise, even after the extent of the Chernobyl disaster and its after effects have been revealed, of a more alert pre-planning for immediate, effective and open action should such an event recur at a nuclear plant in the West.

For a discussion of these issues and of their undoubted relevance in the event of a nuclear war one has to turn to *Chernobyl: The Final Warning*, by Robert Peter Gale and Thomas Hauser. This book examines the scientific background both to the Chernobyl disaster and to nuclear power in general, including the nuclear weapons industry, and picks up many of the points made in the various books referred to in this chapter. It is also a chatty, personal account of Dr Gale's actual experiences in Moscow where he went to help with the victims of the disaster, and it paints a very different picture from Julia Voznesenskaya's novel. It outlines clearly the problems caused by the unexpectedness and scale of the disaster, but reflects also the concern and efficiency of the Moscow hospital, where many of the injured were sent, in dealing both with the victims and their relatives. Gale comments:

Overall, I'd say the Soviets responded well to the crisis. Clearly, their initial announcement regarding the accident was late in coming and they were fortunate that prevailing winds carried the radioactive plume away from population centres rather than towards Kiev. However, beyond that, they handled the situation reasonably well, particularly after they realised the rest of the world could be trusted to deal responsibly with the situation. Much of the credit for the generally constructive Soviet response goes to Mikhail Gorbachev. He has a flexibility and dynamism hitherto unknown in Soviet leaders, and his policies, while not without problems, offer hope for the future.

The final section of Gale's book was written in collaboration with Thomas Hauser, and is directed towards an assessment of the significance for the rest of the world of the Chernobyl disaster. Its most important lesson, they tell us, is to remind us that:

Once, if a hydro-electric dam burst on another continent, we could sit back and say, 'That's their problem'. But if a Soviet nuclear reactor explodes, it's our problem too. We have a substantial stake in how safely the Soviets manage their nuclear power programme; they have a comparable interest in ours; and we both have cause to be concerned with reactors in other countries, particularly in politically unstable and underdeveloped areas of the world.

For these are the areas where nuclear reactors are most vulnerable to sabotage, terrorism or war. And as the authors remark, 'In the end, we all live near Chernobyl.'

Gale and Hauser examine dispassionately the possibilities of such an accident occurring elsewhere, and list a truly frightening number of ways in which accident or deliberate sabotage could happen.

Our society has enormous faith in technology, but nuclear power systems stretch that faith to its boundaries. They're extraordinarily complex, with thousands of pumps, valves, pipes, circuits and motors. Problems can arise from errors in design, manufacture, installation, maintenance, operation and external sources like floods, fire, earthquakes and tornados. Corrosion, vibration, stress and simple deterioration can result in a single small defect. One defect can lead to another. The second can cause a third, which no computer can foresee or control.

To this formidable list must be added 'the most fallible component of any nuclear power plant – the men and women who operate it. People get tired; they have bad days; they act without thinking and make mistakes.' Or even, like the technician at the station in Arco, Idaho, in 1961, they may be under such psychological stress that they stage a 'murder-suicide' action and explosion within the control room. Also to be considered is the possibility of terrorist activity or war – even conventional weapons exploded over power stations could leave the surrounding area devastated. So Gale and Hauser ask pertinently how ready we all are to act decisively in the event of a major nuclear disaster near a large population centre.

> Evacuation requires moving people from high-risk to low-risk areas, using distance as a defence. The term implies an orderly planned exodus but, in the aftermath of a serious nuclear accident in the United States, and particularly near a large city there would more likely be panic and chaos.
>
> How do you evacuate? Who will run the buses and trains? Should children and pregnant women be moved first? What about hospital patients? Should medical personnel be asked to stay behind to care for the bedridden if the general population is moved? How do you empty a prison and control prisoners in the aftermath of a nuclear power plant accident?

These and many other questions, they warn us, still remain to be answered, in spite of the extraordinary courage shown on site after the Chernobyl explosion.

A cautionary tale on a different aspect of the nuclear scene is David Bischoff's *Wargames*, based on the successful American movie of the same name in which a young 'computer freak' sent the nation's defences into turmoil, and almost caused a Third World War by his rash ventures into computer wargames. For computer buffs this will be a fascinating story. Its disadvantage is that once the reader closes the book, the 'willing suspension of disbelief' which has kept him rivetted, almost inevitably gives way to the sense that 'this is only a story'. Nevertheless, the picture of the underground command post where grown men really are manning computers and playing out war fantasies for real is indeed as frightening as Christa Wolf's novel suggests. The most disturbing and realistic sections of the book are the chapters in which Jerry Hallorhan's nerve is being tested by a simulated exercise in which he thinks he is actually being required to press 'the button', and in which the top commanders face similar decisions 'for real'. With a place like this in existence, and men like these in charge – thoroughly credible portraits, given what we know from experience of two world wars of army commanders – how can we continue to rest easy in our beds?

The stories discussed in this chapter attempt to alert readers to the issues relevant to the nuclear age. They do this through direct involvement with movements or incidents actively opposing or calling into question current policies or attitudes towards existing nuclear arms or power. A number of stories have been inspired by actual events, some by accidents at nuclear power stations, the seriousness of which was kept from public knowledge until long after the event. Chernobyl has undoubtedly been the most alarming accident to date, since it led to the wholesale evacuation of people in its neighbourhood, to anxious checks on consequent radioactive contamination of large areas of Europe and Great Britain, and to fears that over the next 50 years as many as 50,000 more people world-wide may die of cancer as a result.

This alerted the general public, once again, to the fact that nuclear fall-out knows no geographical or ideological boundaries, and that, in addition to the dangers presented by the nuclear power industry, the making and deployment of nuclear weapons are also creating conditions in which disaster could occur. A disturbing study of this topic, *Nuclear Weapons Accidents – a Handbook*, was published in the spring of 1988 by the Bradford School of Peace Studies.

There is another aspect of the arms race which should also be considered. The Third Congress of International Physicians for the Prevention of Nuclear War, meeting at the Hague in June 1983, remarked:

> The cost of the arms race is not only the vast sums being diverted to armaments in a world where tens of thousands of human beings die each day of treatable diseases. The cost is also in the great psychological damage that is being done, particularly to young people and children who fear they will have no futures.

Some of the comments of such children are included in a section of Humphrey and Lifton's anthology, *In a Dark Time*. The editors have called this section 'There's a Nuclear War Going On Inside Me', quoting the words of an eleven-year-old from Massachusetts. How can we answer these anxieties; what comfort can we offer these young people, unless by sharing their fears and suggesting effective ways of making them heard?

Stories of nuclear protest will have a strong appeal for such children, who may look to find in them either reassurance or a spur to active protest on their own account. But they will also be attracted, though with mixed feelings, by those many novels now in existence which imaginatively create a vision of a future nuclear disaster, or of a world after a Third World War when nuclear bombs have finally been exploded upon this unheeding planet.

11

What Kind of Future?

The nuclear threat has inspired many and varied novels of warning or prophecy about what the future may hold. It is a vast subject, so individual authors concentrate on a few aspects only of a future nuclear conflict and its immediate or long-term consequences for life on this planet.

One of the best known of anti-nuclear-war fictions is *When the Wind Blows*, by Raymond Briggs, a picture book for readers of all ages. The story-line is simple enough. Jo Bloggs has retired. He spends much of his time reading the papers, while his wife spends hers cleaning and cooking. They are a typical, not very bright couple, entrenched in their rather ordinary lives and sex-roles as is revealed by a low-key strip cartoon dialogue. But Jo has brought home rumours of war, and their gentle nostalgic reminiscences of the last war are soon interrupted by news of an imminent nuclear attack. With simple faith they follow the County Council's inanely futile instructions for building and stocking an indoor shelter; but Briggs interleaves his account of their placid, unhurried preparations with large, frightening double-page illustrations of the missiles, bombers and submarines which are bringing the nuclear strike closer. As we laugh at their simplicity, we realise with growing horror that only a Jo Bloggs and his wife could for one moment suppose that such feeble preparations – or any preparations – could avert the disaster which is about to overtake them. We realise also that our superior knowledge and sophistication in nuclear matters has left us no better off. Why aren't we all screaming now? The message is precisely the one Tony Drake's youngsters were seeking to get across to the unheeding public in *There Will Be a Next Time*; but how much more effective is this devastating picture book, its stark, fearful message uncluttered by teenage love-interest and petty in-fighting!

By the end of Briggs's book we know that Jo Bloggs and his wife will die. But will there be *any* survivors?

Nevil Shute answers this question in the negative in his novel *On the Beach*, which was hailed when it appeared in 1957 as his most important novel so far. It is set in the most southerly tip of Australia, not far from Melbourne, one of the last places to be afflicted by the cloud of nuclear dust which has gradually encircled the globe since an exchange of nuclear weapons in the northern hemisphere. The precise scenario for this war remains obscure; though the impression is given that there has been as much fumbling incompetence and panic as serious grounds for conflict, and that relatively 'minor' powers such as Egypt and Albania have helped to create some of the confusion. As in *Wargames*, this part of the 'message' fosters an uneasy sense of the irresponsibility of those who hold the world's fate in their hands. The main story, however, concerns some of the individuals waiting their turn to be affected by radiation sickness and die: Dwight Towers, the US naval commander; the Australian naval officer, Peter Holmes; his wife, Mary, and their baby daughter, Jennifer; Mary's friend, Moira Davidson, and the scientist, John Osborne.

Perhaps the most chilling aspect of the narrative is the way the survivors remain determined to the end to pursue their daily concerns in complete disregard of their knowledge that death is a few months away. Dwight Towers is detailed to make a final cruise in his submarine, *Scorpion*, to the western seaboard of USA, to see what he can discover about conditions there, with Peter Holmes on board as liaison officer, and John Osborne as the scientist who will try to calculate, as far as he can, how long it will take for the dust to reach Melbourne. Towers knows that he cannot allow his men to land, since everywhere will be too radioactive. He can only observe the seafronts through his periscope, take measurements of radioactivity, and maybe send one observer suitably protected to examine a station which still seems to be transmitting messages. Yet he persists in trying to find presents for the wife and two children who must now be dead. Similarly Mary refuses to face the possibility that she may have to kill her baby, or leave the child helplessly suffering after her own death. Instead she amuses herself with planning and planting her garden, though no one will be alive to see the fruits of her loving labours. Moira Davidson, who is drowning her sorrows in endless glasses of brandy, Sir Douglas Froude, who is steadily drinking his way through the club's vintage port to prevent its going to waste, and John Osborne, who intends to spend his final days recklessly racing in the last Australian Grand Prix, have a slightly different but no less bizarre, inappropriate and irresponsible attitude to a disaster of this magnitude. Peter Holmes seems the only one of the group more or less rational and farsighted in his preparations for the end.

The various ways in which these people turn away from what is inevitably going to happen reminds one of stories both of those Jews who refused to understand that the journeys they willingly undertook would end in the extermination camps, and of those Germans who also refused to know what was being done to former friends and neighbours by Hitler's government. It reflects the dangerous ostrich-like behaviour of all those who still suppose that a nuclear war could be fought and won.

The journey of the *Scorpion* and its crew is symptomatic. In the event they find little of interest in America except a few dead people, still, a year after the event, sitting round a table on a veranda with their cocktails in front of them, the women's summer frocks fluttering in the light breeze – as though nothing untoward had happened. This, too, is a chilling aspect of the story: everyone seems to have died so tidily – without any accompanying mess or corruption. 'It's what animals do,' John Osborne says, 'Creep away into holes to die. They're probably all in bed.' And when the end comes for all these characters, they, too, find relatively tidy ways to die.

The story leaves one deeply dissatisfied, longing for someone to step out of line, even for the more realistic descriptions of mob desperation, greed and agony of other novels. But Shute attempts little in the way of analysis of events or attitudes – only an occasional wry observation of the irrationality of individual responses to the situation. Whether by resolutely ignoring it or by a quiet stoicism, his characters seem to accept the end to human life with a fatalism which finally becomes exasperating. It is epitomised by the US commander's insistence on continuing to observe meticulously US naval requirements to the very last moment. This refusal to do anything contrary to tradition because 'Uncle Sam wouldn't like it' seems most heartlessly futile when Towers takes the *Scorpion* just outside Australian waters to sink her with all hands on board, but will not allow any of the crew's women-folk to join their men in this mass-suicide. Instead the women are left forlornly on shore to die on their own. It does not occur to anyone that this fanatical obedience to orders, whether military or political, could have been a significant factor in the nuclear disaster, or that it is surely now of greater importance to show at last some consideration for the welfare of the living, now facing their final moments.

Most stories, however, – no doubt less realistic in this respect – assume some possibilities of survival, in pockets here or there, though it is interesting to see that these pockets are usually located in areas of white populations – North America, Britain, New Zealand – and not in those Third World countries who are, after all, not yet in the nuclear arms race.

In contrast to Shute's avoidance of any direct scenes of bombing, devastation or violent death, Danny, the hero of Robert Swindells' novel, *Brother in the Land*, is immediately in the centre of the nightmare. The story begins with a fearsome impressionistic description of the first nuclear attack, one which rained alike on the 'Frimleys' and the 'Bukovskys', annihilating both British and Russian towns and families.

Down came the missiles. Some had just the one warhead, others had several, ranging from the compact, almost tactical warhead to the large, family size. Every town was to receive its own, individually-programmed warhead. Not one had been left out.

They struck, screaming in with pinpoint accuracy, bursting with blinding flashes, brighter than a thousand suns. Whole towns and city-centres vaporized instantly; while tarmac, trees and houses thirty miles from the explosions burst into flames. Fireballs, expanding in a second to several miles across, melted and devoured all matter that fell within their diameters. Blast-waves, travelling faster than sound, ripped through the suburbs. Houses disintegrated and vanished. So fierce were the flames that they devoured all the oxygen around them, suffocating those people who had sought refuge in deep shelters. Winds of a hundred-and-fifty miles an hour, rushing in to fill the vacuum, created fire-storms that howled though the streets, where temperatures in the thousands cooked the subterranean dead. The very earth heaved and shook as the warheads rained down, burst upon burst, and a terrible thunder rent the skies.

Then came the radioactive fall-out; so deadly that only by a great effort of imagination can the reader believe that anyone at all could be left alive. Of the people who miraculously do survive, many will die more slowly, including Danny's young brother; many also will die from violence, either at the hands of the 'Commissioners', the men in power, and their soldiers, or at the hands of bandits of various kinds, all desperate to go on living no matter at whose expense. For Swindells is more aware than Shute that it is not only the virtuous who will survive. He is particularly sceptical about those whose positions of authority before the war had guaranteed a place in a bunker. Though they might be expected to take charge in a positive attempt to make life possible for all other survivors, in Swindells' story they have turned themselves instead into a Nazi-style power group. They seize all available commodities, systematically eliminate all those still alive who are unproductive and use the remainder as slave labour. Only a few people, including Danny and his friend, Kim, manage to resist, and try to organise a better way of surviving. With this group is an old man, Branwell, who tells Danny sadly:

'We watched death and destruction on TV newsreels till it meant nothing to us – till it didn't shock us any more. If we'd realized in time what was happening to us, if we'd clung on to our reverence for life, then we'd never have launched those missiles. That's what I think, anyway.'

Though this is undoubtedly a simplistic analysis of what may lead us to nuclear war, its message for our present violent society bears thinking about.

Many issues are brought alive through the experiences of Danny and Kim; the cruelty, greed and banditry of some individuals and groups, the comparative selflessness of others, the pain, suffering, death, despair, and the hopes, some vain, of reviving the earth's surface to take growing crops once more, and of renewing the earth's population with children, in spite of the all-pervasive radiation and the trauma of a future beset with genetic hazards. Though it can be faulted in various respects, *Brother in the Land* seems a more realistic assessment than *On the Beach* of the immediate effects of the war upon those left behind.

Z for Zachariah, by Robert O'Brien, is told in documentary fashion through the diary of Anne Burden. It does not attempt to engage with the reasons for the war, or with the immediate scenario of the nuclear attack, but concentrates instead on the fortunes of two chance survivors. Anne is 16 when she is left at home alone to fend for herself in a valley apparently untouched by nuclear fall-out, preserved by some freakish chance which is never explained. She has been insulated in her valley from the worst effects of the nuclear war. She has seen the mushroom cloud at a distance, and the 'forest fire in the dead woods', and she has heard of the dead birds and people, and of the 'grey wasteland, empty highways and dead cities and towns', and seen the one radioactive stream in her valley with its dead fish and the dying vegetation along its banks, but she has had little direct experience of the effects of the bombing. Over a year later she is joined by John R. Loomis, a scientist who has survived so far with the help of a radiation-proof tent and suit, and it is through his account of his wanderings in search of other survivors and a possible place to live that Anne, like the Australians in Shute's novel, at last learns at second-hand what has happened to the rest of the world.

The central theme of this novel, however, is Anne's increasingly tense and frightening battle of wits with Loomis, who has become crazed by an obsessive determination to live regardless of anyone else, a theme in keeping with Swindells's vision of the embattled post-nuclear world. The nightmarish quality of life after the bomb which the advent of Loomis has introduced into Anne's quiet valley is made more poignant because of its juxtaposition with the quietly realistic detail of ordinary life. But the final impact of her ordeal – and therefore of the nuclear horror – is lessened for the reader as O'Brien reasserts sanity and a measure of hope for the future. Anne prepares to leave her valley to the crazed scientist and go in search of other people, who, it is suggested, will prove to be more friendly and welcoming.

In *Wolf of the Shadows*, Whitley Streiber has also concentrated his story on the fate of a few survivors, but he has attempted a more comprehensive scenario which includes the fate of the animal kingdom. North America has been left devastated and in the grip of a nuclear winter. But the survivors include a wolf pack led by Wolf of the Shadows, and two humans, mother and daughter, who are eventually accepted into the pack, and struggle hundreds of miles south with them in search of a warmer valley, out of the freezing ice and cold, where both wolves and humans can find food.

The flaw in this vivid and imaginative story is the anthropomorphic picture of the wolf leader himself, whose self-abnegatory reluctance to win leadership of the pack and willingness to stay out in the 'wilderness' on his own rather than fight the existing leader is hard to credit, and interferes with the reader's ability to suspend disbelief in the rest of the story. The sense of unease is increased by the mixture of human and wolf points-of-view in the narrative; apparent, for instance, in the persistent reference to motor-cars as 'round-pawed things', or to the woman's knife as a 'silver claw'. Jean George managed this mixture of wolf and human consciousness much better in her story, *Julie of the Wolves*, through a more objective third person narrative for both Julie and the wolf pack.

Streiber was inspired originally, he tells us, by a letter commenting that innocent animal life would perish helplessly with human life in a nuclear winter. He chose to illustrate the truth of this through a wolf pack because of his 'own personal experience of wolves, and knowledge of Native American ways of viewing the wolf, which are so different from the modern image of wolves as vicious enemies of man'. He quotes some telling details from John G. Neihardt's account in *Black Elk Speaks* of American Indian beliefs which still have a serious message for us today; and declares that 'lack of respect for living, growing things' soon leads to 'lack of respect for humans too'. Viewed in this light, and for young readers who can accept this as the theme of the story, and overlook the uneasiness of using 'humanised' wolf-consciousness as the vehicle for the narrative, this is a moving exposition of the horrors which would follow a nuclear war.

Taronga, by Victor Kelleher, shares something of the vision of *Brother in the Land* and also of the interest shown in *Wolf of the Shadows* in the fate of animals as well as of human beings. It is set in Australia, two years after the 'Last Days', as the nuclear holocaust is euphemistically called. The survivors are united in refusing to look back at the disaster, so there are none of the scenes of bombing, fall-out and death which are so vivid in Swindells's story. But, like Swindells, Kelleher is concerned with the human imperfections which had made nuclear war inevitable, and which still motivate those who have survived it. He perceives that it is the blinkered selfishness of modern civilisations and of those who profit from nuclear industries which most seriously threatens our future existence, both through the ecological disasters our greed and disregard for the environment daily make more inevitable, and through our myopic refusal to collaborate with all other human beings for the greater good of each one of us. In his vision of a post-nuclear society struggling for survival, he, like Swindells, sees and fears the consequences of this every-man-for-himself philosophy.

His hero, Ben, is acutely aware of his own shortcomings, and deeply conscious of the betrayals he is constantly led into by his need to go on living. Like several other characters in post-nuclear fiction, Ben has developed unusual mental powers; in his case it is a telepathic ability to control animals, which he reluctantly uses and abuses to provide himself with food or safety. When he eventually finds himself in Taronga Zoo, in the heart of Sydney, he feels that at last he has reached an oasis of safety, a Garden of Eden, where he need no longer betray trust in order to survive. But he is soon disabused. Ellie, an aboriginal girl who refuses to ignore or deny the past, helps Ben to see the truly sinister nature of the power structure in Taronga. Ellie, like the American Indians quoted by Streiber, believes that the land should be held in partnership, with equality between all living things. But Molly and Steve, the two people most securely in charge, admit no others, human or animal, to equality, and will go to any lengths to preserve the zoo for their exclusive use.

This is an exciting and tense story, full of action; with Kelleher's unique ability to create a sense of rapport with the animal kingdom as well as with his characters. Unlike Streiber he does not attribute human attitudes to his animals. Ben's continual and symbolic battle with the formidable tiger, Raja, is a powerful element in the story and in his own development to maturity and understanding; but the will to freedom, the anger and ferocity and finally the acceptance of the ambivalence of their relationship are played out in keeping with Raja's nature as tiger.

There is violence and cruelty in *Taronga* – the tigers are man-eaters, and the humans are unremittingly ruthless towards each other. It is decidedly the law of the jungle which prevails in post-nuclear Australia – kill or be killed. But Kelleher's use of violence in his story is always under control, employed only where it is essential to his theme – namely that in our willingness to use violence towards each other lie the seeds of our own destruction. This message is contained in the scene in which Ben finally realises that Molly is prepared to destroy Taronga and all the animals in it rather than surrender it to the enemy at its gates. Molly explains:

'The point lies in the threat ... Like any threat, it's a weapon, that we'd be foolish not to use. Just think about it – destroy us and you destroy Taronga. Doomsday. Even a child can understand that. It's what people used to call the ultimate deterrent. A last line of defence.'
   'But that's like Last Days!' he burst out.

Recognising the correspondences between Molly's 'Doomsday' plan and past reliance on nuclear deterrence brings Ben and Ellie to their own choice; to save the animals of Taronga at the expense of both sets of warring, implacably cruel humans. It is not an easy decision, and involves Ben in further betrayal; but the arguments, the agonies of conscience and their resolution are worked out in original terms which are well worth the reader's consideration.

Most of these books have closed with the future still to be determined, but there are one or two which hazard a guess about the direction life may take for generations living long years after the bomb. *Children of the Dust*, by Louise Lawrence, begins with a bleak account of the days after a nuclear attack, and the stifling claustrophobia and isolation of the room in which Sarah and her family hide from the bombs and wait out the slow days of increasing radiation sickness which gradually kills all but eight-year-old Catherine. There follows a caustic account of the politicians, the military leaders and the scientists who had taken refuge in the bunkers. They are not evil, like those in power in Swindells's story. Indeed, some of them are selflessly hard-working and conscientious in their determination to create a new and better future for all. But as they stubbornly persist in the rigid authoritarian thinking which had led to the nuclear holocaust they are seen still to be incapable of devising sufficiently imaginative strategies for survival. In her analysis of their failure to adapt, the author seeks to penetrate into some of the human weaknesses which brought about the disaster and which may well, she starkly suggests, persist into the future unless we seek actively to learn from our past mistakes.

Unfortunately, in spite of this promising beginning, a different kind of comforting wish-fulfilment fantasy now takes over. Led by Catherine, the survivors are able within the space of 50 years to adapt physically to the ultra-violet rays penetrating to earth after the destruction of the ozone layer, and mentally to the desperate need for cooperation and non-violence by a parallel growth of psychic mental powers and thought control. This leads to the author's main thesis, a notion that somehow there is hope for a future after the bomb – 'the continuity of creation ... an unbroken perfect pattern that bestowed a meaning upon everything, little fragments of the mind of God which nothing could destroy'. The book concludes with the bland reassurance that: 'Dodos and dinosaurs and *Homo sapiens* had not been wasted. The human race no failed evolutionary experiment, their nuclear war no ultimate disaster. It had happened because it was meant to happen and nothing was lost ...'

In spite of the realistic detail of some parts of Louise Lawrence's book, and the clearsightedness with which she condemns the blinkered vision of the survivors in the bunker, this 'Noah's Flood' aspect of her story seems insensitive, curiously repellent and even dangerous in its complacent acceptance that all things, even a nuclear disaster of this magnitude, will work out for the best. A nuclear holocaust, with its accompanying radiation and raging fires, hurricanes and sudden disastrous fall in temperature which would kill vegetable and animal life world-wide would be a man-made global catastrophe for which no antidote exists other than its prevention. Neither in this nor in any other respect could it reasonably be compared to Noah's Flood.

The Chrysalids is an earlier and vastly superior story, in which John Wyndham, though not attempting to predict the future, is using the post-nuclear scenario for his own purposes. Like Louise Lawrence, he, too, seems to have been fascinated by the possibility of a superior breed, able at last to work cooperatively through developing some new capacities for thought transference. Wyndham's society exists in Labrador some one or two thousand years after the 'Tribulation'; but is still as hostile as the bunker people of *Children of the Dust* to the consequent genetic mutations in plant, animal or human life. In order to protect themselves from such deviations from the 'norm', these people have developed a rigidly censorious religion which sees even the most insignificant mutations as manifestations of evil, to be rooted out by destruction, slaughter or sterilisation and exile to the 'Fringes'. Anyone daring to suggest 'that deviations, so far from being a curse, were performing, however slowly, a work of reclamation' was accused of heresy.

David, the narrator of the story, has a 'deviation' which no one in authority yet suspects, though he soon realises that he shares it with several other people. It is an ability to communicate wordlessly, by thought transference, at a distance. This new quality of mind could, as in Louise Lawrence's novel, provide a way forward by producing societies able think together in harmony instead of separately and in conflict. And although David's ability is sternly and fanatically rejected by his own society, including his rigid and uncompromising father, it is a quality actively developed and encouraged by the 'Sealanders', a race of survivors from New Zealand. They tell David:

'The essential quality of life is living; the essential quality of living is change; change is evolution: and we are part of it.

'The static, the enemy of change, is the enemy of life, and therefore our implacable enemy. If you still feel shocked, or doubtful, just consider some of the things that these people, who have taught you to think of them as your fellows, have done. And consider, too, what they intended to do to you, and why ...'

The Chrysalids is not only a tense and exciting story of David's escape to freedom, it is also an attempt to discuss those beliefs and attitudes which have led to division and conflict and so to the 'Tribulation' which almost destroyed the planet. Unlike *Children of the Dust* it does not suggest that the nuclear holocaust was 'part of God's plan', nor does it attempt any dogmatic statement about the right way forward. David remains critical of his new friends, their 'overwhelming' rhetorical style, their apparent callousness over the wholesale slaughter necessary to rescue David and his precious younger sister, Petra, and their extreme satisfaction with themselves. Refreshingly, though, they do accept that 'sometime ... we ourselves shall have to give place to a new thing'.

Its analysis of the nature of the conflict generated between the forces for progress and a fiercely orthodox community, and its staunch defence of the need for constant reappraisal of beliefs, attitudes and strategies bring to *The Chrysalids* a moral and artistic dimension far superior to the anodyne conclusion of *Children of the Dust*.

How effective are these novels as a means of alerting young readers to a sense of responsibility towards the nuclear dangers still facing mankind, and towards current nuclear policies? In choosing from such fiction it is important first to consider a general warning given by W. Warren Wagar in *Terminal Visions*, in which he surveys fictions about 'last things':

There is the further problem of the extent to which literature is designed to satisfy the hunger of its readers (and sometimes of its writers) for violence and death ... a sense of powerlessness can invoke all the devils of Thanatos: uncontrollable rage, bitter hatred, insatiable gluttony and lust, the desire to destroy supposed enemies and oppressors, self-loathing and cravings for humiliation and death. All sorts of scenes in terminal literature serve these devils well, especially the visions of mass destruction during the catastrophe itself, whatever it may be, and the reigns of lawlessness and terror that so often follow.

On the whole the authors of the novels discussed above have avoided this danger, and have been careful to use scenes of violence in a controlled way, either as part of an analysis of the social mores which made the nuclear deterrent acceptable in the first place, or as a necessary ingredient of nuclear panic.

It has to be admitted, however, that the novels have another limitation: their fictional character readily allows them to be replaced on the shelf and dismissed as sci-fi fantasy by readers who are perennially unwilling to face unpalatable truths. For though many writers, scientists, politicians, novelists, poets and playwrights have seen 'the rapidity with which war was becoming impossible' and have done what they could to warn us, they have not yet succeeded in turning us aside from the nuclear arms race. As long ago as 1829 Robert Southey wrote in his 'Colloquies on the progress ... of society':

The novel powers which, beyond all doubt, will be directed to the purposes of destruction, are so tremendous, and likely to be so efficient, that in their consequences they may reasonably be expected to do more towards the prevention of war than any or all other causes.

We can now see that Southey, though correct in his assessment of the increasingly destructive power of future weapons, was sadly mistaken in hoping that this might be an effective deterrent.

This calls seriously into question also our own faith in 'the novel powers' of nuclear weapons to prevent war, and our current helpless acceptance of the risks to which we are already being exposed in order to maintain them. It is disconcerting to find that in 1914 H.G. Wells, in his prophetic *The World Set Free*, was already giving unmistakable warnings against the course we are still doggedly following:

Certainly it seems now that nothing could have been more obvious to the people of the earlier twentieth century than the rapidity with which war was becoming impossible. And as certainly they did not see it. They did not see it until the atomic bombs burst in their fumbling hands. Yet the broad facts must have glared upon any intelligent mind. All through the nineteenth and twentieth centuries the amount of energy that men were able to command was continually increasing. There was no increase whatever in the ability to escape. Every sort of passive defence, armour, fortifications and so forth was being outmastered by the tremendous increase on the destructive side.

(Quoted in I.F. Clarke, *Voices Prophesying War*)

Writing in *Surviving the Holocaust* of the Nazi extermination programme, Bruno Bettelheim tells us:

Denial is the earliest, most primitive, most inappropriate and ineffective of all psychological defences used by man. When the event is potentially destructive, it is the most pernicious psychological defence, because it does not permit taking appropriate action which might safeguard against the real dangers. Denial therefore leaves the individual most vulnerable to the very perils against which he has tried to defend himself.

He reminds us that those terminally ill cancer patients 'who face what is in store for them with clarity soon also gain considerable equanimity of mind; they do everything that can and needs to be done, realizing how little time they have left to do so'. But the majority, unfortunately, refuse to accept that they are dying. 'They claim that they are getting better, making ambitiously large and unrealistic, even delusional plans and arrangements for their future.' The same refusal to face reality 'when the event is potentially destructive' leads too many authors and their readers to prefer that class of 'delusional' post-nuclear fictions described by Angela Carter in *Over Our Dead Bodies* (ed. Dorothy Thompson):

One of the most curious phenomena of the post-war period has been the growth of fictions about the blissfully anarchic, tribal lives the lucky fifteen million survivors are going to lead in a Britain miraculously free of corpses ... The post-nuclear catastrophe novel has become a science fiction genre all of its own, sometimes as a warning – more often the saddest and most irresponsible kind of whistling in the dark.

I.F. Clarke in *Voices Prophesying War* defines this trend in fiction in terms which reflect more sympathetically Bettelheim's insight into human behaviour.

All these tales have the same theme of destruction and rebirth. They describe disasters as great as any nuclear war but controllable because the earth has not been poisoned, and some human beings, sound in mind and body, have survived. They represent a powerful demand for a second chance, for a fresh start. This has the effect of returning the human race to the Promethean stage of a desolate world and the solitary group destined to start off once more the whole sequence of development from tribe to nation. So, the return to an aboriginal or to an uncomplicated pastoral condition ... brings comfort to an anxious world.

If we re-examine post nuclear catastrophe novels in the light of these comments we can see the danger implicit in such a resolution of the nuclear problem. Subtly it offers reassurance: all will not be lost; we can be soothed into inaction in the belief that there will be a better future, 'the human race no failed evolutionary experiment, their nuclear war no ultimate disaster' (*Children of the Dust*). It is clear that as well as the powerful impact of the novelists' imagination we need the correction which can be given from the sober forecasts of those scientists who are seeking to predict as accurately as possible what may happen. For the impact fiction can make upon its readers' final attitude to nuclear power or to the nuclear 'deterrent' must depend not only on its imaginative strengths but also on its credibility.

How close to reality are any of these nightmare fantasies of a nuclear accident, of the dangers of nuclear 'dumping' or of a future after a nuclear war? John Strachey suggests in *On the Prevention of War* (1962) that nuclear fiction may fall short of the truth:

> The brutal facts of the new military technologies describe the disaster of nuclear warfare in terms that fiction cannot better. Indeed, one expert in this field has claimed that 'even writers of fiction have failed to give us a deep impression of the nature and extent of this catastrophe. Perhaps even they cannot truly visualize what it would mean to survivors to see fifty, eighty or a hundred million people killed within a few days or hours, and tens of millions grievously ill, living without hope in hovels amidst poisonous radio-active debris.'

The expert in question was Professor Oskar Morgenstern, and the quotation comes from *The Question of National Defence*, published in 1959. In 1966 Clarke in his turn quoted this extract in *Voices Prophesying War*, and added:

> After the last bomb had fallen, and after the survivors had waited ninety days in their shelters to escape the worst dangers of local fallout, they would emerge into a blasted world, a desolate planet inhabited by the insects and bacteria. Possibilities of this magnitude make it futile to describe the shape of a nuclear war.

Since then ever more closely reasoned and grim prophecies of the aftermath of nuclear war have been made by scientists. There is an excellent exposition of many of their arguments in J.J.

Wellington's book for secondary school pupils, *The Nuclear Issue*, in which he dispassionately sets out for discussion many of the issues raised by both nuclear power and the arms race. Amongst the many other books written on the subject are *Fire and Ice: The Nuclear Winter*, by Michael Rowan-Robinson and *The Night After ... Climatic and Biological Consequences of a Nuclear War*, an account, edited by Yevgeni Velikhov, of 'the main research on the subject by Soviet scientists conducted under the auspices of the Soviet Scientists' Committee for the Defence of Peace Against Nuclear Threat'. Both these books argue that 'a nuclear war would be a crisis not just for western civilization but for *all* life on the planet'.

In *Fire and Ice*, Robinson writes:

Changes in the earth's climate which have become known as the 'nuclear winter' would have catastrophic biological consequences, with widespread extinctions of plants and animals. Leading biologists are now not able to rule out the possibility that the human species might become extinct.

Quietly and lucidly he explains the theories and reasoning which have led 'scientists from many different fields of study ... on both sides of the Iron Curtain' to this conclusion. He demolishes with biting irony the futile advice given in the British Home Office pamphlet, *Protect and Survive*, and describes the effect upon the earth and its inhabitants of a nuclear war.

There would probably be survivors scattered throughout the southern hemisphere. But would these small groups of people be able to survive? They would be forced back into a hunter-gatherer existence, but ... they would be facing a new and malign environment, with high radiation levels, a severely damaged natural world, and unprecedented weather conditions. Social, economic and cultural systems would be shattered and human beings would face immense psychological stresses. It was the consensus of the group of distinguished biologists who met in Washington that 'We could not exclude the possibility that the scattered survivors simply would not be able to rebuild their populations, that they would, over a period of decades or even centuries, fade away.'

The Third Congress of International Physicians for the Prevention of Nuclear War, meeting at The Hague in June 1983, also declared:

If even a single nuclear weapon is exploded over one of our major cities, hundreds of thousands will be killed. If many nuclear weapons are exploded, radioactive fallout and disturbance of the biosphere will cause suffering and death particularly from starvation, radiation illness, infectious diseases and cancer – without regard to national boundaries.

The remaining medical facilities and personnel will be inadequate to help the wounded. An all-out nuclear war would end our present civilization.

An Information Paper of an Assembly of Presidents of Scientific Academies and other scientists from all over the world, convened in 1984 by the Pontifical Academy of Sciences, added its word to this bleak picture, pointing out that in addition to all the other disasters, the weakening of the human immune system would 'threaten large numbers of survivors'.

In more recent years some of these findings have been challenged; we have been told, for instance, that the 'nuclear winter' may be no more than a 'nuclear autumn'. But at the same time scientists are discovering even further dimensions to possible effects – upon the algae which begin the food chain in the oceans; or upon the world-wide weather cycles in which failure of normal patterns of rainfall and of the monsoons, for instance, could devastate crops over whole regions of the earth.

But yet, as Rowan-Robinson rightly concludes in *Fire and Ice*, the precise details of the catastrophe matter less than the undisputed fact that 'the direct consequences of nuclear war are so appalling that humanity must draw back from this abyss'. The doom-laden prophecies of responsible scientists compel us to immediate action. We cannot indeed 'let human existence on this beautiful planet be snuffed out'.

When we examine these pronouncements we can see that even the most horrific of the fictions we have been discussing fall short of the reality of what could happen. In their imaginative projections into the consequences of such a disaster, for example, only *On the Beach* by Nevil Shute faces Rowan-Robinson's prediction of a future without any hope at all for mankind. But even here the bleakness of the final annihilation of mankind is tempered by a softening of the tragedy, harshness and chaos which scientists predict will attend the last scenes of all.

It is not surprising that many novelists have drawn back from following through to its logical end the predicted death of all organisms save, perhaps, insects, bacteria or those in the depths of the ocean which do not depend on solar energy. It is, after all, difficult to contemplate. It is, moreover, the clinical objectivity of the scientists' accounts which heightens the nightmare. It is impossible to escape from them into a soothing belief that we are only reading science fiction, that these horrendous forecasts are only the result of an over-powerful imagination. How, then, one might ask, can we continue to ignore such warnings?

The personal dimension of nuclear war is nevertheless clearly one respect in which the novelist can offer us more than scientists, with their natural emphasis upon factual realities. In *Fictions of Nuclear Disaster* David Dowling suggests that:

> To read these fictions is to place oneself imaginatively in a position of personal suffering and global despair, not in any chiliastic paroxysm, but in an attitude of calm enquiry. If nothing had prompted our fore-fathers, then Hitler's Holocaust at least compelled us in the latter twen-tieth century to consider the nature of man *in extremis*. The nuclear threat now provides the most effective scenario for doing this.

Several of the novels discussed here, as we have seen, have tried to enter into the feelings of despair, fear, courage or hope appro-priate to their characters in extremity. The presentation of this aspect of survival has varied from the relatively cosy resignation of Nevil Shute's novel to the extreme anarchism and crude self-preservation tactics shown by some of the characters in the novels of Robert Swindells or Annabel and Edgar Johnson (see Chapter 10). For others, though, the prevailing mood has been that described by Dowling earlier in his book:

> Even within the immediate confines of the disaster and its aftermath, the human imagination finds fortitude and inspiration. The popular current movement of 'Survivalism' is part of this reaction against intol-erable despair, and many fictions portray man as resourceful, obstinate and ennobled by facing this ultimate challenge.

Perhaps we need to remind ourselves that in the reality both of Hitler's Holocaust and of the bombing of Hiroshima and Nagasaki, the few who remained 'resourceful, obstinate and ennobled' did so at intolerable cost, and were far outnumbered by the many who did not. As Bettelheim says in *Surviving the Holocaust*:

> Those who wish to learn from these events for the future must accept not only the possibility, but the probability, that most people are neither heroes nor martyrs – that under great stress and misery a few become heroes, but most people deteriorate rather rapidly, and that inhumanity could be found among both Nazis and their victims.

This complexity of human motivation and behaviour can indeed be found in many 'disaster' novels, perhaps most strikingly in *Taronga, Brother in the Land* and *Z for Zachariah*. But there is one aspect of survival which has found little place in novelists' projec-tions of the future after the bomb. This is the overwhelming sense of guilt, experienced often more acutely by the surviving victims than by their persecutors. In *Surviving the Holocaust* Bruno Bettelheim has discussed this phenomenon as it occurred in the

extensive 'survivor syndrome' literature dealing with both concentration camp survivors and survivors of Hiroshima and Nagasaki.
His analysis reveals the extent of the problem which would face
any survivors of a future atomic war. How can they cope both
with the guilt of having lived through the years in which they
made no effective protest against nuclear arms, as well as with this
other guilt, that they have remained alive when so many others
have perished?

Another aspect which remains relatively little explored in
nuclear war novels is the complicity of scientists in the development and manufacture of nuclear weapons. Many scientists
laboured hard to prevent the bombs from being dropped, arguing
passionately that a demonstration, or at least a forewarning which
would enable civilians to be evacuated, would serve the avowed
purpose of ending the war. Some scientists steadfastly refused to
become involved in work to destroy so many lives. Helen Smith
turned away from physics altogether and took up jurisprudence,
while Hans Bethe, in an article for *The Scientific American* which
was later confiscated and pulped by government agents, declared:

> I believe that we would lose far more than our lives in a war fought
> with hydrogen bombs, that we would in fact lose all our liberties and
> human values at the same time, and so thoroughly that we would not
> recover them for a long time.

On the other hand, as Robert Jungk tells us in *Brighter than a
Thousand Suns*, even some peace-loving scientists like Einstein
eventually allowed themselves to become involved with the
nuclear bomb. Jungk examines the stages by which they finally
reconciled themselves to what was being projected, contributed to
its manufacture and, even after the horrifying effects of these two
bombs had been fully documented, were still willing to work to
produce even more deadly weapons. Although 'a number of
American scientific investigators hostile to armament work'
formed a Society for Social Responsibility in Science to protest
against the development of arms techniques, Jungk tells us, 'it
never comprised more than about three hundred scientists in
America, though by 1950 Einstein and Max Born were members'.
He adds:

> Unfortunately they could exert little influence. They were even refused
> admittance to the organization comprising all the scientific bodies in
> America, the American Association for the Advancement of Science.
> Protests soon died away. After a while no more was heard in public
> about the hydrogen bomb. Once again, 'flaming indignation' had
> proved to be only a fire of straw.

This can be compared with Bettelheim's observations on the complicity of scientists and technicians in the construction of gas chambers:

> But this delusion could not have wrought such havoc of human lives had it not been paired with a ruthless and heartless technology which concerned itself only with efficiency, never mind the human cost ... Without such faultless technology (in the manufacture of the cremation ovens etc.) the holocaust could never have been as effective, as it took the organisational genius of an Eichmann to transport all these many Jews over such long distances in such a short time in wartime to these faultlessly constructed gas chambers. That this could have been easily made impossible by an Allied bombing of the tracks leading to Auschwitz, and that this the Allied commanders refused to do despite pleas to thus save hundreds of thousands, this is another story, but still one which tells about the priorities according to which technical considerations have to take precedence over human ones. All I wanted to suggest here is that this deadly co-operation of most efficient technology with pseudo-scientific delusion is an outgrowth of our century and hence a real danger.

Although, as Bettelheim points out, there are ways in which the two situations differed widely, nevertheless, for the ordinary scientists and for the man and woman in the street the moral dilemma and the guilt of contributing to mass murder remain acute in both instances. How on either occasion were people able to come to terms with their own guilt, or the guilt of close friends and relatives?

How can we now fail to see, also, that our present violent world, the endless wars, the oppressive regimes, the prisons and tortures used to suppress opposition in so many countries and the counter-violence of terrorists and freedom-fighters are themselves a legacy from two decades of war and violence in the 1930s and 1940s? Or that we are preparing a similar legacy for our descendants through the cold war and the nuclear arms race which continue to make respectable a reliance on mass murder as a possible argument?

12

A World of Violence

There are those who would argue that the world has always been a violent place, and that our present awareness of this violence marks no real change. Its pervasive appearance as a theme in the arts, and the way it has been treated, particularly in books for young people, has, however, rightly given rise to concern. In 1974 John Fraser produced his book, *Violence in the Arts*, as 'a personal essay' examining 'some of the ways in which, to borrow from D.H. Lawrence, "our sympathies flow and recoil" in our dealings with violence in the arts, and why it is that some violences seem to make for intellectual clarity and a more civilized consciousness, while others make for confusion.' His analysis prompts us to ask how many books for young people successfully hold the balance between, on the one hand, the depiction of violence as a necessary part of the book's theme and a reflection of the author's social conscience, and, on the other, its indulgence in ways which should seriously be called into question.

If, for instance, one reads Robert Cormier's novel, *After the First Death*, quickly, purely for the thrills, it can seem an accomplished, vivid and tense drama, legitimately exploring that modern phenomenon, the young terrorist. But once one begins to examine it in the light of Fraser's analysis, the dubious nature of its depiction of violence and the consequent 'confusion' in the response it elicits from young people become painfully apparent.

One aspect of this is the presentation of the central character, sixteen-year-old Miro, for whom the hi-jacking of a bus-load of five- and six-year-old children is to be his initiation into 'manhood'. He is detailed to kill the driver – his first killing in cold blood. This he contemplates with an increase of tension, but:

> He was not a child anymore. And inflicting death did not bother him. Neither did the contemplation of the act. He had been waiting for four, almost five years now. How else could he justify his existence, make his life meaningful before it was taken from him? His brother, Aniel, had died too soon, before making his mark, before fulfilling his promise.

No, Miro was not apprehensive about the delivery of death; he worried only that he would not do a professional job.

Cormier's cool analysis of Miro's state of mind is entirely credible, in keeping, indeed, with the comments John Fraser makes on such fictional characters:

> What stands out in a number of representative men of violence, whether a smiling murderous bar-room brawler like McPartland's King McCarthy, or Twain's Sherburn, or Achilles coolly putting to death a dozen Trojan prisoners to avenge Patroclus's death, is the completeness of their commitment to courses of violence from which there can be no retreating and in which others may legitimately be no less violent towards them.

Miro has been trained from the tender age of twelve to accept the rightness and inevitability of inflicting violence on innocent victims – including children of five or six. He sees such activities as 'justifying his existence', 'making his life meaningful', 'fulfilling his promise'. He accepts without question that before long his own life will be 'taken from him' as violently as his brother's had been a short time before. Fraser remarks:

> It is the entailed revelation of absolutely unbridgeable differences – of the absolute unshakeableness with which ideas or value-systems that one considers wicked or foolish can be held – that at bottom is so disquieting and challenging about the violences of such men. And what especially disturbs the liberal viewer or reader is the kind of mentality for which destruction – deliberate destruction, with full knowledge of what is being destroyed – appears perfectly right and natural.

We can see this attitude in Miro as he contemplates his first victim, the bus driver, Kate, and focuses his attention on 'the girl's temple near that flow of yellow hair', the spot at which he intends to aim his pistol.

> Do it quickly, Artkin had advised, and do not hesitate. Artkin had often said they were not interested in needless cruelty. They had a job to do and the job concerned death. Do not prolong it more than necessary. Deliver it as efficiently as possible with the least mess. We are not animals, after all, he said, but merely a means to an end.

Put like that it sounds almost a humane operation.

> And Artkin had told him that there were many laws in the world, good laws and bad laws, right laws and wrong laws. According to the wrong laws, their mission, their work, was condemned. But these laws were made by their enemies.

So they are justified in breaking them, even when in doing so they must commit the atrocities for which Miro has been so carefully trained.

What should trouble all responsible people is that values such as these are implicitly endorsed by the way in which young readers are invited to empathise with Miro. Kate, a potential victim, naturally sees Miro as 'a monster'; but the reader is led to admire him for the courage and resolution which, after the death of his mentor and putative father, Artkin, enables him triumphantly to survive the terrible events of the previous few days and to persist, 'past pain and exhaustion', in his mission 'to carry on the work'.

We do not know precisely what 'the work' is – apart from the killing it entails; only that it is connected with Miro's previous life of deprivation, growing up in a refugee camp, alone save for the older brother who has so recently been killed, and finally found there and trained by Artkin for the hostage-taking, publicity-seeking, bomb-placing existence of the ruthless terrorist. What particular cause they are fighting for does not seem to matter. What is important is that in spite of everything that has happened in the intervening pages, by the end of the story Miro has not changed.

> He thought of the girl ... he remembered how her flesh glowed in the dimness of the bus. He had been filled with that something he could not put a name to. The girl had asked him once: Don't you feel anything? Perhaps he had been filled with feeling at that moment. He did not know. He did not care. He would not let himself be filled with anything again. He would keep himself empty, like before.
>
> A car stopped nearby. A station wagon. The driver got out of the car, a man, short and fat. The man looked around and began to walk toward the woods at the edge of the roadway, fumbling with his trousers, apparently seeking a place to urinate. Miro recognized his good fortune. He decided he would not waste a bullet but would use his hands.
>
> He moved out of the bushes into the world that was waiting for him.

It is on this note that the story ends. Sixteen-year-old Miro has achieved adulthood, now that 'the first death', the killing of the girl, has left him ready to 'fulfil his promise' with further deaths which will now cost him nothing; no feeling, no remorse, no hesitation, no thought even.

Fraser remarks that people usually prefer to believe that atrocities are committed not by ordinary, decent men and women, but 'by people who have either been victims themselves (as in wartime or in the slum-childhood kind of criminality) or who wear very obviously the marks of monstrosity and of their own eventual downfall'. Presenting Miro as the 'victim' of his deprived childhood makes it possible for readers to distance themselves from his actions whilst they empathise with him in an impulse of pity similar to that which momentarily stirs Kate. 'In the thrall of Miro's words' as he tells her of his past life – 'the boy stumbling through refugee camps, no parents, his brother dead, taught violence in an underground school' – Kate is 'on the edge of pity' for him. But then, she realises:

> Their two lives had brought them here to the bus where she was a victim, not the boy. His life had prepared him for this moment. Hers hadn't. He was prepared to hurt and kill. She was prepared for nothing. Certainly not to be brave.

So Kate's pity soon gives way once more to disgust at his complete lack of feeling for his victims:

> He had seduced her with his pathetic tale of wandering through the camps as a child ... But now she recognized him for what he was: a monster. And the greatest horror of all was that he did not know he was a monster. He had looked at her with innocent eyes as he told her of killing people ... But innocence, she now saw, could be monstrous.

The shock of the atrocities which Miro has been describing, and of the atrocities that he and Artkin are ready to commit against the small children on the bus is, for Kate, all the greater because she has, in Fraser's words, 'tended to feel previously that at bottom life is essentially benevolent – that Good always wins over Evil because of the essential nature of things'.

Kate is a sympathetic and courageous character who can be seen as a foil to Miro, presenting the other point of view. But the 'flow and recoil' of sympathy between, on the one hand, the terrorists Miro and Artkin, and, on the other, Ben and his father, whose activities combine to rescue the children, is heavily weighted in the terrorists' favour. Certainly Artkin has been willing to sacrifice both Miro and his brother in the cause for which he is fighting, and has ruthlessly trained them to that end, but at least he is always open with Miro about the risks he is facing, prepares him thoroughly for them, shares the danger with him, and himself dies willingly for the cause. Ben's father, sitting safely in his office, betrays his son into a situation the boy is not prepared for and cannot cope with, in ways and with results which leave Ben asking bitterly, 'Is a country worth that much, Dad?' When he learns the truth of the role he has unwittingly been led to play, Ben commits suicide. 'How,' he asks, 'could I have gone through life knowing what I had done? Knowing that my cowardice had served my country? Where did that leave me, Dad?' Whereas the end of the story sees Miro going on to further atrocities, with firm- ness, courage and conviction, both Ben and his father are destroyed mentally and emotionally by the role each has played.

Our admiration is withheld from Ben and his father, in part at least, because they are not tough and ruthless enough. Ben's anguish, and his father's, too, strike us as over-intense, self-pitying and hysterical, slipping over the edge into insanity, far from the trained 'admirable' coolness of Miro and his fellow terrorists. And although we are asked to admire the dedication shown in varying degrees by all participants in the drama, we are not invited to examine seriously a scenario in which duplicity, violence, and total disregard for ordinary, vulnerable people seem acceptable to those on both sides – no more than 'a means to an end'.

As is the case with many of Cormier's books, this story leaves a sour taste in the mouth, a cynicism which, in the impressionable young reader, could easily lead to a belief in what Fraser calls 'the essential awfulness of man, the inevitable cruelty of existence', fostered here by a writer 'supposedly so unflinching, so devastat- ingly honest' that for a while at least his views are accepted unquestioningly. Only the mature reader will perceive how 'pat- ently selective' Cormier has been in his presentation of character and events.

How have books like this gained such ready acceptance, even praise? Are they a symptom of the unease, cynicism and despair which, Fraser suggests, resulted from the revelations of the unbe- lievable cruelty of the Nazi extermination camps? At one time, he says:

> Violences ... were not a problem intellectually: the overwhelming majority of people in civilised countries didn't commit them, civilised states didn't commit them, and their perpetrators obviously couldn't offer defences of them that would carry even a tincture of validity for civilised people.

The large-scale revelations from Nazi Europe caused the collapse of those certainties for the even moderately reflective. On the one hand there was the politicisation of violence, the incorporation of atrocious violences into the very fabric of society, and hence a demonstration of the possibility of the legitimation of the illegal, the centralisation of the eccentric. And on the other, given the large number of perfectly ordinary people involved in one way or another in the perpetration of hitherto unthinkable horrors, there was the disquieting intimation, not only that there are latent possibilities for frightfulness in a great many people, but that relatively small shifts in social structures can permit those possibilities to realise themselves.

Fraser places the blame mainly on Nazi tyranny. But the callous use of nuclear bombs against Japan by supposedly 'good' nations, followed by years of Cold War strategies and further threats of possible nuclear war must also have played a significant part in leading young people to a despairing view of the world. From acquiescence in such policies follows also the increase of violence we have seen in young and old, rebellious and authoritarian, both within, against and on behalf of modern states in so many different contexts.

This questionable use of violence by or against the dissident individual has been the theme of a number of novels for young readers and for adults. How do these novels tackle the difficult problem of its presentation? It has to be admitted, unfortunately, that Cormier's writing undoubtedly has a power and a skill which is not often matched by contemporary authors, that his very involvement with the violence he depicts can itself exert a strong appeal, and that worthiness of motive is no guarantee that books without such involvement will prove attractive to young readers.

What motivates a writer is, however, important. Violence does not occur in a vacuum. It is significant therefore that Cormier has chosen to take Miro's actions out of any real life context which might give them specific meaning, and to concentrate instead on the violence which is central to the young terrorist's philosophy. Like Cormier, James Watson frequently uses scenes of violence in his political novels for teenagers, but in his books the focus of concern is the context which has led to violence rather than the violence which results. In *Where Nobody Sees* it is the suppression of demonstrations against nuclear waste dumping; in *The Freedom Tree* it is the Spanish Civil War; and in *Talking in Whispers* it is the murder of Miguel Alberti in Chile on the eve of the elections and the subsequent reign of terror imposed by the military junta. In each case Watson is using violence primarily in the service of a social conscience, to draw our concerned attention to its existence in the modern world – 'the incorporation of atrocious violence into the very fabric of society' – and to mobilise his young readers against its use, not to shock, thrill or disturb them. When we look, therefore, at his descriptions of murder or torture in *Talking in Whispers*, we are conscious of a revulsion against the murderers, not, as in *After the First Death*, an empathy with them. There is, for instance, an occasion when Andres, hiding for his own life in the wood, sees the cold-blooded execution by machine-gun fire of a number of political prisoners. 'He saw them as they fell; some where they stood, like slow-sliding rocks; some hurled into death like doors smashed from their hinges ...' Watson gives a lengthy description of this incident, but does not gloat over these deaths.

He conveys instead the numbing sense of shock experienced by Andres in contrast to the casual, emotionless brutality of the executioners. This is encapsulated in Andres's observation, as the soldiers, their mission accomplished, drive off in their trucks: 'He saw their faces. He saw no meaning.'

Later, Andres is caught and tortured. The torture scene is given in detail, yet with restraint.

> A charge of electricity shuddered his body. He was a puppet, handled not with love and skill and care, but by a mad operator, his strings yanked in fury. In the chaos of his brain he seemed to feel the strings. And they were attached to his knees, to his hands, to his ears, jerking his head violently from side to side.

The metaphor used here presents vividly the contrast between this mishandling of his living body by the torturers, and the loving, skilful care of his friends, Beto and Isa, whose puppet show is used both to entertain little children and daringly to satirise the military regime. In this way, and with the introduction even of a little wry humour, Watson manages both to involve the reader in Andres's agony and yet to keep sufficient distance from it to make it less unbearable, to strike that difficult balance between a realistic portrayal of violence as a necessary part of the theme, and indulgence in horrific scenes of brutality.

A similarly thoughtful attitude to the use and abuse of violence can be seen in Michael Smith's story, *The Hostages*. In this story, set in the Sudan, Nick, Sue and their parents are captured by Dinka revolutionaries, and, as in *After the First Death*, are held to ransom in a political struggle. The capture is violent and ruthless: Mr Millward is hit over the head, the children, Nick and Sue, are thrown into the back of the lorry like a couple of parcels, and they are all driven headlong off across miles of grassland. But in spite of this initial ferocity, and although Nick discovers that their tribal initiation ceremony involves scarring their faces with traditional patterns cut to the bone to make themselves look appropriately fierce as future warriors for the tribe, he finally reflects:

> When you got to know the Dinkas they were all right. They were kinder, for instance, than the people you met round the oil site at Bentiu. There you would quite often see an owner belabouring his donkey. Here you would never see a Dinka ill-treating an animal. Nor, despite their strange practice of mutilating themselves with scars, were they unkind to children or to each other. He had never, the whole time he had been among the Dinkas, seen a Dinka strike a child.

His subject matter gives Michael Smith the opportunity for scenes of violence, but he chooses instead to explore the different attitudes towards its use in a 'flow and recoil' of sympathies between the Dinkas and their hostages which genuinely requires the younger reader (of twelve or so) to think more clearly about the question.

When we come to books for older readers and adults the criteria we apply are superficially different: we assume that maturity brings the ability to face even the extremes of suffering and violence. But the underlying, deeper judgement is still crucial: how far is violence an essential element in the book's theme, deployed in ways which 'make for intellectual clarity and a more civilised consciousness', rather than for confusion?

The perils facing the author wishing to incorporate scenes of violence into a novel can be illustrated by reference to *A Stricken Field*, by Martha Gellhorn. This is a serious and concerned novel for adults, which is unfortunately flawed in its attempts to handle violence. Perhaps, as she was later to suggest, the author's profound sense of anger and helplessness at the fate of the victims of Nazi oppression had disturbed her artistic judgement. In her Afterword she confesses to a sense of shame at 'taking a fictionalized share' in a tragedy which was not her own, and adds: 'I know something very wrong has happened to me about this last book but as yet I don't know how or why ... with a little time I will find it and correct it.'

There are two torture scenes in the novel. The first has been written, like most of the novel, in the terms of 'a compelling piece of reporting', and is the more effective for its low-key statement of fact. At the end of the novel, however, a similar scene is enacted when Rita is secreted by chance in a coal cellar directly below the torture chamber precisely at the moment when her lover, Peter, is being subjected to similar brutalities. This time the torture scene is reconstructed in detail. The author is clearly motivated by a desire to involve the reader in the reality of the agonies of these unfortunate and tragic people, but the scene is overwritten to an extent which provides an excuse to escape from the true painfulness of the situation into a critical withdrawal from it: a retreat to the knowledge that 'it is only fiction'. Our sympathies, though strongly aroused, are in danger here of the kind of 'flow and recoil' which threatens to 'make for confusion' rather than 'for intellectual clarity' and the 'more civilized consciousness' which had been the author's aim. Fortunately in this novel it is also possible to see behind these flaws to the intolerable pain of what the author is seeking to describe, with an appropriate stirring of conscience on behalf of the protagonists.

There have been a number of novels and memoirs similarly inspired by a desire to mobilise anger and opposition at the suffering and violence abroad in the world, particularly that generated in South Africa as a result of the policy of apartheid. It is interesting to compare two of these, *Gone with the Twilight*, an autobiographical account by Don Mattera, and *Tsotsi*, a novel by Athol Fugard, with the picture of Miro presented in *After the First Death*.

Both South African books highlight the way in which apartheid provides a breeding ground for crime within the deprived, oppressed and resentful communities huddled together in the black townships. Mattera describes how he became leader of a notorious streetland gang of *tsotsis* in Sophiatown, and explicitly links his deterioration towards crime with his position as despised 'coloured'. His grandfather was an Italian sailor who jumped ship in 1904, married a black South African woman, and settled down in Cape Town. Though socially such a marriage was unacceptable, it was not yet illegal. But in August 1955, 'by order of an act of the white parliament' the young Don joined a long queue of people waiting 'to be classified or reclassified either as "pure" coloureds or as "natives"' according to the whim of the officials. Mattera writes:

Heart-rending stories, filled with bitter humiliation and anguish, daily made newspaper headlines in the late fifties. Some victims of the reclassification trauma chose suicide to bail them out of their absurd misery. Whole and stable families were shattered overnight as brothers, sisters, sons and daughters were ripped apart by the cruel laws of race separation. Relentless pass raids netted in hundreds of 'borderline' cases.

He adds, bitterly:

It is only in this mad and frightened portion of the world, bedevilled as it is by race consciousness and pigmentocracy, that human beings are classified under the law into sub-tribal and sub-human units.

Mattera had also to contend with a childhood dogged by feelings of personal as well as social rejection, of alienation from his father and most of the family. By the age of 16, he had become 'a street fighter and a thug for whom violence and obstinacy were the golden rule in the game of self-preservation'. The tale of violence and crime which he relates is brutal enough, but in contrast to Cormier's tone towards his anti-hero, Miro, it shows an unequivocal awareness of the unacceptability of his chosen way of life as well as of the appalling combination of neglect and apartheid which nurtured it. Freedom and justice are vital to man or boy,

Mattera says, but: 'What did they mean when a policeman was shooting at you in the dark? ... Freedom and justice can only mean something to a boy when that boy has been taught to mean something to himself.'

There were fortunately a few individuals, teachers, nuns and churchmen, including Father Trevor Huddlestone, who impressed Mattera as being genuinely concerned at the harsh lot of non-white people in South Africa. Perhaps partly through their influence, he eventually left the life of crime, with its murders, frequent and brutal imprisonment, gang warfare, despair and degradation, and began to identify himself as 'black' and become both a political activist and 'a literary figure with a growing international reputation'.

Tsotsi, by Athol Fugard, written 20 years ago, but published only recently, also explores the relationship between deprivation and gangsterdom in the apartheid world of the black townships. But as a novel it has an artistic unity and purpose which it is interesting to compare with the relatively untidy emotional and intellectual fluctuations of 'real life' and the mixture of reportage, polemic, dramatic narrative and highly coloured 'poetic' passages which make up Mattera's autobiographical account.

Fugard's anti-hero, Tsotsi, like Cormier's character Miro, was an orphan, who deliberately emptied himself of all intrusive emotion.

> His second rule ... was never to disturb his inward darkness with the light of a thought about himself or the attempt at a memory. He was not only resigned to not knowing about himself, he didn't want to know anything.

The novel traces the gradual breakdown of this rule, its consequences for Tsotsi in his personal life, and its symbolic relationship with the fate of South Africa. It begins when Boston, the most recent member of Tsotsi's gang, breaks his young leader's third rule of life, to allow no questions about himself; for questions, catching him without answers, 'sounded the vast depths of his darkness, making it a tangible reality'. An emotional blankness, it will be remembered, was a condition to which Miro, in Cormier's novel, actively aspired, seeing it as a necessary prerequisite to his life as a terrorist.

Boston was a comparatively educated young man, who had retained his ability to 'feel'. Though he joins in the killing with the rest of the gang, he is nauseated by it. His intrusive personal questions lead to a bitter fight with Tsotsi, in the course of which Boston warns him: ' "You'll feel something one day. Ja Tsotsi. One day it's going to happen. And God help you that day, because when it comes you won't know what to do. You won't know what to do with feeling." '

Tsotsi's own early trauma, precipitated when his mother is dragged from her bed by the police, and 'disappears', is related to the ever-present fear and violence of an apartheid state. It is symbolised by the anguished memory he had been determined to erase of 'a dog, a bitch, a yellow bitch ... crawling towards him ... in great pain', and finally dying giving birth to a still-born litter. His gradual progress towards the ability to feel once again is the theme of the book, and is summed up in the image of the bitch; and in the later imagery of light and darkness, used to express Tsotsi's eventual groping towards understanding of the feelings which had been aroused in turn by four individuals who had broken through the hard shell of his indifference and cruelty: his victim, Gumboot, the gangster Boston, the cripple Tshabalala and the baby.

> What is sympathy? If you had asked Tsotsi this, telling him that it was his new experience, he would have answered: like light, meaning that it revealed. Pressed further, he might have thought of darkness and lighting a candle, and holding it up to find Morris Tshabalala within the halo of its radiance. He was *seeing* him for the first time, in a way that he hadn't seen him before or with a second sort of sight, or maybe just more clearly. The subtleties did not matter. What was important was that in the light of his sympathy the cripple was revealed.
>
> But that wasn't all. The same light fell on the baby, and somehow on Boston too, and wasn't that the last face of Gumboot there, almost where the light ended and things weren't so clear anymore? And beyond that still, what? A sense of space, of an infinity stretching away so vast that the whole world, the crooked trees, the township streets, the crowded, wheezing rooms, might have been waiting there for a brighter, intense revelation.

The nature of this revelation eludes Tsotsi. Fugard refuses to resolve it, leaving the reader instead with a final equivocal image to symbolise Tsotsi's experience of life and imperfect fumbling towards understanding. He is killed in his vain attempt to save the baby from the bulldozers sent by the impatient white town to hasten its slum clearance scheme.

> All agreed that his smile was beautiful, and strange for a tsotsi, and that when he lay there on his back in the sun, before someone had fetched a blanket, they agreed that it was hard to believe what the back of his head looked like when you saw the smile.

Through these images we are made conscious always of the
emotional background to Tsotsi's violence, of the feelings determinedly repressed which nevertheless persist in breaking through.
This is an aspect of Fugard's understanding of Tsotsi's personality
which is in marked contrast to Cormier's portrayal of Miro. We
are not invited to understand Tsotsi's deprived background so that
we may excuse his behaviour or sentimentalise over his fate when
his repressed softer feelings finally betray him to his death. Nor
are we invited to admire his toughness unreservedly as an ideal.
But we see both aspects of his nature as part of the unresolvable
ironic tragedy of his situation as a black man in South Africa. It is
one also with the persistently difficult dilemma of those who, like
Holbrook (Chapter 5) or the various victims of the Nazi death
camps (Chapter 7) see that to kill, or even to survive in intolerable
situations of war or threat of death one must empty oneself of
feeling, harden oneself against compassion or concern for others;
for the alternative is to go under.

The conscious artistry with which the individual lives of the
various protagonists in Fugard's novel are woven together illustrates powerfully the potential beauty of South Africa itself,
behind which lurks always the ugliness, hatred, fear, suspicion,
violence and brutality forced on its people by the state policy of
apartheid. It makes its point in different terms from those used in
Mattera's personal story, but concludes with a dual image which
complements Mattera's final half-despairing but passionate protest
at the 'violence, immorality and squalor' of the 'twilight people'
herded into the 'coloured' township, and his contrasting declaration of hope that 'in another day, another time, we would emerge
to reclaim our dignity and our land'. In the last analysis both
these books are informed not with the underlying cynical admiration of the violent personality evident in *After the First Death*, but
with an overriding anger against the state and a corresponding
compassion towards those oppressed by its policies and driven
therefore to a life of crime.

Faysal Mikdadi, too, is concerned as a writer with the problem
of violence. Though he now lives in Britain, he was brought up in
Beirut, the son of a Palestinian father and Lebanese mother. His
novel, *Tamra*, was inspired by his deep anger, horror and personal
involvement with the catastrophic events in the country of his
birth. It is certainly not a novel for the squeamish: Mikdadi writes
in unsparing detail of the chaos and bloodshed, violence and
tragedy, rape, torture and murder which are daily events in Beirut.

His two main protagonists are Tamra, a brilliant university
student whose family are Maronite Christians, and Leyla, her
closest friend and fellow-student, who is a Palestinian refugee,

thus reflecting the city's divided loyalties. Fittingly, therefore, Mikdadi is evenhanded in his condemnation of all sides in the atrocities, many of whom take drugs to enable them to carry out unspeakable acts of cruelty against each other. They are inspired by fanatical hatred, motivated also, like Tamra's father, Pierre, by grief and rage at what has happened to people they love. They commit actions which are appalling, unbelievable when associated with ordinary people. When Tamra's mother is raped and murdered along with the ten-year-old girl she had stayed to protect, Pierre's revenge is to lead an answering massacre, rape and torture of Palestinians in the refugee camp, and, later, to kill his daughter's friend, Leyla. There are certainly no invitations to share vicariously in the violences committed. The reader's sympathies will be drawn instead to those few protagonists who retain some sense of humanity, the chief of these being the two girls, Tamra and Leyla, whose deep friendship for each other protects them from joining in the excesses of hatred and anger.

In the context of this story one remembers wrily Artkin's instructions to Miro. 'Do it quickly', he had said. 'Deliver [death] as efficiently as possible with the least mess. We are not animals after all ... ' But as Mikdadi shows so clearly, killing brutalises more surely than it ennobles, and war provides both aggressors and their victims with an excuse for more killing and worse atrocities. Mikdadi's story rightly arouses horror and outrage at the crimes against humanity committed on all sides by men and by women too, under the influence of passions of hatred and revenge, reinforced by drugs. It is difficult to see how anyone can emerge from reading it without a conviction that war is senseless, brutalising, an escalation of reciprocal revenge and atrocities so horrible that no eventual reconciliation of the warring parties could be possible. But it makes clear also that where innocent people are to be the victims, like Leyla, or the children and their young bus driver in Cormier's story, it is no more acceptable to kill them cleanly, dispassionately, without feeling or mess as Miro had been trained to do.

Reviewing these stories with their varying attitudes to the use of violence and its role in the context of their narrative, one can see clearly the unacceptable dimensions to Cormier's novel. Fraser's remark: 'What especially disturbs the liberal viewer or reader is the kind of mentality for which destruction – deliberate destruction with full knowledge of what is being destroyed – appears perfectly right and natural', applies particularly to Cormier's protagonist, with whom the reader empathises most strongly. The other authors are concerned to show clearly and unequivocally their horror at deliberate violence, their rejection of it as a legitimate means of persuasion, and their anger and anguish on behalf of what is being destroyed – that is, both the physical bodies of the victims and also the emotional and intellectual health of the destroyers and of the communities which support them.

13
Legitimising Violence

Nearly 2,000 years ago Seneca wrote: 'We restrain manslaughter and isolate murders ... but deeds of cruelty are done every day by command of senate and popular assembly, and servants of the state are ordered to do what is forbidden to the private citizen.' In his conversations with Albert Einstein in 1932, 'Why War?', Freud points out that the situation has not changed. He says:

> Thus we see that right is the might of a community. It is still violence, ready to be directed against any individual who resists it: it works by the same methods and follows the same purposes. The only real difference lies in the fact that what prevails is no longer the violence of an individual but that of a community.
>
> (Quoted in Fraser, *Violence in the Arts*)

The novels and memoirs which concern individuals who have experienced 'the violence of a community' are painful to read: but they too are seeking not to exploit a perverse interest in the horrors they depict, but to call the attention of the world to cruelties and injustices which should never be tolerated anywhere.

Alicia Partnoy grew up in Argentina, and, with several of her closest friends, became active in the Peronist Youth Movement, working in a literacy campaign in one of the shanty towns. Like many of her young contemporaries she thought that the Peronist Movement 'bore the seeds of change to socialism'. But Peron died in 1975, and in March 1976 'the military – along with the national oligarchy and backed by multinational corporations – launched a coup'. Alicia was a student at her home town university in Bahia Blanca, but attending classes now became hazardous, for she 'had to pass between two soldiers who were sitting with machine guns at the entrance to the building'. Her Identity Card was then checked daily to see if she was on the list of 'wanted' activists. Soon, therefore, through a mixture of fear and anger, she stopped going to university and became active in working for a better society. She 'clandestinely reproduced and distributed information on the economic situation, the workers' strikes, and the repression'. In the end both Alicia and her husband were arrested, and kept for five months with no means of discovering what, meantime, had happened to their nine-month-old daughter. All this Alicia Partnoy tells us in the introduction to her book, *The Little School*, which then describes, in a series of short, quiet, but terrifying vignettes, her daily life in this centre for 'dissidents'. They were kept perpetually blindfolded, their hands bound, half-starved, allowed to visit the latrine only twice a day – 'three times when the guards felt generous' – punished if they spoke, constantly threatened, abused, beaten and tortured.

> When it rained, the water streamed into the rooms and soaked us. When the temperature fell below zero, we were covered with only dirty blankets; when the heat was unbearable, we were obligated to blanket even our heads. We were forced to remain silent and prone, often immobile or face down for many hours, our eyes blindfolded and our wrists tightly bound.

One of Alicia's friends, Graciela, was five months pregnant at the time of her arrest. She told Alicia:

> The trip from Cutral-Co to Neuquen was pure hell ... They knew I was pregnant. It hadn't occurred to me that they could torture me while we were travelling. They did it during the whole trip: the electric prod on my abdomen because they knew about the pregnancy ... *One, two, three, four* ... Each shock brought that terrible fear of miscarriage ... and that pain, my pain, my baby's pain. I think it hurt more because I knew he was being hurt, because they were trying to kill him ... Sometimes I think it would have been better if I had lost him.

Graciela's son was eventually delivered by the guards. When she finally 'disappeared', 'her son, according to the guards, was given to one of the interrogators'.

It is the small, quiet details of these stories which hurt the heart: the trips, still blindfolded, to the latrine, where the guard, watching and waiting, would hand the prisoner not a piece of newspaper, but sandpaper; the treat of quince jam and cheese given to 'celebrate' the capture of new prisoners; the friend, Benja, chained to the foot of Alicia's bed so that Alicia can hear and feel the impact of the punches. Aware that Benja has recently been tortured, Alicia cunningly finds ways to ameliorate his lot. She distracts the guard's attention each time he comes to punch him yet again; she cuts her precious cheese into pieces, and puts the pieces between her toes to pass them surreptitiously to Benja. But in the end, Benja, too, disappears. With his girlfriend, 17 years old like himself, he is shot.

The might of this community, directed with ceaseless violence against these individuals, most of them in their teens or early twenties, has been recorded here with clarity and pain, but also with courage and hope, by one of the few survivors of 'the little school'. The act of publishing these stories, Alicia tells us, helps her to feel the voices of her dead friends growing stronger, so that they 'will not pass unheard'.

In a very different, but equally powerful book, *The Stones Cry Out*, Molyda Szymusiak records memories of her childhood in Cambodia under the infamous Pol Pot regime during the years from 1975 to 1980. Molyda was not imprisoned; indeed, as a twelve-year-old she was little interested, in spite of frequent 'education' sessions, in the political aspects of her country's ordeal. The violence used against herself and her family took the form of forced labour in appalling conditions. Her book is a daily record of her struggle to survive under a harsh, unpredictable regime in a land devastated both by civil strife and by its growing involvement in the Vietnam War and the consequent 'heavy American bombing'. She tells us: 'During five years under the Khmer Rouge, I endured hunger in the most fertile country in the world, thirst in the most irrigated region of Asia, mourning and massacres in that paradise that was my Cambodia.'

Her story begins in April 1975, when 'the victorious Khmer Rouge entered Phnom Penh, whose population had been swollen by refugees from 600,000 to over 2 million; within days, all of its inhabitants were evacuated to the countryside'. Molyda and her family were forced to move at a moment's notice, with only those few possessions they could carry on the two ends of a bamboo pole. This was the start of five terrible years of hardship for the whole family, of whom only Molyda and three of her cousins managed to survive.

The deaths of so many members of Molyda's family were the result not of deliberate 'liquidation' but of being ruthlessly overworked in spite of the starvation which weakened their bodies and the unhealthy living conditions which further undermined their resistance to disease. Those who did not work did not eat; so, ill and exhausted as he was, Molyda's father continued to go to the rice fields until one day he fell into the mud and had not the strength to pull himself out. When his family found him, it was too late. Time and again Molyda also is forced to go on working, though shaking with fever, thin and weak. The story of her sufferings, and of the deaths of her grandmother, parents, and brother and sisters is detailed and harrowing. She tells of coming across bodies of people who had been 'eliminated', sometimes on flimsy pretexts, and of the torture and executions of some of the

Mekongs (leaders) who had fallen out of favour. Finally, after incredible hardships and near escapes, Molyda and three surviving cousins escaped via Vietnam to France, where at last they could hope for a secure future. But, she remarks, quietly, 'The years of slavery, fear and starvation have left their mark deep within us.'

Molyda's experiences can be compared with those of Haing S. Ngor in *Surviving the Killing Fields*. Ngor was more politically aware than Molyda. He tells us what had led up to the seizure of power by the Khmer Rouge; the riots, the racial grudges operating between the Cambodians and the Vietnamese, the coup by Prince Sisowath Matak and General Lon Nol, the American intervention, the fighting and bombing and finally the counter-coup by the Khmer Rouge all of which left the country devastated.

As a doctor, Ngor was in constant danger from Khmer Rouge purges, and on three separate occasions was imprisoned and tortured. He gives detailed acccounts of the beatings, the spring-loaded vice at his temples, the water torture and other efforts to make him talk, and of the tortures and executions he witnessed during his imprisonment; first considerately warning that 'readers with sensitive feelings might want to skip over the next few pages and begin reading again towards the end of the chapter'.

He too records the prevailing sickness and death which overtook so many of the city-bred people as a result of the punitive regime relentlessly forced on them by the leaders of the Khmer Rouge. 'The greatest single factor in this public-health disaster,' he concludes, 'was malnutrition.' And after the long, painful ordeal of these years, which none of the rest of his family survived, he, like so many other victims of traumatic experiences, continued to suffer from nightmares long after he reached the safety of the USA. 'It didn't take much to set off my nightmares – the sound of water dripping from a faucet was enough. It put me back in prison, looking up at water dripping from a hole in a bucket.'

Both writers have a terrible story to tell, but recount their experiences with quiet restraint, making no capital out of their sufferings, concerned only to win international recognition of the plight of their country, and so offer some hope for its future. The continued UN recognition of the Khmer Rouge as the legitimate government and the continued financial support given to Pol Pot, however, bears tragic witness to the real values and priorities of so-called civilised states.

The situation in Thailand, too, was one of hard work, misery and starvation, this time the result of a combination of prolonged drought, poor harvests, rapacious landlords and a repressive government. In an excellent and thoughtful novel, *Rice Without Rain*, Minfong Ho describes the plight of the peasantry, and the oppressive measures used against anyone seeking to oppose the crippling rent exacted by absentee landlords. A small group of young students, who have come to experience life on the land for themselves, persuade the village headman to refuse to pay the full rent demanded, with the result that he is injured whilst attempting to escape arrest, and dies in prison. His daughter, Jinda, briefly joins the students in a peaceful protest rally in Bangkok, which nevertheless ends in a terrible massacre, recounted in vivid but pertinent detail. Jinda returns sadly to her village, determined to work towards a better future, but without resorting to or inviting further violence. But Ned, the young student she loves, has come to the opposite conclusion. He feels that violent resistance is now inevitable, since the peaceful means he has tried – 'liberal dissent, parliamentary reform – all the things that're supposed to work in a democracy' – have got them nowhere. He tells her, 'The only thing the military understands is force. They shot at us; we've got to shoot back at them. It's that simple.' Jinda is not convinced. 'Killing people,' she says, miserably, 'is never that simple.' The case for and against an attempt to solve the problems of the people through answering violence is thus cogently presented through the fortunes of Jinda and her family in the village of Maekung, and of the students and their abortive attempts to help.

Oppression knows no boundaries of race or creed, as can be seen in Wole Soyinka's account of his imprisonment in Nigeria in *The Man Died*, and in Andrew Ekwuru's description of the genocidal massacres during the Biafran War in *Songs of Steel*, a novel which follows the fortunes of one extended family in Eastern Nigeria to near-extinction. Again, while colonial repression in Kenya has been recorded by Jomo Kenyatta in *Suffering Without Bitterness* and by Josiah Kariuki in *Mau Mau Detainee*, Ngugi wa Thiong'o has given a bitter account in *Detained* of his imprisonment by the Kenyan authorities *after* Independence. He writes: 'The British jailed an innocent Kenyatta. Thus Kenyatta learned to jail innocent Kenyans. Is that the difference?'

In company with the prison literature inspired by the Stalinist period in the USSR (*Darkness at Noon*, by Arthur Koestler, *Into the Whirlwind*, by Evgenia Ginzburg and *One Day in the Life of Ivan Denisovich* by Alexander Solzhenitsyn, for instance), these books were written to mobilise public opinion against the cruelties inflicted upon political prisoners in the name of state security. But it still goes on. In South Africa the 'might of the community' is notoriously 'ready to be directed against any individual who resists it'; and the violences of those in authority are creating a responding escalation of violence and bitterness in those who, under an iniquitous system of apartheid, feel themselves to be victimised by the state. Some of the many books of fiction and autobiography from South Africa have been discussed in Chapter 10 of my book, *Different Faces*. But there are many more which bring into focus the plight of opponents of the system.

Chain of Fire, by Beverley Naidoo, is one of several anti-apartheid novels for younger readers. It takes us to the village of Bophelong, where Naledi and Tiro live with their small sister, Dineo, and their grandmother. They are poor, living on what their mother can send them out of her meagre earnings as a domestic servant, and what their old grandmother can earn locally on a nearby farm, and we are given a vivid sense of the struggles of daily life in this small village. When the children discover that the whole village is to be forcibly uprooted and sent to a barren so-called 'homeland', where life will be even harder to sustain, Naledi helps to organise her schoolfriends into making a peaceful protest march. But here too the non-violent young demonstrators are dispersed violently by police with dogs, whips and rifles; and some are seriously hurt. In subsequent protests other villagers are arrested and subjected to further violence, and the father of Naledi's friend is shot dead. The story concludes with Naledi's vision of a 'chain of fire' which will bind together all those still defiantly persisting in the 'long struggle for freedom' from legalised state oppression.

Waiting for the Rain, by Sheila Gordon, is suitable for slightly older readers of 13 or so. Though its central character, Tengo, finally decides that 'violence was not for him', in the conditions still prevailing he too feels it to be inescapable. 'He could see its necessity for the struggle that was taking place, that was making normal life impossible.'

Tengo grows up in close friendship with Frikkie, a white boy of his own age, on whose uncle's farm Tengo's parents are both working. But Tengo is slowly awakening to the unsatisfactoriness of his position of unquestioning inferiority, and soon is no longer content to follow gratefully behind his white friend. Single-mindedly, Tengo sets himself a goal, to get the education which he discovers the state provides free for Frikkie but which his own parents must pay for. But as, gradually, his intelligent, questioning mind and his unflagging determination lead him towards the end he seeks, so he becomes increasingly estranged from Frikkie.

The story of Tengo's progress towards understanding and of his changing relationship with Frikkie is fascinating, told with economy and a sensitive appreciation of the tensions and difficulties which await him when he finally manages to go to school in Johannesburg. For it is the time of the Soweto riots. In spite of himself, Tengo is eventually caught up in a confrontation between the army and the mourners at the funeral of 'seven people – four of them schoolchildren – who had been shot the previous week after stone throwing had broken out when the police had fired on a group holding a protest'.

As Tengo is running from the scene he and Frikkie (who is currently undergoing his military service) confront each other in very different circumstances from their earlier friendship. Their angry encounter makes clear the tragic impasse now obtaining between two young men who might under other circumstances have remained friends. Tengo tries desperately to pierce the armour of Frikkie's incomprehension, and of his stubborn attempt to deny complicity in the present state of affairs. But Frikkie still obstinately refuses to see that he cannot plead innocence; that he is actively supporting the establishment through the military service which has now brought the two boys into a situation of confrontation; and this Tengo cannot forgive.

Ironically, however, this encounter enables Tengo to realise that, 'rather than the blacks, it was Frikkie and whites like him who were the victims, trapped and cornered as they were by the narrowness of their vision'. Their meeting, with its mixture of insights, pent-up fury, incomprehension, fear and pity and even affection surviving from their old friendship encapsulates with a clarity which forbids sentimentality Tengo's shocked perception of the intransigence of their opposing points of view, and the unacceptability of the inevitable choices facing him. It is a tribute to the power and vision of the novel that the sense of tragedy and the sympathy is not confined to Tengo's broken dreams; any future within South Africa seems bleak for both boys as long as apartheid and state oppression of the black majority persists. Yet this novel ends on a note of hope, tenuous, but resting, in spite of everything, on Tengo's decision to let Frikkie go free, and his certainty that Frikkie will not betray him, either, to his fellow-soldiers.

In Mary Benson's adult novel, *At the Still Point*, the central character, Anne Dawson, like the heroine in *A Stricken Field* (see Chapter 12), is a journalist, concerned with her own personal affairs, yet also drawn deeply into the tragedy being enacted in the country she is visiting. Anne's perceptions of Andrew Fox, whose former 'positive quality' of 'a brightness' has been 'drained' by his arrest and 'statue torture'; Paula, who is in prison for her political activities and relates the horrors of apartheid to the experiences of her fellow Polish Jews under the Nazis; the young Afrikaaner dominee (or minister) on the train, whose Christian compassion for 'Bantu families divided, the children and mothers made to live apart from the fathers' does not extend to those who make either a political or a violent protest; Anne's own conformist relatives and liberal friends; Matthew Marais, the radical defence lawyer who is becoming increasingly involved in anti-apartheid activities; Beatrice Qaba whose case he is defending, and Nathaniel, Beatrice Qaba's younger brother, soon to take up arms against the state, epitomise the divisions and tensions of her native South Africa. The novel is lively, compelling, varied, but uneven in quality, suffering perhaps from the same intensity and closeness to its subject which had flawed Martha Gellhorn's novel. Its indignation is directed against the complacency of the white population, pursuing their petty personal affairs in the bland assumption that it is the destiny of the black peoples to serve them; against the iniquitous pass laws, the injustice of the courts, police brutality and torture, the violence of the state used relentlessly against defenceless individuals who are driven thereby to answering amateur violence. Nathaniel, fleeing finally across the border with Anne's help, is not, he tells her, going to take up the scholarship arranged for him in England, but to train to fight his oppressors.

'I, too,' he said, 'I had not learned before what it is, truly, to hate. And I wanted to kill, blindly. That's bad, wasteful. Afterwards ... I saw that there is no way forward except through violence, only it must be controlled, it must be very carefully and deliberately planned ... I am going for guerilla training. Our brains, our bodies, must be made one with our weapons. How else can we destroy these devils? How else can we, the black people, win back our land and our dignity?'

The book concludes in favour of violence and terrorism as a means of overthrowing an unjust regime, but it does so in terms which require the reader to consider, seriously, the issues involved.

The Children of Soweto, by Mbulelo Vizikhungo Mzamane is part autobiography, part reportage. It presents a bleak view of the future for South Africa. It is an account of the grievances which led to the Soweto uprisings of June 1976, a rebellion which had been simmering for a long time, in the students' growing dissatisfaction with the limited and restricted education deemed appropriate to their lowly status under apartheid. In the first section of the book, 'My Schooldays in Soweto', Mzamane describes how they gradually established their own study cells and combined to form a highly organised and flourishing student movement. But their initially peaceful activities inevitably attracted the attention of the Special Branch, and students were pulled in for questioning. This led to the escalation of action, strikes, demonstrations and, inevitably, to violence by and against the state.

The second section, 'The Day of the Riots', recounts what happened to one man, caught unexpectedly in the township on the day of the riots in the company of a white man, a fellow employee whom he was driving home. This brief episode is a comic interlude in a day of tragedy; illustrating the ambivalent relationships possible between black and white even under apartheid.

The third and longest section, 'The Children of Soweto', is an analysis of what happened to one group of young activists: the deaths of black youngsters when the police fired at random into the demonstrators; the consequent rioting; the arson and looting; the spread of disturbances to other townships; the serious meetings of the groups of students seeking both to organise resistance and to escape arrest; and their plans to unite the township in a week of mourning before the funerals of the victims. There are also quiet, factual but bitter accounts of the interrogations endured by arrested students; and the savage interruption of the peaceful funeral ceremonies by the police. With others of his friends, the author escaped into exile, still defiant.

> We were the children of the new diaspora, we, the children of Soweto, germinating everywhere we went little new seeds of vengeance, hatred, bitterness, wrath, on the fertile soil of our hearts, watering our cherished seeds with our own blood, sweat and tears and that of our people.

In spite of the unacceptable levels of violence and terrorism on both sides, Mzamane's analysis of the situation prompts a reaction different in kind and quality from that evoked by Cormier (see Chapter 12) on behalf of his ruthless young terrorist. For Mzamane never loses sight of the essential humanity and anguish of the children of Soweto, displayed in their warmth and humour and close yet self-critical solidarity. There is in this book a clear perception of mistakes, of good and ill within both black and white communities, and always an invitation to the reader to exercise his or her own judgement as rigorously as do the students themselves, caught up in events not of their choosing.

Following the riots in Soweto came uprisings and protests in other townships, and on 11 August the troubles finally hit Cape Town, where Maria Tholo lived in the township of Guguletu. Maria Tholo was a respected schoolteacher, her husband a supervisor in a retail chain, with an excellent salary. They had two daughters, and the entire family were 'staunch church-goers'. An American journalist, Carol Hermer, who was in Cape Town at the time, made a 'series of weekly, tape-recorded interviews' with Maria between 11 August 1976 and the following February. These form the core of *The Diary of Maria Tholo*, and provide a first-hand account of the events in Guguletu during the riots and the succeeding months. The diaries, supplemented by commentaries from Carol Hermer, are a unique record of the experiences and views of a thoroughly respectable and concerned woman, who is sympathetic to the grievances of the children, and horrified at the violence which they met at the hands of the police. Maria reports instances of police brutality; of a baton charge by riot police on children peacefully eating their lunch, followed by a teargas attack on the staffroom where they then sought shelter; of one young girl with 158 pellets in her back as she fled from the unprovoked attack, and of a young man, innocently cycling home from work, hit in the eyes by pellets from police guns. These and other disturbances and injuries to young people leave Maria confused, afraid and desperately anxious about the future for herself, her family and friends.

Imprisonment under apartheid has been the fate of many black people. Caesarina Kona Makhoere was 21, but still at school (a consequence of the difficult circumstances in which black people manage to obtain their schooling) 'when she was arrested as an "agitator" following the 1976 student uprising against "Bantu education". She was detained without trial, convicted under the notorious Terrorism Act, and served six years in various South African jails, in solitary confinement and virtually incommunicado throughout'. In *No Child's Play* she describes her experience of prison. The day after her arrest she was taken to a building which housed the Pretoria Security Police.

> I was marched to the first floor, into a small room where, without warning, I was beaten up. Four hefty men, two white and two black, gave me the beating of my life. [They] ... threw me all over the place ... Then they took their jackets off and the interrogation began. Selepe was the most vicious, a sadist! He screamed at me: 'You will not get out of here alive if you don't co-operate! ... I can kill you and think nothing of it – the law is protecting me ...'

So began a period of continual battle against the legal violence and inhumanity of the prison conditions she endured in various South African jails.

In Britain, too, protesters have faced an unacceptable abuse of power by state and police. In *Greenham Women Everywhere* Alice Cook and Gwyn Kirk describe how the determinedly peaceful protests of women against nuclear missiles were met by police violence and by arrest mainly on technical charges. 'Whether a particular direct action is deemed illegal,' they say, 'is in the hands of the authorities. There are laws to cover virtually any situation: for example, simply standing still on the pavement can be deemed an offence.' A typical confrontation with the police is described as follows:

> My impression was that the police were being reasonably restrained and some seemed to be sympathetic ... Some police, however, were ... being deliberately violent. I was dragged once by the hood of my cagoule, which was across my throat, which meant I couldn't breathe; I tried to scream but couldn't, and from the violence with which I was thrown down at the side, I was retching and choking. I am sure that was deliberate ... A woman lay at my feet having her head kicked by a policeman ... The woman next to me had her face kicked and her glasses broken ...

This account concludes charitably: 'They were obviously not used to dealing with totally nonviolent women and some over-reacted'!

Prison for these women was a traumatic experience, if not quite so horrific as for the detainees in South Africa. But, increasingly, deliberately humiliating and unnecessary procedures like the infamous strip searching have been used against Greenham women, and against political detainees in Northern Ireland. In this troubled province, as Margaretta D'Arcy discovered after her arrest in 1980, conditions were inhuman and squalid even before the 'no-wash protest' which was organised by the prisoners during her six months in Armagh Jail. In *Tell Them Everything* she describes what happened to her there and says: 'Since the early 1970s approximately 120 women have been incarcerated in Armagh – for armed rebellion, or civil disobedience, or merely for being known to hold dissident opinions ... '

What state repression means in Northern Ireland has also been recorded by Eileen Fairweather, Roisin McDonough and Melanie McFadyean in *Only the Rivers Run Free*. Their account begins:

> In this book you will meet many Irish women, both Catholic and Protestant. Some are feminists, some are not; some politically involved, some not. They tell their stories – stories about war, grief, comedy, love, poverty, men, children, sex and religion. They aren't comfortable stories, and they frequently have unhappy endings. But they are the truth about women's experiences in the Six Counties of Northern Ireland.

They too describe the squalid and oppressive conditions in the various jails in Northern Ireland, for both men and women. There are accounts, also, of police brutality towards those under arrest. Tom, a young man of 21, was shot in the legs by the RUC as he tried to escape from a hi-jacked van, and again – quite unnecessarily – in the back as he lay helpless on the ground. Though too ill to be moved, he was taken from the civilian to the military hospital, and from there, while still very ill, to the Castlereagh interrogation centre. There, his mother said:

> Tom had been made to stand and lean his full weight on the side that his plaster was, and they interrogated him in that position, hour upon hour ... Then they put him into a straight-backed chair. They kept kicking it ... The chair jarred the spine even more and caused him extreme pain, he was very, very sick.
> The doctor left painkillers there for him. Tom never got those drugs. Tom was in Castlereagh for five days and five nights. They pulled the hair out of him, they beat him, they turned his wrists down as far as they'd go towards the palms of his hands, they pulled his ears back. He got all the beatings they could issue ...
> We had a good idea what Tom would look like after five days in Castlereagh but, God knows, we weren't expecting to see what we saw. He was just a physical wreck.

This is only one of many accounts in this book and in others which remind us of the truth of Freud's comment: 'Right is the might of a community. It is still violence, ready to be directed against any individual who resists it.' Its use as illustrated in these books puts to shame the so-called civilised communities concerned.

What this means for all of us is that there must be some serious consideration of the root causes of violence, and active opposition to those who, in our modern civilisations, condone its use. Though undoubtedly a small factor in the equation, literature, especially books for young people, can have a part to play either in confirming acceptance of violence as an integral and unavoidable ingredient of modern life or as something we must strive to eradicate, so that we may return to the state described by Fraser in *Violence in the Arts*, when 'Violences ... were not a problem'.

14
Cautionary Tales

The problem of power, and the corruption and violence which attend it, has been explored in several novels through the creation of an imagined state. Such novels have certain advantages. The author can create a state deliberately structured to illustrate those aspects of society most important to the theme, in such a way that the problems posed and the questions raised can be seen to have universal significance. Peter Abrahams's novel, *This Island Now*, is, he says, 'a work of fiction, in which all persons and places are figments of the imagination'. But, he adds, 'since the imagination is nurtured by reality the point of departure of this story is the reality of the Caribbean'. His fictional island state is vividly evoked – its landscape, the luxurious green of its vegetation, its warmth, sunlight and colour – and we are also drawn strongly into an awareness of its people, and the special nature of their problems. The aftermath of colonialism has left the island with a legacy of a Western-style government, but one which has been dominated for nearly half a century by the aging and venal President Moses Joshua, whose 'compulsive need to destroy any spirit of independence in those immediately around him' has left, at his death, a Cabinet too accustomed to subservience to be capable of rational and concerted action. The people, too, have had 'so much of their humanity, of their dignity ... destroyed that they are afraid of standing on their own'; and both the island and the people have been consistently exploited by rich capitalists at home and abroad. These capitalists are epitomised in the story by the powerful Isaacs family, and the resentment against them is not merely a question of their money and power, but also of their race. For this is the other central problem for the island; the legacy of centuries of racial oppression, so that skin colour becomes a matter of tremendous importance in the coming battle for power. The course of events is to reveal 'a world of latent prejudice among the dark-skinned people against those whose skins were fair, whether they were native to the island or not'. It is within these parameters, common to countries emerging from colonial

214

status, but of significance also to longer established states where existing democracies are threatened, that the drama is played out.

The Cabinet's division and confusion gives one minister, Mr Albert Josiah, 'a neat, slender little dark-brown man', the opportunity he has been waiting for. He cleverly manoeuvres himself into the Presidency, and quickly assumes absolute control. The merchant Isaacs family, the press, the radio, the people, are all jockeyed by various means into accepting his absolute authority, and it is the methods he uses that come under sharply critical scrutiny in the novel. It is not merely a matter of using naked power, though the routine show of strength is evident from the very beginning in the bodyguards surrounding the President, the 'operators' used by him to get the information he needs to enable him to put on trial anyone who seems to threaten his power, the ruthlessness with which he suppresses all expressions of opposition and, eventually, the pervasive routine show of force which is the culmination of five years of his rule.

The various protagonists within the novel symbolise differing interests in the island and differing attitudes towards Josiah's assumption and exercise of power. Andrew Simpson, though an idealistic young man deeply committed to the cause of the under-privileged, has allowed himself to be persuaded that the ends Josiah hopes to achieve justify the means he is prepared to use. Martha Lee strongly disagrees with Josiah's tactics and with Simpson's support of them. Martha is a journalist, a native of the island, part black, part Chinese, but with a strong sense of love and commitment to her country's interests, an equally strong sense of loyalty to her profession, and an instinctive distrust of Josiah. It is she who reacts most sharply and persistently to Josiah's attempts to control the press and to tell her what she may or may not write, and who perceives immediately the trend of Josiah's actions. 'Tyranny often has small beginnings,' she tells Simpson, 'like inhibiting one journalist a little.' So when Simpson argues that 'there are people ... all over ... the third world ... who will happily trade free speech and free institutions for three square meals a day, a roof over their heads and reasonable health services', Martha is not impressed with these arguments as a reason for the suppression of freedoms that still seem vitally important to her, and remains deeply anxious that her country will pay too high a price for the benefits they expect to flow from Josiah's leadership.

Andy only gradually begins to realise the nature of that price: the sacrifice of the honest John Stanhope, who refuses to be manipulated into actions which contravene the Constitution and are contrary to his own principles; of the white editor of Martha's paper; of the one minister, Freeways, who had attempted to oppose Josiah; and, as a consequence of Josiah's need to rig Freeways' trial, of the judge who refuses to comply.

But what finally convinces Simpson that the price is too high, that the ends cannot justify the means, is his own growing personal disenchantment with Josiah, both as a result of the loss of the girl he loves and through his increasing awareness of the ways in which Josiah's repressive measures have begun to be employed not merely against individuals standing in his way, but against the people themselves.

Josiah too is now forced to realise where his policies have led him:

> This was not how he had wanted it. To use force in order to crush the enemies of the people, yes. That he had done without compunction. To use force against the people themselves because they do not know their own interests, that hurts in a way nobody understood.

Nevertheless, Josiah has started on a road from which there is no going back. Like those men of violence described by Fraser in *Violence in the Arts*, he too is convinced of the rightness of his cause, and of the necessity for the acts of violence he commits. He is cruelly aware that the farther he travels 'this chosen road' the more withdrawn his people will become, and the higher will grow the invisible wall of coldness between them and him, 'as though he were the enemy'. He feels, bitterly, 'I was prepared for everything except this ...'; but he consoles himself that: 'There are no easy ways, no short cuts, no way of doing what had to be done without drinking deeply of this bitter cup of loneliness and harshness.' Now that he has reached this conclusion it is evident that for him, 'in the years that lay ahead, long and bleak and lonely years possibly, this moment of doubt, of weakness would not return again'. In this way we are made aware of the paths by which the leader is himself seduced by his own policies to an irrevocable commitment to violence and repression.

Ironically, at the close of the novel, Josiah is left only with his most clearsighted opponent, Martha Lee, still prepared to remain, even to grow closer to the government she feared and hated. She has nowhere else to go. Josiah's right-hand man and apologist, Andrew Simpson, on the other hand, now disillusioned, is lying in wait for Josiah's car to pass within range of his rifle's telescopic sights, remembering Martha's earlier warnings, and (mistakenly) believing himself now to be ready to shoot down the man he had idolised. In the event he cannot shoot, and the reader is left with the paradox that Simpson's failure to commit this act of violence will leave the island at the mercy of its tyrannical president.

In this book the consequences first to individuals and then to the people as a whole of accepting a single, ruthless leader are clearly analysed, as are the fateful steps by which such power is assumed and consolidated. As Martha Lee had once declared, the blame lies not only with the dictator but also with the weakness of the forces for good, which had failed, at moments of crisis, to stand up powerfully for what was right.

The next three stories are of societies in which the repressive and controlling power is already firmly established. They too examine the consequences for the people as a whole, whose acceptance of such a regime has led to a lowering of the quality of life for all, evidenced in particular in a lessening of compassion and concern of fellow-citizens for one another, and in a concerted willingness to turn and rend any individual who threatens to disturb the status quo.

In Peter Abrahams's story the people are controlled openly by force of arms. In *The Vandal* Ann Schlee has imagined a state which controls its people more subtly and surely by literally drugging their minds into conformity. Taking the controlling drug is a nightly ritual.

The curtains were drawn. The room was lit and bright. His mother came in from the kitchen carrying a little tray with three steaming mugs and a drinking bottle. 'That's yours,' she said to Paul, setting his on the mantleshelf.

'I'll do Gran,' he said. He knelt and put his arms around the old lady and fitted the nipple gently between her lips, tilting the bottle carefully so that the liquid stayed at the right angle. When she had finished he rubbed her back for her. Then he took his own mug from the mantleshelf.

'To you, Paul,' said his father, smiling at him.

The three of them touched their mugs together. 'To the future,' they said. 'To the future. To the future.'

An apparently harmless family occasion, cosy, harmonious, all of them joining in a friendly bedtime drink which leads Paul each morning to a sense of wellbeing.

He was happy. He was loved. His sleepy mind reached out one by one to the people who loved him most, whom most he loved. Mum, Dad, Gran. They were near him. This was his home. The world was a safe place. Home was the safest part of it ...

He reached out and switched on the MEMORY, dialled his identity number and then lay back at his ease while it restored to him what it was necessary for him to know.

The sinister nature of the drink only gradually penetrates to Paul's consciousness; and with it the significance of the computerised MEMORY, which restores to him each morning only '*what it was necessary for him to know*'. He begins to question what memories have been erased by the drink and are *not* being restored to him; who is responsible for this insidious form of mind control, unthinkingly accepted by everyone around him, and why such control should be deemed necessary. '*Nothing lost matters*', he has been assured, and this assurance runs like a refrain through the book. But soon he begins to question this assurance too, and secretly to cheat the MEMORY by recording items he does not wish to forget.

Paul, we soon realise, has a rebellious streak, something not ready to be controlled, a capacity for imagination which, before the story begins, had led him to go for a walk, not for any specific purpose, but for the sake of the experience. He had looked out from the top of the hill towards the coast, and had seen a single patch of darkness within the general glow of street lamps. He tells the psychiatrist, Dr Palmer:

> 'I thought the darkness was a great black hand. I thought of it as very strong. I thought if it wanted to it could move and simply scrape away all those millions of lights, as if they were beads, and leave the entire world black and cold.'

He had been aroused and stirred by the experience; it had set his imagination working dangerously, in a way which revived a sequence of folk memories which the drink had been devised to suppress. In his excitement he had returned to his own estate and set fire to the sports pavilion; seeing in the fire a beauty 'beyond imagining', in the explosions of the stored footballs a sound which 'seemed to be shouts of the fire' which he had found 'particularly satisfying'. It is for this act of vandalism that he has been sent to the psychiatrist. Dr Palmer explains:

> 'You've no way of knowing, but the past is dangerous, terrible; it must be kept out. You think we have always been as we are now, kind, quiet, law-abiding citizens, civilized. But what if that were quite a recent thing, a revolution brought about in modern times by a generation which had the incredible wisdom to see that the technological advance had reached its zenith, and destruction lay ahead? Scientists already had the power to remove the individual memory, but it was not until a common memory bank could be perfected that the individual memory could safely be dispensed with. What followed we refer to as the Enlightenment. It has meant a rebirth of society, a new chance of perfection, just as the world was destroying itself. Before that the human

race was degenerate, vicious, filled with guilt and jealousy and hatred for one another. They even killed animals. They even killed each other.'

It is not concern for the well-being of the human race which motivates Dr Palmer, however. Behind this bland yet drastic solution to the 'jealousy, guilt, hatred' so evident in the wars, oppression and violence that have troubled the world from time immemorial lies the self-interest of its organiser and controller, who we discover is Dr Palmer himself. He is also the man who stands to gain most in power and wealth from the drug-controlled 'Enlightenment' he administers.

In a powerful, highly original story, Ann Schlee reasserts the value and necessity of imagination, of folk memory, and above all of the ability of individuals to refuse to conform, to continue to question the power and the violence of the state, even at a cost. And though part of that cost may include reawakening suppressed feelings of violence and aggression, she does not want a society which is peaceful only because it is drugged, programmed to forget and to ignore anything which might be disturbing. For she sees that excluding aggression and violence by these means also involves excluding love and concern for others, along with the potentially dangerous grief for those rebellious sons and daughters, friends and relatives whom the 'state' in its wisdom has expelled or eliminated.

Jan Mark also has explored the consequences of too close and rigid a control of the people as it is operated by secular power in *The Ennead*, and by the priesthood in *Divide and Rule*. In both books she asserts, as Anne Schlee has done, the damage done to the quality of life in such an authoritarian society, and the right of the individual to challenge its power even if the end is tragedy.

The action of *The Ennead* takes place in Epsilon, a small township on a strange bleak planet, Erato, sometime in the future. Erato is one in a system of nine planets, known as The Ennead. It is administered by a colonial government from Euterpe, the third planet in the system; but the real power in the day-to-day running of the town rests with the wealthy and established immigrants themselves, those with power being the employers of labour, and the miners. These people are devoted to the doctrine of extreme self-interest. No one does anything on anyone else's behalf; any favour, however small, has its price; in the interests of security and of preserving already existing privileges, power and wealth, both freedom of movement and freedom to marry and breed are rigidly controlled. Those who contravene these regulations as well as those who become unemployed, and therefore a liability, are immediately deported, even though the odds are against their surviving the journey to another of the planets in the Ennead.

Isaac, the main protagonist of the story, is isolated within this community in several ways: he is the sole survivor of a now-dead planet, Orpheus; he has been rescued and adopted by Mr Swenson, who has also died; and he depends on the patronage of his half-brother, Theodore, who would willingly be rid of him. He has, moreover, a friendly and imaginative disposition, which receives little encouragement in the cold, materialistic and philistine society of Epsilon. Having, by desperate trickery, succeeded in establishing himself as Theodore's steward, Isaac rashly tries to relieve his isolation by persuading his brother to hire a sculptor, hoping thereby to acquire a grateful, friendly protégé. In Eleanor, however, he has introduced into the community a disruptive force that he cannot control. As becomes a dedicated artist, she is too fiercely individual to be humbly grateful, or to conform to the restrictive requirements of Epsilon society. She wilfully flies in the face of all that is asked of her, inevitably involving in her protest Moshe, Isaac's only other 'friend' in Epsilon, and finally Isaac himself. The importance of this story is the contrast it presents between the relentless logic of a society bent single-mindedly on its material self-preservation and lacking all tenderness and understanding towards others, and the compassion and the moral and artistic integrity of Moshe and Eleanor, and of Isaac himself. For in spite of his acerbic attitude towards this uncomfortable artist he has brought to Theodore's house, Isaac repeatedly betrays in his actions a wistful desire for comradeship and a less materialistic existence. As in Anne Schlee's novel, it is the quality of imagination which acts as a catalyst to the rebellion against that requirement to conform which is destructive of life because it denies the right to think and choose for oneself, and shuts off any true empathy with or concern for fellow human beings.

Although at first sight the society of *Divide and Rule* seems less coldly self-interested than that of Erato, its effect upon Hanno is quite as disastrous. His fellow citizens pay lipservice to a religion dominated by a powerful priesthood. Though they have passed beyond human sacrifice, they still demand a year's service from a symbolically 'unwilling' individual chosen to be 'Shepherd' through a complicated ritual and then forced to remain a close prisoner in the Temple, watched at all times by the unfriendly Temple guardians. Hanno is a more than usually 'unwilling Shepherd', since he is forced to serve a god in whose existence he does not believe. His initial incredulity and rebellion when he is chosen are slowly subdued into unwilling conformity, but even this proves not enough to help him survive the year. The details of his servitude, his humiliations, his resentful chafing against his enforced idleness and isolation, and his rising panic and fear of the final outcome are powerfully described in a story which analyses with disturbing clarity the worst aspects of organised religion. The narrative moves inexorably, frighteningly, gathering momentum to the point at which he is required to take part in a vast deception intended to restore the failing faith of the people. When he realises the cynicism with which the Temple 'fool' has been murdered and the 'sacred' Book unscrupulously altered, Hanno makes his lone stand, desperately trying to thwart the Temple plot. He is nevertheless cleverly jockeyed into the position they require, and then, having been made use of, as relentlessly pushed aside, sick, destitute, speechless, broken and apparently hopeless.

What is so powerful and so disturbing in both these stories by Jan Mark is the sense they give of the power of the majority over the rebel, the non-conformist. It is not only the might of the law, the state, the priesthood, whoever actually has authority; it is also the consent of the majority of the people, who at the time of crisis gladly themselves hunt Eleanor to destroy her, or sigh with disappointment when they realise that they will not 'see the Shepherd suffer death for what he had done'. Ann Schlee's society has been drugged out of this mob lust for blood: Jan Mark is too much of a realist even in her futurist fiction, too well aware of the complicity of ordinary people in unspeakable cruelties to present a society so tamed. Like Peter Abrahams in this respect, she attaches blame to those who connive in supporting an unjust state as well as to those directly responsible for it.

Both Ann Schlee and Peter Abrahams take into account the fact that rebellion against authority may involve the rebel as well as the state in acts of violence. Jan Mark's rebels, on the other hand, are victims: when they survive it is, like Isaac, by cunning and by concealing their rebellion. When they are openly defiant it is by a non-violent refusal to conform, to acquiesce in the trickery or corruption of a state they cannot hope to overthrow. In very different ways, therefore, these four imagined societies present scenarios within which the author has been able to raise and discuss questions fundamental to societies of today. How do we preserve individual freedom, the right to think and to oppose authority, and yet maintain an ordered state strong enough to withstand those pressures which constantly bedevil us? How do we control greed, whether for possessions or power? How do we prevent power from corrupting even those who have been trusted to exercise it for apparently moral and benevolent purposes? How do we prevent the violence of the powerful used for their own ends against the weak, and yet not resort to violence ourselves? What are the forces, the strengths and weaknesses in human living which make it so difficult for us to live in peace and tolerance with each other, and which seem so continually to drive us to aggression and conflict? Are aggression and violence inevitably the reverse side of the emotional coin on which are also love and compassion, so that if, as in *The Vandal*, we seek to suppress the capacity for the 'evil', aggressive impulses within us we suppress also the capacity for 'good'? (The suggestion that this may be so has also been made, interestingly, by the ethologist Konrad Lorenz in his book *On Aggression*.)

Though they ask these questions, these novels cannot provide adequate answers. But they can alert readers to the nature of the problem of power exercised corruptly and repressively, and to the appallingly difficult yet pressing need to find some answer to the world's ills other than violence.

15

No End to War

After each of the two World Wars there was a hope, even an expectation, that the scale and horror of the destruction they had caused would turn mankind once and for all to more peaceful ways of settling disputes. But in spite of the League of Nations, and later of the United Nations, armed conflict within and between states has continued to be a feature of the second half of the twentieth century. Of the 'Great Powers', the USA, Great Britain and the USSR have each been involved in wars on territories other than their own: and although no nuclear war has yet broken out, the 'cold war' with its accompanying escalation of nuclear arsenals and the endless testing of nuclear bombs and warheads has caused death and misery to innocent victims of fall-out or of displacement from testing grounds; and germ or chemical warfare, napalm and other weapons designed specifically for use against civilians have been employed in a number of conflicts.

Some of these conflicts have been reflected in novels for young readers and adults. The setting for *Andi's War*, for instance, Billi Rosen's thoughtful novel for readers of eleven or twelve, is the civil war which raged in Greece from 1946 to 1949, bringing tragedy into the lives of Andi and her younger brother, Paul. Through their encounters with former friends, neighbours and relatives now openly or secretively hostile to each other and active on one side or other of the conflict, and also through their more ordinary everyday concerns and childish feuds, Billi Rosen has created an immensely readable story about the effects of war on young children, and the waste and tragedy involved.

The second half of the twentieth century has also seen devastating wars in Korea, Cambodia and Vietnam. *The War Orphan* by Rachel Lindsay, a story for readers from twelve to fourteen, gives a graphic account of the sufferings of the peasant families caught up in the conflict in Vietnam. It brings vividly to our attention the way war brutalises its participants, changing innocent, sensitive 18-year-old American recruits into cynical killers, regarding their victims as subhuman nuisances to be eliminated without compunction so that they may get back safely and quickly to their own home comforts. Even more vividly it brings home to us the dire effects of war upon the innocent victims, upon children as well as adults traumatised beyond repair in a nightmare of war, with its consequent bombing, defoliants, starvation, misery and suffering. *On Loan*, by Anne Brooksbank, set in Australia after the end of the Vietnam war, tells of the memories and subsequent fortunes of Lindy, a Vietnamese girl of 14. She had been adopted into an Australian family at the age of three, and now faces a conflict of loyalties. Her father, who at the time of her adoption was fighting with the Viet Cong, has traced her whereabouts and wishes to reclaim her; a situation which had its parallels after the Second World War, particularly for Jewish children saved from death through adoption into non-Jewish families. Her story is quietly told, but effectively conveys the pain and disruption war brings to the lives of ordinary people.

But though these past wars, the continuing wars in the Middle East, and the various conflicts in Ethiopia or Central America have attracted some genuine concern and help from a few conscientious and hardworking organisations and individuals in Britain and elsewhere, they have seemed remote from the consciousness of most British people. The Falklands War, on the other hand, brought home forcibly the ease with which war fever can still seize hold of the British public, regardless of the personal tragedies it involves. This is the predominant theme of *The Falklands Summer*, by John Branfield, a novel which sets out clearly the effect upon his hero, Matthew, of the mood of jingoistic nationalism so readily evoked in defence of these remote and little-known islands.

Matthew was barely 16 when the conflict in the Falklands began to stir his imagination to such a pitch that his quiet Cornish moors were transformed daily into a battleground. As he walks home from the bus after his final GCE examination:

A helicopter passed overhead on its way to the coast. All the small birds round about scattered in alarm. He pressed himself against the bank, so as not to be seen. Just before it went out of sight over the hillside, he fired an imaginary missile at it. He looked for the flash of flame, listened for the explosion as it crashed in the next valley, but the engine faded away and then grew loud again as the helicopter circled around and came into view. He threw himself into the tall bracken around the stream on the other side of the road, and took cover. He lay low as it passed overhead, disappearing into the south west. He had not been spotted.

Still absorbed in his vivid fantasies of the Falklands War, Matthew goes down towards the beach and, meeting his friend, Robert, joins him in a commando-style war-game. Though the two boys are in fact observing closely the wildlife, the birds and a family of foxes in the peace of a Cornish summer, their activity is transformed into a scene from San Carlos bay.

> With the moorland and the sea, it was very much Falklands country ... There was plenty of cover for snipers ... There were no boats in sight. The warships retired beyond the horizon during the day, to come in close to the beaches under the cover of darkness to begin their bombardment of the enemy positions ... A kestrel strayed into the airspace of the valley. It was a total exclusion zone and the swallows saw it off. They flew above it and dived down, buzzing it closely. They escorted it back to the cliffs.

This war play might seem a harmless enough fantasy in younger boys, like Derek and his friends in *Dawn of Fear* (see Chapter 6), but Matthew's involvement with it has become an obsession which is threatening to change into reality. He contemplates the history of the war so far: 'The Task Force was despatched to recapture the islands. The very name *Task Force* stirred him deeply. It made it sound like a band of tough, highly trained men setting out on a mission.' He longs to be 'one of the heroes sailing away to the South Atlantic'. He 'wanted a fight'. So he is overjoyed when the Argentine battlecruiser, the *General Belgrano*, is sunk.

> It wasn't clear whether it was inside or outside the Total Exclusion Zone, or whether it was steaming towards the British Fleet or heading for the mainland. But what did it matter? They had asked for it.
> It sank quickly, with a thousand sailors on board. A British hunter-killer submarine had proved a match for the Argentine Navy. 'GOTCHA!' he rejoiced, while his dad looked glum.

The tragic fate of the *Belgrano*, and the equivocal mixture of feelings surrounding its sinking are brought out clearly in Branfield's narrative. Matthew was not alone in his rejoicing: such callous disregard of human life ('They had asked for it') is a normal accompaniment of the kind of patriotic fervour aroused in those supporting a war from a safe home base. It is worth noting that those actually involved in the fighting are often less willing to gloat over the enemy dead.

But by the time Matthew's exams are over, the Falklands War has ended too. 'And,' he regretfully observes, 'now the news was just about strikes again.' Nevertheless, he still dreams war, now imagining himself building a nuclear shelter in the disused underground workings of the old lead mines, 'so that they could live down there for at least two weeks while the nuclear fallout was dropping like snow outside'.

His parents lecture him about his 'obsession' with war, and tell him 'it was time he grew up and realised what it really meant'. Matthew defensively tells himself that he does know what it means – he had been 'haunted by the three men from Central Europe' who had crashed on the 'wild and stormy cliff top in Cornwall' in the 1940s and had never returned home. He knew, too, all about those returning home from the South Atlantic, 'with burnt hands like blackened stumps in plastic bags', some 'so badly deformed that they weren't even going to be allowed to appear in the victory parade'. Then, still defiantly pursuing his fantasies of action and glory, he goes off to the recruiting office for brochures about joining the army, and finds that he is by no means the only youngster to have been inspired with similar dreams. The office has been 'inundated with enquiries, absolutely inundated'.

But before he can actually take the plunge and join up, he must wait for his examination results. Meantime he contents himself with organising a daring expedition with his three friends to a small island off the coast, where they will hoist the Cornish flag of St Piran in protest at the business enterprise which has taken over the land and is razing the woods, destroying the scrub which was 'an important habitat for many creatures', including the family of foxes which the boys had been watching every day. This enterprise might seem a worthwhile direction for his frustrated energies, and one which belongs comfortably with his genuine interest in the flora and fauna of the countryside. The trouble is that it is a madcap scheme which nearly results in Robert's death. Then Matthew realises where his fantasies have led him. But for the chance of being seen by fishermen, 'they would have drifted out to sea, and the boat would probably have sunk before morning. They might have been drowned; whether they sank or not, Robert almost certainly would not have survived the night.'

As he faces 'the fear and guilt that he had not felt at the time', Matthew begins to understand that although ostensibly his expedition had been undertaken in a worthy cause his real motives had been to seize the opportunity for 'acting out a fantasy'. So he realises at last the connection between his rash adventure and the fantasies of war acted out for real by grown men.

With a bit of luck, with better weather, they could have brought it off. And then it would have been a fine example of the adventurous spirit of British youth, rekindled by the Falklands War. It was all right for adults, he thought, to act out an adolescent fantasy; that was valour. But if you were an adolescent, it was 'foolhardiness'.

The implications are clear. Matthew had been fascinated by war since his primary-school days, when 'he did project after project' about the Second World War, 'filling books with detailed drawings of the uniforms and armaments, the tanks and aircraft used on both sides', and filling 'sack after sack with twisted scraps of old metal, instruments and bullets' found at the site of a wrecked plane. Matthew is not alone, of course, in deluding himself that war is heroic, glamorous and glorious. Many others, old and young, joined at the time in the excitement of the Falklands War, betrayed by an upsurge of patriotism into supporting what a short time before, in a different context, they might have condemned. For them, too, the glamour and nostalgia of the Second World War was quickly revived in the thrills of 'the landings at San Carlos Bay, the fighting off of the attacks by Super Etendards of the Argentine Air Force armed with Exocet missiles, the recapture of Goose Green and Port Stanley'.

One unusual feature of this story, though, is the absence of actual scenes of violence or fighting. The glamour and thrills are all in the mind, all play-acting. By contrast both Jan Needle's *A Game of Soldiers* and Eduardo Quiroga's *On Foreign Ground* take us to the war itself.

For the three children in *A Game of Soldiers* (see Chapter 1) war was not a fantasy: it was a reality which was steadily creeping closer, and terrifying eight-year-old Thomas, Sarah, who was older, and even the 'tough' Michael, as they lie awake in their several homes in the Falklands listening to the bombardment outside. As Michael lies dreaming of his own heroic part should the enemy invade his house:

> Suddenly, his bedroom wall was illuminated as if by a lightning flash. In the intense whiteness a British marine surged forward from the poster, all white teeth and rifle. As it faded, Michael discovered to his shame that he was whimpering.

The poster is part of his private glorification of the war and the British commandos; but the 'shell, or bomb, or missile' which has illuminated it so dramatically has 'switched Michael's brain from bloodthirsty fantasy to fright'. This is the theme of the book: that war, at close quarters, is a nasty, brutal business, involving, in this case, as the children discover next day, a 16-year-old Argentine soldier hiding nearby, too severely wounded to move from the hut where he has taken shelter.

> And he was young. Despite the greyness of his skin, despite the stubble, despite the gun, he was young. Sarah, for some reason, was deeply

shocked by this. He was not much older than she was, or Michael. A matter of a few years. He was a boy.

This terrified lad, soon to be shot down in cold blood, was the same age as Matthew and his friends, who, in *The Falklands Summer*, were acting out war fantasies in the safety of the Cornish moors. But for the Argentinian boy there were no heroics, only pain, and fear and death.

The same fate is to meet the young Argentine soldier in *On Foreign Ground*. Enrique is 22 by the time he finds himself on the 'foreign ground' of the title. But his experiences of violence stretch back to the years of the Peron reign of terror, when his 18-year-old brother, Juan, was arrested. Under torture Juan implicated in activities against the government anyone he could think of, innocent or guilty. One name and address he gave in his extremity was that of Enrique's innocent 15-year-old friend Monkey, who consequently is also arrested. A few days later, Enrique remembers:

We were all in Monkey's house, trying to think of a way of finding out what had happened. Suddenly the bell rang and Mrs Cohen went to open the door. Her scream brought us out in a flash ... There on the step was a small huddled body, naked and covered in purple bruises, hardly recognisable if not for a shock of red hair. Around his neck was a thin black line like a collar: a nylon thread was embedded in the skin. His bloated tongue peered through his split lips. His eyes were mercifully closed. He seemed incredibly old.

It is against this grim background, in which there is no room for the comfortable fantasies of Matthew and his friends, or of Michael's brief dreams, that Enrique goes to war. But first he has a few idyllic weeks with an English girl in Paris, and his story is told in letters to her which she will never read, and which he writes from his camp, somewhere near Port Stanley. Interwoven with his warm memories of their brief weeks in Paris and later in Brazil, and his recollections of the misery and terror of the Peron years, is the account of the Falklands War, not heroic or exciting, but 'tedious, waiting, never moving, incomprehensible, dully painful, like toothache'. War means rain, snow, endless marching, 'cutting through sheets of rain like mock-soldiers in an opera through large decors of gauze', an action in which, 'in the midst of it, we know nothing. We have lost track of the fighting'. Now and again he comes face to face with reality in the death of comrades, sometimes only reported, sometimes seen, and always grim and sickening. His experiences have left him numbed, with no belief in anything. He writes:

I told you I could believe in God but not imagine him. Imagination requires understanding, it requires the elements to build up an image, and I said I had none. To me He is a shapeless incoherent force, mad and senseless, inhuman as anything is inhuman, stone or water or fire. I believe in Him as I believe in fire and in the rain, relentlessly carrying on, among us but indifferent, unconcerned – because concern cannot be one of His qualities. Mercy, kindness, charity, benevolence, tenderness – He can feel nothing. Nor wrath, revenge, fury. He grows like a wave that crashes down by His sheer force, and we are dragged along behind, believing that when we ride the crest or are drowned in the depth there is a reason. In truth we are just carried away from wherever we happen to be, like seaweed.

This bleak philosophy echoes the bleakness of Enrique's short life, and reflects the truth and pain of the repression, callousness towards human life, and brutality in peace and war he has seen. This is a moving story, powerful in its spare, quiet prose, telling without self-pity or over-emphasis of events which go beyond heroism or glorification of suffering. The book ends with the simple statement: 'Enrique Molina died in an ambush ten miles west of Port Stanley on Friday, 11 June 1982.'

Robert Lawrence, like Matthew in *The Falklands Summer*, began with a heroic dream of army life. At 16, he tells us in *When the Fighting is Over*, he decided to join the Scots Guards. He says:

I saw my time in the Army as an opportunity to have a bit of a *Boy's Own* existence. The big thing that also appealed to me about it was that everything I did in the Army *mattered*. Every decision I made as a young man mattered ... There are eighteen-year-olds running around in Northern Ireland, for instance, and if they make the wrong decision over something, someone else could get blown up tomorrow in Belfast or London.

The thought of this degree of responsibility given to boys just out of school is terrifying; for Robert Lawrence's story is not fiction. Though his attitude to the war is painfully close to that of Matthew in *The Falklands Summer*, it is actual experience. In his twenty-second year, Robert was on his way to the Falklands. What happened to him there was the subject both of *Tumbledown*, a television film by Charles Wood, and of this personal account 'of the battle for Tumbledown Mountain and its aftermath', written independently by Robert and his father, John.

It is disturbing to realise how unquestioningly Robert had been imbued with the conventional image of war and of the 'macho' male role fostered both by the media and by our public schools, the influence of whose view of 'the glory of an early sacrificial death in battle' has rightly been put under critical scrutiny by Peter Parker in *The Old Lie* (see Chapter 3).

By his own account, the sense of unreality, of being part of some heroic drama, accompanied Robert even to the battlefield. He writes:

> And this is a very interesting aspect of war, I think, since the advent of television ... the idea of this big circle, where people going to war find themselves acting as they have seen people act in films about people going to war.

Even during the skirmish on Tumbledown, he catches himself thinking 'this was just like the movies'; while seconds before he was seriously wounded in the head, he 'turned to Guardsman McEntaggart as we went along and, for some inexplicable reason, suddenly cried out, "Isn't this fun?"' Yet not long before he had faced a reality which was grim enough, not 'fun', even to the eager young Guards officer. Coming upon an Argentinian, lying face down, he sticks his bayonet into the man's arm to find out if he is dead or alive.

> He spun wildly on the ground, and my bayonet snapped. And as he spun, he was trying to get a Colt 45 out of an army holster on his waist. So I had to stab him to death. I stabbed him and I stabbed him, again and again, in the mouth, in the face, in the guts, with a snapped bayonet.
> It was absolutely horrific. Stabbing a man to death is not a clean way to kill somebody, and what made it doubly horrific, was that at one point he started screaming '*Please* ...' in English to me. But had I left him he could have ended up shooting me in the back.

Neither this incident nor Robert's own wound belong with the fictional dream of a heroic war. The reality of pain, fear and the accompanying revulsion from 'the killing fields' is too strong. The reader notices, wryly, both the wildness of the stabbing, 'in the mouth, in the face, in the guts', and the ironic connotations of the phrase which comments, 'not a clean way to kill somebody'; as though sanitising the process could somehow have made it more acceptable.

Although he has 'received a high-velocity bullet through the head leaving him with a six-by-two-inch hole in the skull and a significant hemiplegia of the left-hand side of the body which manifests itself in a paralysed left arm, a spastic left ankle and a certain amount of incontinence', Robert nevertheless retains his idealised concept of war. He 'envies those who were still on the Falklands'. While he 'had missed out on all the fun' they were 'running around with all the Argentinian equipment. The victors. It would have been like Christmas.'

Christmas, ostensibly a time for the celebration of 'peace on earth', seems an odd choice of metaphor. The reader, indeed, becomes painfully aware of the naivety of this young man's outlook on war, even whilst being impressed at the same time by an almost incredible toughness of body and personal courage in face of irreversible disabilities. Yet greater courage was needed to come to terms with his anguish at the unexpectedly cool reception he met in England, where he was hustled out of sight because 'they didn't want the severely injured people, the really badly burned and maimed young men, to be seen'. He says: 'I'd wanted to come off that plane as a soldier – a heroic soldier, what's more, who had just helped to win a war. I was still pretty naive then, I suppose ... '

It was the ingratitude of his reception at home, rather than his brief experiences of the battlefield, which disillusioned him; the indifference of the general public; the humiliation of being ignored and kept out of sight during the various victory celebrations; the heartless, petty bureaucracy which pursued him as he tried to get a disabled person's driving licence and a disability pension from the army. He says:

And I had, and still have, this white-hot pride. The kind of pride that the Army trains young soldiers to build up. The kind of pride that enables them to go off to war and fight and kill for what they are taught to believe in; principles like freedom of choice and of speech.

What I didn't realize, until, like so many others, I came back crippled after doing my bit for my country, was the extent to which we had been conned. Conned into believing in a set of priorities and principles that the rest of the world and British society in general no longer gave two hoots about. We had been 'their boys' fighting in the Falklands, and when the fighting was over, nobody wanted to know.

He adds: 'People have been told how bloody the First World War was, and how bloody Vietnam was, but they have not been told how bloody the Falklands war was ... '

It is a disturbing story, of a courageous and determined young man, fed by school and family tradition, and by fiction, film and television to regard war as 'fun', an opportunity to prove oneself, a 'transition period from school to the real world'; who finds himself and his illusions made use of and then flung aside. But his experience raises fundamental questions which go far beyond his individual bitterness and trauma. And though he concludes: 'I have a duty now, I believe, to inform my generation not only about what the fighting was like, but about what can happen to you if you get injured, in some sort of attempt to make them think twice about getting involved in another war', few can doubt that the same inducements and the same betrayals await future young men, as ready as he to be 'conned' by 'the old lie'.

For a final, brief, savagely satirical commentary on the Falklands War and its mythology we could turn to Raymond Briggs's picture book for readers of any age, *The Tin-Pot Foreign General and the Old Iron Woman*. Briggs does not name the place or the warmakers; but there is no mistaking the 'sad little island ... down at the bottom of the world', inhabited only by poor shepherds who 'spent all their time counting their sheep and eating them'. In this story neither the 'tin-pot foreign general' nor the 'old iron woman' are real; they are made of metal, not flesh. They only want to 'bagsie the sad little island' for their own aggrandisement, and care nothing for its fate, or for the fate of the soldiers who were to be shot, drowned, burned alive, blown to bits or only 'half blown to bits'. 'Hundreds of brave men were killed,' we are told. 'And they were all real men, made of flesh and blood. They were not made of Tin or Iron.' At the end of the war, the poor shepherds are left still counting their sheep and eating them, but this time on a devastated island, littered with the debris of war, while a boat loaded with bodies returns the dead to their native land. The surviving soldiers of the winning side are given medals and included in a Grand Parade, 'but the soldiers with bits of their bodies missing were not invited to take part in the Grand Parade, in case the sight of them spoiled the rejoicing'.

It is the pictures which make the most powerful impact in this excellent book. They are restrained, but vivid. The injured men and the families of the dead tending the graves are rendered in a soft pencil gray, which aptly indicates their sad retiring insignificance amidst the bright and brash colours of the banners and guns in the parade.

As a continuous background to these 'live' conflicts the second half of the century has been overshadowed by the 'cold war' between the super-powers, never flaring into direct confrontation, but nevertheless having unacceptable consequences for the rest of the world. Some of these have already been discussed in earlier chapters: but Jane Dibblin's book, *Day of Two Suns*, illustrates very clearly that although the nuclear arsenals relentlessly built up by the 'Great Powers' have not yet been used against an enemy, testing them has already disrupted peaceful communities and cost lives. The victims, whether soldiers or civilians, were not given medals or recognition for their 'services', and found it even more difficult than Robert Lawrence to extract compensation for their injuries. Unlike Lawrence, however, the Marshall Islanders had not been asked whether they wished to sacrifice their lives or their lands for a country not their own. Their subsequent history and that of the Polynesians under France and of the Australian Aborigines demonstrate clearly enough that where a powerful government's interests are concerned, the lives and well-being of individuals who happen to be in their way are of small account. Those 'principles like freedom of choice and of speech' for which Robert Lawrence was prepared to fight and die have had little meaning for these people. Whose freedom, they might well ask; whose choice?

Their experience and their warnings have relevance for us all. The Pacific is not the only place commandeered for tests, nor the only place where superports and military bases are sited, and submarines and bombers are deployed. Nor is it the only place where 'the balance between nature and humankind' is being destroyed 'for the sake of a brief commercial gain', where 'alien colonial political and military domination' persists, or 'the racist roots of the world's nuclear powers' are in evidence; all of which are rightly condemned in the People's Charter for a Nuclear Free World drawn up by the Marshall Islanders. Our environment, as well as theirs, 'continues to be despoiled by foreign powers developing nuclear weapons for a strategy of warfare that has no winners, no liberators, and imperils the survival of all humankind'.

As Marjorie Mowlam reminds us (quoted in Thompson (ed.), *Over Our Dead Bodies*), decisions about nuclear power and nuclear weapons involve choices about how we want to live our lives. The ethos which supports the nuclear arms race is the same as that which fostered support for the Falklands War. It divides the world into 'them' and 'us', with the grim determination that 'we' shall stay on top whatever the cost. It is fed by fantasies of power, of glory, heroism and fame, though these at best are uncertain and transitory in any conventional war – and it is even more difficult to see what power or fame could survive a nuclear war.

Yet, as Caroline Moorehead sadly remarks in *Troublesome People*, conventional war, at least, remains, 'as the Falklands War proved all over again, more exciting and more politically attractive than peace'. In her admirable account of pacifism this century in Britain, the United States, West Germany and Japan, she concludes that protests against both conventional and nuclear weapons have had little effect so far on militarism:

> On this level, it is a story of almost pure failure. Thousands of men and women have gone to prison to uphold their opposition to war and

234 Old Lies Revisited

armaments and they have altered virtually nothing. As an influence on military decisions, the women of Greenham, the Graswurzelrevolution, the Berrigan community in Baltimore and those who track the great white train [carrying nuclear warheads] across America have been powerless. The world in 1986 is a more militant and a more dangerous place than it was in 1916.

In *Day of Two Suns* Jane Dibblin adds a further word of warning. The Marshall Islanders so far have chosen the route of determined but peaceful protest and struggle; but peaceful protest can itself finally turn to violence if repeatedly frustrated.

The European and North American peace movements have often assumed that non-violent direct action is a recent creation, inspired by Gandhi but with no wider roots. It is an assumption which ignores the Black civil rights movement in North America, the history of non-violent marches by Black South Africans and the support given to them by the mostly white 'Black Sash' women, the vigils of the mothers of the disappeared in Central and South America, and the protestors of Kwajalein atoll. It forgets that almost all of the liberation movements around the world *which finally resorted to guns* had struggled for years to make their point *in every other way.* [my italics]

Nevertheless, as Caroline Moorehead more optimistically reminds us, there are still a few crumbs of comfort for peaceful protesters. Nuclear protest is still growing, is still peaceful, 'and, arguably, in small ways at least, having an effect'. Moreover, she concludes:

The pacifists, the nuclear protesters, all those who take their individual stand against the machinery of war, are keeping alive the tradition of individual freedom; their importance can only grow. Conscience has not been altered by violence.

For such people, she adds, Thoreau's words in *On the Duty of Civil Disobedience*, published in 1849 'well over a hundred years ago', are still valid. Incurring 'the penalty of disobedience to the state', he declared, is a smaller price to pay than the loss of self-respect which would accompany silent acceptance of the state's war machine. The choice is ours.

16

Women and War

Much of this book has naturally been concerned with the role of men in warfare: war, aggression and violence, are, after all, more commonly associated with the stereotypical image of 'macho' man. What part, then, do women play in time of war? In the novels and memoirs discussed so far we have already seen women in a variety of roles, sometimes incidental to the action, sometimes as the main protagonists. They have been victims in the death camps, ghettos, bombed cities and devastated countries; they have been victims of rape or prostitutes 'comforting' the troops; they have seen service as soldiers actively fighting at the front, or as partisans or secret agents behind the lines; they have been war correspondents; and they have been left behind at home, sometimes actively supporting the war machine, but also grieving, suffering, endlessly waiting for news. They have also, throughout history, been on record vigorously and selflessly campaigning for peace. So there are an increasing number of memoirs, novels and anthologies which look at war and its aftermath specifically from the woman's point of view.

Not so Quiet ... Stepdaughters of War, by Helen Smith, is a vivid account of the author's experiences in France in the First World War, first as an ambulance driver, and then as assistant cook in the WAAC. It is also an impassioned denunciation of war, of the obscenities perpetrated on the living flesh and minds of those involved in it, and of the opportunities it gives not for heroism but for petty tyranny, and for wilfully blind and nauseatingly hypocritical jingoism. In France as an ambulance driver, Helen must wait night after night for the 'trainloads of broken human beings' to be transported to hospital:

Half-mad men pleading to be put out of their misery; torn and bleeding and crazed men pitifully obeying orders like a herd of senseless cattle, dumbly, pitifully straggling in the wrong direction, as senseless as a flock of senseless sheep obeying a senseless leader, herded back into line by the orderly, the kind sheep-dog with a 'Now then, boys, this way. That's the ticket, boys,' instead of a bark; men with faces bleeding through their hasty bandages; men with vacant eyes and mouths hanging foolishly apart dropping saliva and slime; men with minds mercifully gone; men only too sane, eyes horror-filled with blood and pain ...

In contrast to Helen's perception of the sordid and tragic reality of war is the attitude of her mother at home with her endless committees, and her self-centred rivalry in patriotic fervour with her neighbour. Even at the end, with her neighbour's son, Roy, permanently disabled, she can still write: 'Isn't it wonderful that Roy has had the MC? Wonderful and sad. Our poor blinded hero.' And add in rival self-commendation:

> 'I gave my youngest girl to England, my little Trix, whose medals I always wear on official occasions. But, in the midst of my grief, I can still smile and thank God she died in the service of her country – a country that will never forget.'

Meantime, in France, the devastation continued. Helen records a conversation with a fellow driver, newly engaged to a soldier who had lost his leg in the war. Edwards rejoices that her future husband will never go to war again; and denounces the 'pig-headed, sentimental, brainless old block that got us out here' with patriotic speeches about 'fighting for world freedom'. Helen comments:

> I am glad I am not Edwards. She will never be able to forget these days and nights of war horror. All her life she will have the reminder with her in the Australian husband with one leg. Limp, limp, limp ...
>   When I marry it will be someone whose straightness and strength will erase from my mind these mangled things I drive night after night.

But, ironically, at the end of the war Helen agrees to marry a man blinded, with one leg amputated, and no longer able to have children. She does so in a state of mind from which, for the moment at least, all feeling has been expunged.

> Outwardly I am Smithy, assistant cook; inwardly I am nothing. I have no feelings that are not physical. I dislike being too hot or too cold. My body is healthy, my mind negative. I have no love or hate for anyone. Long ago I ceased to love Roy; long ago I ceased to hate my mother. Both processes were gradual. I am content to drift along in the present. The past has gone; I have no future ... I want no future. With this mental atrophy my physical fear has vanished, for fear cannot exist when one is indifferent to life.

Shortly before being told of Roy's crippling wounds, she antici-
pates without emotion the news she imagines the Unit
Administrator is about to give her:

> Roy? Killed, I suppose? I am not surprised. Trix was wiped out in an air-
> raid on the hospital five months ago, Etta Potato was torpedoed
> crossing the Channel within the last three weeks ... everyone is killed.
> If the submarines, the aerial torpedoes, the poison gas, the liquid fire,
> the long-distance guns, the hand grenades, the trench mortars, and all
> the other things injure without killing them, they are sent back again
> and again after being patched up until they are killed. It is only a ques-
> tion of time. Why should Roy expect to escape? He is better dead.

When she is told what has in fact happened to Roy she remains
apparently unmoved, only remarking: 'I go back to my trestle
table where the onions and carrots are waiting.'
It is the contrast between this emotional deadness and the liveli-
ness and anger of her earlier account of her experiences as
ambulance driver which is so terrifying. Earlier, worn down by the
anguish of so many men so terribly wounded; of the relentless
persecution of the tyrannical, unfeeling commandant; of the cold,
the nausea, the stench, the oppression of never-ending driving
and cleaning out blood and vomit from the ambulances; of punishment fatigues, and the deaths of her friends, she has asked
passionately:

> What is to happen to women like me when this war ends ... if ever it
> ends. I am twenty-one years of age, yet I know nothing of life but
> death, fear, blood, and the sentimentality that glorifies these things in
> the name of patriotism ...
> What will they expect of us, these elders who have sent us out to
> fight? We sheltered young women who smilingly stumbled from the
> chintz-covered drawing-rooms of the suburbs straight into hell? ...
> I see us a race apart, we war products ... feared by the old ones and
> resented by the young ones ... a race of men bodily maimed and of
> women mentally maimed.
> What is to become of us when the killing is over?

Although in the final paragraph of her book she seems to have
accepted the hopelessness of the situation, and deliberately shut
out all emotion, the fact that she was able, in 1930, to publish this
record of her experiences suggests an eventual return to the
feeling she so strenuously denied herself at that time, perhaps
even a hope that her fierce denunciation of war might now find a
response.
Helen Smith was a nurse at the Front, in a typical, caring, nur-
turing role; but sickened, frustrated and exasperated by the

senseless futility of her efforts on behalf of men who were patched up only to be sent back to the Front. Her feelings in this respect are echoed by Vera Brittain in *Testament of Youth*. She, too, came from a prosperous middle-class background; one which in no way prepared her for the role she was later to assume in the VAD.

From early days she had rebelled against her 'father's persistent determination' that she 'should be turned into an entirely ornamental young lady'. Her immediate ambition was to go to university, like her younger brother and his friends; but in the event, she went up to Oxford on her own. Her brother Edward and his friend Roland who should have gone up with her went instead to join the army and to fight for King and Country. *Testament of Youth* is a detailed account of the progress of 'her' war; of her fears and anguish when she knew her beloved brother was in danger at the Front; when, one by one, Edward's friends, including her fiancé, Roland, were killed, and when, finally, Edward himself died in action in Italy in July 1918.

Vera decided to join the VAD at the end of her first year at Somerville; motivated in part by the need to escape from the 'prolonged apprehension', the 'gnawing anxiety' of 'days upon days of miserable speculation' about the fate of those at the Front; the endless wait for letters which was to last, 'with only brief intervals, for more than three years', the knowledge that 'even when the letters came they were four days old, and the writer since sending them had had time to die over and over again'. After Roland's death, she volunteered for service overseas, where her experience included nursing desperately wounded British soldiers and German POWs in Malta and in France. She sums up the strain and exhaustion they all felt in the hospitals in France, and contrasts it bitterly with the complaints of civilians at home:

> The enemy within shelling distance – refugee Sisters crowding in with nerves all awry – bright moonlight, and aeroplanes carrying machine-guns – ambulance trains jolting noisily into the siding, all day, all night – gassed men on stretchers, clawing the air – dying men, reeking with mud and foul green-stained bandages, shrieking and writhing in a grotesque travesty of manhood – dead men with fixed, empty eyes and shiny, yellow faces ...

But a brief return home makes her realise the degree of strain and grief felt there too, from which she had indeed sought to escape into active service.

> It seemed to me then, with my crude judgments and black-and-white values, quite inexplicable that the older generation, which had merely looked on at the War, should break under the strain so much more

quickly than those of us who had faced death or horror at first hand for months on end. Today, with middle-age just round the corner, and children who tug my anxious thoughts relentlessly back to them whenever I have to leave them for a week, I realise how completely I underestimated the effect upon the civilian population of year upon year of diminishing hope, diminishing food, diminishing light, diminishing heat, of waiting and waiting for news which was nearly always bad when it came.

Testament of Youth also gives us insight into the aftermath of war, its consequences for her own generation.

With aching persistence my thoughts went back to the dead and the strange irony of their fates – to Roland, gifted, ardent, ambitious, who had died without glory in the conscientious performance of a routine job; to Victor and Geoffrey, gentle and diffident, who, conquering nature by resolution, had each gone down bravely in a big 'show'; and finally to Edward, musical, serene, a lover of peace, who had fought courageously through so many battles and at last had been killed while leading a counter-attack in one of the few decisive actions of the War ...
For the first time I realised, with all that full realisation meant, how completely everything that had hitherto made up my life had vanished with Edward and Roland, with Victor and Geoffrey. The War was over; a new age was beginning; but the dead were dead and would never return.

Vera emerged from the war a lifelong pacifist. Her daughter, Shirley Williams, tells us: 'I still remember her in her seventies, determinedly sitting in a CND demonstration, and being gently removed by the police.' But Vera recognised the difficulty of her task. She says:

Since those years it has often been said by pacifists – as in a brave, lop-sided pamphlet which I read only the other day – that war creates more criminals than heroes; that, far from developing noble qualities in those who take part in it, it brings out only the worst. If this were altogether true, the pacifist's aim would be, I think, much nearer of attainment than it is. Looking back upon the psychological processes of us who were very young sixteen years ago, it seems to me that this task – our task – is infinitely complicated by the fact that war, while it lasts, does produce heroism to a far greater extent than it brutalises.

The 'heroism' in question here is presumably that produced in men – the role of most women in wartime is less obviously dramatic.
Certainly *Firing Line*, Richard Holmes's exhaustive survey of the soldier in battle, confirms that though the actualities of war can

be endlessly tedious, with few and relatively brief opportunities for exhilarating action, nevertheless, both in prospect and in retrospect men still see it as an adventure, and a rite of passage to manhood. But the price of this adventure is paid by women as well as men. Whatever the balance of heroism and brutality – and who can assert with certainty which way the scales might tip? – war can hardly be justified by the opportunity it may offer for displaying heroism in action. For when you consider Martin Gilbert's estimate (*Observer* 20 August 1989) that though 'the total number of those killed in the Second World War will never be known with precision ... certainly it was more than 45 million', and that 'more than two-thirds of those killed, and killed in cold blood, were civilians – innocent bystanders to the conflict', this is demonstrably an unacceptably high price to pay for the satisfaction of those few who feel that they have thereby 'proved their manhood'. Moreover, as Peter Parker points out in *The Old Lie: The Great War and the Public School Ethos*:

> That during the course of the War many individual acts demonstrated a kind of chivalry does not mean that the war was about chivalry ... That men died for an ethos does not mean that the ethos was worth dying for.

The 'indoctrination of a generation with old lies about the moral value of war', in fact, merely led many of them to fight and die, whether heroically or otherwise, 'for the wrong reasons'.

Meanwhile, women continued to suffer. Vera Brittain takes her story to the post-war years, to the problems and changes in the lives of the women of her generation brought about by the war. Many of them recovered with difficulty from their personal experience of tragedy and loss. Vera herself suffered the 'hallucinations and dreams and insomnia' which are 'normal symptoms of overfatigue and excessive strain' and an 'exhausting battle against nervous breakdown' which she 'waged for eighteen months'. Women also faced the conflict within themselves and with society generated by their new-found independence. Vera felt that 'a nation from which the men who excelled in mind and body were mostly vanished into oblivion had never so much required its more vigorous and intelligent women to become the mothers of the generations to come'. Yet a 'growing number of women ... would refuse marriage rather than give themselves up to years of exclusive domesticity and throw away their training and experience'.

The Second World War found Vera still determinedly struggling to maintain those values which are most threatened in wartime.

In spite of her detestation of the doctrines and atrocities of Nazism she remained a convinced pacifist. During the war she wrote and published 170 letters addressed to like-minded people, a selection from which has been edited by Winifred and Alan Eden-Green and published under the title *Testament of a Peace-Lover*.

The outbreak of war in 1939 brought a renewal of problems and conflicts to a new generation of women. Even before war began Helen Forrester was no stranger to hard work and deprivation. She was brought up in a Liverpool slum by uncaring parents who had once been prosperous and were now continually on the bread-line. She tells the story of her early years in *Twopence to Cross the Mersey*, *Liverpool Miss* and *By the Waters of Liverpool*; but the main account of her war experiences – spent in Liverpool and Bootle – is to be found in the fourth book of her autobiography, *Lime Street at Two*.

In August 1940, Helen's fiancé was lost at sea. She bore her sorrow alone, and the strain of her unexpressed grief 'in a body made frail by much illness and, at times, near starvation' had a devastating effect upon her. Every evening as she returned home through the darkened streets she 'would stumble along ... weeping openly ... in the safe knowledge that no one could see [her] ... and wishing [she] was dead'. But she, too, found strength to survive.

Her work in a charity office brought her into contact with other Liverpool women suffering similar bereavement and her quiet, compassionate observation of the effect of war on ordinary women is a significant part of her account. She writes:

> Our waiting room was daily filled by rows of weeping mothers and wives; every ship that went down seemed to have a Bootle man aboard. My mind is filled with memories of the overwhelmed resources of our little office, when the *Athenia*, the *Courageous*, the battleship *Royal Oak* and hundreds of others, big and small, were lost in 1940 and 1941.
>
> Sometimes the position was reversed, and a seaman's family was lost in an air raid.
>
> My senior, Miss Evans, and I often faced a stony-eyed or openly weeping merchant seaman or a serviceman, sent home on compassionate leave because his home had been bombed and his family killed.

Bootle, where Helen worked 'was to have, for its size, the doubtful honour of being the most heavily bombed area in the British Isles', and Helen and her family suffered endless sleepless nights, 'nodding on the basement steps, trying to get what rest we could, while the diving planes screeched overhead and the guns in Princes Park roared unceasingly'. Frequently, next morning, she had to walk the five miles to Bootle, in company with 'a long line of much older women' who 'plodded along stolidly on swollen feet ... putting first one cautious foot over scattered chunks of brickwork or electric cables and then lifting the other one over'. These were the cleaning ladies of Liverpool, trudging faithfully to work, often leaving behind them their own damaged homes, sometimes to find 'nothing left to clean, only a dangerous mountain of rubble or a burning skeleton of a building'. But their services were invaluable to those businesses damaged, but still left standing, and 'to the nervous, excited clerks and shop assistants, when they arrived later, these women were quiet symbols of stability'.

As soon as Helen arrived at work, she was 'besieged by bewildered people, many of whom had been bereaved the previous night and had lost their homes'; or, perhaps, had escaped comparatively lightly, but with 'their little store of food ruined, tins squashed or pierced, bread, milk and margarine filled with dust or sand, and their handbags or precious ration books lost in the mess. They had no money to buy fresh food and did not know where to get a new ration book on a Sunday.'

The quality of Helen Forrester's book lies in the atmosphere created through the small but carefully observed detail of everyday life, of dogged courage, refusal to be beaten in spite of grief, poverty, emotional and physical exhaustion from sleepless nights, anxiety for loved ones, and bereavement. When first VE Day and then VJ Day finally arrived, Helen had little to celebrate: her second chance of happiness had died with Eddie in the final months of the war. As she stands with the other office girls for a celebration photograph, she reflects:

> One of the six had been widowed and, like me, must begin again, one had a merchant seaman for a fiancé, mercifully spared, one was engaged to a civilian, and two were still fancy free. I smiled for the photographer, but I remember that I wanted to scream at the unfairness of life ...
>
> I felt dreadfully alone.

She remarks also:

> For years afterwards, one would come across brick walls with *Welcome home Joey* or *George* or *Henry*, splashed across it, in drippy, faded whitewash.
>
> I never saw such a message painted for the Marys, Margarets, Dorothys and Ellens, who also served. It was still a popular idea that women did not need things. They could make do. They could manage without, even without welcomes.

In her customary quiet, wry fashion, she adds: 'But these were the women who would give impetus to the feminist movement. At the time of demobilisation they did not realise it, but they were going to do a lot more marching.' This is an honest, direct, moving and understanding book, recapturing with unforgettable vividness the bleak, harsh years of the Liverpool blitz; and the thoughts and feelings of both men and women caught up in a terrible and traumatic war.

Linda McCullough Thew grew up in a pit village, and left school at fourteen to work in the village store, as she relates in *The Pit Village and the Store*. Her second book, *From Store to War*, is an account of her service in the women's army, the ATS, in a very different environment from Helen Forrester's Liverpool. This is a vivid, detailed and robust account of daily life in the army; the discipline, the fatigues, square-bashing, spud-peeling, and also the camaraderie in spite of occasional jealousies and conflicts. On the whole, Linda took a pragmatic view of her experiences, and threw herself into some aspects of army life with an enthusiasm which sometimes left her colleagues standing.

Army life began badly: to her horror and distress Linda was infected with scabies from forced cont; : v. th the clothing of two girls ahead of her in the medical queue. Army discipline and an autocratic, unimaginative and harsh corporal were responsible, and Linda was to find herself in conflict with several such 'steely' NCOs. However, she was soon sent to a gun-site to train as a radar operator – the nearest, she was told, she could get to active service – where she was responsible for pinpointing the position of enemy planes.

By the end of the war, Linda, in contrast to Helen, has something to celebrate. The war had taken her from the humdrum life in the 'store' and given her opportunities and the chance of the further education which civilian life had not afforded her. True, her 'happiness existed almost entirely in the work aspect' of her life, but though she had had emotional disappointments, and at times had thought she 'was destined to be part of the flotsam of army life, rising and falling with the tide, helpless to do other', the vigour of her personality and the unexpected recognition of her intellectual potentialities enabled her finally to achieve her goal.

Linda's role as radar operator brought her a direct responsibility for enemy deaths, which was experienced by few women in either war. She recalls:

During these raids in the early part of 1944, wave after wave of targets came over and one was entirely impersonal about them. They were dots on the screen to be deflected, to be fired at so that our fighters knew where the planes were, or to be fired at and brought down. In a big raid the concentration required was such that we were totally unaware of what was going on. When the raid was not a heavy one in our area, and when one lone plane appeared on the screen, in spite of my trained automatic response, I was always apprehensive. What if it was one of ours limping home off course with his IFF shot away or out of action?

And then there would be the sickening realisation, kept at bay during heavy raids, that those dots were really planes full of young lives.

The realisation of what was involved in bombing raids for young German as well as British lives was brought home to her also in a letter sent from the frontline during the final days of the war:

Your friend need have no worry about retribution to the German people. It has become a common sight to pass through cities and towns which look like graveyards, to see weeping women, despairing refugees and the dead. The whole thing is tragic and no matter what nationality or creed is involved one cannot help deploring the fact that there has been such a war which has shattered the entire life of Europe and caused devastation of life and property on all sides.

When this reciprocal aspect of air warfare first struck Helen Forrester her response was harsher. At the time she was indignantly trying to convince a convalescent bomber pilot 'that the war was on his doorstep' in the devastation she could show him in Liverpool and Bootle. 'People forget that London isn't the only target,' she told him.

He did not reply immediately, and then he said, 'I am not sure that it is a good idea for me to know precisely what bombs do to civilians.'

This remark stopped the conversation in its tracks. It had not occurred to me that our bomber pilots might not get much satisfaction from wreaking havoc in German cities. I did not care if German cities were reduced to ashes.

Though normally a compassionate person, Helen had doubtless been too close to the miseries of British victims to be able to feel sympathy for German counterparts. She had also known more than most people about 'the dreadful situation of European Jews'. Since 1933 she 'had seen a steady stream of refugees' go through her office, and 'each of them had his own shocking story'. When she realised the import of these stories, she was 'both horrified and terrified'.

Vera Brittain had personally experienced the saturation bombing of London, but she did not share Helen's view. She remained passionately concerned at the sufferings of the victims of war on both sides of the conflict. In one of the letters in *Testament of a Peace Lover* she writes:

I listened for an hour to the sound of our heavy bombers flying out to sea, and felt more sick at heart than I have ever been made by the clatter of the German raiders, like a set of vibrant descending tea-trays, over the heads of London's population. To realise that one's own people are suffering damage is grievous, but to know they are about to inflict it is detestable ...

How many children in Germany, I wondered, would die before the morning? ... Our belligerent editors and vituperative politicians often write and speak as though Hitler, Goering and Goebbels were personally damaged by every raid that we make on Germany. But it is not Hitler upon whom our bombs fall. Our air-raids, like his, wreck humble homes and decimate families living in the East Ends of industrial cities, or close to the dockyards of naval and commercial ports. It is not the Nazi leaders but the children of the German and Italian workers whom they destroy.

Realisation of 'the terrible nature of the attack being carried out down below,' she felt, would in later years afflict 'the more sensitive of these young flyers when in future years they ... have time to think about it'. She adds:

Some of their victims – those who are still there – may perhaps forgive them, but will they ever forgive themselves? What aftermath of nightmare and breakdown will come? Has any nation the right to make its young men the instruments of such a policy?

These are the questions that you and I should be asking ourselves today. Thousands of mothers of young airmen must already be asking them in their hearts.

Compassionate awareness in women, as well as in men, takes different forms.

In the Introduction to her translation of I. Grekova's novel, *The Ship of Widows*, Cathy Porter reminds us of the devastation experienced also in the USSR during and after this war.

Everyone had lost someone, and suffered in various terrible ways. Russia had lost twenty million of her people, a further twenty million had been injured or disabled, twenty million were homeless, 11,710 towns and 70,000 villages had been destroyed ... Some four million children's fathers were killed or missing, their mothers out all day toiling in the factories.

The Ship of Widows is about the lives of five women in Moscow during and after the war. Olga Ivanovna, the narrator, loses her entire family, and herself suffers permanent disability. After a raid:

Mother and Natasha perished – I didn't. I was saved by a miracle, as they say. A miracle! Rather one of those negative miracles, miracles of

> evil, wrought by the devil himself. My spine, a leg and both arms were fractured ...
>
> I was encased in plaster from head to foot, and could neither struggle nor move my arms, nor kill myself.

Olga survives, along with the four other widows in the apartment she shares, to make what she can of the remainder of her life.

In spite of strains and tensions, clashes of background, interest and personality, an indomitable quality of strength, a will to survive, is evident in each of the women in Grekova's novel. Even Vadim, Anfisa Gromova's illegitimate son, eventually wins through to the hope of a 'new life', though he, along with many of his contemporaries, had grown up filled with anger and an unfocused desire for revenge for a childhood deprived of the normal family security, and a conviction 'that he'd been given less than other people, done out of his rightful share of things'.

There is, often, an additional trauma in the loss and bereavement suffered in wartime. Jeremy, the RAF officer with whom Linda McCullough Thew had become friendly, vanished without trace. When Helen Forrester's young man was lost at sea, a sympathetic neighbour said to her, 'What you need is a body and a good wake. Gives you a chance to cry yer head off ... There's lots like you, luv, and all they can do is light a candle.' This homely comment highlights one of the hardest aspects of war: the death of loved ones without the tangible proof which gives the survivors the opportunity to mourn in the conventional manner. This is the central theme of *Widows*, a novel by Ariel Dorfman, set ostensibly in Greece under Nazi occupation but inspired by the fate of the women of the author's native Chile, for whom – though it was peacetime – the 'disappearance' of their menfolk was a daily occurrence. Initially the women in his novel can do no more than grieve helplessly, and wait without hope for news of fathers, husbands, brothers and sons who have disappeared without trace. But they band together to call the world's attention to their plight, and create a bizarre situation in which each of them is claiming the same battered, unrecognisable body as *her* father, husband, brother or son, and each is therefore demanding that it be given up to *her* for burial. In this way they make public protest both at the fate of their loved ones and at the cruel desolation of the situation in which a ruthless, repressive and inhuman authority has left them without certain knowledge of what has been done to their menfolk and without even a body to give substance to their mourning.

This impressionistic and evocative novel is not intended as a realistic account of life under any specific military regime; it creates an archetypal situation which is symbolic of the courage, endurance and refusal to succumb, whatever the cost, which these women demonstrate through their united action.

Closer at hand both in place and time are the problems daily besetting women in Northern Ireland. In the early 1980s Melanie McFadyean went to Belfast to record interviews with ordinary women from both sides of the conflict. With the help of Roisin McDonough and Eileen Fairweather she has told their stories in *Only The Rivers Run Free*, a book which, she explains, is not intended as a work of history, but 'is more like a documentary film in prose which takes the reader into the living rooms and kitchens, the prisons, churches and streets where women in the North live out their lives under British occupation'. Whatever their political or religious commitments, the overriding concerns of these ordinary women are anguish and fear for their menfolk and their children, dismay and grief at the state of their own lives and the lives of those around them, bitter unceasing struggle to keep going, and fear, sometimes hopelessness, for the future.

The authors recall their impressions of Belfast during the three years they spent interviewing:

There were whole areas littered with the jetsam of destruction.

But the riots are beyond a question of point or reason. The internment 'commemorations' are an expression of frustration, the frustration of a generation of kids brought up in the ghettos of Northern Irish cities, and they take that anger to the streets where they can explode it in the rioting. Those streets bear the scars of many a skirmish between Republicans and the security forces. The burnt-out buses, hollow charred cars, broken pavements, the stones pulled out for missiles, much broken glass. Not all the violence in the ghettos is political in motive. The war has bred a generation for whom nothing is certain, and whose rage and despair are sometimes expressed by wrecking, violence and vandalism. Windows are broken by plastic bullets and badly aimed retaliatory missiles; they are also smashed by kids for kicks, kids for whom 'law and order', even their own community's sense of law and order, is without meaning.

In ghettos like these, the women conduct their private battle to feed, clothe and bring up their kids, often without help from the absent husband and father. Mary, for instance, 'a weary single parent with three children', drags her son home from one such scene of violence saying bitterly:

These kids are old before their time. They've seen what they've seen, injustice and brutality every day of their lives. Then they see the politicians on the TV and all that teaches them is that when you're in the ghetto nobody cares.

Like the townspeople of Auschwitz, who resolutely ignored the smoking chimneys and the inmates of the deathcamp nearby, we look the other way.

Only the Rivers Run Free tells of children in the firing line; of children as young as five or six 'lifted' by the police for questioning; of 'a young girl shot dead in a gun battle'; and of the eventual 'rebelliousness in the women, the paradoxical positive aspect of the war which has taught women the hard way, incited in them an independence and awareness that they might well never have encountered had Ireland gone on the way it was going before Civil Rights'.

But this independence also is purchased at a high cost in suffering and death; resulting from the riots, from police brutality and from imprisonment, particularly in the notorious Holywood barracks, a 'torture centre for which Britain was indicted at the European Court of Human Rights'. There, one 13-year-old girl claimed, her brother was deliberately maimed by a 'butcher's needle' inserted into his leg, to take part of the marrow away; an act one compares with horror to the experiments at Ravensbruck recorded by Wanda Poltawska (see Chapter 7). Indeed, it is difficult to read the accounts given here of the jails and internment camps of Northern Ireland without feeling a combined distaste, horror and despair for the human race similar to that evoked by the records of daily life in the German concentration camps. There is no mass extermination programme, to be sure, but according to the women whose experiences are recorded in this book, there are extremely uncomfortable parallels in the callous disregard shown towards men, women and even children, and in the reports of brutality, inhuman cruelty and torture.

Women's concern at the consequences of civil or international conflict to their own families or to other women and their families has been reflected recently in a spate of books and reports by women. There are also a number of excellent and thoughtful anthologies of women's writings on war, and firsthand accounts of women's war experiences. As a reporter Martha Gellhorn covered many areas of conflict, from the civil war in Spain in 1936 to wars in Finland, China, Europe, Java, Vietnam, Israel and central America, and was led by her experiences to a firm repudiation of war as a means of settling anything, and an abiding anger at the stupidity of mankind. In the 1967 introduction to *The Face of War*, her collection of articles and reports from various theatres of war, she writes:

> War happens to people, one by one. That is really all I have to say and it seems to me I have been saying it forever. Unless they are immediate

victims, the majority of mankind behaves as if war was an act of God which could not be prevented; or they behave as if war elsewhere was none of their business. It would be a bitter cosmic joke if we destroy ourselves due to atrophy of the imagination.

Her book has justly been described as 'a work of vision and compassion', a 'commitment to humanity, life and peace'. She brings to her reporting her own vivid sense of the waste, suffering and destruction caused by wars to property, environment and life. She reports from the Canton front in 1941; from the small Dutch town of Nijmegen, recaptured by the Allies, but surrounded still by the retreating German armies; from Dachau in 1945 and from the Nuremberg trials; or from the city of San Salvador, which she found terrifying in 1983; and observes quietly but powerfully the small details of life in wartorn Saigon. Sometimes there was personal danger to be encountered in obtaining her reports; but always underlying her accounts there is the same anger at the plight of the victims, whoever they may be.

Women in War concentrates on the role of women as active combatants during the period from the Second World War to El Salvador. In her Introduction Shelley Saywell remarks that when she first began her research she was quickly 'reminded that women have always been in battle'. She says:

There is hardly a nation that does not have in its history at least one martial heroine. What astounded me was the extent to which women have faced combat in modern war – nursing, reporting, fighting, spying, bombing, killing, dying.

She travelled round the world to interview women and record their experiences and opinions, and found:

The things I expected to hear and perhaps, in the beginning, wanted to hear were not always said. I wanted to hear that women are in every respect as capable as men: instead I heard about their weaknesses as well as their strengths. I expected to hear a great deal about male chauvinism, but I also heard about men who treated the women they fought beside as equals, as comrades. I wanted to hear that women are innately more pacifist than men, but I learned that they can be every bit as determined in their willingness to kill and die for their beliefs. At the same time I was often told that ultimately women are mothers and want above all to nurture and preserve life.

This variety of attitude, reflected in so many recent anthologies, and in the fiction, autobiography and other writings by or about women discussed in the course of this book, is testimony to the range of women's involvement in time of conflict. We see in these books both active support for war, and also continuing deep concern to arouse public consciousness to the tragedy, waste and futility of seeking to resolve problems by recourse to war. But the feeling which still has the greatest power to shape women's attitude to war can perhaps be summed up in the words of Olive Schreiner, an influential South African writer and campaigner on behalf of women, who wrote in 1911:

> There is, perhaps, no woman ... who could look down upon a battlefield covered with the slain, but the thought would rise in her, 'So many mothers' sons ... So many months of weariness and pain while bones and muscles were shaped within; so many baby mouths drawing life at women's breasts; all this, that men might lie with glazed eyeballs, and swollen bodies, and fixed, blue, unclosed mouths, and great limbs tossed – this, that an acre of ground might be manured with human flesh ...' No woman who is a woman says of a human body, 'It is nothing.'
>
> (Quoted in Cambridge Women's Peace Collective, *My Country is the Whole World*)

This is the feeling that has informed so much of women's protest against the horror and fear of wars past and to come; and which still powerfully stirs them in their current world-wide campaigns for peace.

17

The Poetry of War

What can poetry convey to us about war which has not already been encapsulated in prose memoirs or novels?

Sometimes there is in the poetry of war a freshness of experience and vision absent from much of the prose, since with the exception of a few collections of letters from the Front, novels and memoirs have usually been written at a distance from the events, ten, twenty or even thirty years later. Some of our most cherished war poetry also has the added poignancy that the authors died in the course of the action they so movingly evoke. In these poems there is often a distillation of experience, a power lent to them by the concentration of emotion, imagery and thought found only in good poetry. For 'poetry of a high order', as Vernon Scannell observes in his critical survey, *Not Without Glory*, 'is able to strike resonances, suggest ambiguities and pack layers of other possible meanings beneath [its] anecdotal surfaces that are beyond the scope of the novelists'.

Neither Wilfred Owen nor Isaac Rosenberg survived the First World War: their poetry matured within the context of events still being experienced; and all that had gone to shape their short lives, literary, personal, social and cultural, was concentrated into the final product. In considering poems like Owen's 'Futility', 'Exposure' and 'Spring Offensive', or Rosenberg's 'Dead Man's Dump', 'Break of Day in the Trenches' and 'Returning We Hear the Larks' we are confronted not merely with a single, self-contained event but with a total and considered response to the meaning for the poet of his life and threatening death.

Owen's poetry has survived in manuscripts which show how carefully he worked over each poem, requiring time and solitude to perfect each line, assembling with each new composition all that he had learned of his craft, up to that moment, from previous study of other poets and from close, detailed thought about exactly what he wished to convey. After his meeting with Sassoon at Craiglockhart War Hospital, according to Dominic Hibberd in *Owen the Poet*: 'Owen responded to his new friend's first advice,

"Sweat your guts out writing poetry!", with characteristic enthusiasm, making use of everything he could learn from Sassoon's
work.' And during the period following his recovery from shell-
shock, he rented a cottage to which he could retreat in order to
write. Hibberd comments:

> His method of working deserves to be recognised as an extraordinary
> undertaking – a young subaltern training by day for the fighting that
> would almost certainly kill him, and in the warm spring evenings
> walking down a country lane to shut himself away in a windowless
> room and open his 'inward eye' to the intensity of those feelings and
> experiences that had brought him close to madness a year before.

The concentration and seriousness of Owen's approach to his
work is evident in 'Exposure', a poem which recreates for us, with
an immediacy not possible within a more lengthy prose exposition, the many hours of inactivity, tedium and apprehension
spent in the trenches.

> Our brains ache, in the merciless iced east winds that knive us ...
> Wearied we keep awake because the night is silent ...
> Low, drooping flares confuse our memory of the salient ...
> Worried by silence, sentries whisper, curious, nervous,
> > But nothing happens.

The contrast with the drowsy sensuousness of Keats's 'Ode to a
Nightingale' ('My heart aches, and a drowsy numbness fills my
sense') has inevitably been commented on. These minds are weari-
somely alert in the unaccustomed and unnerving silence,
restlessly trying to tease out what might be in preparation. But
though there is no physical action from the enemy, the 'merciless
iced east winds' both numb and pierce their brains' unavailing
effort. The flares which might have offered illumination, or at
least a brightness to counteract the dark and the silence, are low
and drooping, like the men's spirits; they blur the memory and
add to the confusion and sense of helpless apprehension. The sen-
tries, whispering, betray that they, too, are anxious, and their fears
are quickly communicated to the men as they lie sleepless,
straining to anticipate what is happening.

But though their eyes remain open and watchful they see
nothing in the darkness save the distant flickering of gunbursts.
More insistent even than the guns rumbling far off 'like a dull
rumour of some other war' is the wind nearby. It brings to their
imagination nightmare scenes of men twitching in their last
agonies in the barbed wire entanglements of no-man's-land. This
hostility of the elements adds to their feeling of the senselessness

of their position; reinforced as the dawn sky, far from bringing its traditional sense of renewal and hope, seems also to be in alliance with the enemy.

> The poignant misery of dawn begins to grow ...
> We only know war lasts, rain soaks, and clouds sag stormy.
> Dawn massing in the east her melancholy army
> Attacks once more in ranks on shivering ranks of grey,
>   But nothing happens.

Action when it does come in the form of sudden flights of bullets is, paradoxically, 'less deathly' than the 'sidelong' flakes of snow, 'wandering up and down the wind's nonchalance'. The flakes 'fingering' their faces suggest simultaneously an erotic tenderness and a casually treacherous stealth from which they shrink back into confused dreams. Their 'snow-dazed' impression of warmth and spring is so far removed from the reality that it seems like the fantasies prefacing death. In this bleak stillness they become absorbed in 'their dying'.

Their 'ghosts drag home' unwillingly, not hopefully, to find their reluctance justified: they are shut out. The home fires they are defending are sunk. Though the 'jewels' encrusting the dying coals suggest the beauty and value the fires of home still have for these soldiers, they are now costly in a more sinister sense, being red like the blood from their comrades' wounds. Even the perception that the 'innocent' mice are now in possession and 'rejoice' recalls the predatory rats which infested the trenches. But, in ironic contrast to the doors of home closed against them, the soldiers still reiterate their belief in the cause for which they are suffering – how else could they continue to endure?

> Since we believe not otherwise can kind fires burn;
> Nor ever suns smile true on child, or field, or fruit,
> For God's invincible spring our love is made afraid;
> Therefore, not loath, we lie out here, therefore were born,
>   For love of God seems dying.

But in the context of the indifference and hostility of the elements and of sunken home fires and closed doors, their declared belief in the cause for which they are dying, in the love of God or the invincible nature of His spring, becomes too fragile to maintain. All these reasons for living, for fighting, for hope for the future are threatened, and are dying in the trenches with soldiers for whom the future seems bleak.

> Tonight, this frost will fasten on this mud and us,
> Shrivelling many hands, puckering foreheads crisp.
> The burying party, picks and shovels in shaking grasp,
> Pause over half-known faces. All their eyes are ice,
>   But nothing happens.

In ways quite outside the powers of the prose writer Owen's verse enacts the plight of the men. At times the rhythm halts and swerves with the falling snowflakes, or falters with the men's numbing misery; then urges the reader forward with their strained expectation of an attack or with the urgency of their will to believe, only to be checked yet again by the dull flatness of 'But nothing happens'. Owen's subtle use of assonance echoes the mood, as the ear is repeatedly cheated by a rhyme which each time misses the expected completion of the verse.

Rosenberg's 'Dead Man's Dump' by contrast is full of movement and action and a positive anger; but the sense of futility and death is strong here too.

> The plunging limbers over the shattered track
> Racketed with their rusty freight,
> Stuck out like many crowns of thorns,
> And the rusty stakes like sceptres old
> To stay the flood of brutish men
> Upon our brothers dear.

It is not those at home, or in the future, who are here to be protected; but fellow soldiers in the trenches nearby, as the 'limbers' plunge over a track already shattered with shell-fire. The freight of rusty barbed wire and stakes indicates the time already spent fruitlessly on this action and the fragility of their defence: the imagery of 'crowns of thorns' and 'sceptres old' conveys both the sacrificial nature of their enterprise and its quality of ages-old experience.

> The wheels lurched over sprawled dead
> But pained them not, though their bones crunched,
> Their shut mouths made no moan,
> They lie there huddled, friend and foeman,
> Man born of man, and born of woman,
> And shells go crying over them
> From night till night and now.

The immediacy of this brings home painfully the sprawled helplessness of the dead, now making 'no moan', though the crunching bones recall the pain and anguish suffered before they gained this immunity through death, and underline the growing callousness of the drivers who 'lurch' as indifferently over them as

over the holes and craters. The futility of their sacrifice is demonstrated by the indiscriminate huddle of friend and enemy, being
ground now into the earth together: their common heritage
emphasised by their parentage, 'man' presumably begetting the
warrior in them, 'woman' bewailing their death. But here it is only
the shells which cry over them, 'from night till night and now'; a
phrase which makes vivid the incessant threat of their wailing.

> Earth has waited for them
> All the time of their growth
> Fretting for their decay:
> Now she has them at last!
> In the strength of their strength
> Suspended – stopped and held.
>
> What fierce imaginings their dark souls lit?
> Earth! have they gone into you?
> Somewhere they must have gone,
> And flung on your hard back
> Is their souls' sack,
> Emptied of God-ancestralled essences.
> Who hurled them out? Who hurled?

There is a sense of inevitability and betrayal in the perception that
Earth – normally portrayed as 'life-giving' – has all the time been
'fretting for their decay', triumphing in their sudden and fruitless
end even in the midst of their strength. This prompts a desperate
questioning of Fate and of the purpose of lives so ended.
'Somewhere they must have gone'! But who has been responsible
for the violence of their end? And if their essential being, their
souls, were composed of 'God-ancestralled essences', what now
has happened to these, as the empty sack lies abandoned on the
hard earth?

> None saw their spirits' shadow shake the grass,
> Or stood aside for the half-used life to pass
> Out of those doomed nostrils and the doomed mouth,
> When the swift iron burning bee
> Drained the wild honey of their youth.

These men were young; the 'wild honey' now drained by 'the
swift iron burning bee' held sweetness and promise; their souls,
now dark and empty, were once 'lit' by 'fierce imaginings': the
sense of the waste and tragedy of their 'half-used lives' is vivid and
poignant. Even for those still living, still 'immortal seeming',
death is nevertheless imminent in the ceaseless explosions, as is
foreshadowed in the lines:

> Timelessly now, some minutes past,
> These dead strode time with vigorous life.

But as 'Maniac Earth' is now 'seared' by the 'jagged fire' of shrapnel piercing it in 'savage' love, Heavens and Earth combine to give birth to new dead. In an ironic reversal of erotic imagery, Rosenberg fuses all these thoughts of a confused conspiracy against mankind through the deadly and furious combination of Nature, of God and of Man himself. For it is also Man who is blindly contributing to his slaughter, digging out in like madness both the iron for his own destruction and the earth for his own tomb.

Even as the stretcher-bearers carry their load, they are splattered with the brains of the newly dead; the wounded man they are carrying himself slips 'drowning', and 'sunk too deep for tenderness'; and the dying, desperately crying out for help, die before help can reach them.

> Here is one not long dead;
> His dark hearing caught our far wheels,
> And the choked soul stretched weak hands
> To reach the living word the far wheels said,
> The blood-dazed intelligence beating for light,
> Crying through the suspense of the far torturing wheels
> Swift for the end to break
> Or the wheels to break,
> Cried as the tide of the world broke over his sight.
>
> Will they come? Will they ever come?
> Even as the mixed hoofs of the mules,
> The quivering-bellied mules,
> And the rushing wheels all mixed
> With his tortured upturned sight,
> So we crashed round the bend,
> We heard his weak scream,
> We heard his very last sound,
> And our wheels grazed his dead face.

It is the individual lives here which attract our answering anguish and anger, both on behalf of the dying men and of the stretcher-bearers and mule-train drivers for whom the newly dead must now be seen only as additional obstacles over which to lurch to their own temporary safety.

In both 'Exposure' and 'Dead Man's Dump' the length and structure of the poem correspond to the needs of the mood and subject matter. But quite different, tighter, more formal structures like that of the sonnet were used by many poets to convey other and varied effects. Brooke's 'The Soldier' and 'The Dead' owed much of their appeal to the persuasive rhythms of the sonnet form; and though the naivety of their war ethos is now rightly questioned, remain moving testimony to the sadly misplaced idealistic aspirations of an inexperienced young man. The versatility of this form is exemplified by Charles Sorley's answering 'When you see millions of the countless dead', in which he counters the sweep of Brooke's verse with his own sterner lines. Consider, for instance, Brooke's:

> There are waters blown by changing winds to laughter
> And lit by the rich skies all day. And after,
> Frost, with a gesture, stays the waves that dance
> And wandering loveliness ...

The first two lines of this extract have a persuasive movement which carries the reader momentarily to an acceptance of the imagery, with its deceptive sense of the beauty of death and sacrifice, quite unlike Owen's image of the frost 'shrivelling many hands, puckering foreheads crisp'. But the movement of Sorley's sonnet is harsh, with its clipped, taut sentences, and the brutal realism of 'gashed head' and 'blind eyes'.

> Give them not praise. For, deaf, how should they know
> It is not curses heaped on each gashed head?
> Nor tears. Their blind eyes see not your tears flow.
> Nor honour. It is easy to be dead.

Both Owen and Sorley were acutely aware of the physical presence of the 'countless dead', and have created images and used rhythms in ways appropriate to their knowledge.

Sassoon too was skilful in his use of verse structures. He often chose a tight, brief verse form which would enable him to conclude with some devastating riposte:

> But he did for them both by his plan of attack.
>
> ('The General')

> And when the war is done and youth stone dead,
> I'd toddle safely home and die – in bed.
>
> ('Base Details')

> no doubt he'll die today.
> But *we* can say the front-line wire's been safely mended.
>
> ('Wirers')

> And the Bishop said: 'The ways of God are strange.'
>
> ('They')

In the context of the poem itself and of the frequency of this pattern in Sassoon's verse the caustic satiric intent of each of these concluding lines is unmistakably effective, as a more detailed examination of 'Lamentations' will show. The abrupt opening line of this poem immediately alerts the reader to the expectation of some trauma.

> I found him in the guard-room at the Base.

The rhythm becomes more tentative, its pauses matching the blundering intrusion of the narrator and the incomprehension and hesitant explanations of the sergeant:

> From the blind darkness I had heard his crying
> And blundered in. With puzzled, patient face
> A sergeant watched him; it was no good trying
> To stop it; for he howled and beat his chest.

The verse then moves to a climax of indignant verbs which convey both the soldier's grief and the sergeant's gathering impatience at what he sees as his unreason. This begins with a rush of words after the opening, hesitant 'And':

> And, all because his brother had gone west,
> Raved at the bleeding war; his rampant grief
> Moaned, shouted, sobbed, and choked, while he was kneeling
> Half-naked on the floor.

It is at this point that Sassoon explodes his punch-line; the sourly judgemental withdrawal of sympathy:

> In my belief
> Such men have lost all patriotic feeling.

The reader's response of answering sympathetic indignation at such callousness and of anger at the tragedy of waste is assured.

But though many of the poems of the present century have been concerned in one way or another with a similar sense of the pity and tragedy of war, both for themselves and even, at times, for the enemy, there are many war poems quite different in character. In *The Oxford Book of War Poetry*, edited by Jon Stallworthy, the opening extract from Exodus is an exultation at the wholesale destruction of the Egyptian army:

> The Lord is a man of war: the Lord is his name.

Pharoah's chariots and his host hath he cast into the sea; his chosen captains also are drowned in the Red sea.

The depths have covered them: they sank to the bottom as a stone.

Thy right hand, O Lord, is become glorious in power: thy right hand, O Lord, hath dashed in pieces the enemy.

In his survey of war poetry from the earliest recorded times to the present day, Stallworthy charts its many changes in tone, mood and direction. It was, for instance, the function of the great early European poets and minstrels to celebrate glorious actions in war and encourage others to emulate the deeds of past heroes. So Homer, as Sorley reminds us, told:

> Tales of great war and strong hearts wrung,
> Of clash of arms, of council's brawl,
> Of beauty that must early fall,
> Of battle hate and battle joy ...

Homer, Virgil and other classical poets, Stallworthy points out, were familiar both to aspiring poets and to young officers of the early twentieth century, and became, indeed, part of the public school tradition of patriotism and of the virtues of conquest and heroic valour.

Stallworthy also includes in his volume a number of battlesongs from British history, celebrating the Battle of Maldon and other less well-known affrays; as well as later poems in the heroic vein of Tennyson's 'The Charge of the Light Brigade', Julian Grenfell's 'Into Battle', or Herbert Asquith's high-sounding but meretricious verse, 'The Volunteer', a fulsome tribute to the city clerk who now, the poet would have us believe:

> lies content
> With that high hour, in which he lived and died.
> And falling thus he wants no recompense,
> Who found his battle in the last resort;
> Nor needs he any hearse to bear him hence,
> Who goes to join the men of Agincourt.

Even from the earliest times, however, 'content' was a word sparingly applied to the dead in battle. 'Lament of the Frontier Guard', for instance, Ezra Pound's translation of an eighth-century Chinese poem by Rikahu, ends with bitter grief and anger at the fate of the guards and at the 'barbarous kings' who have turned a 'gracious spring' to 'blood-ravenous autumn', bringing:

               sorrow, sorrow like rain.
Sorrow to go, and sorrow, sorrow returning.
Desolate, desolate fields,
And no children of warfare upon them,
    No longer the men for offence and defence.
Ah, how shall you know the dreary sorrow of the North Gate,
With Rikahu's name forgotten,
And we guardsmen fed to the tigers.

Ten centuries later from Britain, comes 'The Drum', an anti-war poem by John Scott of Amwell.

    I hate that drum's discordant sound,
    Parading round, and round, and round:
    To thoughtless youth it pleasure yields,
    And lures from cities and from fields,
    To sell their liberty for charms
    Of tawdry lace, and glittering arms;
    And when Ambition's voice commands,
To march, and fight, and fall, in foreign lands.

    I hate that drum's discordant sound,
    Parading round, and round, and round:
    To me it talks of ravaged plains,
    And burning towns, and ruined swains,
    And mangled limbs, and dying groans,
    And widows' tears, and orphans' moans;
    And all that Misery's hand bestows,
To fill the catalogue of human woes.

In the context of Stallworthy's anthology, celebrating so many countless centuries of wars and war dead, the anger to be found in Richard Eberhart's poem of the Second World War, 'The Fury of Aerial Bombardment', is savagely underlined:

    You would feel that after so many centuries
    God would give man to repent; yet he can kill
    As Cain could, but with multitudinous will,
    No farther advanced than in his ancient furies.

Unfortunately he is infinitely further advanced in his technical ability to kill, and the century has brought wars without end all over the globe. After its detailed scrutiny of the two World Wars, Stallworthy's anthology moves on to poetry of the horrors of Vietnam, Northern Ireland, El Salvador and the possibility of a future nuclear war, presaged by William Stafford's 'At the Bomb Testing Site', by Peter Porter's well-known 'Your Attention Please' and by Richard Wilbur's plea for sanity in 'Advice to a Prophet'.

In his poem 'In the Dordogne' John Peale Bishop made his own protest at the futility of war and at the naive innocence of the soldier's hope for a future made 'safe' by his action.

> And each day one died or another
> Died: each week we sent out thousands
> That returned by hundreds
> Wounded or gassed. And those that died
> We buried close to the old wall
> Within a stone's throw of Perigord
> Under the tower of the troubadours.
>
> And because we had courage;
> Because there was courage and youth
> Ready to be wasted; because we endured
> And were prepared for all endurance;
> We thought something must come of it:
> That the Virgin would raise her Child and smile;
> The trees gather up their gold and go;
> That courage would avail something
> And something we had never lost
> Be regained through wastage, by dying,
> By burying others under the English tower.

But when he died in 1944 he could not have foreseen the wholesale obliteration of life foreshadowed in Wilbur's poem, with its plea to mankind to envisage the ending of *all* things in nature through a nuclear holocaust.

> Ask us, prophet, how we shall call
> Our natures forth when that live tongue is all
> Dispelled ...
>
> Ask us, ask us whether with the wordless rose
> Our hearts shall fail us; come demanding
> Whether there shall be lofty or long standing
> When the bronze annals of the oak-tree close.

In attempting a coverage of war poetry through the ages Stallworthy has produced a varied and finally a chilling record of war. There are many other more specialised anthologies of war poetry, particularly from the First World War, and so many critical studies, too, that there is an embarrassment of material for readers.

One of the most authoritative anthologies of the Great War is Jon Silkin's *First World War Poetry*, first published for Penguin Books in 1979 and revised in 1981 to enlarge the original selection of poems in translation. Of these Jon Silkin and his co-editor,

David McDuff remark that though, unlike their British counter-parts, European poets were writing 'even *before* the war with tense foreboding':

> When we come to the *experience* of war there is greater congruity between British and European poets. The individual's experience of war is at the same time the negative critical experience of a civilization, comradeship or its equivalent freemasonry notwithstanding.

In this respect they cite 'the atrocities Klemm unfolds, the shaking of foundations, a sense of which is re-created by Ungaretti' as comparable to the themes present in the work of Sassoon, Herbert Read, David Jones, Owen and Rosenberg. It is natural, for instance, to compare Owen and Rosenberg's vivid sense of the relationships between the soldiers and nature with that of the Italian poet, Ungaretti. In his poem, 'Agony' (translated by Charles Tomlinson), nature participates in the agony and in the hostility; the quail, like the embattled men left helpless and hope-less, has lost the will to continue the fight against its foes; and the blinded finch is seen to be less fortunate than the dead. The pity of war is the theme also of 'San Martino del Carso' (translated by the editors), in which the empty, desolate houses contain only 'fragments of memory'; leaving the poet mourning: 'My heart is / the most tormented country of all'. But perhaps the most memor-able of Ungaretti's poems is the plea of 'No More Crying Out' (translated by Jon Silkin):

> Cease murdering the dead.
> If you hope not to perish, if you
> Want sound of them again,
> Stop crying out, cease
> The crying out of it.
>
> They have a barely heard whispering,
> No more than the increase of grass,
> Happy where no man passes.

Two poems by Wilhelm Klemm, both entitled 'Clearing Station', convey the stench and horror of suppurating wounds, of agony in dying, and of a sense of God's anger and of useless sacrifice with as direct, grim and gruesome accuracy as comparable British poetry (the gas attack in 'Dulce et Decorum Est', for example, or the descriptions of the dead in Sassoon's 'The Counter Attack' or of the dying man in 'The Death-bed').

The Lost Voices of World War I, edited by Tim Cross also gives generous space to poetry from Europe as well as from Britain and

America. This massive volume of prose and poetry was produced for the Armistice festival of 1988, and contains brief biographical details and critical comments on the writers, all of whom had been chosen for inclusion because they had been killed in the war. But the work selected does not itself necessarily have a direct bearing on their war experience: its relevance to the occasion is the sense of waste generated by contemplation of talents thus lost to posterity. We are told: 'An appendix lists some eight hundred writers of all nationalities who are known to have died as a result of World War I. Even that figure can only serve as an example of the millions of lives lost. But it is a potent example.'

The volume also contains an interesting Introduction and Conclusion in which Robert Wohl discusses a number of topics relating to the war experience, including the impact of the war on writers and the relation of the literature they produced to contemporary attitudes to the war. Like Richard Holmes (see Chapter 15) he remarks:

> Thus though it is necessary to emphasize, as so much of the war literature of the late 1920s and early 1930s did, the terrible disillusionment suffered by the enthusiastic volunteers and conscripts of 1914–1915, it is also – and equally – true that the war was experienced by many intellectuals as a privilege, a rite of passage, and a revelation of mysteries and emotions not available to men in times of peace.

He cites as an example, however, some of Alan Seeger's lines, claiming that 'despite the stilted rhetoric and the echoes of stentorian verse' they 'expressed what many felt':

> There we drained deeper the deep cup of life,
> And on sublimer summits came to learn,
> After soft things, the terrible and stern,
> After sweet Love, the majesty of Strife.

The tired clichés strike a discordant note which calls into question the sincerity of such lofty sentiments and casts doubt upon Wohl's claim that they are a true representation of attitudes genuinely held. Nevertheless this is an impressive collection of writing from many different points of view. In a volume of over 400 pages, about 70 are given to British writers; about 180 to German, about 120 to French and the remainder to other combatant nationals, to Italian, Polish, Czech, Bulgarian, Hungarian, Serbian and Armenian writers. This gives a distinctive flavour to the volume, introducing many poems unfamiliar to a British audience, and offering usefully the original version along with its rendering into English, so that those who know the language concerned can better savour the literary value of poems which inevitably suffer in translation.

Useful and interesting in a different way is Martin Stephen's anthology, *Never Such Innocence*. This book also attempts to give a new slant on the poetry of the war by including in its selection a number of poems which did not ignore 'the horrors or the follies of the First World War' but yet 'produced from them a mood that was neither markedly left- nor right-wing'; which is 'rather more varied ... than is normal in anthologies of First World War verse', and which, like a Norfolk gentleman farmer whom Stephen interviewed, 'remembered the war with sadness, sometimes with repulsion, but more often with pride'. Though it is hard to see why a Norfolk gentleman farmer's views should be considered particularly representative of those of the rank and file, it is fair to point out that many anthologies do have a decided bias towards the officer-poet group, so that it was reasonable to try to represent the ordinary infantryman by the inclusion, for instance, of a scattering of poems by less well-known ordinary soldiers and also some of the lighter, bawdier soldiers' songs. Stephen also devotes sections to other fields of battle than the traditional trench warfare in Europe. So there are poems of the war in Africa, the Dardanelles and Gallipoli, and the neglected areas of air and sea warfare. In addition, Stephen puts the war poetry in a context both of poetry which preceded it, and that which came after. He gives further help to the reader through some extremely useful factual information about the mechanics and technology of the war, and brief chronological notes on its progress which help to set in perspective and illuminate particular poems. There is also a section on the Home Front, in which can be found one or two poems on the sufferings of the women left behind – 'Lamplight', by May Wedderburn Cannan, and 'Train', Helen Mackay's painful account of a woman's parting from her soldier-husband with its agonised motif:

> Will the train never start?
> God, make the train start.
>
> She cannot bear it, keeping up so long;
> and he, he no more tries to laugh at her.
> He is going ...
>
> God, make the train start!
> Before they cannot bear it,
> Make the train start!

The tension of their parting, their desperate attempts to remain cheerful in spite of mutual knowledge that these may be their last moments together, and their longing nevertheless for the train to start and the parting to be over are poignantly realistic. Comparing this cry from the heart with the final poem in that section, 'The Send-Off', by Wilfred Owen, brings alive the opposing visions of the same anguish, as the men set off for the Front Line, and makes its own comment on the famous lines:

> Nor there if yet they mock what women meant
> Who gave them flowers.

Indeed, observing that though 'We know of the male agony of the trenches from the poetry of soldiers like Sassoon and Owen, we know little in poetry of what that agony and its millions of deaths meant to the millions of women who had to endure them', Catherine Reilly has gathered together in her anthology, *Scars Upon My Heart*, a record of other poems like these in which 'much more modestly yet still truly' women poets 'speak for women whose own lives were often blighted by that miserable loss'. In her Preface to this book, Judith Kazantzis remarks, 'The voices of despair and endurance and anger are quiet, yet they mount steadily into a cumulative effect.'

This is a just assessment, though the poems included vary considerably in quality. Perhaps the most moving in its quiet way is Anna Gordon Keown's brief poem, 'Reported Missing', which encapsulates in a few lines the sadness, bewilderment, heartbreak and initial refusal to accept the truth of their loss revealed in memoirs of women like Helen Forrester, Vera Brittain and Helen Smith (see Chapter 15).

> My thought shall never be that you are dead:
> Who laughed so lately in this quiet place.
> The dear and deep-eyed humour of that face
> Held something ever living, in Death's stead.
> Scornful I hear the flat things they have said
> And all their piteous platitudes of pain.
> I laugh! I laugh! – For you will come again –
> This heart would never beat if you were dead.
> The world's adrowse in twilight hushfulness,
> There's purple lilac in your little room,
> And somewhere out beyond the evening gloom
> Small boys are culling summer watercress.
> Of these familiar things I have no dread
> Being so very sure you are not dead.

This was the experience of so many women in time of war: long slow months of hopefulness and steadfast refusal to accept the reality of the missing soldier's death; which in the end must gradually but inevitably have given way to the pain and acceptance of loss.

There are many anthologies of the poetry of the Great War and more books and articles have been written about the literature of this period than about that of any other conflict. Jon Silkin has some particularly penetrating comments to make on some of the major poets in his critical book, *Out of Battle: The Poetry of the Great War*, and gives a detailed analysis both of the context in which they wrote and of the merits of individual poems.

There is general agreement that the work of poets of the Second World War is neither as outstanding in quality nor as well known, but while relatively speaking there are fewer critical works or anthologies devoted to their writing, Vernon Scannnell has made a good case for it in his critical volume, *Not Without Glory*. Ian Hamilton's anthology, *The Poetry of War 1939–1945* is a notable collection of verse written by members of the armed forces serving during that period, and Catherine Reilly has produced a companion volume to *Scars Upon My Heart* in *Chaos of the Night: Women's Poetry and Verse of the Second World War*. From these and other sources we get a very varied picture of the many different theatres of war – air and sea, desert and land, though naturally there are few of the trench poems which formed the bulk of the output of the previous war.

Roy Fuller's poem, 'Waiting to be Drafted', perhaps provides a starting point:

> It might be any evening of spring;
> The air is level, twilight in a moment
> Will walk behind us and his shadow
> Fall cold across our day.

The words 'any evening', 'level', and 'walk' set a quietness of tone which is quickly belied by 'Fall cold across our day'. The scene, with the 'usual trees', is transformed by the agitation of the mind, in which ordinary things unexpectedly excite feelings of disgust and pity. With such fluctuations of emotion comes 'constantly the sense of time / Retreating, leaving events like traps'. The unreality of this interval of time spent (as Saul Bellow puts it in his novel of that name) as a 'dangling man' awaiting the draft leaves the poet unrelentingly aware of the menace of the future, the trap waiting for him and for his friends.

> My comrades are in the house, their bodies are
> At the mercy of time, their minds are nothing but yearning.
> From windows where they lie, as from quiet water,
>   The light is taken away.

Twilight, no longer a peacefully normal ending to the day, has become a deliberate act of deprivation which presages their death: 'The light is taken away'.

The menace is felt, too, in Frances Cornford's poem, 'Soldiers on the Platform'; as the soldiers, with their 'young, bare, bullock faces', wait for the train to take them to the slaughter. Though they each seek to conceal their knowledge, imagining it to be peculiar to themselves they all know:

> With a simplicity like drawing breath,
> That out of happiness we fall on woe
> And in the midst of life we are in death.

Or as Keith Douglas remarked in 'Canoe', 'Well, I am thinking this may be my last / summer'.

But first come the 'Lessons of the War', detailed in Henry Reed's remarkable poem, beginning with the section best known, 'Naming of Parts'. It is the juxtaposition of the harsh admonitory tones of the instructor, with the gentle tenderness, the almost dreamlike quality of the japonica and the almond blossom, which makes so effective the contrast between the lesson in the art of killing, in the functions of the upper and lower sling swivel, the safety-catch and the bolt of the lethal guns, and the life-giving natural processes of bees and flowers, now no longer relevant to the new recruits, as they are being transformed from sensitive men to 'things'. This is also the tenor of Randall Jarrell's savage poem, 'The Lines'.

> After the centers' naked files, the basic line
> Standing outside a building in the cold
> Of the late or early darkness, waiting
> For meals or mail or salvage, or to wait
> To form a line to form a line to form a line;
> After the things have learned that they are things,
> Used up as things are ...

This depersonalising process in the training of new recruits has been the theme of many memoirs, but nowhere as incisively expressed as here, in the chilling 'After the things have learned that they are things'.

In Alan Ross's poem, 'Mess Deck', the men still make show of being living humans; but they too take on qualities of death, as, 'laid out on lockers, some get waylaid; / And lie stiff, running off films in the mind's dark room'. A similar set of images is found in Louis Simpson's 'The Battle', which begins with a vision of the men marching without identity of any kind, as though they were no more than their clothes:

> Helmet and rifle, pack and overcoat
> Marched through a forest.

But here, eventually, their ordinary humanity seeps through the impersonality of the battlelines:

> Most clearly of that battle I remember
> The tiredness in eyes, how hands looked thin
> Around a cigarette, and the bright ember
> Would pulse with all the life there was within.

The fragility of 'all the life there was within' is the subject of many of Randall Jarrell's poems. He served as a sergeant-pilot in the USAAF, and remained fully conscious of the destruction to life and cities consequent upon his operational and later his instructional activities. 'Eighth Air Force' attempts to come to terms with this knowledge, as he watches the puppy innocently drinking in the hutment, a tribute to the humanity of its inmates, the drunken sergeant whistling as he shaves, the men playing games of Pitch ... These men are all 'murderers', 'wolf to man', in spite of their apparent innocence and their natural fears lest the next mission be their last. 'Still, this is how it is done', in time of war. Of necessity, they thrust off the knowledge of their murders:

> Men wash their hands, in blood, as best they can:
> I find no fault in this just man.

The ambiguity of the final words is their most telling attribute, leaving a wry taste in the mouth, a sense of the bitterness lying behind the justification in its wartime context as in its original moment of utterance by Pontius Pilate as he delivered Christ to his death. Indeed, Jarrell's poetry is, in Scannell's words, 'one of the most bitter condemnations of war's waste and futility to have been written in the past half century or so' (*Not Without Glory*). One of the most savage is the brief poem, 'The Death of the Ball Turret Gunner', who woke from his 'dream of life' to 'black flak and the nightmare fighters. / When I died they washed me out of the turret with a hose.'

Many of his poems are concerned with actual or impending death. 'A Field Hospital' focuses upon the single wounded airman, painfully coming to consciousness; but even as 'He stirs, beginning to awake', the nurses advance with the hypodermic syringe to plunge him back, away from the terror of slowly returning memories, to renewed oblivion, where he 'sleeps, comforted'. The memories he is thus evading are encapsulated in 'A Pilot from the Carrier':

> Strapped at the center of the blazing wheel,
> His flesh ice-white against the shattered mask,
> He tears at the easy clasp, his sobbing breaths
> Misting the fresh blood lightening to flame,
> Darkening to smoke; trapped there in pain
> And fire and breathlessness ...

They are there also in 'The Dead Wingman', where the pilot stubbornly circles in search for his dead comrade; 'the eyes distending / With hatred and misery and longing, stare / Over the blackening ocean for a corpse.'

A significant part of Jarrell's bitterness was his judgement that wars in the end are fought not for ideals, but from more sordid motives. In 'The Range in the Desert' he concludes:

> Profits and death grow marginal:
> Only the mourning and the mourned recall
> The wars we lose, the wars we win;
> And the world is – what it has been.
>
> The lizard's tongue licks angrily
> The shattered membranes of the fly.

The sense of waste and of the imminence of death is paramount in so many of his poems, and in those also of Keith Douglas. In poems like 'Simplify Me When I Am Dead' and 'Dead Men' Douglas seems to face his own death and those of his comrades almost with a detached resolution; in 'Time Eating' the approach is simultaneously philosophic and intensely personal. 'Ravenous Time' is seen to devour everything he creates:

> But as he makes he eats; the very part
> where he began, even the elusive heart,
> Time's ruminative tongue will wash
> and slow juice masticate all flesh.
>
> That volatile huge intestine holds
> material and abstract in its folds:
> thought and ambition melt and even the world
> will alter, in that catholic belly curled.

But in spite of this huge abstraction of the image of all-devouring time, Douglas closes with an assertion of his own uniqueness, which, destroyed, can never be remade. It is the same sense of the loss of something irreplaceable which informs Tim Cross's endeavour to bring together in his anthology the writings of those who had died in the Great War, and which informs also Sarah Stafford's poem, 'The Unborn', in which, combining the protests of Owen's 'Strange Meeting' and 'The Parable of the Old Man and the Young', she writes:

> So, when a man lays down his lusty life
> To save his land, he says with dying breath,
> 'Here, people, since you need it, is my life
> And my son's life, yes, and my son's son's life,
> And my wife's joy, and all our sums of joy
> And God knows what of richness and delight
> That might have flowed from me. You make me now
> In death, a sad perpetual Abraham –
> Slaying my son, slaying my son for ever.
> You know there is no thicket and no ram
> And no reprieving angel at my side.'

Poetry of War can have a uniquely powerful impact on the individual reader: but what can it do to change the course of history? When Louis Simpson was asked to contribute a few autobiographical statements for Ian Hamilton's anthology, *The Poetry of War 1939–1945*, he wrote:

What, in these poems, was I trying to do that had not already been done? i did not wish to protest against war. Any true description of modern warfare is a protest, but many have written against war with satire or indignation, and it still goes on.

Though the selection of poetry for this chapter has necessarily been limited, it sufficiently demonstrates the wide variety of attitudes to war shown by combatants and civilians, some acceptance, even sometimes a sense of pride and glory, but above all an increasing measure of protest and indignation. Yet Simpson, so far, unfortunately is right: war still goes on. There is still support, even, for the so-called 'nuclear deterrent'. What more must we do to change this, and to make effective in life the protests that poets have repeatedly made in literature?

In his poem, 'Jews at Haifa', Jarrell pictures Jews who have survived the holocaust and are now standing at the rail of a freighter, 'gray with rust', at last entering the harbour. They 'stare till their looks fail / At the earth that they are promised', with its hope of safety and of some kind of future.

> Here on the edge

> Of the graves of Europe
> We believe: truly, we are not dead;
> It seems to us that hope
> Is possible – that mercy is permitted
> To men on this earth,
> To Jews on this earth ...

But even in Haifa the camps to which they are initially taken threaten their fragile hopes:

> The huts, the trembling wire
> That wreathes us, are to us familiar
> As death.

It is only with difficulty, therefore, that they are able to cling to a hope which is thus clouded with dread, and to reaffirm to themselves: 'Truly we are not dead'. There is a tragic irony now in this poem undoubtedly not intended by Jarrell. But could Jarrell or anyone else at that time have foreseen what was to happen in the Middle East within the lifetime of many of those thankfully finding refuge and a haven in their Promised Land?

Nevertheless, their painful hopes are still ours; that somehow in spite of all the strife that even yet continues unabated all over the world, 'truly we are not dead', but may cling to some hope for a future for ourselves and those we love.

Or are we always to be the victims of a cynical dependence on the power of the gun and the bomb, lampooned so bitterly in Nancy Price's parody of a popular wartime song?

> Johnny, take a gun – take a gun – take a gun,
> Killing's to be done – to be done – to be done,
> Never want to run – want to run – want to run,
> Finish with your fun – with your fun – with your fun.

> Handle steel – love the feel – death you'll deal,
> Pity, mercy crush,
> Remember they are mush,
> Thousands dead,
> Keep your head.
> Then you may
> Beside your pay
> Have a medal pinned –
> Hooray!

Afterword

In the sonnet found in his kit after his death on the Western front in 1915 Charles Sorley had written:

> When you see millions of the mouthless dead
> Across your dreams in pale battalions go,
> Say not soft things as other men have said,
> That you'll remember. For you need not so.

These lines took on an added irony after the outbreak of the Second World War. I well remember the Armistice Days of the 1930s, when each eleventh day of November at precisely eleven o'clock the sirens called for the two minutes' silence for us to remember the 'millions of the mouthless dead', and in the towns and even on the country roads the traffic stopped, while in schools and churches and other public places we sang Kipling's 'Recessional'. In spite of its unabashed imperialism, its regretful backward glance at past power and glory as 'farflung the armies melt away / The captains and the Kings depart', our emphasis was on its exhortation towards 'a humble and a contrite heart', its awareness of the transience of 'pomp', of the unacceptability of 'frantic boast' and 'foolish word', and on its plangent refrain, 'Lest we forget. Lest we forget.' To my youthful innocence, at least, it was a ceremony in remembrance of the *enormity* of the sacrifice, and the renewal of a pledge that no generation of young people should ever be called upon to make such sacrifice again. I remember, too, when this ceremonial ceased; because in spite of everything done and said since the end of the 'Great' War, we had, it seemed, forgotten.

Reading now statistics produced in the history books and quoted in *Never Such Innocence* and in another recent anthology of verse and prose on the theme of war and peace, *In a Dark Time*, the force of Sorley's 'millions of the mouthless dead' strikes even harder. '31 July–6 November 1917;' Martin Stephen writes in his Preface to the 'combat' section of his anthology: 'Third Battle of

272

Ypres (Passchendaele). British casualties over 300,000; German casualties under 200,000.' The palm for killing at this single battle clearly goes to the Germans. His record continues until finally he writes, 'The First World War is at last over. Of more than 65 million men mobilised by all the combatants, 37.5 million have become casualties – killed or died, missing, wounded or prisoner.' Nicholas Humphrey and Robert Jay Lifton, the editors of *In a Dark Time*, give figures of soldiers killed in both World Wars, quoting from those produced by Gwyn Prins, editor of *Defended to Death* and from Francis A. Beer in *Peace Against War*. These include 7,500,000 men from the USSR alone in the Second World War, a figure double the German losses in this war, and far outstripping the total number of soldiers killed from France, Britain and the US. But the staggering total of soldiers killed worldwide in the 1914–18 war is given as 8,418,000, and in the 1939–45 war as 16,933,000. Remember that these figures relate this time only to the dead, and take no account of those missing or injured; or of civilian deaths, which during the raids on large cities of Europe, during the advance of the German army into USSR, and during the conventional bombing runs over Japanese cities and the two brief nuclear raids on Hiroshima and Nagasaki mounted to uncountable millions more.

The numbers stun us. In writing of Eberhart's 'The Fury of Aerial Bombardment', Scannell remarks that the final stanza, added later, with its specific reference to two actual names of the dead (Of van Wettering I speak, and Averill / Names on a list, whose faces I do not recall) enables Eberhart to come 'down from the upper regions of abstract speculation to the plain earth where ordinary men who lived and died prematurely are remembered', and this is what 'makes the poem so effective'. It is indeed true that figures of themselves can only numb the mind with a sense of their horror: it is the individual lives, deaths, injuries, tragedies which make war real to us.

It is the function of the novels, memoirs and poems discussed in this book to make real what is rapidly receding into folk memory and myth by specifically entering into the individual lives and tragedies of those who suffer in time of war and to make real, too, our fears for the future, which with its possibility of inconceivable, unimaginable totality of destruction apparently yet remains mythical, unbelievable to those who still cling pathetically to a reliance on 'the nuclear deterrent'.

Of course, in writing, and indeed in reading a book of this kind or the literature it reviews it is necessary to keep perpetually in mind Brecht's poem, 'Literature Will Be Scrutinised', with its warning:

> Whole fields of literature
> Written in choice phrases
> Will be scrutinised for signs
> That then too there were rebels in the midst of oppression.

I have been very conscious of the ease with which books, and passages from them, can be found to support my own view of war, of peace, and of the use of violence in literature and in life. But though my firmly pacifist stance will be abundantly clear in these pages, I have certainly felt it to be important to present also books and passages written from a different standpoint; and have in any case attempted as far as possible to allow books and authors to speak for themselves. My belief that each individual must make up his or her own mind on all issues, particularly on the most vital issues of life and death, holds good in this area, too. I am not afraid to admit that my extensive reading of war literature has at times forced me to think again, carefully, about my own pacifist convictions. Can they be upheld at all times and in all circumstances? Perhaps the book which most gave me pause was Primo Levi's *If Not Now, When?*, read in the context of other literature of the Nazi period. That I sustained my views, nevertheless, is due mainly to the perception that however great, indeed pressing, may be the temptation to resort to killing in self-defence or in an attempt to defeat unscrupulous evil, the end result provides only a temporary solution, and one which in the process inevitably hardens and changes for the worse both the people involved and the cause for which they fight. There has to be some other way than confrontation and violence.

It may seem useless and hopeless to reiterate that few problems would not yield to cooperative effort if only we were to put as much energy and resources into finding peaceful solutions for the world's wrongs as we do both into preparing for war, and into actually carrying out the wholesale destruction which is modern warfare. Yet this is still true. Indeed, the combined international efforts required to solve such persisting problems as world hunger and disease would be a wholly desirable and constructive way of directing and controlling human aggressive impulses, as was suggested by Konrad Lorenz in 1963 in the optimistic conclusion to his book, *On Aggression*. The question still remains, how to convince others, and to convince them in sufficient numbers to make the required effect.

One way is through education. But here it becomes vital to recognise that it is necessary not to be too selective in one's choice of material, but to present opposing arguments as openly and honestly as possible. For just as one cannot achieve a lasting peace through violence, so one cannot achieve lasting conviction either by confrontation or by preaching unremittingly to the young one point of view only. Discussion has to be free and open, genuine and untrammelled. The books and poems are there, carrying their weight of actual experience; they should be encouraged to do their own work. If they fail – and it is uncomfortable to reflect with Louis Simpson, Caroline Moorehead, Dorothy Rowe and other writers on the subject that there is as yet little evidence of a sufficient change of heart – then we face a bleak future, perhaps no future at all. For this reason, and whatever reservations or scepticism we may have, we must nevertheless do our best, take what opportunities may present themselves, work untiringly for the world's peace and the world's future.

Perhaps we could begin by paying serious attention to the warning quoted earlier from Dorothy Rowe's *Living with the Bomb.*

> The warnings are there all the time for us to see. The planes fly overhead, the missiles are installed. Our newspapers, radio and television show us in words and pictures what cruelty we inflict on one another, either directly by killing and maiming, or indirectly by allowing such cruelty to continue. Some of us heed these warnings and try, in ways which seem puny and ineffective, to alter the course of human history so that the human race will not only continue to exist but will live with greater love and understanding. However, most of us are ignoring the warnings and go on living as if all is well and life will continue for ever on this bountiful planet. But denial of reality, that is, lying to yourself, is the most costly error you can ever make. Reality does not become unreal. You do. Our present world is full of people who are unreal to themselves, who do not know themselves. It is they who will destroy us all.

The way would then be open to consider responsibly and positively how to put into effect the wish for peace already widely expressed in literature and by various existing pressure groups. It is not, as Muriel Rukeyser has pointed out in her optimistic little poem, 'Peace the Great Meaning', merely a matter of negative opposition to the prevailing ethos, as though 'peace' were only an absence of war. It does require positive and responsible action to create a world in which values upholding and admiring violence and toughness as virtues, as a viable way of achieving goals, finally give way to the active promotion of a rich and cultured society which has the courage to place its reliance not upon force and competitiveness but on mutual tolerance, understanding and active and concerned cooperation.

In the few years since the emergence of *perestroika* in the USSR, there have been throughout the world some disturbing outbreaks of communal violence. But there have also been sporadic stirrings of action in various countries, movements towards the resolution of disputes which had seemed intractable, movements away from confrontation and towards more relaxed discussion of differences followed by compromise and a readiness to work together. Hesitant, fragile and incomplete though some of these movements may seem, they are a signal of hope. In Muriel Rukeyser's words:

> Peace the great meaning has not been defined.
> When we say peace as a word, war
> As a flare of fire leaps across our eyes.
> We went to this school. Think war;
> Cancel war, we were taught.
> What is left is peace.
> No, peace is not left, it is no canceling;
> The fierce and human peace is our deep power
> Born to us of wish and responsibility.

Bibliography

Keegan, John and Holmes, Richard, *Soldiers*, London: Guild Publishing 1985 (adult)

Foreword

Cambridge Women's Peace Collective, *My Country is the Whole World*, London: Pandora Press 1984 (adult)

Moorehead, Caroline, *Troublesome People*, London: Hamish Hamilton 1987 (adult)

Rowe, Dorothy, *Living with the Bomb*, London: Routledge & Kegan Paul 1985 (adult)

Swanwick, Helena M., *The Roots of Peace*, London: Cape 1938 (adult)

Chapter 1   A Tough Nut to Crack

Bettelheim, Bruno, *The Informed Heart*, London: Thames & Hudson 1961, Paladin 1970 (adult)

Clarkson, Ewan, *The Many-Forked Branch*, London: Hutchinson 1980 (ages 11–14)

Cormier, Robert, *The Chocolate War*, New York: Pantheon 1974; London: Gollancz 1975, Fontana Lions 1978 (ages 12–14)

Diop, Birago, 'Sarzan', from *Modern African Stories*, ed. Charles Larson, London: Collier-Macmillan, Fontana 1970 (ages 16 and over)

Golding, William, *Lord of the Flies*, London: Faber 1954 (ages 14–adult)

Holmes, Richard, *Firing Line*, London: Jonathan Cape 1985 (adult)

Hughes, Thomas, *Tom Brown's Schooldays*, London: Ward Lock 1857 (ages 14–15)

Kipling, Rudyard, *Stalky and Co*, London: Macmillan 1899 (ages 14–15)

Levi, Primo, *The Periodic Table*, London: Michael Joseph 1985, Sphere Books 1986 (adult)

Moorehead, Caroline, *Troublesome People*, London: Hamish Hamilton 1987 (adult)

Needle, Jan, *A Game of Soldiers*, London: Collins (Fontana Lions) 1985 (ages 12–15)

Snedeker, Caroline Dale, *Theras*, London: Dent 1925 (ages 10–12)

Southall, Ivan, *To the Wild Sky*, Ringwood, Victoria: Angus & Robertson 1967, London: Puffin 1971 (ages 11–13)

Storey, David, *This Sporting Life*, London: Penguin 1960 (ages 16 and over)

Sutcliff, Rosemary, *Warrior Scarlet*, London: OUP 1958 (ages 12–14)

Westall, Robert, *The Machine-Gunners*, London: Macmillan 1975, Puffin 1977 (ages 13–15)

Chapter 2 A Dream of Heroes

Blythe, Ronald (ed.), *Writing in a War: Stories, Poems and Essays of 1939–1945*, Harmondsworth: Penguin 1966, rev. 1982 (adult)

Bryher, *The Fourteenth of October*, London: Collins 1954, Puffin 1964 (ages 11–13)

Carter, Peter, *Madatan*, London: OUP 1974 (ages 11–14)

Cormier, Robert, *The Chocolate War*, 1974, London: Gollancz 1975, Fontana Lions 1978 (ages 12–14)

Hodges, Walter, *The Namesake*, London: Bell 1964, Puffin 1967 (ages 12–14)

Picard, Barbara Leonie, *One is One*, London: OUP 1965 (ages 11–13)

Shakespeare, William, *Henry V*

Sutcliff, Rosemary, *Eagle of the Ninth*, London: OUP 1954 (ages 12–14)

——, *Warrior Scarlet*, London: OUP 1958 (ages 12–14)

——, *Knight's Fee*, London: OUP 1960 (ages 11–13)

——, *Sword at Sunset*, London: Hodder & Stoughton 1963, Peacock 1965 (ages 13–16)

——, *Mark of the Horse Lord*, London: OUP 1965 (ages 12–14)

——, *Song for a Dark Queen*, London: Hodder & Stoughton 1978 (ages 13–15)

Treece, Henry, *The Viking Saga*, London: Bodley Head 1955, 1957, 1960, Puffin (one volume) 1985 (ages 11–14)

Welch, Ronald, *Knight Crusader*, London: OUP 1954, Puffin 1977 (ages 11–13)

Chapter 3 Mud, Blood, but not much Glory

Anand, Mulk Raj, *The Village*, New Delhi 1939, Orient Paperbacks (ages 14–adult)

——, *Across the Black Waters*, New Delhi 1940, Orient Paperbacks 1980 (ages 14–adult)

——, *The Sword and the Sickle*, New Delhi 1942, Orient Paperbacks, Liverpool: Lucas Publications 1986 (ages 14–adult)

Cawley, Winifred, *Down the Long Stairs*, London: OUP 1974 (ages 11–13)

Clarke, I.F., *Voices Prophesying War*, London: OUP 1966 (adult)

Crane, Stephen, *The Red Badge of Courage*, New York: Appleton 1895, London: Penguin 1983 (ages 14–adult)

Darke, Marjorie, *The First of Midnight*, London: Kestrel 1977 (ages 13–15)

——, *A Long Way to Go*, London: Kestrel 1978, Puffin 1982 (ages 14–16)

Fussell, Paul, *The Great War and Modern Memory*, New York and London: OUP 1975 (adult)

Greene, Bette, *The Summer of my German Soldier*, New York: Dial Press 1973, London: Hamish Hamilton 1974 (ages 12–14)

Hill, Susan, *Strange Meeting*, London: Hamish Hamilton 1971, Penguin 1974 (ages 14–adult)

Leonard, Alison, *An Inch of Candle*, London: Angus & Robertson, 1980 (ages 13–15)

Lunn, Janet, *The Root Cellar*, Canada: Lester & Orpen Dennys 1981, London: Puffin 1983 (ages 11–13)

McCutcheon, Elsie, *The Summer of the Zeppelin*, London: Dent 1983 (ages 12–14)

Parker, Peter, *The Old Lie: The Great War and the Public School Ethos*, London: Constable 1987 (adult)

Thompson, Brian, *Trooper Jackson's Story*, London: Gollancz 1975, Puffin 1982 (ages 13–15)

Welch, Ronald, *Knight Crusader*, London: OUP 1954, Puffin 1977 (ages 11–13)

——, *Tank Commander*, London: OUP 1972 (ages 12–14)

Chapter 4   From the Horse's Mouth

Barbusse, Henri, *Under Fire* (France 1916), trans. Fitzwater Wray, London: Dent 1926 (ages 15–adult)

Blunden, Edmund, *Undertones of War*, London: Cobden-Sanderson 1928 (ages 15–adult)

Clarke, I.F., *Voices Prophesying War*, London: OUP 1966 (adult)

Frank, Rudolf, *No Hero for the Kaiser* (1931), trans. Patricia Crampton, London: Dent 1986; New York: Lothrop, Lee & Shepherd 1986 (ages 13–15)

Fussell, Paul, *The Great War and Modern Memory*, New York and London: OUP 1975 (adult)

Graves, Robert, *Goodbye to All That*, London: Cassell 1929 (ages 15–adult)

——, *But It Still Goes On*, London: Cassell 1930 (ages 15–adult)

Hill, Susan, *Strange Meeting*, London: Hamish Hamilton 1971, Penguin 1974 (ages 14–adult)

Manning, Frederic, *The Middle Parts of Fortune* (1929), London: Peter Davies 1977 (ages 16–adult)

Parker, Peter, *The Old Lie: The Great War and the Public School Ethos*, London: Constable 1987 (adult)

Remarque, E.M., *All Quiet on the Western Front* (1929), trans A.W. Wheen, London: Putnam 1929 (ages 15–adult)

Renn, Ludwig, *War* (1929), trans. Willa and Edwin Muir, London: Martin Secker 1930 (ages 15–adult)

——, *After War* (1930), trans. Willa and Edwin Muir, London: Martin Secker 1931 (ages 16–adult)

Richards, Frank, *Old Soldiers Never Die*, London: Faber 1933 (ages 15–adult)

Rutherford, Andrew, *The Literature of War*, London: Macmillan 1978 (adult)

Sassoon, Siegfried, *Sherston's Progress*, London: Faber 1937 (ages 15–adult)

——, *Complete Memoirs of George Sherston*, London: Faber 1937 (ages 15–adult)

——, *Siegfried's Journey*, London: Faber & The Book Society 1945 (adult)

Welch, Ronald, *Tank Commander*, London: OUP 1972 (ages 12–14)
Wells, H.G., *Mr Britling Sees It Through*, 1916 (ages 16–adult)

Chapter 5 The War Machine

Cozzens, James Gould, *Guard of Honour*, New York and London: Longmans Green & Co., 1949 (adult)

Douglas, Keith, *Alamein to Zem Zem*, Oxford: OUP 1979 (ages 16 and over)

Fatchen, Max, *Closer to the Stars*, London: Methuen 1981, Puffin 1983 (ages 11–13)

Hamilton, Ian (ed.), *The Poetry of War 1939–1945*, London: New English Library 1972 (ages 15 and over)

Heller, Joseph, *Catch–22*, London: Cape 1962 (adult)

Holbrook, David, *Flesh Wounds*, London: Methuen 1966, Longmans 1968, Buchan & Enright 1987 (ages 15–adult)

Hough, Richard, *Razor Eyes*, London: Dent 1981 (ages 14–adult)

Mailer, Norman, *The Naked and the Dead*, London: Wingate 1949 (adult)

Malgonkar, Manohar, *Distant Drum*, New Delhi: 1960, Orient Paperbacks 1974 (ages 16 and over)

Richter, Hans Peter, *The Time of the Young Soldiers* (Paris: Verla Alsatia 1967), trans. A. Bell, London: Kestrel 1976 (ages 13–15)

Scannell, Vernon, *The Tiger and the Rose*, London: Robson Books, 1983 (ages 16 and over)

——, *Argument of Kings*, London: Robson Books 1987 (ages 16 and over)

Smith, Graham, *When Jim Crow Met John Bull*, London: I.B. Tauris 1987 (adult)

Southall, Ivan, *What About Tomorrow?*, London: Angus & Robertson 1977 (ages 12–14)

Chapter 6 A Civilian's War

Bawden, Nina, *Carrie's War*, London: Gollancz 1973, Puffin 1974 (ages 12–14)

Burton, Hester, *In Spite of All Terror*, London: OUP 1970 (ages 12–14)

Cambridge Women's Peace Collective, *My Country is the Whole World*, London: Pandora Press 1984

Cooper, Susan, *Dawn of Fear*, New York: Harcourt Brace 1970, London: Chatto & Windus 1972, Puffin 1974 (ages 10–12)

Evenhuis, Gertie, *What About Me?* (The Netherlands: Deltos Elsevier 1970), trans. Lance Salway, London: Kestrel 1974 (ages 10–12)

Hannam, Charles, *A Boy in Your Situation*, London: André Deutsch 1977 Adlib Paperbacks 1988 (ages 13 to adult)

Hartman, Evert, *War Without Friends* (Rotterdam: 1979), trans. Patricia Crampton, London: Chatto & Windus 1982 (ages 13–15)

Kerr, Judith, *When Hitler Stole Pink Rabbit*, London: Collins 1971 (ages 11–13)

——, *The Other Way Round*, London: Collins 1977 (ages 13–15)

Klaussner, Wolf, *Survive the Storm*, London: Methuen 1984 (ages 13–15)

Koehn, Ilse, *Mischling, Second Degree* (New York: Greenwillow 1977), London: Hamish Hamilton 1978, Puffin 1981 (ages 14–18)

Lutzeier, Elizabeth, *No Shelter*, London: Blackie 1984 (ages 10–13)

Magorian, Michelle, *Back Home*, London: Viking Kestrel 1985 (ages 12–14)

——, *Goodnight, Mr Tom*, London: Puffin 1983, Viking Kestrel 1987 (ages 12–14)

Rees, David, *The Exeter Blitz*, London: Heinemann (New Windmill) 1981 (ages 11–12)

Serraillier, Ian, *The Silver Sword*, London: Cape 1956, Puffin 1960 (ages 11–13)

Stockum, Hilda van, *The Winged Watchman*, New York: Farrar, Straus & Giroux 1962 (ages 11–14)

Trease, Geoffrey, *Tomorrow is a Stranger*, London: Heinemann 1987 (ages 12–14)

Walsh, Jill Paton, *Fireweed*, London: Macmillan 1969, Puffin 1972 (ages 12–14)

Westall, Robert, *The Machine-Gunners*, London: Macmillan 1975, Puffin 1977, New York: Morrow 1976 (ages 12–15)

Wicks, Ben, *No Time to Wave Goodbye: True Stories of 3,500,000 Evacuees*, London: Bloomsbury 1988 (ages 15 and over)

Further Reading

Calder, Angus, *The People's War: Britain 1939–1945*, London: Cape 1969, Panther 1971 (adult)

Grafton, Pete, *You, You, and You! The People Out Of Step with World War II*, London: Pluto Press 1981 (adult)

Harrisson, Tom, *Living Through the Blitz*, London: Collins, Mass Observation reports 1976 (adult)

Moorehead, Caroline, *Troublesome People*, London: Hamish Hamilton 1987 (adult)

On Evacuation

Fyson, Nance Lui, *Growing Up in the Second World War*, London: Batsford 1981 (for schools)

Jackson, Carlton, *Who Will Take Our Children?*, London: Methuen 1985 (adult)

Westall, Robert, *Children of the Blitz*, London: 1985, Isis Large Print Books 1989

Contemporary Accounts

Croall, Jonathan, *Don't You Know There's a War On? The People's Voice 1939–45*, London: Hutchinson 1989 (adult)

Children and War

Ballard, J.G., *Empire of the Sun*, London: Heinemann (New Windmill) 1984 (13 and over)

Hughes, Patricia, *Children at War*, London: BBC Books 1989 (for schools)

Lingard, Joan, *Tug of War*, London: Hamish Hamilton 1989 (14 and over)

Chapter 7   The Final Solution

Balderson, Margaret, *When Jays Fly to Barbmo*, London: OUP 1970 (ages 12–14)

Bauman, Janina, *Winter in the Morning*, London: Virago 1986 (ages 15–adult)

Bettelheim, Bruno, *The Informed Heart* (New York: The Free Press 1960), Thames & and Hudson 1961, Paladin 1970 (adult)

Carter, Peter, *Bury the Dead*, Oxford: OUP 1986 (ages 14–16)

Fenelon, Fania, *The Musicians of Auschwitz* (Paris: Opera Mundi 1976), trans. Judith Landry, London: Sphere Books 1979 (ages 17–adult)

Frank, Anne, *The Diary of Anne Frank* (Amsterdam: Contact 1947), trans. B.M. Mooyart-Doubleday, London: Vallentine Mitchell 1952, Pan 1954 (ages 13 and over)

Hannam, Charles, *A Boy in Your Situation*, London: André Deutsch 1977, Adlib Paperbacks 1988 (ages 13 and over)

Hart, Kitty, *Return to Auschwitz*, London: Sidgwick & Jackson 1981, Grafton Books 1983 (adult)

Hartman, Evert, *War Without Friends* (Rotterdam: 1979), trans. Patricia Crampton, London: Chatto & Windus 1982 (ages 13–15)

Kielar, Weislaw, *Anus Mundi: Five Years in Auschwitz* (first published in Polish, Krakow: 1972), trans. from the German by Susanne Flatauer, London: Allen Lane 1981, Penguin 1982 (adult)

Klaussner, Wolf, *Survive the Storm*, London: Methuen 1984 (ages 13–15)

Korschunow, Irina, *A Night in Distant Motion* (1979), trans. Leigh Hafrey, Boston: Godine 1983, London: Hodder & Stoughton 1984 (13–15)

Laird, Christa, *Shadow of the Wall*, London: Julia Macrae Books 1989 (ages 12–14)

Levi, Primo, *If This is a Man* (Turin: Einaudi 1958), trans. Stuart Woolf, London: Bodley Head 1966, Orion Press 1968, Sphere Books (Abacus) 1987 (adult)

Levoy, Myron, *Alan and Naomi* (New York: Harper & Row 1977), London: Bodley Head 1979 (ages 13–16)

Orgel, Doris, *The Devil in Vienna* (New York: Dial Press 1978), London: Simon & Schuster 1989 (ages 12–14)

Poltawska, Wanda, *And I am Afraid of My Dreams* (Poland: 1964), trans. Mary Craig, London: Hodder & Stoughton 1987 (17–adult)

Reiss, Johanna, *The Upstairs Room*, London: OUP 1972 (ages 12–14)

Rhue, Martin, *The Wave*, New York: Dell 1981, London: Puffin 1988 (ages 14–16)

Richter, Hans Peter, *Friedrich* (Nürnberg: Sebaldus Verlag G.m.b.H. 1961), trans. E. Kroll, London: Longman 1970, Kestrel 1971, Heinemann (New Windmill) 1978 (ages 12–14)

——, *I Was There*, (Freiburg: Verlag Herder KG 1962), trans. E. Kroll, London: Longman 1972 (ages 12–14)

Suhl, Yuri, *On the Other Side of the Gate*, New York and London: Franklin Watts 1975 (ages 12–14)

Wolf, Christa, *A Model Childhood*, trans. Ursula Molinaro and Hedwig Rappolt, London: Virago 1983 (adult)

Chapter 8 Hiroshima and After

Bruckner, Karl, *The Day of the Bomb*, trans. by Frances Lobb from *Sadako Will Leben*, Vienna: 1961, London: Burke 1962 (ages 13–14)

Burchett, Wilfred, *Shadows of Hiroshima*, London: Verso 1983 (adult)

Clarke, I.F., *Voices Prophesying War*, London: OUP 1966 (adult)

Coerr, Eleanor, *Sadako and the Thousand Paper Cranes*, Australia and London: Hodder & Stoughton 1981 (ages 10–14)

Hart, Kitty, *Return to Auschwitz*, London: Sidgwick & Jackson 1981, Grafton Books 1983 (adult)

Hersey, John, *Hiroshima* (*New Yorker* 1946), London: Penguin 1946 (adult)

Maruki, Toshi, *The Hiroshima Story*, London: A. and C. Black 1983 (ages 9 and over)

Mattingley, Christobel, *The Miracle Tree*, Sydney and London: Hodder & Stoughton 1985 (ages 9–12)

Mayhew, Patrick (ed.), *One Family's War*, London: Hutchinson 1985, Futura 1987 (adult)

Oe, Kenzaburo (ed.), *Fire from the Ashes*, London: Readers International 1985 (adult)

Thompson, Dorothy (ed.), *Over Our Dead Bodies*, London: Virago 1983 (adult)

Townsend, Peter, *The Postman of Nagasaki*, London: Collins 1984, Penguin 1985 (adult)

Further Reading

Chisholm, Anne, *Faces of Hiroshima*, London: Cape 1985 (adult)

Chapter 9 Fighting Back and the Challenge of Conscience

Burton, Hester, *In Spite of All Terror*, London: OUP 1970 (ages 12–14)

Cambridge Women's Peace Collective, *My Country is the Whole World*, London: Pandora Press 1984 (adult)

Cook, Alice and Kirk, Gwyn, *Greenham Women Everywhere*, London: Pluto Press 1983 (adult)

Cross, Tim (ed.), *The Lost Voices of World War I*, London: Bloomsbury 1988 (adult)

Hart, Kitty, *Return to Auschwitz*, London: Sidgwick & Jackson 1981, Grafton Books 1983 (adult)

Hartman, Evert, *War Without Friends* (Rotterdam: 1979), trans. Patricia Crampton, London: Chatto & Windus 1982 (ages 13–15)

Hayes, Denis, *Challenge of Conscience*, London: Allen & Unwin 1949 (adult)

Levi, Primo, *If Not Now, When?*, (Turin: Einandi 1982), trans. William Weaver, New York: Simon & Schuster 1985, London: Michael Joseph 1986, Abacus 1987 (adult)

Mayhew, Patrick (ed.), *One Family's War*, London: Hutchinson 1985, Futura 1987 (adult)

Moorehead, Caroline, *Troublesome People*, London: Hamish Hamilton 1987 (adult)

Richter, Hans Peter, *I Was There* (Freiburg: Verlag Herder KG 1962), trans. E. Kroll, London: Longman 1972 (ages 12–14)

Saywell, Shelley, *Women in War*, Canada: Penguin Books 1985, Tunbridge Wells: Costello 1987 (adult)

Scannell, Vernon, *Argument of Kings*, London: Robson Books 1987 (ages 16 and over)

Suhl, Yuri, *Uncle Misha's Partisans*, New York: Four Winds Press 1973, London: Hamish Hamilton 1975 (ages 14–16)

Walsh, Jill Paton, *The Dolphin Crossing*, London: Macmillan 1967, Puffin 1970 (ages 11–13)

Watson, James, *The Freedom Tree*, London: Gollancz 1976, Fontana Lions, 1986 (ages 13–15)

Chapter 10   Anti-Nuclear

Bischoff, David, *Wargames*, New York: Dell Publishing 1983, London: Penguin 1983 (adapted), Puffin 1983 (ages 12–14)

Bradford School of Peace Studies, *Nuclear Weapons Accidents – a handbook*, Bradford 1988 (adult)

Dibblin, Jane, *Day of Two Suns: Nuclear Testing and the Pacific Islanders*, London: Virago 1988 (adult)

Drake, Tony, *There Will Be a Next Time*, London: Collins 1984, Fontana Lions 1986 (ages 14–15)

Gale, Robert Peter and Hauser, Thomas, *Chernobyl: The Final Warning*, New York: Warner Books, London: Hamish Hamilton 1988 (adult)

Hoy, Linda, *The Damned*, London: Bodley Head 1983 (ages 14–15)

Humphrey, Nicholas and Lifton, Robert Jay, *In a Dark Time*, London: Faber 1984 (adult)

Johnson, Annabel and Edgar, *Finders, Keepers*, New York: Four Winds Press 1981 (ages 14–15)

Lingard, Joan, *The Guilty Party*, London: Hamish Hamilton 1987 (ages 13–15)

Pitcher, Caroline, *On the Wire*, London: Blackie 1989 (ages 11–13)

Sampson, Fay, *The Watch on Patterick Fell*, London: Dobson 1978 (ages 12–13)

Strugatsky, Arkady and Boris, *Roadside Picnic*, trans. Antonina W. Bouis (New York: Macmillan 1977), London: Gollancz 1978, Penguin 1979 (adult)

Swindells, Robert, *A Serpent's Tooth*, London: Hamish Hamilton 1988 (ages 13–15)

Voznesenskaya, Julia, *The Star Chernobyl* (Munich: Roitman Verlag 1986), trans. Alan Myers, London: Quartet Books 1987, Methuen 1988 (adult)

Watson, James, *Where Nobody Sees*, London: Gollancz 1987 (ages 13–15)

Wolf, Christa, *Accident*, London: Virago 1989 (adult)

Woodford, Peggy, *Monster in Our Midst*, London: Macmillan Children's Books 1988 (ages 13–15)

Chapter 11   What Kind of Future?

Bettelheim, Bruno, *Surviving the Holocaust*, London: Fontana (Flamingo) 1986 (adult)

Bischoff, David, *Wargames*, (New York: Dell Publishing 1983), London: Penguin 1983 (adapted), Puffin 1983 (ages 12–14)

Briggs, Raymond, *When the Wind Blows*, London: Hamish Hamilton 1982, Penguin 1983 (ages 12–adult)

Clarke, I.F., *Voices Prophesying War*, London: OUP 1966 (adult)

Dowling, David, *Fictions of Nuclear Disaster*, London: Macmillan 1987 (adult)

Drake, Tony, *There Will Be A Next Time*, London: Collins 1984, Fontana Lions 1986 (ages 14–15)

George, Jean, *Julie of the Wolves* (New York: Harper & Row 1972), London: Hamish Hamilton 1973, Puffin 1976 (ages 12–14)

Jungk, Robert, *Brighter than a Thousand Suns* (1956) trans. James Cleugh, London: Gollancz and Hart Davis 1958, Penguin 1960 (adult)

Kelleher, Victor, *Taronga*, London: Hamish Hamilton 1988 (ages 13–15)

Lawrence, Louise, *Children of the Dust*, London: Bodley Head 1985 Fontana Lions 1986 (ages 13–14)

Neihardt, John G., *Black Elk Speaks* Lincoln: University of Nebraska Press 1932 (adult)

O'Brien, Robert, *Z for Zachariah*, London: Gollancz 1975 (ages 13–15)

Rowan-Robinson, Michael, *Fire and Ice: The Nuclear Winter*, Harlow: Longman 1985 (adult)

Shute, Nevil, *On the Beach*, London: Heinemann 1957, Pan 1966 (ages 14–adult)

Strachey, John, *On the Prevention of War*, London: 1962 (adult)

Streiber, Whitley, *Wolf of the Shadows*, New York: Alfred A. Knopf 1985, London: Hodder & Stoughton 1986 (ages 12–14)

Swindells, Robert, *Brother in the Land*, Oxford: OUP 1984 (ages 13–15)

Thompson, Dorothy (ed.), *Over Our Dead Bodies*, London: Virago 1983 (adult)

Velikhov, Yevgeni (ed.), *The Night After ... Climatic and Biological Consequences of a Nuclear War,* Moscow: Mir Publishers 1985 (adult)

Wagar, W. Warren, *Terminal Visions*, USA: Indiana University Press 1982 (adult)

Wellington, J.J., *The Nuclear Issue*, Oxford: Basil Blackwell 1986 (teachers' book for pupils 14 and over)

Wells, H.G., *The World Set Free*, London: Hogarth Press 1988

Wyndham, John, *The Chrysalids*, London: Hutchinson 1955 (ages 13–15)

Chapter 12   A World of Violence

Cormier, Robert, *After the First Death*, London: Gollancz 1979, Armada Lions 1980 (ages 14–15)

Fraser, John, *Violence in the Arts*, Cambridge: CUP 1974 (adult)

Fugard, Athol, *Tsotsi*, S. Africa: Donker (Pty) Ltd 1980, London: Penguin 1983 (adult)

Gellhorn, Martha, *A Stricken Field* (New York: Duell, Sloane & Pearce 1940), London: Cape 1942, Virago 1986 (adult)

Mattera, Don, *Gone with the Twilight*, London and New Jersey: Zed Books 1987, S. Africa: Ravan Press 1987 (adult)

Mikdadi, Faysal, *Tamra*, London: Martin Brian & O'Keeffe 1988 (ages 16 and over)

Smith, Michael, *The Hostages*, London: Hodder & Stoughton, 1987 (ages 11–13)

Watson, James, *The Freedom Tree*, London: Gollancz 1976, Fontana Lions 1986 (ages 12–15)

——, *Talking in Whispers*, London: Gollancz 1983 (ages 14–15)

——, *Where Nobody Sees*, London: Gollancz 1987 (ages 12–15)

Chapter 13   Legitimising Violence

Benson, Mary, *At the Still Point* (Boston: Gambit 1969), London: Virago 1988 (adult)

Cook, Alice and Kirk, Gwyn, *Greenham Women Everywhere*, London: Pluto Press 1983 (adult)

D'Arcy, Margaretta, *Tell Them Everything*, London: Pluto Press 1981 (adult)

Ekwuru, Andrew, *Songs of Steel*, London: Nelson, Panafrica Library 1980 (ages 17 and over)

Fairweather, Eileen, McDonough, Roisin and McFadyean, Melanie, *Only the Rivers Run Free*, London: Pluto Press 1984 (adult)

Fraser, John, *Violence in the Arts*, Cambridge: CUP 1974 (adult)

Gellhorn, Martha, *A Stricken Field* (New York: Duell, Sloane & Pearce 1940), London: Cape 1942, Virago 1986 (adult)

Ginzburg, Evgenia S., *Into the Whirlwind* (Milan: 1967), trans. Paul Stevenson and Manya Harari, London: Collins/Harvill 1967 (adult)

Gordon, Sheila, *Waiting for the Rain*, New York and London: Orchard Books 1987 (ages 13–15)

Hermer, Carol, *The Diary of Maria Tholo*, Johannesburg: Ravan Press 1980 (adult)

Ho, Minfong, *Rice Without Rain*, London: André Deutsch 1986 (ages 14 and over)

Kariuki, Josiah Mwangi, *Mau Mau Detainee*, Oxford: OUP 1963 (adult)

Kenyatta, Jomo, *Suffering Without Bitterness*, Nairobi: East African Publishing House 1968 (adult)

Koestler, Arthur, *Darkness at Noon*, trans. Daphne Hardy, London: Cape 1940, Penguin 1947 (adult)

Makhoere, Caesarina Kona, *No Child's Play*, London: The Women's Press 1988 (adult)

Mzamane, Mbulelo Vizikhungo, *The Children of Soweto*, London: Longman Drumbeat 1982 (ages 16 and over)

Naidoo, Beverley, *Chain of Fire*, London: Collins 1989 (ages 11–14)

Ngor, Haing S., *Surviving the Killing Fields*, London: Chatto & Windus 1988 (adult)

Ngugi wa Thiong'o, *Detained*, London: Heinemann 1981 (adult)

Partnoy, Alicia, *The Little School* (Pittsburgh: Cleis Press 1986), London: Virago 1988 (adult)

Solzhenitsyn, Alexander, *One Day in the Life Of Ivan Denisovich* (Moscow: *Novy Mir* 1962), trans. Ralph Parker, London: Gollancz 1963, Penguin 1963 (adult)

Soyinka, Wole, *The Man Died*, London: Rex Collings 1972, Penguin 1975 (adult)

Szymusiak, Molyda, *The Stones Cry Out: a Cambodian Childhood 1975–80*, London: Cape 1987, Sphere 1987 (adult)

Whitehead, Winifred, *Different Faces*, London: Pluto Press 1988 (adult)

Chapter 14   Cautionary Tales

Abrahams, Peter, *This Island Now*, London: Faber 1966 (adult)

Fraser, John, *Violence in the Arts*, Cambridge: CUP 1974 (adult)

Lorenz, Konrad, *On Aggression* (Vienna: 1963), trans. Marjorie Latzke, London: Methuen 1966 (adult)

Mark, Jan, *The Ennead*, London: Kestrel 1978 (ages 14–16)

——, *Divide and Rule*, London: Kestrel 1979 (ages 14–16)

Schlee, Ann, *The Vandal*, London: Macmillan 1979 (ages 14–16)

Chapter 15   No End to War

Branfield, John, *The Falklands Summer*, London: Gollancz 1987 (ages 12–15)

Briggs, Raymond, *The Tin-Pot Foreign General and the Old Iron Woman*, London: Hamish Hamilton 1984 (9–adult)

Brooksbank, Anne, *On Loan* (Australia: McPhee Gribble Publishers and Penguin 1985), London: Puffin 1988 (ages 12–14)

Cooper, Susan, *Dawn of Fear* (New York: Harcourt Brace 1970), London: Chatto & Windus 1972, Puffin 1974 (ages 10–12)

Dibblin, Jane, *Day of Two Suns: Nuclear Testing and the Pacific Islanders*, London: Virago 1988 (adult)

Lawrence, John and Robert, *When the Fighting is Over*, London: Bloomsbury 1988 (adult)

Lindsay, Rachel, *The War Orphan*, Oxford: OUP 1984 (ages 12–14)

Moorehead, Caroline, *Troublesome People: Enemies of War 1916–1986*, London: Hamish Hamilton 1987 (adult)

Needle, Jan, *A Game of Soldiers*, London: Collins (Fontana Lions) 1985 (ages 12–13)

Parker, Peter, *The Old Lie: the Great War and the Public School Ethos*, London: Constable 1987 (adult)

Quiroga, Eduardo, *On Foreign Ground*, London: André Deutsch (Adlib Paperbacks) 1986 (ages 14–16)

Rosen, Billi, *Andi's War*, London: Faber 1988 (ages 11–13)

Thompson, Dorothy (ed.), *Over Our Dead Bodies*, London: Virago 1983 (adult)

Chapter 16 Women and War

Brittain, Vera, *Testament of Youth*, London: Gollancz 1933, Virago 1978 (adult)
——, (ed. Winifred and Alan Eden-Green), *Testament of a Peace Lover*, London: Virago 1988 (adult)
Cambridge Women's Peace Collective, *My Country is the Whole World*, London: Pandora Press 1984 (adult)
Dorfman, Ariel, *Widows*, London: Pluto Press 1983 (adult)
Fairweather, Eileen, McDonough, Roisin and McFadyean, Melanie, *Only The Rivers Run Free*, London: Pluto Press 1984 (adult)
Forrester, Helen, *Twopence to Cross the Mersey*, London: Cape 1974, Bodley Head 1979, Fontana 1981 (ages 11–14)
——, *Liverpool Miss*, London: Bodley Head 1979, Fontana 1982 (ages 12–14)
——, *By the Waters of Liverpool*, London: Bodley Head 1981, Fontana 1983 (ages 13–15)
——, *Lime Street at Two*, London: Bodley Head 1985, Fontana 1986 (ages 14–16)
Gellhorn, Martha, *The Face of War*, London: Virago 1986 (adult)
Gilbert, Martin, *The Second World War*, London: Weidenfeld & Nicolson 1989 (adult)
Grekova, I., *The Ship of Widows* (Moscow: *Novy Mir*), trans. Cathy Porter, London: Virago 1985 (adult)
Holmes, Richard, *Firing Line*, London: Cape 1985 (adult)
Parker, Peter, *The Old Lie: The Great War and the Public School Ethos*, London: Constable 1987 (adult)
Saywell, Shelley, *Women in War: First Hand Accounts from World War II to El Salvador* (Canada: Penguin Books 1985), Tunbridge Wells: D.J. Costello 1987 (adult)
Smith, Helen Z., *Not So Quiet ... Stepdaughters of War*, London: Marriott 1930 (adult)
Thew, Linda McCullough, *The Pit Village and the Store*, London: Pluto Press 1985 (adult)
——, *From Store to War*, London: Pluto Press 1987 (adult)

Further Reading

On Ireland
Bernard, Margie, *Daughter of Derry*, London: Pluto Press 1988 (adult)
D'Arcy, Margaretta, *Tell Them Everything*, London: Pluto Press 1981 (adult)
Ward, Margaret, *Unmanageable Revolutionaries: Women and Irish Nationalism*, London: Pluto Press, 1983 (adult)

Miscellaneous Anthologies of Writing on War
Blythe, Ronald, *Writing in a War: Stories, Poems and Essays of the Second World War*, London: Penguin (rev.) 1982 (adult)
Florence, Mary S., Marshall, Catherine E., and Ogden, C.K., *Militarism versus Feminism*, London: Virago 1987 (adult)
Humphrey, Nicholas and Lifton, Robert Jay, *In a Dark Time*, London: Faber & Faber 1984 (adult)

Thompson, Dorothy (ed.), *Over Our Dead Bodies: Women Against the Bomb*, London: Virago 1983 (adult)

Chapter 17 The Poetry of War

Hibberd, Dominic, *Owen the Poet*, London: Macmillan 1986
Scannell, Vernon, *Not Without Glory: Poets of the Second World War*, London: Woburn Press 1976
Silkin, Jon, *Out of Battle: The Poetry of the Great War*, London: OUP 1972
Wyk Smith, M. van, *Drummer Hodge: The Poetry of the Anglo–Boer War (1899–1902)*, London: OUP 1978

Anthologies

Cross, Tim (ed.), *The Lost Voices of World War I*, London: Bloomsbury 1988
Gardner, Brian (ed.), *Up the Line to Death: War Poets 1914–18*, London: Methuen 1964
——, *The Terrible Rain – The War Poets: 1939–1945* , London: Methuen 1966
Hamilton, Ian (ed.), *The Poetry of War 1939–1945*, London: NEL Books 1972
Harvey, Anne (ed.), *In Time of War*, London: Blackie 1987, Puffin 1989
Reilly, Catherine, (ed.), *Scars Upon My Heart*, London: Virago 1981
——, *Chaos of the Night: Women's Poetry and Verse of the Second World War*, London: Virago 1984
Selwyn, Victor (ed.), *Poems of the Second World War: The Oasis Selection*, London: Dent 1985
——, *More Poems of the Second World War*, London: Dent 1989
Silkin, Jon (ed.), *The Penguin Book of First World War Poetry*, London: Penguin 1981
Stallworthy, Jon (ed.), *The Oxford Book of War Poetry*, London: OUP 1988
Stephen, Martin (ed.), *Never Such Innocence: A New Anthology of Great War Verse*, London: Buchan & Enright 1988

Individual Poets

Asquith, Herbert, *Poems 1912–33*, London: Sidgwick & Jackson 1934
Bishop, John Peale, *Selected Poems*, New York: Charles Scribner's Sons 1941
Brooke, Rupert, *Poetical Works*, London: Faber 1946
Cornford, Frances, *Travelling Home*, Cresset Press 1948
Douglas, Keith, *The Complete Poems of Keith Douglas*, ed. Desmond Graham, London: OUP 1978
Eberhart, Richard, *Collected Poems 1930–1986*, New York: OUP 1988
Fuller, Roy, *Collected Poems 1936–1961*, London: André Deutsch 1962
——, *New and Collected Poems 1934–84*, London: Secker & Warburg 1985
Hardy, Thomas, *The Dynasts*, London: Macmillan 1930
——, *The Collected Poems*, London: Macmillan 1952
Jarrell, Randall, *The Complete Poems*, London: Faber 1971
Keown, Anna Gordon, *Collected Poems*, Caravel Press 1953

Mackay, Helen, *London, One November*, London: Andrew Melrose 1915

Muir, Edwin, *Collected Poems 1921–1958*, London: Faber & Faber 1984

Owen, Wilfred, *Collected Poems*, ed. C. Day Lewis, London: Chatto & Windus 1963

Pound, Ezra, *Collected Shorter Poems*, London: Faber & Faber 1984

Price, Nancy, *Hurdy-Gurdy*, London: Frederick Muller 1944

Reed, Henry, *A Map of Verona*, London: Jonathan Cape 1946

Rosenberg, Isaac, *Collected Poems*, ed. Gordon Bottomley and Denys Harding, London: Chatto & Windus 1937

Rukeyser, Muriel, *Collected Poems*, New York: McGraw-Hill 1982

Sassoon, Siegfried, *Collected Poems 1908–1956*, London: Faber 1971

Scannell, Vernon, *Soldiering On: Poems of Military Life*, London: Robson Books 1989

Seeger, Alan, *Poems*, London: Constable 1917

Simpson, Louis, *Collected Poems*, New York: Paragon House 1988

Sorley, Charles Hamilton, *Marlborough and Other Poems*, Cambridge: CUP 1932

Stafford, Sarah, *I Burn for England*, London: Leslie Frewin 1966

Wilbur, Richard, *New and Collected Poems*, London: Faber & Faber 1989

Afterword

Humphrey, Nicholas and Lifton, Robert Jay (eds.), *In a Dark Time*, London: Faber 1984

Levi, Primo, *If Not Now, When?* (Turin: Einandi 1982), trans. William Weaver, New York: Simon & Schuster 1985, London: Michael Joseph 1986, Abacus 1987 (adult)

Lorenz, Konrad, *On Aggression* (Vienna: 1983), trans. Marjorie Latzke, London: Methuen 1966 (adult)

Martin, Stephen, *Never Such Innocence*, London: Buchan & Enright 1988

Rowe, Dorothy, *Living with the Bomb*, London: Routledge & Kegan Paul 1985

Rukeyser, Muriel, 'Peace the Great Meaning', *Collected Poems*, New York: McGraw-Hill 1982

Index

Acknowledgements

Permission to reprint copyright poems in whole or in part is gratefully acknowledged. Every effort has been made to locate copyright-holders, but apologies are offered where this has proved impossible. The author and the publishers would be glad to hear from anyone concerned.

Bishop, John Peale: 18 lines from 'In the Dordogne', reprinted with permission of Charles Scribner's Sons, an imprint of Macmillan Publishing Company, from *Selected Poems* by John Peale Bishop. Copyright 1933 by Charles Scribner's Sons, renewed 1961 by Margaret G.H. Bronson.

Cornford, Frances: 3 lines from 'Soldiers on the Platform', reprinted from *Travelling Home* by Frances Cornford, with acknowledgement to the author and to Random Century Group Ltd.

Douglas, Keith: 8 lines from 'Time Eating', reprinted from *The Complete Poems of Keith Douglas*, edited by Desmond Graham, 1978, with acknowledgements to the author and to Oxford University Press.

Fuller, Roy: 8 lines from 'Waiting to be Drafted', reprinted from *New and Collected Poems 1934–1984* by Roy Fuller with acknowledgements to the author and to Secker & Warburg.

Jarrell, Randall: 7 lines from 'The Lines', 6 lines from 'A Pilot from the Carrier', and 10 lines from 'Jews at Haifa', reprinted from *The Complete Poems* by Randall Jarrell, by permission of Faber & Faber Ltd, and Farrar, Straus & Giroux Inc, New York.

Keown, Anna Gordon: 'My thought shall never be that you are dead', from *Collected Poems* by Anna Gordon Keown, published by Caravel Press, 1953.

Muir, Edwin: 14 lines from 'The Horses', reprinted from *Collected Poems 1921–1958* by Edwin Muir, by permission of Faber & Faber Ltd, and Oxford University Press, New York.

Pound, Ezra: 8 lines from 'Lamentations of the Frontier Guard', reprinted from *Collected Shorter Poems* by Ezra Pound, by permission of Faber & Faber Ltd, and New Directions Publishing Corporation, New York.

Price, Nancy: 'Johnny Take a Gun' from *Hurdy-Gurdy*, published by Frederick Muller Ltd, 1944.

Rukeyser, Muriel: 'Peace the Great Meaning' from *Collected Poems* by Muriel Rukeyser, published by McGraw-Hill, by permission of William L. Rukeyser.

Sassoon, Siegfried: 'The Dugout' and 'Lamentation' reprinted from *Collected Poems 1908–1956*, London: Faber & Faber, 1961, by permission of George T. Sassoon and Viking Penguin, a division of Penguin Books, USA, Inc.

Simpson, Louis: 6 lines from 'The Battle' reprinted from *Good News of Death and Other Poems* (Scribner's), by permission of the author.

Stafford, Sarah: 11 lines from 'The Unborn', reprinted from *I Burn for England*, edited by Charles Hamblett, published by Leslie Frewin Ltd, 1966.